NAZI PARIS

NAZI PARIS

The History of an Occupation,
1940–1944

Allan Mitchell

Berghahn Books
NEW YORK • OXFORD

Published in 2008 by
Berghahn Books

www.berghahnbooks.com

Library of Congress Cataloging-in-Publication Data

Mitchell, Allan, 1933–

Nazi Paris : the history of an occupation, 1940–1944 / Allan Mitchell.
  p. cm.
Includes bibliographical references and indexes.
ISBN 978-1-84545-451-7 (hbk. : alk. paper)
  1. Paris (France)—History—1940–1944. 2. France—History—German
occupation, 1940–1945. I. Title.
D802.F82P37535 2008
944'.3610816—dc21

2008020324

British Library Cataloguing in Publication Data

A catalogue record for this book is available from
the British Library.

Printed in the United States on acid-free paper

Photographs are courtesy of the Établissement Cinématographique et Photographique de l'Armée, Ivry-sur-Seine (EPCA-Ivry), and the Bundesarchiv, Koblenz (BA-Koblenz).

For Catherine and Alexandra

"My love is like a red, red rose ..."

CONTENTS

PREFACE

It cannot be entirely coincidental that this study was researched and written during the American military engagement in Iraq. Even the most reclusive historian cannot ignore the daily association between newspaper headlines and scholarly pursuits. Surely all occupations of an invaded territory by a foreign power share some identifiable mutual characteristics, and the homilies to be drawn from a comparison of them soon become disarmingly simplistic: do not expect the conquered populace to throw flowers; beware of undue reliance on the local police; prepare to be blamed for absolutely everything that goes awry; and so forth.

Yet I have kept clearly in view that Paris is not Baghdad, and certainly that the 1940s had little in common with the initial decade of the twenty-first century. The evidence has therefore in no way been trimmed to support easy—and often misleading—generalizations. Sufficient unto the day is the evil thereof. Unavoidably, nonetheless, the vocabulary necessary to describe or analyze events often has much the same resonance. Use of the designation "terrorists" to identify insurgents was just as common in the four years after 1940 as it would become over six decades later. And, yes, there were in both instances improvised explosive devices, political assassinations, and well-documented incidents of torture—all of which were alternatively justified or condemned in similar terms. Still, the striking differences between then and now, here and there, are profound. One can ignore them only at great peril of distortion. Perhaps what we need to do is found an Institute of Occupation Studies in the hope that our political and military leaders will thereby be encouraged to think twice before embarking on a foreign adventure.

A number of colleagues and friends have offered me advice and encouragement along the way. I want to thank each of the following warmly for their help: Chantal Bamberger, Claude Blay, Karen Bowie, François Caron, Alfred Gottwaldt, Peter Hennock, François Jacquot, Larry Joseph, Joanne Karpinski, Shawn Kendrick, Annemarie Kleinert, Jürgen Kocka, Stefan Martens, Sylvia Roubaud, Tom Skidmore, and John Sweets. It would be remiss of me not to acknowledge here also the unflagging support of my indulgent editor, Marion Berghahn, head of what she likes to call my *Hausverlag*.

INTRODUCTION

T he notion of Vichy France is of course a complete misnomer. All of France was never governed from Vichy, and between June 1940 and November 1942 even the Unoccupied Zone south of the demarcation line was not really autonomous. For more than four years Nazi Germany ruled France, and it did so from Paris, which remained as always the heart and soul of the French nation. For the military administrators of the German Occupation, Vichy was a sometimes troublesome but temporary convenience that relieved part of the strain on their inadequate manpower resources. Besides, whenever important business had to be transacted, French ministers could be summoned to the capital.

In framing an investigation of that topic, as is apparent above, I have finally decided to capitalize the word "Occupation" in reference to the German administration, a practice frequently adopted by French historians of the period. The reader will surely understand that this usage is strictly a literary device to avoid repetition of awkward circumlocutions. By no means does it imply that German authorities in Paris always adopted the same policy or constantly acted in unison. On the contrary, one of the basic themes of this study is necessarily the lack of political harmony and frequent personal clashes among German officials. In many regards, as the evidence will show, the Nazi Occupation was dysfunctional from its outset to its demise.

In recent years, historical treatment of the Second World War in general, as well as occupied France in particular, has undergone a profound and permanent transformation. Many earlier writings were based to a considerable extent on personal memoirs, written or oral, that supplied an invaluable wealth of anecdotal evidence. But the generation of witnesses—those who experienced the events in question as adults—has largely passed away, and their testimony has in any case been amply recorded. Now, much more systematically than was possible before, the documentary record has become available to scholars, who are able to test or flesh out hypotheses and personal impressions of the past. To be specific, in regard to the Occupation, two large guidebooks to the most pertinent archival collections were simultaneously published in the year 2002: one for the holdings of German documents at the Archives Nationales in Paris and another for complementary sources held in the German military archives at Freiburg-im-Breisgau. A search of these materials housed on both sides of the Rhine is henceforth essential for any scholarly investigation of the Occupation.[1]

Such sources need to be supplemented by other repositories, which are indicated in the bibliography of this volume. Obvious and indispensable among them are police files, ministerial papers, and statistical records conserved by the Archives Nationales. Not to be overlooked in Paris as well are the holdings of the Centre de Documentation Juive Contemporaine, valuable not only for light they shed on the fate of French Jews but also for information about the conduct of the Occupation's military administration. On the German side, apart from Freiburg, the main centers of research are now in Berlin, especially at the Foreign Office archives but likewise at the Bundesarchiv, which has consolidated documentation previously scattered during the war at outposts in Potsdam, Merseburg, and Coswig. The Bundesarchiv in Koblenz contains only a few items of direct relevance.

To list these various locations is to suggest that current researchers unavoidably face a daunting task. They must also seek a special niche amid a staggering quantity of secondary historical literature. Among those scholars who have concentrated mainly on the French experience during the war years, a fairly clear pattern has emerged. The first narrative of note was written by Robert Aron barely a decade after the liberation of Paris. Aron took the view that the French, defeated but defiant after 1940, were virtually all sympathetic to, if not indeed active participants in, the Resistance. Their nearly unanimous reaction to the German Occupation, in short, was revulsion.[2] That version of the story was sharply attacked in 1972 by the most influential book ever to appear on the subject, Robert O. Paxton's *Vichy France*, which instead portrayed the majority of the French and their leaders as docile if not quite enthusiastic collaborationists. Paxton thus made what he called "a grave moral case" against French elites because of their complicity with the Occupation, which reached far down into the population.[3] Most of French scholarship during the balance of the twentieth century wavered between these two poles, with a noticeable albeit not uncritical tilt toward Paxton. So many books, often excellent, have treated the history of wartime France that it seems almost invidious to single out but a few. Yet if one must choose, the three most important general accounts appear to be those of Jean-Pierre Azéma, Jean-Louis Crémieux-Brilhac, and the Swiss historian, Philippe Burrin.[4] In addition, note must be taken of the extraordinary outpouring of works devoted (as the Germans invariably put it) to the Jewish question. Although the plethora of fine monographs precludes an adequate listing here, the incredibly meticulous sleuthing of Serge Klarsfeld surely deserves special praise.[5]

Curiously, German historians have produced a much less impressive body of work on the subject. Three texts require emphasis. First, the pioneering study of Eberhard Jäckel provides a general context, although it lacks solid footing in the primary sources of the period because it appeared very early.[6] The same does not apply to Hans Umbreit's superb analysis of the Occupation's military administration. If somewhat narrowly conceived, without consulting documentation gathered in France, Umbreit's depiction of the invaders' regime in Paris is nonetheless grounded in a myriad of details scrupulously drawn from German archives, and it remains generally reliable.[7] Third, the monographic treatment of the complicated interaction of French and German police forces by Bernd Kasten represents an original contribution to our understanding of collaboration.[8] This listing could of course be longer, and my apologies are due to other authors whose writings are cited only in the notes and bibliography.

Where, then, does this study fit into such a large and crowded field? The best answer can perhaps be given by comparison with two books, one mentioned and one not, that must rank high in any review of volumes concerning France's dark years of German Occupation. The first is Paxton's *Vichy France*. Well-researched and vigorously written, this early account indisputably remains a reference point of interpretation. Yet the author made a small but telling error (corrected in his later work), because he did not realize at the time of publication that there were actually two German military commanders in Paris named General von Stülpnagel—the cousins Otto and Heinrich. As a consequence, he conflated their careers and awarded them only one confusing entry in his index. This mistake by no means vitiates the powerful main argument of Paxton's book, but it does indicate that he was still far from uncovering the inner administrative workings of the Occupation in Paris. In the main, my purpose has been to fill this research lacuna, which is easily explicable due to Paxton's lack of access in the late 1960s to all of the German archival resources that are now catalogued in Paris and Freiburg and that constitute the basis of my study. The resulting difference is largely one of tone, since in my view Paxton did not fully recognize the extent to which French functionaries were monitored and dominated by their German counterparts, an insight that might have led him to nuance some of his judgments about collaboration.

The second tome, appearing nearly three decades later in the year 2001, is the perceptive and remarkably comprehensive overview by the British historian Julian Jackson. There is no better synthesis of the French experience during the Occupation and no shrewder summary of the previous historical literature on that topic. But this weighty volume fundamentally differs from my approach in two crucial regards. First, Jackson concentrates exclusively on the occupied, whereas my focus is mostly on the occupiers. This basic distinction between our viewpoints explains much about our respective narrative voices and modes of analysis. Furthermore, whereas his conclusions are based entirely on secondary sources and published memoirs that are to be found in a library, my research was largely conducted among primary materials that can be gathered only from archives. To be precise, Jackson has neither cited nor apparently read a single one of the hundreds of German documents that provide the foundation and the framework of my investigation. Again, this is not at all to disparage the genuinely significant scholarly contribution of a fellow Anglophone outsider but to point out its understandable limitation. My objective has therefore been not to contradict Jackson's findings but to complement them by providing a missing element.[9]

A word should be added about the structure of the work in hand. It is divided into chronological periods, based on the assumption that the character of the German Occupation of France evolved with the progress of the war. Within each of the three main phases before the Allied invasion of Normandy in June 1944, five themes are developed. These thematic chapters are presented in the same order in each phase. Thus, it is possible to read the text either horizontally (phase by phase) or vertically (theme by theme). Anyone particularly concerned, for example, with problems of the French economy could tackle chapters 3, 8, and 13; or, for the Jewish question, chapters 5, 10, and 15. Presumably, however, it makes more sense to peruse the text from start to finish. I can only hope, in any event, that the reader will discover this subject to be as interesting as I found it to research and write.

Finally, the notes. Although I have attempted to organize them in a unified and consistent manner, the sheer variety of sources—drawn from several different archival collections in two countries—defies that effort. Moreover, there are frequent and delicate problems of attribution. It is not trivial to know whether a certain dispatch or memorandum was personally composed by an individual in a position of authority or was simply sent in his name by a faceless bureaucrat as a matter of routine. Are we really dealing with the banality of evil? That question obviously arises in particular regard to the execution of hostages or the deportation of Jews to Auschwitz. When I could be certain of authorship, I have indicated that by name; when not, by title or office. After all, the main purpose of the notes, as I understand, is to enable another researcher to locate readily a given document in order to check its content. Such has been my intention, however imperfectly realized.

PART I

TAKING OVER
(June 1940–June 1941)

Chapter 1

LAW AND ORDER

B rilliant as the planning and execution of German military operations had been in May and early June of 1940, the same cannot be said of the Occupation that followed. France had fallen, but now it needed to be governed. Entering into the details, one can only be astonished at the lack of foresight and the extent of resulting administrative confusion. An early indication was that the first official military staff communiqué from occupied Paris was released on 14 June as German troops were still entering the city, yet a second did not follow until more than a week later. In the meanwhile, soldiers and civilian administrators fanned out in the capital, randomly requisitioning hotels, public buildings, offices, and other quarters wherever they could find them. Not quite a ghost town, Paris was nonetheless strangely silent. Most of its bakeries, bars, bistrots, restaurants, cinemas, and boutiques were closed and shuttered. The streets were nearly empty and quiet, except for the occasional clatter of passing German military vehicles, horse-drawn caissons, motorcycles, or marching squads of gray-clad soldiers. On the sidewalks and squares a few uniformed French police officers stood about, lacking reason or motivation to direct the sparse traffic.[1]

This scene of desolation has often been described in eyewitness and subsequent accounts, and it provides the appropriate setting for a brief outline of the slowly emerging administrative structure of the German Occupation that attempted to gain control of a chaotic situation. Initially, to reduce matters to their simplest terms, the basic problem was that the German command itself

was in virtual chaos. The first phase of the Occupation was therefore characterized by a welter of titles, acronyms, ill-defined prerogatives, and overlapping
duties as the German bureaucracy struggled to adapt itself to the particular
circumstances of occupied France.[2]

That the invaded French territory should be placed under a military occupation was not a conclusion foregone. Occupied portions of Poland, for instance,
were left largely to the cruel mercies of the SS. Alsace and Lorraine were in
effect annexed to Germany and put under a Nazi Party *Gauleiter*. The Neth-
erlands and Luxemburg were accorded civilian administrations. But France
and Belgium were still considered unfinished business in the summer of 1940,
since the conflict with Great Britain remained in progress, for which the German Wehrmacht was supposedly preparing Operation Sea Lion. Hence, the
fateful decision was made to leave the main Occupation in military hands
while the French nation was being carved up into palatable morsels. Besides
the loss of Alsace and Lorraine, the two northern Atlantic departments of
the Nord and Pas-de-Calais were detached to military headquarters in Brussels. Mussolini's Italy received a thin slice (later expanded) of Alpine region
opposite Switzerland. And, famously, the southern third of France was placed
under the political authority of Marshal Pétain's quasi-independent regime
at Vichy. The rest, cut off from the Midi by an arbitrary demarcation line,
thereby became the fiefdom of the German army. It included three-quarters of
the French population, most of its industrial complex, all of the Atlantic and
Channel coastline, and of course crucially the capital city of Paris.[3]

It would be proper to speak of four layers of German military administration insofar as occupied France was concerned. At the top, needless to
insist, was the supreme command of all combat forces, the Oberkommando
der Wehrmacht (OKW)—in a word, Hitler. Ever since the ouster in 1938 of
generals Blomberg and Fritsch, both of whom faced scandal charges, and the
subsequent resignation of the estimable Ludwig Beck, who protested the risk
of a European war over Czechoslovakia, as chief of staff, the German military
establishment remained securely in the grasp of the Führer. This proved to
be of capital importance for France, because, as countless documents testify, a nod from Hitler's headquarters put an end to every argument. In the
Third Reich and its conquered territories, a personal dispatch signed by Hitler
(*Führererlass*) was the final word. As a rule, it was Hitler's chief adjutant, Field
Marshal Wilhelm Keitel, who dealt directly with Occupation authorities in
Paris. But Hitler's wish was unquestionably Keitel's ukase, and there was never
an instant of doubt that instructions from OKW meant an order to do the
master's bidding. Distant and aloof as he seemed, the Führer actually took a
keen interest in France for a while and did not hesitate, from time to time, to
intervene in affairs of the Occupation. Yet there were two manifest difficulties
with such a procedure. The first was Hitler's almost total ignorance of Paris,

which he rapidly toured once in his life at dawn on 28 June 1940, soon after signing the Armistice at nearby Compiègne. His immortal pose for photographs that morning at the Trocadéro in front of the Eiffel Tower was just that, a pose, indicating no familiarity whatever with things French. The second difficulty, as it proved, was that Hitler exercised his unchallenged authority over France in ways that too often turned out to be self-contradictory. Symptoms of this disruptive tendency would become apparent in the initial phase of the Occupation and were to persist as the months passed.[4]

Beneath the OKW ranked next the chief commander of the German army, the Oberbefehlshaber des Heeres (OBH), General Walther von Brauchitsch. Usually withdrawn at the castle of Fontainebleau, 30 kilometers southeast of the capital, or with increasing frequency removed altogether from French soil in Berlin, Brauchitsch essentially became an absentee landlord. During the first months of the Occupation, he did participate actively in determining its administrative structure, but the repeated shifts of personnel and constant revision of job descriptions indicated that this was an improvisation without carefully considered objectives. Technically, the phlegmatic Brauchitsch functioned throughout the opening weeks of the Occupation both as OBH and as Militärbefehlshaber in Frankreich (MBF), the military commander in France. On 25 October 1940, the latter post was formally relinquished by Brauchitsch, and that date in effect marked his permanent abdication from the military governance of France. At most, he remained as a kind of moral preceptor for the officers and troops stationed there, irregularly issuing sermons about the importance of proper conduct in order to preserve the "reputation" (*Ansehen*) of the German army. Apart from that sacred and tirelessly repeated concept of military honor, it is fair to conclude that Brauchitsch left no deep impression on the Occupation.[5]

The third level of authority was the one abandoned by Brauchitsch and bestowed on General Otto von Stülpnagel late that October. For all practical purposes, the position of MBF had heretofore been filled by an elderly career officer, General Alfred von Streccius, who rather ineffectually labored under the awkward title of Chief of the Military Administration in France (Chef der Militärverwaltung in Frankreich). Since this designation was simply abolished when Stülpnagel took office, Streccius was not literally his predecessor, although that was actually a distinction without much difference. Stülpnagel thus soldiered on under the mistaken assumption that he would thereafter be solely in charge of all French affairs in the Occupied Zone. The reality was different. Behind the administrative curtain, a central theme of his tenure as MBF was the steady erosion of Stülpnagel's authority, which was finally to culminate in his resignation in early 1942. Everyone, it seemed, had a direct line to some higher power in Berlin—Göring, Goebbels, Himmler, Eichmann, Ribbentrop, Rosenberg, Speer, Canaris, or Hitler himself, to name only the most obvious. Personally sensitive and excitable, Stülpnagel attempted in vain to assert his primacy in Paris while others deliberately set about to undermine it. Still, his strenuous efforts were abetted by a dedicated bureaucratic cadre that included several outstanding military and civilian administrators. Housed on the Avenue Kléber in the sprawling Hotel Majestic, which instantly became a sort of huge ugly Vatican of the Occupation, they were divided into a military staff (*Kommandostab*) and a parallel administrative staff (*Verwaltungsstab*). Of these, the latter soon became more significant, due in large measure to its capable director, Dr. Jonathan Schmid, and to the emergence of the astute Dr. Werner Best as its central figure. The military staff was confined mostly to technical matters concerning German troops stationed in France, although the influence within it of a young and efficient German officer, Lt. Major Hans Speidel (a post-war NATO commander), was not negligible. Also worthy of specific mention, for future reference, was Dr. Elmar Michel, who headed the MBF's Economic Section and who was later to succeed Schmid after his departure from Paris in August 1942.[6]

The fourth rung in this chain of command was represented for most of the first phase of the Occupation by Lt. General Ernst Schaumburg, an officer too frequently neglected by historians. In the earliest flowcharts depicting the German administration of the Occupied Zone, two separate posts had been created to handle the quotidian problems of administration in the capital: a municipal commandant of Paris (Stadtkommandant von Paris) and, again awkwardly, a Chief of the Military Administrative District of Paris (Chef des Militärverwaltungsbezirks Paris). The latter included oversight of the entire Department of the Seine as well as the adjacent departments of Seine-et-Oise and Seine-et-Marne. As this arrangement proved both unwieldy and redundant, however, the eventual result was that the two jurisdictions were unified (minus the two neighboring departments) under a single title: Kommandant von Gross-Paris. The sobriquet of "Greater Paris" thereby became synonymous with the Department of the Seine, meaning the city and immediate environs, the famous Parisian *banlieue*. This consolidation, which began on 1 March 1941, gave Schaumburg immense authority over the day-to-day regulation of the Paris region and enabled him to dominate his French counterpart, the Prefect of the Seine. With his residence centrally located on the Right Bank in the swanky Hotel Meurice, on the Rue de Rivoli across from the Louvre, Schaumburg kept watch over the interaction of the municipality and its troops of occupation. Also indicative of his importance in the military hierarchy is the fact that Schaumburg ordinarily functioned as the MBF during Stülpnagel's frequent furloughs from the capital.[7]

As the acknowledged second-in-command in Paris, Schaumburg's role was further enhanced by his duties as the supervisor of police in the Department of the Seine. France had no national chief of police, so it was natural for German authorities in the capital to deal with the Prefecture of Police in Paris, even though its legal jurisdiction was only departmental. Under German pressure, the former Prefect of Police was replaced in late June by the compliant Roger Langeron. The problem was that many municipal police units had disappeared during the collapse of the Third Republic, and the formidable Garde Mobile Républicaine, considered too militarized by the Germans, was dissolved. The police structure therefore needed to be reconstituted under close surveillance of the principal German security agencies—the Sicherheitspolizei (Sipo), Sicherheitsdienst (SD), and Geheime Feldpolizei (GFP)—which together came indiscriminately to be identified and feared by the French as the Gestapo. This reorganization of police forces in the Paris region proved to be one of the first and most crucial forms of collaboration.[8]

Numbers told the story. A memo in mid-October 1940 accounted for exactly 26,010 French municipal police and rural gendarmes in the departments of the Seine, Seine-et-Oise, and Seine-et-Marne. One must recall that this area in and around Paris contained an estimated population of 6,785,000, according to the memo. At the same time, the manpower of the German police force in all of France probably exceeded no more than 3,000 and was never to become far more numerous. It was therefore imperative for the Occupation to gain the cooperation of indigenous police units that were coherent and strong enough to maintain control of the streets of Paris and yet were insufficient to become a focus of armed opposition to the German military forces stationed there. Accordingly, side arms were allowed for French minions of the law only with caution and in strictly regulated quantity.[9]

In this regard, the Occupation was largely successful. Dozens of internal German reports confirmed that relations with French police officials, if not always cordial, were "correct" and "without friction." Generally, the French did as they were instructed, although often not with enough efficiency to suit their prompters. One sore point was the so-called obligatory salute (*Grusspflicht*) expected of uniformed French policemen when passing German military personnel. Complaints abounded that the policemen either neglected to give such acknowledgment or did so in an unacceptably casual manner. Trivial as that matter might seem, it bore heavy symbolic importance for the Germans. When reprimanded about this sloppy comportment, Langeron promised conformity to German wishes but noted in reply that the French lacked the same military tradition as that *outre Rhin*.[10] Besides endless guard duties and irregular house searches, Parisian police were required to direct traffic and to assist in roundups or razzias of suspected Communists, Gaullists, and Jews, which became routine. In addition, the police were pushed to the foreground whenever a popular demonstration threatened to erupt. The most significant incident of that sort occurred on Armistice Day, 11 November 1940, when students and schoolchildren gathered on the Left Bank near the Sorbonne in the morning, then marched or rode the subway in the afternoon to the Champs-Élysées. Eyewitness accounts varied considerably. Whereas many French tended to magnify the event as a significant display of protest, the Germans played it down, claiming that the youthful crowds, thanks to the conspicuous assistance of the French police, were "effortlessly dispersed."[11] The only other manifestations of note during the initial phase of the Occupation transpired in May 1941 at the Wall of the Federals in the cemetery of Père Lachaise, where several dozen demonstrators twice gathered to commemorate May Day and the resistance of the Paris Commune in 1871. Yet these events, too, had little public resonance and were easily contained by alerted and supervised French police.[12]

The French constabulary was much involved in two broader actions of law enforcement in the early days of the Occupation. One was the arrest and incarceration of British civilians left behind in June 1940, mostly in Paris, while their troops were hastily evacuated during the disastrous military operations that ended on the beaches at Dunkerque. A German police report in early August listed 662 English subjects who had been jailed at Fresnes, just south of Paris. Other prisoners of various types were meanwhile being held on the fringes of the capital at the former tuberculosis sanatorium of Aincourt, also at Clairvaux and Fort Romainville, and in downtown Paris at the Centre des Tourelles.[13] A second category of special note was composed of Communists, who were described on police blotters as "active" and whose agitation was "ever increasing." These terms were relative, however, and one military staff memo suggested that the populace of Paris was in fact astonished that the Germans were not reacting more harshly to repress them.[14] With the Nazi-Soviet Pact of 1939 still in force, Occupation authorities were apparently content to leave such measures to the French, and the Prefect of Police, as always prodded from above, dutifully began to keep a regular box score of persons arrested and imprisoned. The count reached exactly 988 by 1 December 1940 and more than 1,700 by 20 February 1941, and was to exceed 2,400 by late June 1941.[15] Yet such statistics must be treated with some skepticism, since they were compiled by French police officials eager to ward off criticism by the Germans that they were performing with inadequate zeal. To evaluate these figures properly, one would need to know much more about who was apprehended, why, and to what effect. How were prisoners actually charged? What was their punishment, if any? When were they released? These unanswered questions left ample ambiguity about the actual role of French police and the extent of German oversight. One conclusion nonetheless remains clear: the permanent lack of sufficient German personnel made collaboration between occupiers and occupied a necessity. Without it, circumstances in Paris and the rest of the Occupied Zone would have been far removed from the *Ruhe und Ordnung* prized among Nazi Germany's top priorities in France.[16]

In this context, it is appropriate to record the first mention of the word "hostages" (*Geiseln*) within the German military administration. This tender subject was initially broached in a long memorandum by Alfred von Streccius on 12 September 1940. At its origin were a few incidents in August when German guards were personally attacked in Paris, during one of which three were wounded by gunfire in the vicinity of the Bois de Boulogne. In response, German authorities threatened "measures of retaliation" (*Vergeltungsmassnahmen*) without specifying what was thereby intended. Certainly, one idea discussed was the detention of French civilians who would be made available for public retribution in case of recurring violence. It was this notion that Streccius now sought to define. The selection of hostages, he wrote, must be conducted with the "greatest reserve" out of consideration for a populace with whom the Occupation wished to collaborate. Those chosen as hostages should consequently have an "especially close solidarity" with the presumed criminals, that is, they should come from the same socio-economic group or political affiliation (a transparent allusion to Communist sympathizers in the working class). In all cases, alone as Chief of the Military Administration, Streccius would decide on any possible sentence for the execution of prisoners. Fortunately, during the initial stage of the Occupation, the occasion did not arise.[17] The only other notable reference to hostages at that time came in mid-October when the German Embassy informed Berlin that it had requested the Gestapo to detain fifty French Freemasons, just in case. But this measure did not conform to the precise terms of the previous Streccius memo, and nothing further came of it.[18]

In the vocabulary of the early Occupation, another common term became current: "resistance" (*Widerstand*). Its usage in the autumn of 1940 was at first in loose reference to scattered gangs or groups in unoccupied France, then eventually to those in the Occupied Zone as well. Not until early February 1941 was there explicit mention in Sipo-SD reports of a French "Resistance movement" (*Widerstandsbewegung*) that merited a capital letter. This expression, however, was usually reserved for irregular Gaullist cells detected in such provincial towns as Dijon, Nancy, and Reims. There was no hint of large dissident organizations in Paris despite continued Communist activity there and the mounting number of arrests by French and German police.[19]

In all of this commotion, it is striking that the SS and other German security officials managed to maintain a low profile. There are several explanations. For one, Stülpnagel was determined to preserve military discipline and prestige, often repeating that he did not intend to allow France to become another Poland. For another, the ranks of the Sipo-SD were seriously understaffed and were at first headed by a scholarly young officer, Helmut Knochen, who regarded his assignment to be mostly information gathering and who thus accepted a modest role subordinate to his august superiors at the Hotel Majestic. Perhaps most significantly, as mentioned, the situation in Paris and in France altogether was still generally calm, without the bloodshed that was to occur in the summer of 1941 after the German invasion of Russia, an event that would mark the opening of a second phase of the Occupation.[20]

For the time being, in short, the Occupation seemed to have everything in hand. Relations with the French police went from "correct" to "painfully correct." The criminal police of Paris received special praise for their effort "to execute orders of the German military administration promptly and thoroughly."[21] Among them was the duty of tracking down information provided through "denunciations" (*délations*), frequently anonymous handwritten notes that today choke the archives, in which one French citizen seeking advantage, employment, or revenge tipped off police authorities about some alleged impropriety of another.[22] In the meantime, individual arrests and razzias continued. Of the latter, the most extensive in Paris were those of late August, early October, and mid-December 1940 in which hundreds were taken into custody.[23] Another public campaign, at German insistence, was the rapid removal of Communist graffiti (such as the hammer and sickle), scrawled signs of "V" for victory, and Gaullist crosses of Lorraine. For the most part, the Germans opted to push the French police into action and, as Werner Best described it, to oversee "discreetly" the operations that unfolded.[24] But, if veiled, the iron fist of the Occupation was omnipresent. After an untoward fracas occurred on the day of Jeanne d'Arc, 11 May 1941, Commandant Schaumburg announced in no uncertain terms: "I do not intend to tolerate a repetition." He thereupon issued instructions that French police should henceforth quash any public disorder with necessary force, including the use of weapons. No person arrested by the French, moreover, should be released without Schaumburg's explicit permission.[25]

Like his assistant Schaumburg, Stülpnagel also attempted in the spring of 1941 to buttress his own administrative authority. Shortly after his formal designation as MBF, he issued two sets of policy guidelines. The first delineated the precise duties to be allocated to German police forces, the Sipo-SD, namely, the surveillance of "Jews, Communists, emigrants, [Masonic] lodges, and churches." In addition, the Gestapo should "secure" valuable documents in libraries or archives and throttle any anti-German political activity by Freemasons and the clergy. All of which was to be coordinated with the German Counterespionage Section (Abwehr), housed in the Hotel Lutétia on the Left Bank, along with the law enforcement agents of the GFP, who were patrolling Paris in mufti. Supervision of the French police would remain under the MBF's administrative staff. These details suggested that all police matters would be directed by the military command in Paris rather than from Berlin.[26] The second decree, thirteen pages long, outlined Stülpnagel's policy regarding hostages—or, in official language, "atonement measures" (*Sühnemassnahmen*)—that would be enforced on the French population in cases of major sabotage. In most regards, these guidelines closely followed those already drafted months before by General von Streccius. But Stülpnagel's version was much more emphatic that German retaliation for acts of violence would be conducted with "*all severity.*" He also shifted somewhat the definition of hostages, who originally were to have a similar social or political affiliation with the perpetrators. Instead, hostages would be selected according to geographic proximity—"the populace at the scene of the crime or in the immediate vicinity." Therewith Stülpnagel hoped to place responsibility more obviously in the hands of the local citizenry, "*who must thus in every instance be publicly threatened*" with retaliation. Although he repeated Streccius's caveat that the "greatest reserve" should always be observed in the choice of hostages, with this announcement Stülpnagel openly associated himself with a policy that was later to be his undoing.[27]

Meanwhile, Stülpnagel's firm assertion of his preeminent right to govern in the Occupied Zone brought him increasingly into conflict with the German ambassador to France, Otto Abetz. Fluent in French, married to a French woman, and long a proponent of Franco-German rapprochement, Abetz was an ideal advocate for the vaunted cause of collaboration. At first only a staff member in the Hotel Majestic, he was elevated to ambassadorial rank by Foreign Minister Joachim von Ribbentrop in early August 1940 and moved to the Rue de Lille. There the German Embassy soon became a Left Bank counterweight to the Stülpnagel-Schaumburg regime across the Seine. It was Abetz's contention that his assignment, blessed by the Foreign Office in Berlin and by the Führer himself, was to deal with all matters political in France, whereas Stülpnagel's concern and competence were strictly military in nature. Alas, this view did not sit well in the Majestic, where there was scarce inclination to make fine distinctions between politics and military administration. Harsh words ensued on both sides in early April 1941, until Abetz finally announced that it was "purposeless" to pursue the issue any further.[28] A fortnight later, however, Stülpnagel attempted to resolve the question, not without more recriminations, by concluding that he would henceforth handle all military affairs; should they contain a political aspect, the Embassy would be duly informed. No reply was forthcoming from Abetz until 5 May, when he declared that he was in "complete agreement" and that the debate was after all "totally inconsequential." These categorical phrases very poorly rendered the ambiguity or the outright hostility that existed at the heart of the Occupation and that would fester until its final days.[29]

Yet by the beginning of the summer of 1941, Paris was quiet. The Germans could congratulate themselves on having established a military administration that, although admittedly shorthanded, was functioning efficiently enough to maintain public order in the city and its suburbs. Partly this control had been accomplished through measured doses of force coupled with a latent threat of more severe measures, if required. A system of military tribunals was created in Paris and the provinces of the Occupied Zone, and it was known that on various occasions they had ordered the execution both of German soldiers (usually charged with desertion) and of French civilians who had been caught possessing arms, distributing enemy propaganda, or committing acts of sabotage. Even listening to broadcasts of foreign radio stations carried a possible death sentence.[30] The consequence was the start of another box score. A staff report of the military administration in early March 1941 listed eighteen death sentences for French civilians and three for German soldiers; a month later another added, respectively, eight and two. But not all such judgments resulted in executions, and one study of this question has concluded that only fourteen Frenchmen were put to death at the order of German military tribunals before the beginning of June 1941.[31] Complaints and pleas by French officials to the Armistice Commission at Wiesbaden were of no effect in deterring the military courts under the Commandant of Greater Paris from meting out justice as they saw fit. Consequently, jails and prisons began to fill up, and more were required. Most notorious among them in the vicinity of Paris was a facility near a railway stop at Drancy on the city's northern edge. There a large tenement complex, shaped like a horseshoe, was confiscated by the Germans and converted into what was at first euphemistically called a "prisoner assembly center" (*Gefangenensammelsstelle*) or "internment camp" (*Interniertenlager*). As if it were too crude for Paris, the term "concentration camp" (*Konzentrationslager* or KZ) was for the time being avoided—although it was meanwhile used, for example, to designate a similar penitentiary at Besançon. One can only observe that reality, neither for the first time nor the last, far surpassed official rhetoric.[32]

Chapter 2

RULES AND REGULATIONS

The German presence changed the appearance of Paris. After nearly a century since Baron Haussmann's rebuilding of the city, during which time thousands of private dwellings were heated with bituminous coal and few edifices were cleaned, the capital had a general pallor of dull gray—appropriate, it seemed, for the period of Occupation. Otherwise, much was different. Most conspicuous to the visitor were perhaps the thickets of black-and-white German direction signs on every street corner, pointing the way to this or that military post. Nor to be overlooked were huge banners, hanging from the façade of the National Assembly building and the Eiffel Tower, with their block letters: "DEUTSCHLAND SIEGT AN ALLEN FRONTEN" (Germany is everywhere victorious). There were wooden or metal barriers and hundreds of sandbags strewn in many of the streets, enabling the Germans to cordon off protective zones around hotels and public buildings. Those obstacles quickly became so numerous, in fact, that orders were issued to remove some of them "so that the impression of the urban space will not thereby be disturbed."[1] But Parisians could scarcely avoid the sight of dozens of swastika flags throughout the city or the groups of uniformed soldiers roaming its boulevards. Moreover, the passing traffic looked different. Bicycles were everywhere. Interwar Paris had been crazy about automobiles, but now they were mostly gone, except for official German military vehicles. There were also fewer busses running, so that patronage of the subway system rose suddenly by 25 percent to well over two million passengers a day.[2] In the inner city, around the Place de la

Concorde, everything came to a stop at dawn and dusk to allow passage of an ostentatious parade of German troops and the changing of guards at the main military command post (*Hauptwache*) on the corner of the Rue de Rivoli and the Rue de Castiglione, near the Hotel Meurice where the Commandant resided. Another major transformation occurred at night through a mandatory blackout. Paris was no longer the city of light.[3]

The first and most pressing problem of the Occupation was to house all of the German military and civilian personnel who had flooded into the twenty urban *arrondissements* of Paris and the outlying *banlieue*. The obvious solution was to confiscate or construct barracks for the troops and to requisition hotels for officers with their staffs. A primitive telephone directory of the military administration was issued on 21 June 1940. It was largely a listing of the city's fanciest hotels, fabled names like the Majestic, Meurice, and Lutétia, as well as the Crillon, Raphael, George V, and so forth. These were ideal facilities, providing bedrooms, restaurants, bars, and office space, all with impeccable service at French expense. According to the terms of the armistice, the French agreed to pay daily a tidy sum of 20 million German marks—that is, 400 million French francs—to cover the costs of the Occupation. During the next four years, therefore, German officials would lead a charmed life in the most comfortable and elegant surroundings imaginable.[4]

In the first stage of the Occupation, at least, life for the common soldiers was doubtless less princely but hardly less exciting. German records leave no question that there was a great deal of drinking and whoring, despite explicit orders to the contrary. From Fontainebleau, General von Brauchitsch reminded all officers that they were to be "exemplary representatives of the German army" and that he would therefore expect of them an "iron discipline." This message was passed on down the line. Troops were instructed to observe a model behavior: "every single soldier" would be required to display "the sharpest discipline, exemplary conduct, and enthusiasm for the duties of security and occupation."[5] When walking in the streets, uniformed personnel were prohibited from smoking or loosening their tie. They should observe all French traffic signs and signals at crosswalks. Speed limits were posted (and often ignored) for Paris: 40 kilometers an hour by day, 20 by night.[6] Military persons were forbidden at first to enter French cinemas and were restricted to special *Soldatenkinos* in the inner city. True, restaurants and cafés were another matter. Yet even there regulations applied. Soldiers were confined, like French civilians, to ordering solely three-course meals, and they were warned about illegal cocaine sales at neighborhood bars.[7]

Ideally, military authorities would have wished nothing better than a blanket policy of non-fraternization, but enforcement was impossible. Consequently, before long, the Occupation had created a maze of social restrictions and prohibitions—in sum, an elaborate new public etiquette. There would be no swimming in the Seine, no dancing in public, no singing in the streets, no horse riding in the Bois de Boulogne (to avoid "grotesque scenes" there by the untutored), no purchases of pornography, and certainly no association with "black and Jewish women" (*Negerinnen und Jüdinnen*), both because such contacts were an offense against the Reich's racial laws and because they were simply "unworthy of a German soldier."[8] Also, military persons were discouraged from frequenting French shops (although many did) and from picking up "collectibles." Detailed instructions concerning "spoils of war" (*Kriegsbeute*) were sent from Berlin by Field Marshal Keitel himself. In principle, he noted, everything that was portable could be so classified: gold, weapons, horses, etc. Yet they must be seized only by the state, not by individuals. Plundering, apart from items of urgent military necessity, was forbidden. To be sure, soldiers might obtain souvenirs of little or no monetary worth without official approval, but they must not steal any valuable property.[9] Nor was hoarding ("as has happened") to be tolerated. Whenever possible, shopping should be done at German military department stores and liquor outlets. Organized bus tours in the capital would care for visiting troops, who were deposited at special military boutiques near the Bois de Boulogne to make any desired purchases before leaving the city. When in the capital, soldiers naturally wanted to explore and carouse, despite being told that such behavior was "strictly forbidden." One junior officer complained that these restrictions created an "impossible circumstance" and requested that more free time be accorded for strolling and shopping. Military personnel stationed in Paris were meanwhile urged to spend their time at *Soldatenheime*, in effect, army clubhouses where they could find newspapers, snacks, and parlor games to play.[10]

But, understandably, some men had other ideas. They moved about freely in Paris, frequently making use of the metro to do so. It was thus a common experience for French civilians literally to rub shoulders with German soldiers during a subway ride. Reserving first-class carriages for Germans ("ABTEIL FÜR DEUTSCHE") did not entirely solve the problem of close quarters at rush hour. The French especially objected to young German passengers in uniform occupying seats normally reserved for the elderly, the handicapped, or pregnant women. While recognizing the justice of that complaint, Commandant Ernst Schaumburg was nonetheless firm: "In general, the director of the metro has been advised that all German military personnel have priority over the French." Here a single sentence unmistakably spoke volumes.[11]

German soldiers also went to brothels. Indeed, from beginning to end, prostitution was one of the Occupation's insoluble problems. A list of forbidden brothels had been circulated in late June 1940, along with an admonition that most French whores carried venereal disease. In mid-July more than 300 restaurants and 750 hotels were declared off limits because of "wild" prostitution. Then, during the months of that autumn, several notifications of brothels approved for German troops appeared. At first more than thirty were so designated, a number that was later winnowed down to seventeen in the inner city of Paris and seven in the suburbs.[12] Countless reports later conceded that these restrictions were rarely observed. For example, in early November three cafés in the Boulevard de Clichy were proscribed due to the presence of prostitutes, pimps, and drugs. A fortnight later, the Hotel Fairyland (sixty-four rooms) at the nearby Place Blanche was also sanctioned because of an altercation there between soldiers and shady women. In December, a nightclub next to the more decorous Moulin Rouge came under the same order. Such instances, among many others, were sufficient to preserve the already established international reputation of the area around the Place Pigalle.[13]

To control all of this sexual enthusiasm was well beyond the capacity of Occupation authorities. They did appoint a "morality commission" (*Sittenkommissariat*) for the city, which ordered French police to close down 300 locales that allegedly had "colored" (*farbige*) or Jewish owners and guests.[14] They also sent patrols to some of the more disreputable Parisian hotels, where it was confirmed that soldiers were taking prostitutes to their rooms. The German Commandant let it be known that this practice, if unchecked, would be "damaging in the highest degree to the reputation of the army" and that those guilty would receive "severe punishment."[15] Yet the truth remained that the sex business was thriving in Paris and that police raids on hotels and "houses" were ineffective in containing it. Alarmingly, as a consequence, measures to combat the spread of venereal disease were "practically unenforceable," as the army's chief staff physician admitted, since it was simply impossible for German doctors to examine every prostitute in Paris. The matter would have to be left to the French.[16]

By no means was this the Occupation's only unresolved issue. Another was the enforcement of a curfew in the entire Occupied Zone, which was thought a suitable means to curtail untoward activity at night. But its application proved to be vexing and variable. In the first place, all clocks in occupied France had to be set to German time. Rural dwellers were required to be in their homes by 9:00 PM, whereas in cities the curfew hour would be fixed by each local military commander. Initially, that limit was put at midnight for Paris, with restaurants and cinemas forced to close at least a half hour earlier in order to allow enough time for guests to return to their residence to meet the deadline. This rule was later tightened to 11:00 PM but then relaxed once more to midnight.[17] The ensuing confusion was manifest, compounded by various exceptions and violations too numerous to count. Repeatedly, there were reports of both German soldiers and French civilians on the streets after midnight, and yet "an intervention by the French police," one report read, "was nowhere to be observed." In part, this indiscipline was encouraged by the blackout regulations forbidding public lighting or open fires after dark. Hence, it was relatively easy to avoid detection. As usual, French police were instructed to exercise "strict control" of non-compliance, and placards were mounted throughout the city with a warning that violations would be "most harshly punished." But neither uniformity nor regularity was ever achieved, and the question of a curfew remained a source of irritation for everyone concerned.[18]

Even the most harmless forms of public comportment in Paris could be a headache for the Occupation. It must be recalled that many of the occupying troops were young boys far from home who were dazzled by the big city and who harbored no hostile or haughty attitude toward its citizens. The report by a Lieutenant Dietsch to his military superiors in November 1940 described a Catholic mass in the cathedral of Notre Dame at which about twenty German soldiers were seated in the congregation among French worshippers. Either they did not realize that such commingling was forbidden, Dietsch remarked, or else they were knowingly violating army regulations. "A sense of nationality seems to escape these soldiers altogether," he concluded.[19] At the same time, French youth also presented difficulties. Particularly bothersome for the police was the rowdy behavior of audiences at Parisian cinemas. Packed together, seated in the dark, they would emit "loud whistles" during newsreels at the appearance of Hitler or Göring, and there was "strong applause" for scenes of destruction caused in Germany by British bombers. On one occasion, English soldiers were shown on the screen singing "It's a Long Way to Tipperary," whereupon about fifty voices joined in the chorus, which ended with vigorous clapping and cries of "Vive l'Angleterre."[20] The Germans were eager to quell such outbursts and issued orders through the Prefecture of Police that movie theater managers, at the first sign of disorder, should turn on the house lights. If the trouble continued, the cinema was to be emptied and, if necessary, closed. Strict enforcement in this case did eventually achieve some success. By the summer of 1941, restrictions were lifted and Parisians could once again watch newsreels in a fully darkened auditorium.[21]

While on the subject of public behavior, it is fitting to add a word about rats. The Occupation, as it turned out, had to contend not only with human beings but also with small gray beasts with long tails who were veteran residents of the capital and who now thrived on a new bonanza of German trash, for which no regular collection was at first provided. From the perspective of Parisian rats, the Germans had by far the best garbage in town. No wonder they began flocking from their usual habitats to nearby military installations. Alarmed German commanders therefore ordered retaliation by poison, while declaring the need for a "general rat annihilation." Again, it was necessary for that purpose to mobilize the Prefecture of Police, which responded by unleashing a special Service de Dératisation for the city.[22] Finally, in the spring of 1941, a concerted extermination campaign began. As the new Prefect of Police, Admiral François Bard, explained, it would be impossible to determine precisely how many rats might actually be killed, because the poison being used took several days to take effect and many rats would expire uncounted in their holes. Still, he promised "a marked improvement" at once and anticipated another slaughter in the near future.[23]

In general, regarding the impact on daily life in Paris under their administration, German military authorities had reason to be pleased with the opening of the Occupation. Yet their evaluations of the "attitude" (*Stimmung*) of the populace were surprisingly frank and unflattering for the Occupation. The mass exodus from the capital during early June 1940 had stunned the Parisians, who lapsed into a state of shock and awe. This numbness soon wore off, however, once the refugees began to return in large numbers. They had not taken full measure of the tragic end of the Third Republic, had not meekly accepted military defeat, and were therefore "less friendly" toward their occupiers. This negative tendency became more pronounced in the autumn, German evaluations agreed, with the onset of food and fuel shortages and the beginning of rationing. Especially in Paris, long lines formed every morning in front of bakeries, meat counters, dairies, and tobacco shops, and in those lines people grumbled, sometimes loudly, invariably blaming the Germans for their collective discomfort.[24]

This consistently pessimistic picture was corroborated in early October 1940 by the head of the MBF's administrative staff, Dr. Jonathan Schmid, in a report to General von Streccius. He listed five reasons for the general decline of public morale in Paris: (1) the realization of defeat sinking in; (2) the visibly worsening economy; (3) the effectiveness of English propaganda; (4) the return of refugees from southern France; and (5) the continuing activity of Communist saboteurs.[25] One month later, a secret Abwehr memo from the Hotel Lutétia, forwarded to the German Foreign Office in Berlin, concurred with this appraisal. It noted that Parisians, grumbling aside, had become "completely apathetic and indifferent" despite a "rather strong" lingering hope in some circles for an eventual English victory.[26] To obtain a second opinion, it is useful to look much farther down the chain of command to the simultaneous reports submitted by more junior military officers who were in daily contact with the local population. Here, in familiar terms that well summarized the first phase of the Occupation, the French were described as "quiet and correct" or "reserved and cautious." Although this repressed atmosphere did not preclude the perception of a growing Germanophobia in Paris, it did suggest that by the early summer of 1941, France had essentially submitted to the dictates of German military order.[27] Nevertheless, it must have been sobering for military superiors to read parallel reports from the administrative staff and its Propaganda Section in the spring of 1941 indicating that French interest in collaboration had "effectively sunk to zero."[28]

Nothing is harder to judge than this subtle interaction of the occupier and the occupied, a combination of irrationality, complicity, and deep resentment.

One of the noticeable factors in this mixture, against which regulations were helpless, was an endless spate of speculations. A general breakdown of communications and of confidence in the impartiality of the media doubtless accounted for this phenomenon. The list of rumors is very long. The British were landing at French ports as well as bombing castles in the Loire Valley. Hitler was living in the Hotel Majestic. There was a revolt in the Balkans. The United States was entering the war. The Germans were going to leave Paris after inflicting a terrible bloodbath on the city. The Vichy government was moving to Paris. The Germans had invaded England. Thirty thousand armed Gaullists would soon be attacking the Occupation army. And so on.[29] Yet at the same time, the Germans were making frequent note of the "absolutely tentative" attitude of the Parisian populace. If some of the upper classes were inclined toward collaboration, the lower were "absolutely uncertain." With his tipsters and plainclothes policemen scattered in the city, Helmut Knochen gathered much of this small talk. He was convinced that the average Frenchman had no taste for politics, cared mostly about his own satisfaction, and regarded the Pétain regime with "a certain indifference."[30]

If there was a tide in the affairs of Frenchmen, that drift was not propitious for the Occupation. Confidential German reports continued to be frank and to paint a bleak picture of stiffening negative public opinion. "The Parisians want the Germans to withdraw soon," said one, because they did "not view the German Occupation favorably."[31] Knochen observed an "increasing anti-German tendency." And Streccius's staff warned that an "anti-German attitude is beginning to gain ground."[32] Otto Abetz agreed, noting in mid-September that personal relations with the French citizenry had "considerably soured" since June and that one could well speak of "passive resistance." He was seconded in that view by Professor Friedrich Grimm, who regularly traveled to Paris and provincial towns to give lectures (in French) for the Groupe Collaboration. If there had been an initial popular depression or at least stupor, he wrote, that was long gone, increasingly replaced by bitter recriminations. As a consequence, in his opinion, "a genuine reconciliation with France is not possible."[33]

Such pessimism could not have taken the military administration by surprise, since its own sources were expressing much the same evaluation. In truth, the fledgling policy of collaboration was apparently failing. Otto von Stülpnagel's own staff was telling him so. Werner Best's unit could not deny "that the majority of the French are still hostile to everything German," while Hans Speidel's office stressed "the deeply rooted mistrust of Germany."[34] Perhaps the whole situation was best summarized by a banal observation on 21 June 1941 by Commandant Schaumburg. He told of a singer at the music hall Alhambra who interjected into her act "sarcastic remarks" about collaboration that were spontaneously greeted by "applause throughout the room."[35] On the next day, news of the German invasion of Russia reached Paris.

Chapter 3

ECONOMY AND ARMAMENT

The confusion and lack of planning so evident in other aspects of the Occupation were also apparent in German attempts to secure a grip on the French economy. In most regards, France's pre-war infrastructure remained intact. Farms and factories had rarely been damaged. However, transportation was a problem because rail junctions had been destroyed by the retreating French army and bridges had been purposely collapsed or buckled in combat, often falling so as to block waterways. The highly inefficient consequence was an initial dependence on trucks, which meant that supplies of food and fuel were slow to reach Paris. Meanwhile, refugees straggled back into the city, and the first signs of mass unemployment became obvious. Yet it was a warm and beautiful summer across the French countryside, where the population seemed quite astonished that the suffering of a conquered nation could be so relatively moderate. By early July the Germans noticed "a certain relaxation" of tensions that had caused the great exodus from the capital.[1]

German organization was slow to take shape. The first administrative innovation was an Inspectorate for Armament (Rüstung) under Major General Schubert, which was assigned to oversee repairs—of machines and vehicles, for example—and to procure unspecified materials "important for the German economy." Meanwhile, an Economic Agency (Wirtschaft) was also created. These two units, usually identified in abbreviated form as Wi and Rü, were soon unified into a single Wi Rü Stab Frankreich, reporting to General von Streccius, with affiliated offices in Bordeaux, Rouen, and Troyes. The officer immediately in charge of this staff, General Franz von Barckhausen, arrived in the capital in early July, with dozens of other functionaries to follow in the next weeks. Not before the beginning of August did this office for economic affairs declare itself to be functioning. As previously noted, a separate Economic Section (Wirtschaftsabteilung) under Dr. Elmar Michel was also meanwhile attached to the MBF's administrative staff.[2]

The most urgent needs of Paris, of course, were fuel and food. Electrical power had to be restored, and for that purpose French employees were "obliged" to cooperate in repairing high-tension lines. Likewise, coal was essential to supply energy for both electrical power and industrial plants—hence the priority given to reopening railways from coal fields in the Lille region, requiring participation by officials and *cheminots* of the Société Nationale des Chemins de Fer (SNCF). Added to this was the necessity by early autumn of mobilizing crews for the coming harvest in which French peasants would be assisted by German military personnel. These were the earliest and most basic forms of "collaboration" (*Zusammenarbeit*). In the original vocabulary of the Occupation, that term was used freely, without the freight of political connotations that later burdened the neologism *Kollaboration*. Such was the message delivered by General Brauchitsch in mid-July and repeated by Streccius in a memo on the urgency of the reconstruction effort in France "insofar as is necessary for the fulfillment of German military, political, and economic objectives." Precisely what those objectives were, it must be observed, still lacked a firm definition.[3]

By late July 1940, then, German reports on the economic situation in France were replete with optimistic appraisals such as "satisfactory," "good progress," "further improvement," and so forth.[4] Yet there were three nagging difficulties for which the Occupation had no ready panacea. The first was unemployment. Predictably, the disruptions caused by military combat and the massive southward flight of population had closed a multitude of businesses and factories in the Paris region. Normalcy could not be rapidly restored. Consequently, a German report on 17 July stated that the Department of the Seine already had 83,000 persons registered as unemployed, of which 60 percent were women and at least 25,000 were either over the age of 65 or "incapacitated" (*unfähig*). Not only was the national economy thereby weakened, but a considerable strain was being put on financial means to provide social assistance for the needy. A portion of the necessary resources would come from employers and the rest, presumably, from the French government. All of this was supervised by the Employment and Social Welfare Section (Abteilung Arbeitseinsatz und Sozialwesen) of the Occupation, which also supplied some alarming statistics: by mid-August social aid in Greater Paris was being provided for 180,000 individuals without work, an increase of 125,000 in one month. No improvement of this trend was in sight.[5]

A second issue was inflation. This problem was forever confounding for the Germans, who never succeeded in calming the ceaseless fluctuation of prices and wages. In principle, their policy was to impose a system of strict price controls, fixing a limit at the level of 1 September 1939. But that proposal proved to be a leaky pot. Symptomatic was an administrative report in late July that identified nearly 8,000 cases of price gouging in Paris requiring investigation. Eighty-nine trials resulted, ending with forty convictions that could bring a maximum sentence of three months in prison and a fine.[6] Moreover, some inflationary pressures could scarcely be contained. Even if food prices were fixed in Parisian shops, the black market was irrepressible, especially as the Germans themselves were among its best customers. Restaurants were required to post menus with announced prices, but what of special dishes prepared to suit personal tastes or group requests? The better restaurants were especially known to charge German officers, without their complaint, more dearly than regular French patrons. Luxury goods in France, notably in the more elegant clothing emporiums, traditionally bore no price tags, and bargaining between owners and customers was a common, long-established practice. Was it really the duty of German finance inspectors to change an entire culture?[7]

Thirdly, and crucially, the Occupation had to contend with an unsettled labor market. A first tip-off came in mid-July with a notification from Berlin that Field Marshal Hermann Göring, head of the famous Four Year Plan, demanded a transfer of miners to the Ruhr from the coalfields of Belgium and northern France. These orders were followed in early August by similar instructions to recruit agricultural labor for the Reich.[8] Later that month the shipment of workers from France began. At first they were entirely foreigners, mostly Poles and Czechs, and largely unskilled. On 15 August 1940, about 500 were sent from Paris to Germany by rail. Further transports departed on 22 and 28 August, including some married couples and a few children aged seven to thirteen. Gruesome to say, but literally true, it was good practice for the German administration and the SNCF.[9]

Beyond the details, a fundamental question about the fate of the French economy was gradually emerging. Was the primary German purpose to integrate or to eliminate the productive capacity of France? This question was explicitly posed when orders arrived from Berlin to ship French machines, tools, and raw materials to the Reich. Yet it was unclear how such instructions could be carried out without at the same time reducing the potential of French firms to supply parts for the German arms and aircraft industry. The Wi Rü staff therefore advised that it would be "hardly possible" to do both at once.[10] The Germans had neither a policy nor a plan for its implementation. That uncomfortable truth was underscored in late September by Hans Speidel, who again raised the overarching issue of whether the objective of the Occupation was to incorporate France into the New Order or to "wipe it out" (*völlig zerschlagen*) as a European and colonial power. Everything, he added, would depend on the answer; until then, "political ambiguity will hinder clear and purposeful effort."[11]

The formulation of an economic policy for France came in bits and drabs throughout that autumn. A first pronouncement by Göring can be traced back to 14 August, when he attempted to draw a distinction between direct and indirect French participation in the war industry. The former, meaning the supply of finished military products, was categorically rejected by him. Hence, France should provide only parts of machines and weapons that could then be assembled in Germany. Such an arrangement was unfeasible in practice, however, and it was never actually implemented.[12] Göring nonetheless persisted, especially in his alternate role as chief of the German Luftwaffe. In September he let it be known that the transfer of machines, parts, and skilled labor to bolster Germany's aircraft industry must be given "unconditional priority." This message was immediately echoed by a Wi Rü staff memo declaring that all efforts must be devoted "to raise the war potential of the German arms industry."[13] A brief visit by Göring to Paris in mid-September was undoubtedly intended to reinforce his authority in the matter, although he seemed to be rather more concerned about inspecting French paintings to be purloined for his private art collection.

Finally, at the end of October, the director of the military administration's Economic Section, Dr. Michel, issued a set of general guidelines (for which he credited Göring) that would now govern the French economy. Succinctly put, they contained four main points: (1) the primary objective was to increase German war potential; (2) to that end, administrators in Paris must identify and promote those French firms useful for military production, even if that meant closing others; (3) civilian consumption in France should be reduced to a minimum; and (4) all Jewish businesses were to be terminated.[14] A supplementary report ten days later declared the policy issue of integration or elimination of French industrial capacity to be thereby resolved, although some practical difficulties of implementation admittedly remained.[15] There is no way to measure the impact of these successive declamations, but it is hard to evaluate them as much more than political posturing that did little in fact to clarify the future course of the French economy. At least the obvious priority was unequivocally stated: the military wants and needs of Nazi Germany would henceforth be paramount.

Policy statements accomplished nothing to improve the standard of living in Paris as the first winter of the Occupation approached. Conditions, as the always alert Helmut Knochen remarked in early October, were becoming "ever more difficult."[16] By the time Otto von Stülpnagel assumed command at the end of that month, it was possible to locate three perpetual sources of discontent. First, there was the unstable labor situation. Unemployment in Paris continued to climb. German staff memos estimated that about 570,000 adults in Greater Paris were without work, which was fully two-thirds of the total in the Occupied Zone. Those numbers, constantly augmented by the return of refugees and the lack of raw materials needed to reopen industrial plants, did not begin to recede until December. Not before the end of January 1941 could a significant reduction be reported.[17]

Second, the recruitment of workers for the Reich was lagging. By the beginning of October 1940, fewer than 6,000 had volunteered. Three months later that figure barely exceeded 20,000. One notable development was the willingness of some French laborers to leave the country in order to find employment at higher wages in Germany. Not until the beginning of February 1941, however, did French recruits outnumber Polish labor exported from France.[18] The laborers came primarily from Paris, where unemployment was highest. Pathetic reports from German recruiters told a lamentable story of their lack of success in attracting candidates outside of the capital. One German official recorded "a very meager result" from his efforts in several rural villages. Instead of wasting further time, he returned to Paris.[19] Another in nearby Orléans found recruits there to be mostly "used," that is, old, ill, or handicapped. Many of them were drifters, often jobless as well as homeless. Competent French laborers were scarcely to be found "because they reject employment in Germany."[20] A different explanation was simply the rising need for labor to be retained within France, especially for farm and forestry work, but also for the Organisation Todt (OT), that formidable German engineering enterprise charged first with restoring French railroads and waterways and then with constructing fortifications of the Atlantic Wall.[21] Thus, the balance slowly began to tip from unemployment to labor shortage, creating a situation that would soon require more drastic measures of recruitment.

Third, the energy supply was insufficient. France had always been a coal-poor country, and that deficiency now threatened to become acute. Simultaneous estimates by Michel and his administrative superior, Jonathan Schmid, stated on 2 October that coal deliveries to Paris were about half of current needs and the total of energy supply no more than 75 percent, which was "completely insufficient." No improvement could be signaled a month later as the weather turned raw.[22] It happened that the winter of 1940–1941 was exceptionally cold. Canals iced over, while many railway tracks in northern France froze and became unusable. Accordingly, food and fuel supplies to French cities, notably Paris, suffered "a considerable degradation."[23] As always, shortages, work stoppages, the lack of heating and hot water, and the high price of cigarettes—to name only a few of the common complaints—were all blamed on the Occupation. One report to the German Embassy in Paris from Nancy described the bitterness expressed by French women lining up before a market, where one cried out: "It's high time that these thieves [German soldiers] were driven out. We women are going to help." Essentially, the same reporter later added, the entire Occupation was a "question of the stomach" (*Magenfrage*). Unless authorities could resolve the bedrock economic issues of jobs, wages, and supplies, any attempt at persuasion of the occupied populace through propaganda would be futile.[24]

Once the Occupation began to operate through rationing and inflation controls, there was no end to complications. Prices were to be fixed by the French but regulated by the Germans, thus creating a broad zone for manipulation and friction between them. And prices had to be set in francs, since the rule (often ignored) was that no German currency could be paid out to French civilians.[25] All this necessitated repeated, elaborately detailed negotiations that wandered through a maze of trivia. For example, one must imagine a grotesque discussion—which actually occurred on 19 February 1941—in which ten senior German military officers convened around a table to determine the price of champagne to be served in Paris nightclubs. The gathering could agree that the currently applied scale of costs was inoperable. They thereupon decided that the normal charge for a bottle of fine champagne would be 200 francs, with a proviso that cheaper brands be made available for 150 or 175 francs. A charge of 250 francs was allowed only in luxury establishments, ten of which (including the Lido, for instance) were approved. The length of this list was later doubled.[26]

A more serious and no less complex issue was the extent of the working week. Given the high rate of unemployment during the first months of the Occupation, French officials thought it wise to limit labor to a maximum of 40 hours a week. But the beginning of recruitment for work in Germany and the decline of unemployment figures in Paris in early 1941 caused a change of policy, although not without debate. Whereas one group in the Wi Rü staff wanted to increase the maximum hours in order to enhance French productivity, another argued that such a measure would be harmful to German interests, namely, in the effort to attract more French labor for shipment to the Reich.[27] For its part, the French regime in Vichy favored maintaining the 40-hour maximum, both to cut unemployment and thereby to discourage further recruitment of workers for Germany. At last, on 26 March 1941, the working day for factory labor in the Occupied Zone was extended to ten hours, with a maximum of fifty-four hours per week. By then it was clear that high unemployment was a thing of the past and that German officials would need to open a more vigorous campaign to "comb out" excess workers from French firms to make them available for shipment from Paris.[28]

Guidelines for labor recruitment, twenty-seven pages long, were issued by the German military administration in mid-April. The program remained strictly voluntary, intended for those "willing and able" to live in Germany. Workers had to be between the ages of eighteen and forty-five. Families with children would no longer be accepted. Foreigners, with the exception of "non-Aryans," were welcome.[29] So much for theory. By the spring of 1941, shipments to Germany averaged about 500 workers a week, and they brought many problems with them. Some were physically unfit or ill-adapted to their assigned jobs. Of 400 French laborers sent to a German airplane factory in early May, a large contingent was summarily returned to Paris. Those who remained were promised furloughs every three months to visit their families, and they were visibly discontent when that offer was withdrawn. Once a year was more often the rule.[30] By the beginning of June, nearly 50,000 laborers had been transferred to the Reich. Incredibly precise (and perhaps therefore dubious) German statistics permit a general profile to be drawn. In terms of skills, 19,205 were metal workers, 18,947 were in construction, and 12,774 categorized as "others" were mostly farm hands. As for nationality, the total included 22,705 French, 7,464 Poles, 6,698 Russians, and an assortment of various Eastern Europeans. These numbers were disappointing for German officials, but no doubt recruitment was an imperfect and tedious process.[31]

Far less precision was possible when evaluating the overall contribution of French production to the German war effort. Statistics were as yet scattered and at best symptomatic. One economic sector stood out and may be considered indicative of Germany's gathering success in harnessing French industry. According to a survey by Occupation authorities, the production of trucks in France between July 1940 and the end of March 1941 reached exactly 37,399 units, of which 29,782 were requisitioned by the German military command. If so, it is safe to conclude that France was supplying the armed forces with an approximate annual average of 24,000 heavy vehicles—not a negligible feat.[32] This significance of France as an economic factor for the Reich was not overlooked by Hermann Göring, who signed a directive on 29 March again calling attention to the overriding need "to coordinate the French economy with necessities of the German war economy." During the initial phase of the Occupation, he professed, this imperative was being adequately fulfilled, but as the war proceeded French productivity was certain to grow ever more important. Surely Göring knew whereof he spoke, since the planning in Berlin for an invasion of Russia was already well advanced, and he was therefore better able than anyone in Paris to peer into the future.[33]

Virtually as a postscript, one further economic matter needs to be mentioned here. In late May 1941, 18,000 French coal miners in the departments of the Nord and Pas-de-Calais briefly went on strike to protest low salaries and tight rations. The German response was uncertain and hesitant. A long shutdown of the mines would severely reduce coal supplies to Paris—and shipments did in fact decrease in early June to half of normal capacity. What concessions, if any, should be made? Ambassador Otto Abetz confirmed that the miners' demands were partially justified, and he recommended modest raises in wages and food allotments. But there was apparently also a political aspect to the protests. It could not be the Occupation's policy to tolerate Communist agitators. Fortunately, most of the miners returned to their pits after forty-eight hours. Yet this troubling incident would henceforth need to be appended to the Occupation's long agenda of unresolved dilemmas.[34]

Chapter 4

CULTURE AND PROPAGANDA

In the context of the Occupation, the juxtaposition of propaganda and culture was self-evident. For the Germans, culture was propaganda and vice versa. But the problem of managing the public sphere and of influencing public opinion in Paris was far more perturbing for the occupiers than that simple formulation might imply.

It is well to begin with high culture, in particular, the performing arts of opera, music, and theater, and to observe that the French capital has seldom in its history witnessed such a glorious display of creative endeavor as during the Occupation. Within weeks after the German entry into Paris, the old state theaters—the Opéra, the Opéra Comique, the Comédie Française, and the Odéon—were up and running on a regular schedule. This is not to mention the dozens of smaller stages in the city, which resumed in the autumn of 1940 with performances of Jean Cocteau, Paul Claudel, Jean Giraudoux, and Jean Anouilh, among many others.[1] To this rich diet the Germans added a glittering display of talent, especially musical. Barely three weeks after the Occupation began, the Berlin Philharmonic held two concerts in Paris and another in Versailles. In November, the Parisian elite was treated at the Opéra to Beethoven's *Fidelio*, Mozart's *Figaros Hochzeit*, and Wagner's *Der fliegende Holländer*, while *Parsifal, Der Rosenkavalier*, and Gluck's *Alceste* were announced on the program for January 1941. Orchestral concerts offered by ensembles from Berlin, Cologne, Dresden, and Munich were meanwhile frequent at the Palais de Chaillot and the Théâtre des Champs-Elysées.[2] All of this cultural opulence was clearly intended to coax the discriminating Parisian public into a warmer appreciation of the Occupation and presumably therefore a more collaborative mood by presenting the best that Germany had to offer. One such occasion in late December 1940 deserves special mention. A Bach concert under the direction of Herbert von Karajan at the Chaillot was to be sponsored by Dr. Robert Ley's organization, Kraft durch Freude (Strength through Joy), but a personal request in Berlin by Ambassador Otto Abetz obtained permission for a transfer of sponsorship to the newly founded German Institute in Paris, attached to the German Embassy, with a welcoming speech by Abetz himself. As the first major event of the Institute, it was acclaimed by its director, Dr. Karl Epting, to be a rousing success of cultural prowess and effective propaganda.[3]

Limited by the language barrier, theater was a less promising medium. Yet the Germans spared no effort or expense during the winter months by bringing to Paris, for example, productions of *Kabale und Liebe* performed by Berlin's Schiller Theater and *Ute von Naumburg* by the Lessing Theater.[4] Language was far less a factor when the Zirkus Busch visited Paris several times in the autumn of 1940.[5] Likewise reaching a broader spectrum of the populace were the many open air concerts by German military bands at such venues as the Parvis Notre Dame, the Tuileries, the Buttes Chaumont, the Jardin de Luxembourg, and the Place de la République. At the very least, Parisians must have concluded that young German men made excellent musicians.[6] All this was set against the backdrop of a flourishing Paris nightlife, strongly encouraged by the Occupation in the name of normalcy. One list in early 1941 gave the names of 32 *variétés*—showgirl reviews, music halls, or vaudeville theaters—with famous names like the Folies Bergère, Mayol, Venus, and so on. These full houses were frequented nightly both by French patrons and by stationed or visiting German troops, for whom tickets were made available at half price.[7]

It is of course impossible to quantify the effect of this great German charm offensive. If anything, Occupation authorities tended to exaggerate the salutary impact of officially sponsored events, of which two examples must suffice here. After obtaining clearance from the German Embassy, a predictably unflattering exhibit on European Freemasonry was opened at the Petit Palais in mid-October 1940. Enthusiastic German reports claimed that massive crowds estimated at 50,000 were in attendance daily, a stampede such that the show had to be extended by a fortnight into December. In all, the Embassy insisted, within six weeks over a million Parisians had attended the exhibit, where they were "hammered" by two principal themes: first, that Freemasons and Jews were responsible for all the miseries that had befallen France; and, second, that a French recovery would become possible only by a thorough cleansing of those elements and by adoption of the Nazi *Weltanschauung*. How the restrained and somber throngs, whose numbers were undoubtedly inflated, in fact responded to these blunt messages, the Embassy report could not say.[8]

Less noteworthy but no less indicative was a concert of sacred music given by the Regensburger Domchor in April 1941 at the cathedral of Notre Dame, during which, according to Dr. Epting, 6,000 individuals were present. Although Notre Dame is a very large structure, to be sure, it is altogether improbable that so many persons could have been crowded into it at one time.[9]

That the ill-defined public realm of culture and propaganda was not relegated to a single agency of the Occupation consequently produced its first serious internal conflict. This friction began with Adolf Hitler, who decided in August 1940 that the Paris Embassy should exercise full authority over "the treatment of all political questions," including the most salient media of propaganda: press, radio, publications, film, and theater. These, Abetz was quick to specify, now fell "exclusively within the responsibility of my staff." Visibly flushed with self-importance, the Ambassador conferred with Brauchitsch and Streccius, advising them that the military administration henceforth might handle only censorship duties and otherwise assist in cultural matters, albeit strictly under Abetz's supervision. Learning of this turn of events, the commander of the military's Propaganda Section, Major Heinz Schmidtke, immediately left for Berlin.[10] But his protest there was to no avail. The decision remained, commensurate with Hitler's decree, that the Embassy "alone" would control all matters directly related to political propaganda. Schmidtke would thus be obliged to take orders from Abetz, whose own definition of his expanding mandate seemed boundless.[11]

All of this bickering and personal in-fighting was further complicated by another intervention from OKW in Berlin. This involved Hitler's selection of Alfred Rosenberg to "secure" from French museums, archives, and libraries an unspecified number of art works as well as documents suitable for shipment to Germany. This arrangement was probably at the instigation of Hermann Göring and certainly with his connivance.[12] The upshot was a heated dispute between the Einsatzstab Rosenberg—a special contingent from Berlin established on the Boulevard Haussmann—and the German Embassy in the Rue de Lille. In the limited domain of paintings and manuscripts, as it turned out this time, Abetz was the loser. When he complained to the administrative staff of MBF that some actions by Rosenberg's underlings, such as confiscating the libraries of non-Jews, were politically harmful and that it was "urgently necessary" to restrict them, he was coolly informed by Jonathan Schmid that it was "foremost" up to the Embassy to iron out things with Berlin on its own.[13] The sharpness and at times the pettiness of these frequent bureaucratic exchanges gave a sense of the strains and rivalries engendered in the first phase of the Occupation.

The same reality was apparent when it came to censorship. One thing that all German agencies could agree upon was the effectiveness of Allied propaganda via British radio. What to do about it? Whereas the MBF ordered that listening to foreign broadcasts was forbidden and should be severely punished, the Embassy warned that strict enforcement would be politically inadvisable and in any case unfeasible. Attempts were made to counter Radio London by endowing Radio Paris with "a truly French face" and by avoiding an impression of tight German control over the news. Yet the issue was never actually resolved, and Werner Best's military staff gloomily conceded that "after 6:30 PM English radio rules the airwaves."[14]

Print was another matter. As for the newspaper press, whose daily circulation in the Paris region was nearly three million, censorship was largely self-governing. After all, the Occupation held all the trump cards. If a news report or editorial displeased German censors, an editor could be quickly informed that his allotment of raw paper (mostly imported from Germany and Scandinavia) was to be curtailed or stopped altogether. Nor would military authorities hesitate to order French police to raid editorial offices and simply close them down. All things considered, the press in Paris never proved to be a problem for the Occupation.[15]

Books presented a more delicate and less manageable difficulty. According to German statistics compiled in August 1940, counting *arrondissement* by *arrondissement*, the inner city of Paris contained exactly 1,749 bookstores, 438 kiosks, 71 libraries, and 28 *bouquinistes* along the Seine.[16] The first attempt to establish a grip on this abundance of book dealers was the "Liste Bernhard" of forbidden publications, drafted by the Germans, which was then in September incorporated by the French into the somewhat more extensive "Liste Otto," printed in 40,000 copies and distributed throughout the Occupied Zone. On this basis, the first razzias were conducted by police in Paris, which, still more significantly, were followed by raids on seventy publishing houses. Of these, if we are to believe the remarkable exactitude of German reports, eleven were closed, while 713,382 books were seized and sent to warehouses.[17]

The next step was school texts. In an effort to coordinate this special effort of censorship, a caucus (*Arbeitskreis*) was formed that comprised representatives from two MBF agencies, the Propaganda Staff of Paris (Propaganda-Staffel Paris) and a new unit called "School and Culture" (Schule und Kultur); Karl Epting, acting for the Embassy and the German Institute; and police officials of the SS and GFP. This example of bureaucratic overkill soon resounded with echoes of the disputes already in progress higher in the chain of command. On orders from Abetz, Epting seized the initiative, approving a ban on 187 school textbooks and prescribing alterations in 115 others.[18] These sweeping measures did not sit well with the military administration, which found reason to deplore "the vainglorious politics of the German Institute," whose zealous exercise of censorship had resulted in "inaccuracies and incongruities." The motto of the Hotel Majestic, by contrast, was "no unnecessary interference" in French schools, despite the "hateful insults" of some academic texts and the "widespread Germanophobia" evident in instruction.[19]

A counterattack from the German Embassy was to be expected, and it came in a muted but insulting form. Abetz suggested that the MBF's Propaganda Section and its Paris offspring, the Propaganda Staff, should be restrained and renamed "Censorship Offices" (*Zensurstellen*), since the very word "propaganda" was a liability carefully avoided by the Embassy. The difficulty with this proposal, he admitted, was the political situation in Berlin—meaning that Joseph Goebbels was unlikely to tolerate such a derision of his own title and function.[20] Willy-nilly, then, the Occupation's censorship continued in a muddle of mutual recriminations. If there was any evolution of policy, it was a more vigorous attempt to encourage the French to participate in spreading German propaganda. For that purpose, they would need to be persuaded of "the superiority of German culture, efficacy, and organizational skill," thereby drawing them into full collaboration "from a feeling of their inferiority." Just how this lofty ambition was to be accomplished remained unclear.[21]

One bastion of French self-esteem, and also of perceptible anti-German sentiment, was higher education. In Paris, this term referred essentially to the Sorbonne, the Collège de France, and the *grandes écoles*: the elites of the university system in France. Paris was the obvious fulcrum of French intellectual life, as statistics showed. A census in the summer of 1939 had counted over 35,000 university students in the capital. By December 1940, that number was down to about 30,000, and, demographers noted, the proportion of women to men had markedly increased.[22] The teaching corps was of international standing and precisely for that reason was deemed suspect by the Occupation. Yet during its initial phase, dark thoughts did not lead to much action. There was talk, for instance, of moving the École Normale Supérieure from Paris to the Unoccupied Zone, but German authorities soon thought better of it.[23] At the Collège de France, the arrest of three professors was ordered in late October 1940, yet only one of them was actually incarcerated before being released several weeks later.[24] The most dubious of Parisian educational institutions was Sciences Po (École Libre des Sciences Politiques), where the instruction of history, economics, and politics trod on dangerous terrain. Singled out at this institution as "not compatible" with German interests was the historian Pierre Renouvin, author of acclaimed works on the provocative thesis of German war guilt in 1914. Helmut Knochen, speaking for the SS, advocated closing the school altogether, a move opposed by the Embassy on the grounds that it would only create martyrs and cause more trouble than it was worth.[25] Abetz did agree, nonetheless, that an investigation should be conducted of all faculty members "whose activity contradicts German interests." Knochen was only too willing to comply, and his staff began collecting files on professors at the Sorbonne, the École Pratique des Hautes Études, and the Collège de France, as well as Sciences Po. Again, it was a controversial historian, Edmond Vermeil, known for his specialty in Franco-German studies, who attracted the most attention. After he had fled Paris, Vermeil's personal library was confiscated by the Einsatzstab Rosenberg, which vilified him as "one of the worst agitators against Germany."[26]

Such details serve to document a certain German preoccupation with conducting an academic purge in Paris. To this as yet unrealized intention must be added a distinct strain of collaborationism within the French professorate itself. One noteworthy example was Bernard Faÿ, a historian at the Collège de France, who became director of the Bibliothèque Nationale (BN) in October 1940 after his Jewish predecessor was dismissed. Faÿ was considered "completely loyal" by the German military administration, and he proved it by executing orders that the BN and other university libraries ban the circulation of anti-German publications.[27] Another figure deserving mention in this regard was the classicist Jérôme Carcopino, who was first appointed director of the École Normale Supérieure, then rector of the Sorbonne, and finally Minister of Public Education in the Vichy regime. Siding with Knochen against the more cautious Karl Epting, Carcopino advocated a "cleansing" of the Paris teaching corps. Also, during what can only be described as an outburst of fanaticism in June 1941, he excoriated the "painful episodes," "puerilism," "infantilism," and "naiveté" of French university students, a comportment that exceeded "all decent limits." Hence his categorical statement: "I would approve of all sanctions, even the most severe." Collaborationism had no more fervent advocate.[28]

Here it would be remiss to omit the special case of Frédéric Joliot. A world-renowned expert in radioactivity, a specialist in nuclear fission, and, incidentally, a son-in-law of Pierre and Marie Curie, Joliot was in the process of constructing a cyclotron in his laboratory at the Collège de France when the Germans entered Paris. As such an apparatus did not yet exist in the Third Reich, there could be no mystery why Berlin was interested in Joliot's project. Accordingly, in mid-August 1940, he received a visit from a German physicist, Dr. Erich Schumann, the personal science adviser of OKW Chief of Staff Wilhelm Keitel. Within a month, the Occupation's administrative staff—invoking the right of "an occupying power," according to the Hague Convention—had installed Dr. Kurt Diebner and a few assistants in Joliot's lab with orders that "his instructions are to be followed in every regard."[29] Protracted and intricate negotiations ensued about the terms of cooperation. They sometimes involved hairsplitting over an issue, such as, for instance, whether Diebner's crew was working "beside" (*auprès*) or "with" (*avec*) Joliot. In vain, the French Ministry of Public Education tried to advance the legalistic argument that the Hague Convention "absolutely forbids" seizure of an instructional facility by a foreign power. But the Germans countered that the Paris lab, as well as its affiliate at Ivry-sur-Seine, had previously been used under two military contracts, for which the Hague Convention provided no defense. French objections were therefore "not free of doubt."[30] In short, Joliot was presented with a choice between cooperation and outright confiscation. The laboratories must in any event continue to function, as the German High Command freely stated, "because of their military importance."[31] Whether Joliot, who could not have been unaware of the military implications of atomic energy, deserves criticism as a collaborationist is of course debatable, and it has been debated. Yet a later German memorandum, dated 10 June 1941, affords a broader perspective. It contains an account of a German scientist who had traveled from Berlin to Paris and reported that any French researcher suspected of close collaboration with the Occupation would be boycotted by his colleagues. It would therefore be inadvisable to issue invitations to Paris for French participation in scientific congresses held in Germany. Herein, once more, one finds evidence that Occupation policy had its limits in practice.[32]

As always, in France education was closely tied to religion. Occupation authorities naturally had no interest in stirring enmity within the Catholic Church, but they were troubled, as the military staff commented, by "the international and Germanophobic stance" of the French clergy.[33] At the same time, it was gratefully noted that the Church was adapting to the conditions of the Occupation and generally remained quiet and restrained in public. That impression was strengthened by friendly utterances from members of the higher clergy, including Cardinal Suhard of Paris and Archbishop Baudrillart, the elderly director of the Catholic Institute in the capital. Suhard even made a demonstrative visit to the German Embassy to declare his allegiance to Franco-German rapprochement. But informed and perceptive officers like Hans Speidel warned that the administration should not be deceived by Suhard's amenability because the Church was in fact divided in its feelings. Archbishop Gerlier of Lyon, for example, was notoriously anti-German, and so were many of the lower clergy. Even when Germanophobic tendencies were not openly expressed, they often remained "very deeply felt."[34] Moreover, as Otto von Stülpnagel remarked, Catholic youth groups were "an especially difficult problem." With an estimated membership of 1,200,000, they were rather grudgingly tolerated by the Occupation, although several other youth organizations, including the Boy Scouts, had been officially proscribed. All youth activities in Paris would be closely watched and must be specifically authorized by the German bureaucracy.[35]

Meanwhile, daily religious practice went on as if nothing had changed. In the early days of the Occupation, services for both Catholic and Protestant military personnel were held in Notre Dame, but objections from the Church hierarchy soon put an end to that. Thereafter, Germans held separate services, and one church, Saint Joseph, was formally designated as a sanctuary for military worshipers (*Wehrmachtskirche*) in the Avenue Hoche close by the Arch of Triumph. This apparently harmonious scene was little disturbed by the spring of 1941, even though on one occasion ten priests were briefly detained by the police and a few bishops were reprimanded. Sermons were monitored for hints of anti-German rhetoric, some consistories were investigated, and priests' quarters were searched for weapons. Yet these measures yielded only a "minimal result," as Best's staff confirmed, adding that collaboration had been accepted by the clergy as a practicality, despite the fact that the National Socialist ideology was rejected by them with near unanimity.[36]

A common denominator in the first phase of the Occupation was German restraint. That aspect can be further illustrated by turning to the luxury trades. Nazi Germany had an interest, as Abetz put it, in breaking France's "intellectual monopoly."[37] Certainly, a monopoly existed in fashion, if not in intellect. In late August 1940, Knochen noted fears in Paris that Germany would attempt to suppress the dominant French industry of *haute couture* in order to bolster its own. That was precisely the message brought back from Berlin by the head of the Propaganda Section, Major Schmidtke, who added that a similar policy was also being secretly discussed with regard to the French film industry. Confirmation came straight from Joseph Goebbels himself. Germany's objective, he said, would be to make Berlin "*the* fashion capital of Europe." However, this never happened, as moving an entire industry a thousand kilometers eastward proved to be unfeasible. Runways and fashion houses in the Faubourg St. Honoré were not closed, and Berlin remained in this regard a cultural backwater.[38]

The same was true of the film industry. Apprehensions about German intentions to strangle production caused some French directors and actors—the most prominent including Jean Renoir, Michèle Morgan, and Jean Gabin—to flee from Paris to Hollywood. German Occupation officials soon regretted this and argued against such a policy. It would be better to engage French movie stars in film companies that were openly or covertly regulated by Germany rather than to expel them. Besides, as the special film group of the Propaganda Section observed, maintaining Paris in a pivotal role allowed films to appear on foreign screens without the stigma of being merely instruments of German propaganda. As a result, the French cinema remained a big business throughout most of the Occupation, and, arguably, being freed of Anglo-American competition, it thrived as never before.[39] In Paris alone, by German count, over 300 movie houses operated daily in addition to 1,100 in the provinces. The German role was restricted mostly to censorship of such American confections as Darryl Zanuck's *Chante, bébé, chante* and to the removal of some Jewish-sounding names from theater marquees. With one noteworthy exception, simultaneous efforts to promote the popularity of German films fell flat. That exception was the infamous *Jud Süss*, which played in the French provinces during the spring of 1941 to spontaneous and strong applause and opened that May in 100 Paris cinemas. It was a good showing, no doubt, but hardly evidence that a German intellectual monopoly had displaced the French.[40]

One dog that scarcely barked during the initial phase of the Occupation was French politics. None too coherently, the Germans developed three lines of policy toward political activity in Paris. The first was to accept and indeed to encourage the formation of a single mass party that could be closely watched and tightly controlled. This role was initially assigned to Jacques Doriot's Parti Populaire Français, although its reliability was from the beginning in some doubt.[41] The second was to extend a discreet toleration to other groups with fascist leanings. The problem there, obviously, was to arrive at an approved list, an exercise bound to promote internal altercations. A meeting at the German Embassy on 7 January 1941 identified those organizations, apart from Doriot's, with which the Occupation might cooperate without formally recognizing their statute. The proposed groups included Les Gardes Françaises, Les Francistes, La Cagoule (also known as the Mouvement Social Révolutionnaire), and Le Feu. At that meeting, a third policy decision was unanimously reached: "No group will be allowed to call itself 'party' or 'National Socialist.'" It would therefore be "impossible" to permit any political agitation by the Parti Nationalsocialiste Français of Christian Message ("a permanent source of disorder"), the Parti National-Socialiste Français of Colonel François de la Rocque ("extremely anti-German"), or the all too traditionalist Action Française of Charles Maurras.[42] Disputes arose over the evaluation and treatment of several individuals involved. Message, who was considered "highly undesirable" by the German military administration, was jailed in January 1941 and stayed in detention for ten weeks, during which time his followers slipped away to other rightist groups. Another controversy surrounded Marcel Déat, who was arrested on orders from Vichy but was promptly released in Paris by Stülpnagel. Eugène Deloncle, leader of the Cagoule, attempted to establish an anti-English political club, the Amicales des Combattants de Dunkerque. He found disfavor with the German Embassy when he proposed the release of French POWs who had been captured on Channel beaches in June 1940.[43] Finally, placed in a special category, was the Groupe Collaboration, declared by German authorities to be a "movement" rather than a party. Its main function would be to arrange concerts and lectures, ostensibly under French sponsorship, and thereby to aid the Propaganda Section and the German Institute in their campaign of cultural events.[44]

An issue ancillary to that of political parties was the treatment of trade unions. A tradition of radical French syndicalism, with its repeated threats of a general strike, had been well established since the turn of the century. Consequently, one of the first acts of the German Occupation was to abolish the old unions and, in effect, to decentralize the structure of labor by restricting activity to individual enterprises or branches of industry. Ever at the ready to criticize the military administration's policies, however, the German Embassy gathered complaints about confusion and unrest in labor ranks, caused in large measure by the dissatisfaction of workers over inadequate wages and rations. At the insistence of Abetz, therefore, the matter was forced to a reconsideration, and a new umbrella organization, the Fédération des Travailleurs, was founded. Two difficulties were immediately detected. One, signaled by the Commandant of Greater Paris, was that orders were being circulated for Communists to join the new formation en masse. The other was that a rising pitch of rhetoric at labor gatherings threatened public tranquility, as when one orator exclaimed that worsening labor conditions might require French workers to resort to "their old methods." In other words, as noted, the specter of a major strike now loomed not far away.[45]

In the meanwhile, the German propaganda war against Gaullism and Communism was unrelenting. Of the two, Gaullism was currently far less problematical for the Occupation, as it was mostly still confined to harmless graffiti and clandestine pamphlets. It was true, the Germans thought, that De Gaulle had more real support than Pétain, but his efforts to stir the populace had little effect. As a consequence, few arrests of Gaullists were deemed necessary.[46] Communist agitation seemed more sinister, including minor acts of sabotage—such as cutting electric cables and phone lines, spreading glass and sharp metal objects near German installations, and sometimes causing the derailment of train cars—and occasional scuffles in the streets of Paris, especially in working-class districts. The result was irregular daily reporting by the SD of police actions: eleven arrests, ten arrests, twenty arrests, twenty-five arrests.[47] Yet German records betrayed no sign of undue alarm. The Communists were thought incapable of mounting any serious resistance in Paris, and their propaganda was considered "confused," particularly after the "failure" to carry out mass demonstrations announced for May Day 1941. Hence, Commandant Ernst Schaumburg felt safe in praising the "positive results" of repressive measures taken by the Occupation as that fateful summer came on.[48]

Chapter 5

GERMANS AND JEWS

In the little town of Breisach, overlooking the Rhine near Freiburg-im-Breisgau, there is a tiny plaque inscribed in remembrance of the German Jews expelled to France in 1940. Everything is said in one simple sentence: "In memory of the Breisach Jews who on 22 October 1940, together with all Jews from Baden, the Palatinate, and the Saarland, were deported to the camp at Gurs in the French Pyrenees." Among other things, this inscription is a testimony to the incoherence of German policy regarding the treatment of Jews in France during the early months of the Occupation. Was it actually the intention of the Nazi regime in Berlin to use France as a dumping ground for displaced European Jewry? That appearance, we know, was deceptive and soon proved to be misleading.[1]

From the vantage of the Occupation, the fate of Jews in France was a complex tale of bureaucratic turf wars and personal conflicts. It was in many ways parallel to and related with disputes concerning the confiscation of paintings and documents from French museums, libraries, and archives. In a similar fashion, as the Germans invariably put it, "the Jewish question" provoked a triangular struggle among the military government, the Embassy in Paris, and (in a broad sense) the Gestapo. Thrust into the midst of this configuration, in addition, was the loose cannon of the Einsatzstab Rosenberg. Each of these powerful agencies held a somewhat different notion of the matter, and hence once again the Occupation cannot be said to have had a single policy but rather several. If they had anything in common, it was a shortage of personnel to implement effectively whatever decisions might eventually be reached.

The basic difficulty with the seizure of art and manuscripts was the impossibility of separating the public and private spheres. The Einsatzstab Rosenberg exercised the authority, derived straight from the Führer, to collect Jewish and Masonic documents, whereas the German Embassy claimed the right to search for treasures in abandoned villas, especially those belonging to Jews. For his part, Otto von Stülpnagel objected to any such actions without the express authorization of his staff. This is not to dwell on strenuous objections from the French that all of these operations amounted to nothing more than a flagrant theft of their national patrimony. Finally, at the end of January 1941, Stülpnagel threw up his hands, exclaiming that he wanted "nothing further to do with this question." Bravely, he also criticized Hermann Göring's support for the confiscations as "not very fortunate." Such seizures would only harm the Reich in world opinion, he wrote, because it was doubtful that there could be a legal justification for them. He therefore refused all responsibility for the actions of the others, which he regarded as incompatible with his duty to ensure an orderly Occupation.[2]

Needless to say, no one paid much heed to Stülpnagel's tirade, and the looting continued. At one point a sort of informal alliance emerged between the Sipo-SD and the Embassy against the Einsatzstab Rosenberg, with whom a certain division of labor was arranged. For example, while the Embassy was left to deal with the delicate task of dividing works taken from the Jewish art house Seligmann (affiliated with a related private firm in New York), the Einsatzstab Rosenberg took over an extensive collection gathered at the Louvre, where a special exhibit was being prepared at the nearby Jeu de Paume for a viewing by Göring and Rosenberg in person. This confiscated trove was valued at no less than a billion Reichsmarks, besides which mention must be made of 6,000 cartons of "scientific material." In all, thirty freight cars were readied for shipments to Germany.[3]

These events and altercations were only the proverbial tip of the iceberg. Beneath them lay two layers of anti-Semitic intention, one for public consumption and the other hidden from view in the halls of German administration. The former consisted of decrees, laws, and card files intended to identify all Jews in France and to begin a long process of separating them from the general populace. As this aspect of the documentary record has already been minutely recounted, it may be rapidly summarized here. The first step was a German decree on 27 September 1940 that required Jews to register with the police and to carry a light blue or green card stamped in red with *Juif* or *Juive*. Moreover, Jewish shops and businesses had to display a yellow poster identifying them as such. This census produced the habitually precise German statistics: the Department of the Seine contained 85,664 French and 64,070 foreign Jews, that is, nearly 150,000 in all. There were 7,737 individual enterprises (mostly Paris shops) and 3,456 jointly owned Jewish companies. Rounding these numbers off in late November, the Embassy recorded that 11,700 signs had so far been mounted in store and office windows—not bad for a start.[4]

The second step, on 3 October 1940, was a comprehensive law from the Vichy regime (acting on its own initiative) that mandated the exclusion of all Jews from government service, liberal professions, and public education. For such measures the Germans supplied a suitably ugly word, *Entjudung*, to designate the elimination of Jewish influence from public life. This included, of course, the French economy, which was the specific object of another German decree on 18 October that forbad Jewish ownership, direction, or operation of all business enterprises. That date thus marked the essential beginning of what came to be called "Aryanization" (*Arisierung*), an ambitious program that would occupy countless man-hours and reams of paper until the end of the Occupation—a subject that will therefore require further study.[5]

All of this enterprise, at German insistence, needed to be captured and quantified on paper. The result was the creation of the infamous *fichiers*, detailed catalogues that ultimately attempted to classify every individual Jew and Jewish enterprise in France. At a conference on the last day of February 1941, Helmut Knochen's assistant for Jewish affairs, Theodor Dannecker, reported on the progress of this mighty undertaking, conducted mainly at the Prefecture of Police in Paris. The count stood currently at 65,000 Jewish households in Greater Paris, with a total of more than 200,000 persons. Of these, Dannecker noted, about 75 percent were not French citizens. He thereby singled out the category that would draw the immediate attention of German authorities. A roundup of foreign Jews by Vichy had in fact begun in the Unoccupied Zone, where nearly 40,000 were already relocated into concentration camps (among them, those from southwestern Germany). Under German oversight, naturally, the French would be encouraged to undertake further actions.[6]

The focus on non-French Jews was not a new concept. As early as July 1940, German military authorities in Paris had ordered the Prefect of Police to begin "the identification and supervision of all foreigners."[7] This measure suited the Vichy regime, given Marshal Pétain's outspoken desire to spare French citizens any unduly severe discriminatory measures—the law of 3 October notwithstanding. German police officials were eager to accommodate him, but they were not satisfied to limit such action to territory south of the demarcation line. Knochen considered it his assignment to include the internment of all foreign Jews in the Occupied Zone as well, despite the "considerable technical difficulties" of arresting and incarcerating at least 100,000 individuals in the Paris region alone. The French police should again be prodded to perform that task, while the German role would be to ensure its "complete execution."[8] However, the mills of repression ground slowly, and German impatience grew. The French, it seemed, were displaying insufficient diligence, as Occupation authorities complained in the spring of 1941, and it was consequently decided to found a new central control agency to handle the Jewish question, which the Germans baptized the Zentralamt für die Judenfrage and the French called the Commissariat Général aux Questions Juives (CGQJ).[9] But mass arrests in Paris did not begin until May. On 14 May, over 3,700 non-French Jews, mostly Poles, were apprehended in the capital—"selected" by the Prefecture of Police with German "support"—and sent to two concentration camps in the Loiret at Pithiviers and Beaune-la-Rolande. Meanwhile, sporadic arrests on city streets continued as both French and German police plied their trade of checking papers and identity cards. By mid-June, 166 such inmates were in detention at the Paris Centre des Tourelles, and dozens more were to follow in July.[10]

Behind the scenes, the evolution of German policy toward Jews in France was more elusive. Yet a review of extant documents from the Occupation reveals a reasonably clear image of it. The starting point was a memo prepared by Ambassador Abetz in mid-August 1940 in which he outlined three proposals: (1) immediate orders should be issued to prohibit any Jews who had fled the Occupied Zone from re-entering it; (2) preparations should begin for "the removal of all Jews"; and (3) means should be determined for the expropriation of Jewish property.[11] Safe to predict, this agenda promptly aroused a flurry of controversy in the Hotel Majestic, where Werner Best gathered contradictory reactions. The existing policy of the Stülpnagel administration was notably passive. As the Economic Section observed: "The fact alone that a [French] citizen is a *Jew* does not at present allow special measures against him," although vacated and unclaimed apartments in Paris might properly be requisitioned.[12] In direct response to Abetz, another memorandum stated that the primary objective of the Occupation was to ensure the safety of its troops. "Hence, it is not a matter for the military administration to intervene positively (*verbessernd*) into the internal political conditions of France." Above all, the impression should be avoided of an intention to annex the Occupied Zone, which might be created by the insertion of "the racial question." Measures advocated by Abetz therefore stood "in contradiction" with instructions from General von Stülpnagel, since "their implementation would mean the abandonment of previously observed policy." A change could be justified only if Jews presented a demonstrable threat to Occupation forces by spying, public demonstrations, or nefarious economic activity. In sum, whereas Abetz's first point might present no problem, the second was "impossible," and the third would require at most "the elimination of Jewish business managers."[13]

This relatively moderate view did not pass without opposition. True, as one staff report remarked in early September, no aggressive measures had so far been taken to force Jews from public life, but the Occupation could not long remain static if it were to achieve "the ultimate goals of German policy." Granted, those terms had not yet been precisely defined, but they surely implied that Jewish influence, especially in the French economy, should be "radically eliminated." Such a process must necessarily be gradual, beginning with individual operations that would be all the more effective if completely arbitrary and thus unsettling. By these means, in effect, life could be made increasingly uncomfortable and intolerable for Jews in all of France.[14] The evidence is unambiguous that this line of reasoning soon prevailed, personally endorsed as it was both by General von Brauchitsch in Fontainebleau and by Reinhard Heydrich from Berlin. Further reservations expressed within Stülpnagel's staff were consequently superfluous.[15]

Here was the opening for Dannecker, whose specialty it would be, as he unequivocally defined it in a memorandum dated on 21 January 1941, to prepare a "Final Solution" (*Endlösung*) for the Jewish question in France. Almost to the day, exactly one year before the notorious Wannsee Conference formally adopted this terminology, Dannecker and the Sipo-SD in Paris epitomized Hitler's intentions. Accordingly, they stressed that the formation of a new bureau for Jewish affairs, the CGQJ, was a matter of "urgent necessity." It would be well, as Knochen explained a week later, to start by ridding Paris of all foreign Jews, thereby taking advantage of traditional French xenophobia and creating attractive economic opportunities for social climbers. To do so, admittedly, the Germans would need to organize the extensive police action that was a prerequisite.[16]

Bureaucratic organization followed irregularly. The Prefecture of Police had already installed a euphemistically named "Jewish service" (*Judendienst*), which was busy compiling directories to identify the Jews of Greater Paris. The importance of these *fichiers*, as the Sipo-SD office chillingly confided to Heydrich, should by no means be underestimated "for a sooner or later intended general transport of Jews."[17] But this project was too limited for a much grander undertaking that foresaw the French nation as but one element of a broader European campaign. For that purpose, a new central agency for Jewish affairs would be especially useful "in order to eliminate the reaction of the French people against everything that comes from the Germans." Lamely optimistic, Best commented in a meeting with Dannecker that pushing the French to the forefront of this matter might even allow the military administration to deconstruct some of its decrees and to lean more on laws emanating from Vichy.[18]

Stepping back from the details to gaze across the scene in Paris, one can observe that an unspoken collusion had formed between the German Embassy and the Gestapo. It is no surprise that the most fanatical voices of the Occupation were to be heard at Sipo-SD headquarters in the Avenue Foch. Yet the Embassy, when it came to formulating policy toward Jews in France, was scarcely less strident. Abetz's original three proposals in August 1940 remained the basis of German designs, and in the spring of 1941 he and his staff continued to amplify them. On 24 March, the Ambassador's first assistant in the Rue de Lille, Rudolf Schleier, applauded the commencement of measures against foreign Jews and added ominously: "French Jews should later follow."[19] Within a few days, Abetz received a visit from Xavier Vallat, the newly appointed chief of the CGQJ. The two men could agree, because of demurrals from Vichy, that it would be necessary to proceed cautiously with any new anti-Semitic legislation. But Abetz urged persistence in hastening the detention of all Jews in France and explicitly asked his interlocutor to prepare their emigration. Vallat promised to comply.[20]

Another perceptible development in early 1941 was the erosion of reluctance in the Hotel Majestic. Stülpnagel was no hard-bitten Nazi. If he was not totally unaffected by racial ideology, that mattered far less to him than the maintenance of military discipline and public order. Yet the repeated waves of imprecation from Berlin and the steady undertow of anti-Jewish sentiment within his own administration in Paris were bound to eat away the foundations of his resolve. He trusted no one more than Best, whose attitude was finally less enigmatic than sometimes assumed. The day after Abetz's talks with Vallat, Best suggested to his superior that it would be advisable to negotiate directly with the CGQJ on the progressive elimination of non-French Jews and the planning for "a later emigration also of Jews with French citizenship." Furthermore, as a long-committed SS officer, Best did not lack a clear vision of the ultimate purpose—"the complete *Entjudung* of Europe." Whatever his reservations, Stülpnagel was forced to watch affairs spinning out of his control.[21]

On 10 May 1941, precisely a year after the opening of military hostilities against France, the German Occupation released its third formal decree on the Jewish question (after those of 27 September and 18 October 1940). Its purpose was to emphasize the importance of moving more quickly with the program of Aryanization. Essentially, there was nothing new in this message, apart from its obvious sense of urgency. No later than mid-October 1940, apparently taking a cue from Hermann Göring, Brauchitsch had demanded more alacrity in evicting Jews from the French economy. He complained to Stülpnagel about the slow pace in Paris and requested that the MBF take a personal interest in the matter.[22] In November, Stülpnagel, in turn, passed that order on to Best with specific instructions "to end definitively the Jewish influence in the French economy." But he added a significant caveat: every effort should be made to ensure that businesses continued to function without work stoppages or massive layoffs.[23] The result was a discernible ambiguity in practice. If the theory was "in no case" to retain Jews in important economic positions, their immediate dismissal should be demanded only "insofar as possible." This implied that some Jews might still be retained as technical advisers or in subaltern posts. Stülpnagel's staff warned that a radical solution for Aryanization might otherwise cause "great economic dislocation."[24]

Thus, as dozens of individual dossiers confirmed, progress (as measured by the Occupation) was agonizingly slow. Records of these complex transactions were kept in excruciating detail—now available in kilometers of microfilm—by the office of the Service du Contrôle des Administrateurs Provisoires (SCAP), an agency designated to execute German policy and intended to be its public face. These documents showed a growing frustration among Occupation officials with incomplete and often faulty reporting, despite their firm instructions that Aryanization must be pursued "until the Jewish influence is completely eliminated."[25] It was this bothersome irritation with French bureaucratic meandering that led in the spring of 1941 to the third German decree and to the formation of the CGQJ, into which SCAP was then absorbed.[26]

Vallat's entrance onto the scene soon proved, however, to be a huge disappointment. In conference with German military commanders in early April, after consulting with the Sipo-SD, he confessed some confusion about the real locus of German authority. Stülpnagel's response was that he, as MBF, was "exclusively" in charge of Jewish affairs and that Vallat should report only to Best—a claim that could not fail to ring somewhat hollow in a city where stories about Stülpnagel's loss of grip were already widely circulated. Moreover, Vallat repeatedly cautioned against an excess of anti-Semitic zeal, stressing that the Occupation needed to respect a traditional French sense of justice and to honor with exceptions the special status of Jewish war veterans. Clearly, such qualifications fell short of the stated intention of German personnel overseeing the CGQJ to achieve "complete Aryanization."[27]

Following Ranke's famous dictum about every epoch being "immediate to God," more than one historian has remarked that, in order to analyze events, it is often better to ignore their outcome. Improbable though that may be, there is surely reason to evaluate the first phase of the German Occupation of Paris without reference to the known tragedies that were to ensue. When doing so, three generalizations stand out. The first is that the quotidian circumstances of Paris in the opening months of the Occupation were peculiar to that moment and far different from what they were to become. A single incident in the autumn of 1940 is perfectly adequate to illustrate the point. On an August evening, a gang of French youth cast rocks through the windows of nine Jewish shops on the Champs-Élysées. Detained by the police and charged with a misdemeanor, the boys explained that they were members of the Gardes Françaises, whose prime objective was the complete elimination of Jews from the French economy. An investigation by the Gestapo concluded that this had indeed been a "purely French action."[28] However, that view was contradicted by the military administration, which discovered that the Germans, if not directly involved in the action, had been informed about it and, in fact, had provided office space for the group. Should the matter come before the French courts, therefore, the German role in the affair would unavoidably become known. Hence, there would be no trial and no conviction, and the youths were surreptitiously released.[29] This episode was characteristic of the caution and confusion with which the Germans were treating the Jewish question before June 1941. They were still inordinately concerned about the reputation of the military administration and careful not to tread too heavily on the feelings of the French populace. The policy of the Occupation at that time was to promote Aryanization by all means, but only if it were integrated into the larger political objectives of collaboration.

The second generalization—that the internal conflicts of the Occupation were uncontainable—is also observable in that example. Whether it was political tactics or propaganda, cultural activity or economic policy, confiscation of art or Aryanization of enterprise, there was a striking lack of single purpose. Such issues were seldom assigned to one sole agency. Instead, competing interests and clashing priorities were the rule, while the somewhat hapless Stülpnagel vainly attempted to maintain a semblance of military order. The direct lines to Berlin seemed to extend in every direction, and the MBF and his staff became entangled in the resulting web of intrigues and in-fighting. If unity of command is the first principle of warfare, it was certainly not the guiding tenet of the German Occupation in Paris.

The third generalization is that the beginning chapters of the Occupation demonstrated that it was an inextricable part of the continuum of French history and not an altogether exceptional period to be isolated from the rest. As a political structure, the Third Republic was gone, yet many of the personalities and prerogatives lived on—starting with Pétain, Laval, Darlan, and most of the other depressing figures huddled in Vichy. As for Paris, the Germans had undeniably taken over. But they, too, were obliged to contend with the past. To be specific, if the Occupation was asked to respect an abiding French sense of justice, it could also count on some traditional French xenophobia and anti-Semitism. In regard to the latter, the problem was sometimes dealing with too much of a good thing. Throwing rocks through Jewish shop windows on the Champs-Élysées could hardly be considered a contradiction to German policy, but such public disorder did not represent the countenance that the reigning military administration wanted to present. By the summer of 1941, then, while Nazi Germany indisputably ruled Paris, the Occupation exuded something less than an aura of complete harmony.

German troops entering Paris in June 1940

A mobile unit, reaching Paris, pauses beneath the city's most famous monument

In the shadow of Sacré Coeur, soldiers find something else to admire

Under a huge "V" (for *victoire?*) the banner reads: "Germany is everywhere victorious"

The Paris Opéra decorated with swastika flags

BA-Koblenz

Making friends in front of the Moulin Rouge …

ECPA-Ivry

… and on the Place de la Concorde

Grusspflicht: a French policeman offers a passing German officer the "obligatory salute"

German military personnel at a sidewalk cafe

At the Occupation's outset, ice cream cones all around

Fishermen of the world unite

Frequenting *bouquinistes* on the banks of the Seine

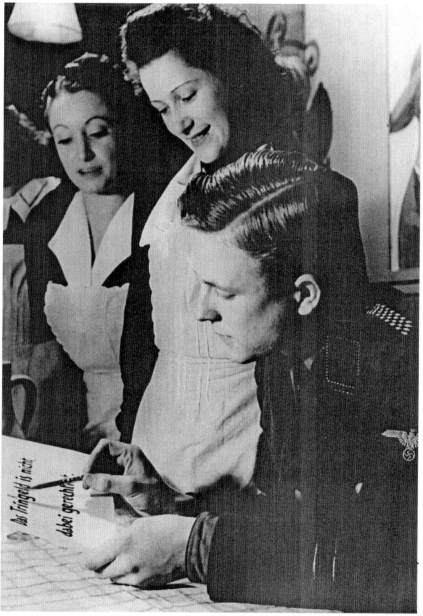

A German officer obligingly corrects the spelling of a sign: "The tip is not included"

PART II

CRACKING DOWN
(June 1941–November 1942)

Chapter 6

THE HOSTAGE CRISIS

A profound surprise." That is how the Prefect of Police summarized reactions in Paris to the arrival of the astounding news on 22 June 1941 of Nazi Germany's invasion of the Soviet Union. Until that date the internal situation in occupied France had been dominated by the Nazi-Soviet Pact of 1939, which dictated a measured restraint on the part of French Communists in their opposition to the Occupation. Now all previous bets were off.[1] It did not take long to detect signs of increased Communist activity, especially in the traditional working-class strongholds in the eastern suburbs. Such reports were soon gathered from Ivry-sur-Seine, the Porte des Lilas (seven arrests), and the Porte d'Aubervilliers (apprehension of ten "notorious Communists"). After the first surprise, it seemed obvious that a concerted pro-Soviet campaign was commencing that encouraged sabotage and other "brutal action," including labor strikes in the capital.[2]

The first reaction of the German military administration may be described as moderate in theory but efficient in practice. General instructions came directly from the OKW's Wilhelm Keitel in Berlin. The Occupation should respond with firmness, he wrote, but its tactics must be weighed in light of relations with the French that might be harmed by "an excessively rigorous procedure." It would therefore be mandatory to consult with Berlin before taking any extreme retaliatory measures, namely, executions, which might be thought necessary.[3] Arrests for suspicious activity in the streets of Paris meanwhile continued at an accelerated pace: in all, 3,052 were recorded during the first month after the beginning of the Russo-German War. Of these, by the end of July 1941, twenty-two French civilians had received death sentences.[4] A spike in acts of sabotage was likewise evident. The total of such incidents reached nearly 3,000 by early August and was listed as exactly 3,250 by the end of that month.[5]

The first bold act of open defiance took place on 14 August 1941, when a Communist manifestation trooped along the Right Bank boulevards between the Place de la République and the Porte St. Denis. A messy brawl erupted at the Porte St. Martin, pitting the police against about eighty French youths, of which six were taken into custody. Within hours, a similar scuffle ensued near the Gare St. Lazare, where seventeen were detained, and another took place at the metro station Barbès-Rochechouart near Pigalle. In the latter instance, the crowd of demonstrators, who were brandishing at least a dozen tricolor flags, was estimated at one hundred. As usual, accounts of these outbursts varied. Whereas French police officials tended to downplay such melees, Helmut Knochen's report for the Gestapo called them "noteworthy."[6]

Indeed they were. Paris was perceptibly a city under increasing tension, and a certain strain became palpable. Otto von Stülpnagel was visibly worried and told Otto Abetz that the differing opinions within the Occupation now made it "urgently necessary" to agree about uniform procedures to deal with a possible insurrection. It was, as an administrative staff report concurred, "absolutely necessary" to restrain public demonstrations. Ominously, in a formal announcement posted throughout the city, Stülpnagel specified that any Communist activity whatever would henceforward be regarded as "abetting the enemy" (*Feindbegünstigung*) and that those found guilty must reckon with a death penalty.[7] On 18 August, Commandant Ernst Schaumburg issued an advisory about the methods of enforcement to be employed. Whenever possible, the French police should be utilized in the first operations of repression. Only when they were "no longer master of the situation" should German security forces be deployed. All must be prepared to use firearms if provoked, since the mere threat of drawing weapons was seldom effective. When on duty or strolling on the boulevards, German soldiers should appear only in groups, and they should in particular avoid carousing in the vicinity of Montmartre. Thus, by mid-August, German apprehensions about potential trouble in Paris had been clearly expressed, and even the most likely location of a serious incident within the city had been identified.[8]

On 18 August, Stülpnagel departed from Paris on a brief furlough, leaving Schaumburg as customary in charge. Three days later, a German naval cadet, Alfons Moser, was shot in the back and killed at the metro Barbès-Rochechouart. What to do? Schaumburg's reaction, in the form of an official "notification" (*Bekanntmachung*), was tentative and cautious. First, any person taken prisoner by or for the German Occupation would be considered a hostage. Second, should a further fatal incident occur, a corresponding number of hostages would promptly be shot. One must be struck by two features of this announcement: that there would be no immediate reprisal, and that the number of executions, if any, was in effect left an open question. Whether Stülpnagel would have responded more forcefully or with less vagueness, had he been on duty in Paris, is of course impossible to determine.[9]

At the same time, Schaumburg also sent a message to military headquarters in Fontainebleau in which he provided additional details on the murder of Moser but remained ambiguous about the policy to be adopted as a consequence. The number of hostages that should be executed in the future, he simply commented, must be "in accordance with the severity of the deed," which might therefore lead to death sentences for "several Jewish-Communist leaders."[10] Mention should be made here of a simultaneous incident at Versailles, where, during a public ceremony, both Pierre Laval and the rightist politician Marcel Déat were wounded by gunmen. Presumably, however, this was the work of anti-government conspirators and was consequently dismissed by German authorities as irrelevant to the events in Paris.[11]

Finally, on 28 August, after a full week had passed since the shooting near Montmartre, a headline appeared in the official German press organ in the capital, the *Pariser Zeitung*: "Three Communists Executed." The accompanying explanation was markedly short on specifics. After the initial judgment of a French special court, the death sentences were carried out at dawn. In addition, other persons—no numbers supplied—were condemned to forced labor.[12] Was it at least established, then, that one German life was worth three French? Not at all, it appeared, when German naval personnel complained that their branch of service was receiving inadequate support from the military administration. The navy had in fact been promised six executions, they claimed, and their commanding officers were "most deeply disappointed." Hence, pressure was exerted, and later requited, for the execution of more hostages.[13]

In the meantime, Knochen's Sipo-SD department warned of "a very large increment" of Communist activity in the capital, a report confirmed by news of a second German murder victim, Ernst Hoffmann, at the Gare de l'Est on 3 September. The engine of reprisal was then revved up as thirteen more hostages were executed on 6 September at Mont Valérien, on the capital's western extremity.[14] Since Stülpnagel had returned to Paris by that time, it must be assumed that this act of a firing squad occurred with his knowledge and tacit concurrence. Nonetheless, it is notable that a French memo was circulated from the office of Werner Best to the effect that, because Communists were the putative perpetrators of most of the violent acts, it would be "unjust and regrettable" to blame the French population as a whole for the murders or to destroy innocent lives as a result.[15]

Another jolt struck in mid-September. This time the operative event was a fatal attack on Captain Wilhelm Scheben, and again OKW responded directly from Berlin with a portentous message: the Führer was demanding "the most severe measures" of retaliation, since previous retributions in Paris had been unable to tamp down the random violence. In this communiqué, unmistakably, there was a scarcely veiled criticism of the Occupation's relative moderation. Yet what measures, precisely, would be deemed sufficient? Tighter curfews were announced, but that was not likely to assuage Berlin. Thus, on 20 September, twelve hostages were executed at Mont Valérien. Three days later, three more passed before a firing squad, evidently intended to placate the naval staff for the Moser murder nearly a month before.[16] The French police were also activated, and, according to a fresh set of statistics, since the invasion of Russia they had made 1,064 house searches and 195 arrests, in addition to confining 638 suspects.[17]

These numbers, let it be said, are difficult to evaluate because of a failure to distinguish carefully among hostages, criminals, and political agitators. So far as can be established, more than fifty executions of French civilians were conducted between late June and the end of September. Because no more attacks on German military personnel had occurred since 16 September, an impression (false, as it proved) was created that calm had been restored and perhaps the hostage crisis resolved. The first half of October appeared to confirm that impression—until news reached Paris on 22 October that a German *Feldkommandant* had been killed in Nantes. Once more Berlin intervened. Orders from OKW were that fifty hostages were to be executed at once, and fifty more if the assassins were not captured within a few days. Manifestly appalled at this prospect, Stülpnagel was thus exposed, as he later wrote, to "the most severe pressure." Reluctantly, he agreed to the first round of executions in Nantes. Then, two days later, reports arrived at the Hotel Majestic that a German civilian official and an army major had been murdered in Bordeaux. Stülpnagel's authority now came completely unraveled. His information was that the assassinations were the work of "small terrorist groups," and consequently he opposed the mass execution of hostages. Yet it was he who had earlier set into motion the Occupation's hostage program and, just hours before, had already approved the elimination of the first fifty hostages for Nantes. Acutely suffering from a bad case of buyer's remorse, he could not now find reason to oppose the same drastic measures for Bordeaux, even though he found them to be "inappropriate" for the Occupation. Yet orders were orders and, *à contrecoeur*, Stülpnagel submitted.[18]

Surely no less squeamish, the Vichy government could only plead for an indefinite delay of the second round of executions, as did Marshal Pétain in a personal letter to Hitler. But, acting as bureaucracies do, the military administration provided a justification to refuse, even though innocents might be put to death, with the argument that the German treatment of hostages rested on "a firmly established legal concept."[19] For its part, the German Embassy in Paris remained unmoved, tending for once to side with Stülpnagel with the observation that harsh reprisals could be justified only if the French populace was overwhelmingly anti-German. But, Abetz contended, after the famous handshake between Hitler and Pétain at Montoire on 22 October, and in view of German military advances into the Soviet Union, that was clearly not the case. He therefore recommended a postponement in implementing death sentences for the second batch of one hundred hostages.[20] There is no golden scale upon which to weigh the relative effect of Stülpnagel's protests, Pétain's pleas, and Abetz's reservations. In any event, Berlin finally relented and agreed to defer further executions to an unspecified future. With undisguised relief, Stülpnagel announced in the *Pariser Zeitung* that the planned retribution was "provisionally suspended" in order to allow the population an opportunity to assist in capturing the criminals, and he expressed the hope of the Wehrmacht that any such measures would become unnecessary.[21]

Parenthetically, we may note a misfired trial balloon from the office of Hans Speidel, according to which the Nantes and Bordeaux attacks had actually been fomented by a small gang ("parachutists!") trained by the British secret service , who were therefore in all probability not Communists but Gaullists. This fanciful hypothesis proved, however, to be a non-starter and was not heard again.[22]

During the months of November and December, Paris remained calm and tense. The shock produced in the capital by the sensational aftermath of events in Nantes and Bordeaux was recorded by the Prefect of Police, who confirmed that Communist activity there had "further slackened." A strict overnight curfew remained in force, and although minor incidents of sabotage continued, no major instances of violence ensued after mid-October. Meanwhile, police activity reached a higher pitch. One razzia in St. Denis, for example, netted 117 arrests.[23] Yet again, because the extant evidence is imperfect and fragmentary, such numbers afford only a faint reflection of the daily reality. A detailed administrative report tallied 249 death sentences between June and late November 1941, of which 108 executions resulted. However, it is impossible to disaggregate statistics of the hostage victims from others. This confusion was compounded by another box score of Jews arrested and condemned, as well as the deportation of persons to the East, to be considered subsequently. The only absolute certainty was that the German military administration continued to gather lists of hostages with no respite in sight.[24]

The beginning of 1942, according to the Prefecture of Police, brought "a brutal conflagration of Communist activity." Indeed, consumed by a "burning hatred of Germans," youth gangs had "redoubled" their efforts in the Occupied Zone, as another spasm of attacks and reprisals seemed in the offing. This heavily charged atmosphere was bound to produce the usual frictions between German authorities and French police. A conference called at the Hotel Majestic attempted to establish clear boundaries of jurisdiction with a declaration that the municipal police were to act strictly in accordance with French laws but "in no case" under German decrees. This hypothetical distinction proved of course impossible to sustain.[25]

Ten more hostages were executed by firing squad on 12 January 1942 in retaliation for the fatal wounding of a German army captain in Dijon a fortnight before. This event, although virtually a banality in the bloody context of the past several months, in fact provoked second thoughts about the Occupation's hostage policy. One suggestion emanating from within the administration was to avoid hostage executions in the future by sending all criminal suspects to military tribunals, which would hand down a generous number of death sentences. The condemned prisoners would be detained in a pool of available victims, who could then be executed whenever the occasion demanded, thereby negating the criticism of the Vichy government and the French people that the Germans were ruthlessly killing innocent civilians for crimes they did not commit.[26]

Stülpnagel himself recommended an alternative procedure to deflect such opprobrium. He began by citing as a fact that, of sixty-eight cases of attacks on German personnel, twenty-two had been solved and the killers brought to justice. Investigations proved that these perpetrators were invariably small Communist groups. The general French public was thus demonstrably not responsible for the incidents, and selecting innocent hostages from among them could not fail to have undesirable consequences for an orderly Occupation. Rather, it would be better to transport the majority of interned individuals to Germany or to "the East" where (about this he was conspicuously vague) they could be dealt with. As a result, Stülpnagel wrote with emphasis, executions would be conducted in France "only in a *limited* number appropriate to the circumstances" (again left to the imagination). Personally, he added for good measure, he could no longer reconcile the mass execution of French hostages with his conscience. Moreover, he explicitly requested that this message be conveyed to General Keitel in Berlin.[27]

This ostentatious fling of a gauntlet initiated the chain of events leading to Stülpnagel's resignation as MBF in mid-February 1942. Unfortunately for him, the crisis of command coincided with the most severe personal strain within the Paris military administration since the onset of the Occupation. That is, it occurred just as he found it necessary to reprimand two of his most trusted underlings, Jonathan Schmid and Werner Best, for airing differences and acting independently on the question of hostages in Nantes. In a fit of pique, Stülpnagel categorically insisted that it was his prerogative "solely and alone" to make policy decisions in Paris, and he sharply chastised Best for "a complete misunderstanding of the entire situation."[28]

It was too much. On 15 February 1942, apparently after suffering a nervous breakdown, Stülpnagel proffered two letters of resignation. The first was a formal statement addressed to OKW in which he gave an explanation that recurrent illness had forced him to abandon his post. Although there was some truth to that assertion (hence his frequent absences from Paris), it was altogether unconvincing—as the second letter demonstrated. This was a private missive to Keitel in which he recounted in detail "the entangled situation" at the Hotel Majestic and cast a net of blame as widely as possible. In addition to members of his own staff (obviously referring to Schmid and Best), who did not always obey his orders, there had been problems with the Sipo-SD (Knochen and Dannecker) and their "not always useful dealings." His choicest words of complaint, however, were reserved for the Embassy (Abetz and Rudolf Schleier), where dubious political manipulations had produced only a more rigid negative attitude among representatives of the Vichy government.

Yet in the end, it was unquestionably the hostage crisis that was the most crucial sticking point, because it had revealed both the impotence of Stülpnagel's regime and the essential difference regarding the Occupation as viewed from Paris and Berlin. Seeing the situation from afar and in the broad context of ruling various occupied territories throughout Eastern and Western Europe, Keitel was convinced that harsh retaliatory measures were necessary and justified to quell the successive waves of public violence. But, as so often noted, Stülpnagel's first priority was to promote collaboration in France by ensuring a firm but fair military administration, a policy he felt better able to formulate "through my intimate knowledge of the mentality of the French people." Accordingly, he favored only a very few hostage executions in France, to be accompanied by the "deportation of great masses of Communists and Jews to the East." This, he maintained, would actually strike more fear into the French and thus be of greater deterrent value than the uninformed and inconsistent instructions from Berlin (for which he specifically blamed Hermann Göring!) to execute large numbers of innocents. "Thus on these issues," he concluded, "I sit among the various powers and, so to speak, among all the stools." Hence, after fifteen months of "strenuous but successful work," Otto von Stülpnagel chose to resign.[29]

He was immediately replaced by his cousin, Carl Heinrich von Stülpnagel, an officer more patrician in bearing than his predecessor, whose clear intention was to calm emotions in Paris and to defuse the hostage issue. Yet Heinrich (as he was always called) had no tabula rasa, and he was far from successful in doing so. One of his first acts as MBF was to forbid the use of the word Geisel because the French equivalent (otage) implied taking into custody some prominent local notability. Instead, only the more technical term Sühnemassnahmen should be employed, thereby stressing the common sphere between persons committing a crime and those selected to pay for it. The new Stülpnagel likewise wished to eliminate from the Occupation's vocabulary "deportation" and "to the East," expressions that he felt were evocative of camps in Siberia under the tsars.[30]

Heinrich von Stülpnagel also took pains to patch up relations with Abetz by reaffirming the nebulous policy that all political questions should be cleared by the Paris military administration through the German Embassy. Nevertheless, the evidence is that hard feelings between the two persisted, especially by proxy through their surrogates, Schaumburg and Schleier. Whereas the former found the Embassy's pretensions to control all propaganda and political matters to be "painful," the latter snapped back that the MBF's strictures were "false and incomprehensible."[31] Nor did the vicious circle of murderous attacks and harsh retaliations cease. On 10 March 1942, twenty Communists were shot, and another twenty had their death sentences deferred (until they were later granted a stay of execution). A month later, after a German sentinel was killed and a bomb was thrown into a German locale, twenty more Communists were promptly executed. If the perpetrators were not captured soon, the threat was that "a certain number" of hostages would meet the same fate.[32]

For good and obvious reasons, relations with the French police remained ticklish. When pressed on the problem, Vichy's current chief of government, Admiral Darlan, admitted that the French constabulary could not shirk the "especially sensitive duties" of transporting prisoners to detention camps, but they must use a maximum of tact in this "particularly delicate" operation. To this tortured statement he added a phrase that betrayed the psychological malaise created by the hostage crisis: the French police should obey orders "while manifestly leaving the entire responsibility for the measures taken to the German authorities."[33] Such caveats or not, it was evident that a certain routine had set in and that everyone was expected to do his part to push the campaign of repression. On 2 May another spectacular shooting occurred in Paris at the Clichy metro stop. Five "Communists and Jews" were executed at once. Another fifteen, it was announced, would follow if the assassins were not soon caught. In addition, without naming their destination, 500 persons would be condemned to forced labor.[34] A nearly identical scenario was repeated after an attack on 27 May: ten persons would be executed and "a greater number" would be transported to a labor camp if the killers were not delivered to the police within ten days. In sum, Paris had become the scene of a roiling seismic insurrection that could neither threaten the public order imposed by the military Occupation nor be entirely repressed by it.[35]

Since there was no imminent end to this story, one can only draw an arbitrary chronological line in lieu of a terminus. The end of May 1942 was greeted by a flurry of statistics concerning the hostage question. Because of the many inconsistencies and discrepancies resulting from overlapping categories, it is impossible to untangle these data with absolute precision. Still, the generalization must stand that the number of hostages executed in the year since Alfons Moser had been gunned down at the metro of Barbès-Rochechouart was approaching the figure of 500. One report set the total at 434, another at 466, and a third at 473.[36] Whatever the exact truth, there could be no doubt that the impact of the hostage crisis had fundamentally altered the ambiance of Paris and therewith inaugurated a new phase of the Occupation.

Chapter 7

A DANGEROUS PLACE

While the hostage crisis naturally gathered all the headlines, daily life in occupied Paris ground on. The difference for the Occupation was a new tone of urgency and severity. Stimulated by the shocking news from the Soviet Union, German and French police conducted mass arrests of suspected Communists. Six hundred of them were taken into custody during the first week after the invasion of Russia. In addition to arrests by the Paris criminal police, the municipal constabulary fanned out in the city, stopping and interrogating citizens in the streets. One report in September 1941 recorded exactly 76,567 such confrontations that resulted in nearly a thousand detentions.[1] These actions were accompanied by tighter and more strictly enforced curfews for bistrots, bars, and cafés. Cinemas and theaters were ordered, temporarily, to be closed by 8:00 PM.[2] Penalties for traffic violations were now to receive "strict application," and instructions were issued to raise the level of alert for possible air raids. No public celebrations would be permitted for the national holiday, the *quatorze juillet*. In short, the grip of the Occupation was being perceptibly strengthened.[3]

The Germans also moved at once to regulate what survived of French political life. No new organizations would be allowed, and those that existed were prohibited from displaying badges, uniforms, and flags. Only a few political parties and "movements" would be authorized or tolerated, while three were explicitly forbidden.[4] A particular problem was posed by the so-called Légion de l'Europe unie, which was headed by Eugène Deloncle. Its members were supposedly being recruited as volunteers in the struggle against Bolshevism—not a principle the Germans had reason to oppose—but Occupation authorities were skeptical about encouraging any such formation, even in a good cause. Nor did the Vichy government support it. Yet after some controversy and delay, Deloncle finally received permission to hold a public rally at the Vélodrome d'Hiver, which was draped with the French tricolors (against orders) and enlivened by a marching band.[5] As it turned out, this gathering on 18 July was much ado about very little. The meeting hall was half-empty, and the loudspeaker system malfunctioned, causing many in the audience to leave before the conclusion. Afterwards, a few small groups struck up a chorus of the "Marseillaise," but the cacophony was such that no police intervention was necessary to break it up. Recruitment for the Légion remained feeble.[6]

To cover these immediate measures of public control, the Occupation meanwhile attempted to maintain a veneer of normalcy. Performances by the Circus Amar and a troop of puppeteers were permitted. And the Piscine Deligny, a swimming pool floating in the Seine near the National Assembly building, was reopened. A new list of authorized brothels for German military personnel was issued, from which the one near the concentration camp at Drancy had been discreetly removed.[7] A list of twenty-one nightclubs whose curfew was stretched to 5:00 AM was published in mid-July, and several weeks later seventy-one restaurants were accorded an extension to 1:00 AM, notably those most frequented by German officers, such as the Tour d'Argent, Maxim's, and Lapérouse.[8] A German tennis club was in full swing, with more members than it could accommodate, and ice-skating rinks were operated in the autumn. Large numbers of German troops from elsewhere in France continued to tour the capital—with instructions to "keep a distance from the French civilian population"—while steamships regularly transported hundreds of German soldiers on cruises up the Seine.[9]

None of these amusements mitigated the wave of violence that swept the Paris region and some provincial towns in occupied France. In addition to the individual attacks on German personnel that provoked the hostage issue, French insurgents began to make more indiscriminate use of improvised explosive devices. Either pitched or planted, these small bombs at some times recalled the anarchists of late nineteenth-century Russia and at others suggested the methods of dissidents much later. From the standpoint of the Occupation, such incidents were recurring with dismaying regularity: in a garden on 18 August, at the Renault factory on 29 August, at the Paris flea market and in the Latin Quarter at a German bookstore in November, and so on.[10] During the two months of December 1941 and January 1942, according to one Abwehr report, seventeen explosions occurred in Paris in addition to eight personal attacks on German military persons. It was, as Commandant Schaumburg commented, "a dangerous development."[11]

One instance was particularly noteworthy. In early October, lethal devices were exploded simultaneously in seven Paris synagogues. Speaking for the Sicherheitspolizei, Helmut Knochen immediately announced this to be "a purely French matter" that should be left to the Paris criminal police. But an investigation by the MBF soon proved otherwise. When interrogated, one of Knochen's subordinates admitted that he had assisted in the action on orders from Sipo-SD headquarters and that the explosives used had actually been supplied from Germany. Otto von Stülpnagel was outraged by Knochen's connivance "behind my back" and "contrary to my intentions." Further cooperation with him would therefore be "impossible," he notified Berlin, while demanding that Knochen be recalled from Paris. As it happened, however, Ambassador Abetz intervened, and Knochen was retained after all, as Stülpnagel was informed, because his "sensitivity" to French politics and his good relations with the German Embassy made him indispensable.[12]

Another striking feature of the "resistance movements" (a term now more common) in and around Paris was a series of attacks on railway installations. Lines were cut, gates disabled, railway ties loosened, and occasional bombs exploded. German authorities suspected French *cheminots* of abetting such actions but lacked definitive proof of their guilt.[13] All that could be done, it was decided, was to post guards along the tracks. The difficulties of implementing that policy were patent. A map of the Paris region revealed that it contained thousands of kilometers of railway. An initial proposal was to post a guard every 300 meters. Werner Best even advocated that guards be placed every 100 meters, where their posts would be manned each night from 10:00 PM to 6:00 AM. Clearly, there were not enough policemen available for such a scheme, and so citizens were to be recruited for the task at a ratio of five to one. But should they be armed? Only with wooden batons (*Schlagwaffen*), it was decided. All of this came to nothing. Gendarmes promised by the Prefecture of Police never arrived in sufficient numbers, and civilians—understandably disinclined to sit up all night—shied away from recruitment. Once again, for lack of adequate manpower, a German program could not be sustained. It was finally determined that mobile guard units rather than stationary posts should watch the railways and that only certain bridges and tunnels would remain under constant observation. Acts of sabotage consequently continued.[14]

Besides these troubling episodes, the Occupation soon had to deal with bombings by the British Royal Air Force (RAF). Two of these raids occurred just before the start of Germany's Russian campaign: one at dawn on 17 May at Le Bourget airport and another at the Dunlop tire factory in the night of 15–16 June 1941. Both were relatively harmless and seemed to be no more than a random alarm. The same was true of a stray bomb dropped on the Avenue Foch in October without apparent purpose.[15] That changed in early 1942. On 3 March, approximately eighty RAF planes attacked and severely damaged the Renault plant in the western suburb of Boulogne-Billancourt. Estimates as always varied, but twelve German soldiers and nearly 500 French civilians were killed, and 200 houses in the vicinity were destroyed.[16] Another major attack, also in the western *banlieue* near Colombes, occurred at the end of April, once again with heavy casualties and extensive damage to vital firms such as Alstom and Goodrich. To the consternation of German military authorities and propaganda officers, the population of Paris responded to these losses with stoic indifference. Such air raids, it was generally acknowledged, were a necessary part of the war effort and an unavoidable sacrifice if France were ever to be liberated.[17] A later military report outlined the damage from a similar raid at nearby Courbevoie and Gennevilliers on 30 May, and it added a convenient list of violent incidents around Paris during the summer and autumn of 1942:

2 July	A grenade is thrown at a squad of marching troops.
15 July	A bomb is thrown at a recruiting office of the Légion.
18 July	A bomb is planted at a German employment office.
28 July	A German officer is shot in the suburb of Suresnes.
6 August	A French policeman is wounded near the Porte de Vanves.
20 August	A fleeing Communist is shot at St. Denis.
26 August	An explosion in a cinema kills one woman, wounds nine.
27 August	A shootout in Puteaux leaves one Communist dead.
4 September	A bomb causes property damage in Suresnes.
8 September	Another explosion in a cinema kills one, wounds nine.
26 September	Minor damage is caused by an explosion in a barracks.
29 September	A German officer is shot and badly wounded at Issy.[18]

Although there is no way to reconstruct a complete record of all the violent acts committed in Paris during the Occupation, such sporadic glimpses suffice to suggest that the capital had indeed become a dangerous place for all concerned. It is no wonder, then, that steps were taken to bolster the city's police force or that the Germans took a keen interest in hastening them. The current Prefect of Police, Admiral Bard, proved eager to please, initiating a reform and recruitment effort after firing fifty officials on his staff who were suspected of Communist or Gaullist sympathies.[19] Yet he had to endure pointed criticism from Schaumburg that the French police were too often "passive" and that their performance on the streets seemed "reluctant and lethargic."[20] Two innovations stood out. First, a mobile unit called the Service de Police Anti-Communiste (SPAC) was organized and specially equipped with weapons and vehicles in an effort to provide additional public security through quick response.[21] Second, regional police brigades were attached to the offices of prefects throughout the Occupied Zone to reinforce the function of *police judiciaire* attached to the French court system.[22] Besides the normal duties of police units in a large city, the French were prodded into performing special

tasks: a search of nineteen metro stations in early October 1941; a raid on illegal gun dealers (with 36 arrests) a fortnight later; removing graffiti from traffic
signs; thwarting incipient demonstrations on Armistice Day; raiding a Communist nest in the Rue Ferdinand Duval, where 250,000 illicit political tracts
were seized; and so forth.[23]

If these actions and the German supervision of them transpired without
much overt friction, there was always an element of ambiguity. Let it be recalled
that altogether about 40,000 to 50,000 men were involved in the *gendarmerie*
and the various police forces of the Paris region. Since the Germans lacked such
numbers for regular law enforcement and special assignments, as Best noted,
they were "forced" to cooperate with the French Ministry of the Interior and
the Prefecture of Police, which required close and constant oversight.[24] Hence,
despite the recurring grumbles by the Germans about the "failure" (*Versagen*) of
the Paris police and the absence of "satisfactory results"—for instance, in suppressing "wild" prostitution—the Occupation continued to count on the French
to make up for the German deficiency of manpower.[25] A good illustration of
this symbiotic relationship was a campaign mounted under German orders to
search the sewers of Paris. In view of the fact that the city had over 2,000 kilometers of underground passages with nearly 5,000 entrances, this project was
well beyond the capacity of the German secret police and uniformed Gestapo
forces. Necessarily, therefore, it was conducted by French police units, who
claimed the seizure of 16,000 revolvers and rifles plus 19 machine guns from the
beginning of September 1941 to the end of March 1942.[26]

At the root of ambiguity was the essential, and essentially unanswerable,
question of how independent the French police should be. That issue was
explicitly broached in a December 1941 memo by the head of the MBF's administrative staff, Dr. Jonathan Schmid. In it, he offered the Delphic formula that
French law enforcement should function with complete independence except
in those cases when German interests were directly or indirectly involved.[27]
But how were those circumstances to be identified? A clarification would not
emerge until many months later, and it came with a startling new development
after the resignation of Otto von Stülpnagel. Manifestly unhappy about the
disharmony and unsettled conditions in Paris, OKW in Berlin took advantage
of the change in regime there to announce the appointment of a "Supreme
SS and Police Leader" (*Höherer SS- und Polizeiführer*) in the person of Carl
Oberg.[28] A Nazi down to his polished black boots, Oberg would formally be
under the MBF's administration in the Hotel Majestic. But his own office in the
Boulevard Lannes and his vast responsibilities were to be in fact separate. He
would preside over both the German and French police forces, participate in
"all questions relevant to France's domestic political situation," and take charge
of all "retributions against criminals, Jews, and Communists."[29] Accordingly,
the GFP directorate of Heinrich von Stülpnagel's command was disbanded

shortly after his arrival in Paris, and the entire staff of Knochen's Sipo-SD unit came under Oberg's authority. The importance of this fresh consolidation of power in Paris was underscored through a visit to the capital by Heinrich Himmler's chief adjutant, Reinhard Heydrich, in early May 1942 (only a few weeks before the latter's assassination), when Oberg was introduced to his new surroundings and underlings. The future significance of his role was perhaps best defined by Stülpnagel, who remarked that Oberg would soon become to France what Himmler was to Germany.[30]

Oberg's official installation on the first day of June 1942 was accompanied by a general shake-up of the military administration. Best was relieved of his duties and made available for "special assignments." In fact, he soon left for Denmark and was replaced by Franz Medicus. Suddenly taken ill, Schmid resigned his post, which was assumed by Dr. Elmar Michel, who also retained his command of the MBF's Economic Section.[31] Yet apart from Oberg himself, the most important change arguably occurred on the French side with the appointment by Vichy of a former prefect, René Bousquet, as Secretary General of the nation's police. Always in favor of more centralization, the Germans thereby obtained what they wanted: a single, ranking police official who would follow Oberg's every instruction in maintaining public order. But Bousquet likewise benefited from the bargain, he felt, because he would be allowed the latitude and independence to do so. A formal accord to that effect was reached late in that summer. As Bousquet put it, there would henceforth be a concerted effort "to reinforce and coordinate the action of the different services" so that the collaboration of French police forces with the German military administration would assume "a totally new importance."[32]

So it did, and with devastating consequences. On 6 July 1942, a military convoy containing a thousand political prisoners, mostly Communists, left Compiègne for the East. Oberg followed shortly with a tough new policy to be enforced on hostile acts against German personnel. Namely, for the first time, he specified that "severe punishment" would be inflicted on the *family* of perpetrators if they were not apprehended within a brief period after the crime. When Bousquet questioned the wisdom of such a regulation, Oberg countered that it was decided in consultation with Stülpnagel and Abetz, and that it had the personal approval of Himmler. His orders were expressly intended to shock the French public, Oberg added, and he had reason to believe they would do so.[33] When the insurrectionary violence nonetheless persisted, Oberg reacted without qualms. In mid-August 1942, he ordered the execution of 95 (allegedly Communist) prisoners, of which 88 were shot by firing squads at Mont Valérien. A month later he condemned another 116 to death, of which 46 also fell at Mont Valérien, the rest elsewhere in the Occupied Zone.[34]

Not since the opening days of the hostage crisis in the autumn of 1941 had executions on this scale occurred under the Occupation. It is obvious that the

Germans were prepared neither by their military training nor by Nazi ideology for the practical problems that were entailed. The killing and disposing of so many humans proved to be a grotesque nightmare, which was rumored throughout the city and recorded by the military administration in graphic detail. Clearly, it was Oberg who took charge of the operation, and he preferred to do so without interference from Heinrich von Stülpnagel. But such on-the-job training was admittedly bound to cause "conflicts of competence," as one German official noted, and therefore "a clarification of the limits of responsibility is eminently and immediately necessary."[35]

Before the eighty-eight executions on 11 August 1942, those who carried them out had but very general guidelines. A death sentence would ordinarily be pronounced only a few hours before the event, leaving just enough time for prisoners to gather their belongings and write a few farewell notes. In provincial towns, the executions would take place near the local prison, but in Paris that was unfeasible, and the condemned would have to be gathered and transported to Mont Valérien. Once the executions had taken place, corpses had to be put in coffins and turned over to French burial officials.[36] But things did not go quite as planned. Those responsible for transportation were not notified until 24 hours before the scheduled executions. Scattered as they were throughout the Paris region, prisoners had to be hastily assembled at Fort Romainville, east of Paris, whence they needed to be conducted through the capital to Mont Valérien, west of Paris. Phone connections were bad. There were not enough busses or trucks, and sufficient fuel for them was lacking. The drivers were uncertain about the routes to be taken, and the vehicles became separated, with resulting delays. There were not enough handcuffs or cords to bind the prisoners during transport or to secure them to stakes once they arrived. Coffins were too few in number, since only twenty-five were delivered (at 42 francs each) on the day of execution. The men of the Ordnungspolizei (Orpo), who were charged with organizing the firing squads, were suffering from "strained nerves" and needed to be supplied with *Schnaps* and cigarettes. Moreover, they refused to untie the corpses and place them into coffins. There were not enough disinfectants or gloves for handling the dead. A precise schedule of executions should have been provided and provisions made for disposal of the personal possessions and final writings of the victims.[37]

As a result of such confusions, the killing at Mont Valérien that day went on for more than four and a half hours—from 7:00 to 11:40 AM—under the direction of an Orpo officer, Major Schütze. That same night, the bodies were loaded onto trucks and taken to the cemetery of Père Lachaise, where they were to be cremated. Unfortunately, one of the two ovens there was out of commission, so that the burning required three days to complete. Thereupon, the urns needed to be picked up and "quietly" distributed for burial in various Paris cemeteries, of which Ivry—again, to the east of the city—afforded the most available space.

When, or indeed whether, the families of the deceased might be notified was a matter of dispute. Oberg's decision was that they should not be informed of the exact site of burial lest they make a memorial of the graves. Parisians neverthe-less flocked to cemeteries to leave flowers and wreaths at freshly dug plots.[38]

More detailed guidelines were made available. All executions of males should be by firing squads, of women by beheading. Each firing squad would comprise ten men in two rows at a distance of five paces. Executions must be conducted promptly after the pronouncement of a death sentence, from which pregnant women and the mentally ill were to be exempted. The commanding officer present should decide how the prisoners were to be arranged, bound, and blindfolded. A chaplain of the prisoner's faith should be in attendance—if possible, a French-speaking German or, if not, a French cleric. While the fir-ing squad stood at ease, a military officer should read the sentence. After the cleric spoke a word, the order to fire would be given. A medical person should confirm the death, and the corpse was then to be removed for cremation (if possible) and burial. If an execution were to be conducted at sea, the body should be pushed overboard at once.[39] These details give some idea of the unexpected complications and difficulties experienced by Occupation authori-ties when faced with an unpleasant reality about which they were clueless. They suggested that in the event that a program of ridding occupied France of undesirables should be expanded and prolonged, some other procedures might need to be envisaged.

Another issue was raised by Bousquet on the same day, 16 September 1942, that the execution of eighty-two more *Sühnepersonen* was ordered for Paris and Bordeaux. He wanted the German military administration to concede that no persons identified and arrested by the French police would be designated for execution or deportation. The Germans received this request with due cau-tion, noting that exceptions were always possible to any principle and that they might act otherwise if (unspecified) conditions required. It would be well in any event to keep reserves of prisoners near Paris for "unanticipated cases." In regard to this question, a census of French prison inmates was meanwhile con-ducted: in twenty French detention centers, including Drancy, a total of 8,362 prisoners currently resided. This number included precisely 2,047 political prisoners (that is, presumably, Communists), 2,162 Jews, 2,169 Gypsies, 591 foreigners, 110 prostitutes, and assorted others.[40] To this, Knochen soon added a list—without exact enumeration of their ever changing population—of Ger-man penitentiaries that included the camp at Compiègne, directly under the Sipo-SD, and the previously mentioned one at Fort Romainville, which served as a collection point of the condemned.[41]

One other telling set of statistics must catch the eye. In early October 1942, Heinrich von Stülpnagel released an account of nearly a hundred executions ordered since 6 April by the German military courts (Feldkriegsgerichte), a number not to be confused with mass hostage shootings. Of these, slightly more than a third, thirty-five of ninety-four, were conducted within the jurisdiction of the Commandant of Greater Paris. But some provincial courts-martial were also quite busy: Dijon (FK 669) was responsible for three, Rouen (FK 517) for eight, and Nancy (FK 591) for twenty. Imperfect as these records may be, they show beyond question that a killing machine had been set in motion as the Occupation struggled to cope with an insurrection it could not contain.[42]

The extent to which the residents of Paris were aware of these facts and how they reacted to them are not subjects that allow definitive proof. Many of the events described here transpired out of sight in distant and forbidding surroundings such as Mont Valérien. Outwardly, the city appeared much the same, although a few aspects of its existence could not have escaped notice. The familiar rear-deck Parisian busses were no longer running, and the passenger use of the metro had consequently risen by 60 percent over pre-war levels. The black market was still thriving, as was the sex trade, sometimes reported in exquisite detail, such as the story of a German NCO's escapades with French women that revealed "how a soldier in the big city can lose every sense of honor."[43] The Germans were in the meantime busy with an inventory of bicycles in the capital, raising fears among Parisians that they might soon be confiscated. Danger in the city streets and bars of Paris remained a concern shared by occupiers and occupied alike, in view of which German military personnel had instructions to carry a loaded weapon at all times, even when off-duty.[44] Yet the military administration remained convinced that the general populace displayed above all a tentativeness born of "resignation and passivity" that bordered on fatalism. Despite the many attacks and sabotages of months past, there was still no major public disturbance in sight. As one observer said it so well, only a few hours before the Allied invasion of North Africa in early November 1942, "the fear of German reprisals is greater than the courage to act."[45]

Chapter 8

STRICT CONTROLS AND
STRINGENT QUOTAS

The relatively stable and prosperous condition of the French economy during the first phase of the Occupation did not survive the second. True,
the winter of 1941–1942 was less severe in France than the year before, and
the harvest from early autumn was somewhat improved. The production of
potatoes, for instance, was better by a third, although still 20 percent below the
pre-war norm. Disruptions and irregularities of foodstuff shipments to Paris
were nevertheless evident. Rations of meat, fruit, and vegetables were reduced
in October 1941. And fuel—coal, wood, electricity, and gas—was at times
scarce. What good were potatoes, some Frenchwomen were heard to mutter, if
there were no hot stoves to prepare them?[1]

The first serious remonstrance about "certain difficulties" in the food chain
was recorded during a conference at the Hotel Majestic in the early summer of 1942. These included "completely insufficient" transportation from
southern France, lack of proper security because of inadequate numbers of
occupation troops, and passive resistance by French peasants when it came
to provisioning the capital. Moreover, it was agreed that "a complete procurement of the necessary quantities is not possible if the requisition apparatus is
composed solely of German forces. Rather, the cooperation of French government agencies is an absolute precondition." This was to touch on the most
sensitive nerve of economic collaboration: just how much could the French be
squeezed before they became recalcitrant? As things stood, Pierre Laval was

willing to meet German quotas for farm products, but he was asking in return certain concessions, including the reattachment of two northern departments (Nord and Pas-de-Calais) to the Occupied Zone, a reduction of daily occupation costs, and the return of POWs from German captivity. A representative of the German Ministry of Agriculture responded to this agenda by promising to submit the question to the head of the Four Year Plan, namely, Hermann Göring, with confidence that modest concessions would secure the delivery of expected food supplies.[2]

Three rounds of talks ensued. First, the current French Minister of Agriculture, Gabriel Le Roy Ladurie, was called in to consult on the anticipated "difficulties of immense proportion," especially the flagging shipments of meat to Germany.[3] Second, Laval was summoned to meet with the chief of the MBF's Economic Section, Dr. Elmar Michel. Laval stated the obvious—that France's capacity to meet agricultural quotas would depend largely on the 1942 harvest. His regime would attempt to observe the prescribed levels of rationing, Laval said, but it would be helpful if the French had greater freedom in fixing prices. That, Michel replied, was a "very delicate" question for German authorities in all of occupied Europe, although Heinrich von Stülpnagel was not personally opposed to certain increases.[4] Third, on one of his infrequent visits to Paris in early August, Göring conferred directly with Stülpnagel. An across-the-board 12 percent reduction in French rations had already been announced. The portly *Reichsmarschall* now insisted that it be enforced and that also newly elevated food quotas for Germany be introduced: over 2,000,000 tons of grain, 350,000 tons of meat, 300,000 tons of potatoes, 150,000 tons of vegetables, 300,000 tons of fruit, and 6,000,000 hectoliters of wine. Furthermore, Göring demanded that a plan for the fulfillment of this program be submitted to Berlin within a fortnight.[5]

Not surprisingly, Stülpnagel and his staff were appalled at the enormity of these disconcerting instructions. Michel's office let it be known in Berlin that it "in no way approves such an absolutely inoperable plan." Stülpnagel himself, after more consultations with the French, concluded that it was "out of the question" that they would accept the quotas, which could not be realized without further cuts in their rations, a corresponding sag in French production, and the risk of strikes by railway workers, which the Occupation would be hard pressed to contain with its "hardly sufficient" personnel. He also contacted his immediate superior, General von Brauchitsch, who agreed that hard feelings produced by excessive German requisitions might have dangerous repercussions in case of an Allied landing on the Continent. Perhaps, then, the entire issue should be reconsidered from a military standpoint.[6]

At another high-level conference in Berlin in September, the matter was again aired, rather plaintively, by Occupation representatives from Paris, but to no avail. The quotas, they were told, must be met. A personal plea from

Stülpnagel to Göring—that "the fulfillment of the total demands ... is not possible"—was likewise rejected.[7] The floodgates were now open. Not only massive quantities of foodstuffs, but all manner of French natural resources and manufactured goods—for example, according to one reckoning in late September 1942, 55 percent of aluminum, 80 percent of magnesium, all locomotives, and countless machines—would be requisitioned for the German war economy. In textiles, France would retain only 30 percent of woolens, 16 percent of cottons, and 13 percent of linens. Food deliveries altogether were to surpass five million tons. No wonder German authorities back in Paris feared a "total collapse" of the French economy and warned Berlin of a "serious danger to the German arms industry in France."[8] Here was one of the few occasions when the German Embassy in Paris fully supported the military administration. The imposition of Göring's quotas was "not possible" without sinking French rations "far below a minimum standard of living," Otto Abetz stated, with the result that "revolts, most serious disruptions of public order, and the immediate resignation or overthrow of the existing regime would be unavoidable."[9] Although these dire predictions later proved to be exaggerated, they at least illustrate once more the extent to which the perspective in Paris differed from that in Berlin.

While these tensions ran their course, problems over price fixing continued to plague the Occupation. Hypothetically, the regulation of wages and prices in Paris was administered by Jacques Barnaud, the French Minister of Economy and Finance, but the Germans had their own Price Oversight Office (Preisüberwachungsstelle), which kept a close watch. As in so many other instances, the policy was to give French officials direct responsibility, with the German military regime intervening only when their performance was unsatisfactory. This arrangement did not function particularly well. The Laval government felt hamstrung by regulations it did not actually control, and inflation was scarcely held in check. Vichy was simply told that wage increases in Paris were *verboten*. If the French needed to earn more to meet unfortunately rising prices, they could either work longer hours or volunteer for labor assignments in Germany.[10]

Exact statistics are as always elusive, but the MBF's Economic Section estimated that, the black market aside, the cost of living in Paris had risen from August 1939 to July 1942 by 65.5 percent. In other words, inflation had jumped by nearly 50 percent since the beginning of the Occupation.[11] One obvious problem was that the black market could not be set aside. A useful barometer with regard to its importance was the surveillance of restaurants. Basic ingredients for cuisine were both scarce and dear. By early 1942, grain prices had doubled or trebled since 1939, and the same was true of potatoes.[12] Since restaurants were obliged to display menus with prices outside the premises, they could easily be checked for signs of inflation. One control in October 1941 forced eight of them to close temporarily. The reasons were various: offering fish or *gigot d'agneau* on the wrong day, serving extra vegetables or some dish not on the regular menu, or allowing clients to carry off extra portions of butter. But an illegal rise in prices was the key.[13] A flurry of similar inspections in the spring of 1942 produced lists of eighteen and eight closures. That July, *Le Petit Parisien* reported that six restaurants *hors classe* had to be reprimanded for violating price controls. To date, the paper said, 686 investigations of restaurants, brasseries, and bistrots had uncovered 183 infractions. A later German memo listed 53 violations alone for the fortnight from 25 June to 10 July 1942.[14] Stülpnagel was not pleased. French attempts to halt price increases had attained "no notable success," he fumed, and allowing restaurants to ignore established limits could "no longer be permitted."[15] One may easily guess the rest: more rigorous rules, sporadic attempts to enforce them, frequent exceptions and evasions.

No less perplexing than obtaining food supplies was the procurement of fuel, especially coal. With the national railway network operating with tolerable efficiency, and the Allied bombing campaign still in its infancy, faulty transportation was seldom advanced as a cause of shortages in the second phase of the Occupation. Two other explanations were more prominent. The first was strikes. A brief walkout of coal miners near Lille in the summer of 1941 caused a temporary shortfall in deliveries to Paris. If not crippling for the French economy, strikes were considered potentially serious enough to convene a series of conferences at the Hotel Majestic in mid-September. What should be done to avert a strike threat? Raise wages? Simply forbid any more work stoppages? Intervene "by all available means"? An eight-page memorandum from the military administration attempted to summarize the agreed-upon answers to these questions. In the event of unrest in mining regions, French police should be dispatched in an attempt to calm the situation "in an amiable manner." That failing, they should arrest any agitators and seize the enterprise in order to isolate the insurrection. German troops might then be deployed, but only as a last resort.[16] Wildcat strikes nonetheless persisted. Yet they were neither intended nor assumed to be revolutionary or part of an organized resistance movement. Rather, they represented scattered protests over wages, hours, and rations. That being said, they were still troubling enough for Occupation authorities to worry about "an increased reserve, even rejection by the populace" of the German presence.[17]

A second explanation for the fuel shortages, strange to say, was the weather. Southern France was undergoing a prolonged dry spell. In the autumn of 1941, a first alarm was sounded. Due to a lack of adequate rainfall, the amount of hydroelectric energy available was restricted, and power for the Paris region would instead need to be produced by coal. Allocations in the capital were therefore reduced for all but the absolutely essential arms industries. Furthermore, in view of this "highly critical situation," it was announced, gas and electricity must be curtailed by 50 percent.[18] There was something almost absurd about the notion that French industrial production depended on the weather. However, consider the following sequence. In late December 1941, notice was given of a 30 percent cut in electricity starting in January 1942. At the outset of February, this order was rescinded due to unexpectedly heavy rainfall in the Midi and snow in the Alps. But at the end of that month, an "acute" coal shortage was again declared, and a 25 percent reduction for the arms industry was demanded by MBF headquarters in the Majestic. This pre-emptory order was "decisively rejected" by the Wi Rü Stab Frankreich on the grounds that it would diminish French industrial production for the Reich. After a prickly debate, the figure for energy cuts in the capital was lowered to 17 percent. In mid-March, these restrictions were also rescinded when a sudden thaw in the Alps once more increased the supply of water power.[19] Such fluctuations and indecision made statistical calculations somewhat dubious, but in general the Germans concluded that the total coal resources supplied to French industry from northern mines had dropped by about 50 percent since pre-war years, and imports from Belgium were down by the same proportion. As an unavoidable result, by the summer of 1942, monthly iron and steel production had declined from 52,000 to 28,000 tons. Perhaps the unkindest cut of all was a notification in October 1942 that in Paris warm water would henceforth be available in German military barracks only twice a week.[20]

The problem of sustaining the productive capacity of industry and agriculture in France, while at the same time harnessing the French economy to the German war effort through quotas and requisitions, pointed to a fundamental contradiction of German policy regarding the Occupation, which can best be illustrated by an examination of labor recruitment for the Reich. Throughout the year 1941, this program was conducted on a voluntary basis and directed by the military regime in Paris. However, the nature of the program changed drastically in 1942, when Germany's manpower requirements, after the invasion of Russia, became ever more pressing. As earlier observed, recruitment efforts began with foreign workers but increasingly shifted to French labor, particularly in the metal trades, which often accounted for more than half of the contingents exported across the Rhine. Large numbers of women laborers were also welcomed, but no children. In some cases, recruiters attempted to attract entire teams of workers from various French enterprises—what the Germans called *Firmenwerbung*. These efforts were not without success, but they manifestly failed to slake Berlin's thirst for labor, notably skilled labor, as the war continued.[21]

Initially, high unemployment in Paris and the promise of substantially increased wages in Germany were inducements to board a train for the Reich. But there were irritating difficulties that held down the number of volunteers. For one thing, it was far more dangerous to work in German factories because of heavier RAF bombing. There was also a question of families left behind in France, for whom adequate compensation was lacking. To this was added uncertainty about the duration of contracts. Recruiters would "try everything" to extend them to a full year, although most French workers were reluctant to sign up for more than six months. Likewise, concerns grew about guarantees of paid vacation for those who stayed on.[22] The negative effect of these issues was compounded by stories circulating back from Berlin about the crowded living conditions to which imported workers were subjected—"all of them miserable" as one letter read—and about intolerable constraints on individual liberty. Such complaints probably explain the tepid support offered by the Vichy regime and the "passive behavior" of French recruitment officials in Paris, to the chagrin of the Germans. As Jacques Barnaud confessed, his ministry was willing to tolerate labor recruitment in the Occupied Zone while "always refusing to favor it."[23]

It was not hard to tell where these circumstances would eventually lead. That path was anticipated at a gathering in the Hotel Lutétia in early February 1942, attended by the Abwehr, the Gestapo, and the military command. Their conclusion was simple: if France did not supply enough volunteers, it would be necessary to institute a draft. This program, the infamous Service du Travail Obligatoire (STO), took shape in the months that followed. During that time, voluntary recruitment gradually lost its last chance. On 18 March, Dr. Michel met with French cabinet ministers Barnaud and François Lehideux, informing them that they would need to furnish 150,000 new recruits within a short time. To free up needed workers, the Germans proposed closing several non-essential factories and increasing the standard working week to 48 hours. But the prospects were not positive. When the Hermann Göring steel plant in Braunschweig signaled an urgent need for more hands, the German Labor Ministry sent a representative to Paris where, alas, he encountered "great difficulties" in a disappointing attempt to persuade workers, temporarily unemployed after the bombing of the Renault factory at Boulogne-Billancourt, to accept jobs in Germany.[24]

Berlin would have to take charge. The man designated to enforce a tighter German recruitment policy was Fritz Sauckel, a veteran SS officer, a true believer in the Nazi creed, and a devoted—if not fanatical—servant of Adolf Hitler. From the beginning, Sauckel asserted that a labor draft would be necessary in France, although at first he held back in mid-April 1942 at an unsettled moment when Admiral Darlan resigned as premier in Vichy and was replaced by the resilient Pierre Laval. That respite was brief, and Laval was soon informed that a new German quota was fixed at 350,000, in what came to be known as the first "Sauckel Initiative" (Sauckel-Aktion).[25] On 13 May 1942, Sauckel flew to Paris, where he conferred at length with Heinrich von Stülpnagel, Carl Oberg, and other Occupation dignitaries. He was not there to negotiate but to inform one and all of his demands. He had the Führer's blessing, which was all that really counted.[26]

A draft was still not formally in effect. Sauckel did relent somewhat, agreeing with Laval to reduce his initial quota to 250,000 and to return one French POW from Germany for every three skilled laborers sent there—the so-called *Relève*. For these measures, Sauckel obtained Hitler's personal support, although the Führer stipulated that the POWs would not actually be released but only furloughed to work on French farms. Meanwhile, Stülpnagel was instructed from OKW in Berlin to stay out of Sauckel's way. The MBF would be provided with any necessary information. When further recruitment nevertheless lagged, Laval was pressured into producing legislation that essentially introduced a draft for all French men aged eighteen to fifty and women twenty-one to thirty-five. Slowly and painfully, despite German accusations of French stalling and several bomb attacks at Paris recruitment offices, Sauckel's goal of 250,000 approached fulfillment.[27]

All of this occurred amid gathering misgivings within the Occupation, where warnings were voiced that such an accelerated pace of recruitment was "technically impossible" and "economically unbearable." These terms clearly referred to the antithesis between culling French labor and maintaining French production. Although it was not immediately apparent, those contrary poles would come to be personified by Sauckel and his ultimate nemesis Albert Speer. On a trip to Paris in June, where the two met, Speer, who was now the German Minister of Armaments and Munitions, was made aware of the increasing strain in the French labor market. At the time, his reaction, which he would later revise, was that both objectives—labor conscription and industrial production—could be fully realized.[28] Besides, Sauckel was able to obtain another *Führererlass* in support of his recruitment program. Stülpnagel, although worried about the consequences in France, duly informed Vichy that any further reticence "must be ruthlessly broken." Otherwise, he would be forced to intervene with "the most severe measures."[29] His orders failed to quiet the "strongest objections" within his own administration, however, and plagued by doubts he finally decided to send a telegram to both Speer and Sauckel, back in Berlin, asking whether they were in accord. Speer replied the same day, 8 October 1942, that he was "totally and completely" (*voll und ganz*) in agreement with the shipment of French workers to the Reich. But he added a remark drenched with equivocation: "The transfer must of course be flexibly and sensibly executed." This seemingly innocuous comment, as it would later become apparent, was to open a wedge between Speer and Sauckel. The two characteristics that Sauckel lacked were flexibility and sensibility. If Speer for the moment deferred to Sauckel's Führer-ordained prerogative, that was not to be the final word on the subject, which would be spoken at a later phase of the Occupation.[30]

The dichotomy of German economic objectives could not fail to have obvious repercussions within the military administration. Its staff in charge of manufacturing, the Wi Rü Stab Frankreich, had been founded on the assumption that harmony existed between the general health of the French economy and the armament needs of the German war machine. Each would enhance the other. To maximize production, and to assure German oversight of it, 917 French firms were designated by the beginning of 1942 as Rü-Betriebe, that is, enterprises essential to the arms industry. In addition, some 3,500 other businesses received a classification of V-Betriebe, meaning in effect that they were subcontractors and suppliers of the main industrial plants. In the Rü category alone, nearly 450,000 French workers were employed, mostly in the immediate vicinity of Paris. Because of fuel shortages, it became necessary to determine which of the ancillary enterprises were more essential than others—hence the creation of the rubrics "Va" and "Vb" in January 1942. The former would be spared from a reduction of 50 percent in the allocation of electricity that was imposed on less essential firms.[31]

Berlin wanted further cuts and, given manpower needs in the East, demanded that the personnel of the Wi Rü Stab Frankreich be depleted by 20 percent. That was only a start. During his visit to Paris in June 1942, Speer raised the question of a general reorganization or, as he liked to put it, "simplification" of the Occupation's entire administrative structure in matters economic. This was the principal topic of his conversations with Laval, who agreed that a certain rationalization of the French economy would thereby be served, although it might create an even heavier burden on his government. Yet "in face of the Bolshevik menace," Laval conceded, "France has an obligation to support Germany with all its might."[32] The upshot was outlined in a memo by General Keitel on 26 June. The Wi Rü Stab Frankreich would be divided, with Wi reporting to OKW in Berlin and Rü placed under Speer's ministry. Not only divided, it was soon abolished as a single unit, with its personnel redistributed and its offices and vehicles turned over to other agencies. These changes became effective on 20 July. Two weeks later, Speer's personal representative, Colonel (soon General) Max von Thoennissen, arrived in Paris to assume control of arms production in France—all of which, as Stülpnagel's staff noted with some detachment, "did not proceed without friction."[33]

To speak of a crisis might be excessive. Yet it is clear that Sauckel regarded these developments with skepticism and that he had reason to do so. At a conference in Paris on 12 October, the telegram, sent four days before from Stülpnagel to Speer and Sauckel, was read aloud and analyzed. In response, Thoennissen commented—in a tone reflecting Speer's own expressed view—that he agreed in principle with the transfer of French workers to Germany but wished that it could be accomplished "at a different tempo."[34] Correctly sensing that a challenge to his authority was afoot, Sauckel returned at once to Paris to determine the reasons for "the hitherto highly unsatisfactory result" of labor recruitment. As of 20 October, he announced, shipments of labor to Germany must reach 7,000 a day, a quota to which Hitler had consented. Once more in Berlin, Sauckel then informed Stülpnagel that he was authorized by the Führer to send a delegate, Julius Ritter, to Paris who would thereafter supervise the operation and who would be "*directly responsible to me.*" Taking up his post in Paris, Ritter was accordingly admonished by Sauckel that he was "bound solely to my instructions." Once more, in other words, the MBF would be the odd man out.[35]

Therewith, more visibly than ever, the lines were drawn. Not for the first time, a power struggle in Berlin was to be replicated by proxy in Paris. Thoennissen and Ritter thus became surrogates in a contest between Speer and Sauckel. As matters stood, Sauckel still held the upper hand, a fact that he made unmistakably clear in a rambling two-hour speech before a gathering of German military officers on 2 November 1942, as Allied landing craft were approaching the shores of North Africa. The thrust of his oration was a vigorous defense of the substance and pace of quotas established for France, which, he commented, "we will fulfill … as long as there are human beings in Europe." He understood that the measures imposed on the French would be hard to bear, but they were "correct and humane." He would accomplish the task ordered by the Führer "against all resistance," with the ultimate objective of ensuring that in all of Europe there would in the future be "*one* rhythm determined by Germany." He then concluded grandly with a clinching sentence: "Whoever in Europe does not work should also not eat."[36]

It would be difficult to conceive of a more unvarnished statement of single-minded dedication to a political cause. Whatever the opposition, and whatever the human cost, Sauckel was driven to acquit his duty. In that regard, he was not unlike Oberg, whose pitiless enforcement of law and order in Paris recognized no limits. Together, these two men epitomized the second phase of the Occupation at a time when Nazi Germany had taken on the world and set out to subdue all of Europe, determined to establish a New Order in which everyone would march to the same drum, struck in Berlin.

Chapter 9

A LOST BATTLE

M uch like the evolution of the French economy, the progress of the propaganda war in Paris depended importantly on the weather. The reason
was simple. After the invasion of Russia, it became axiomatic that German
troops on the Eastern Front advanced during the warm season and retreated
once the cold of winter settled in. Among the dozens of German staff reports
and administrative memoranda that attempted to evaluate public opinion and
popular attitudes (*Stimmung*, as they called it) in the Occupied Zone, there
was one conclusion upon which all could agree: that much depended on events
outside of France and, in particular, on the course of military action in the
East. Hence, broadly speaking, those developments seemed to go well in the
autumn of 1941, badly during the frigid months that followed, swimmingly
again in the spring of 1942, and with difficulty once more as another chill
approached in October and November.

Naturally, the Germans were keen not simply to record this ebb and flow
but to influence it. Their efforts to do so were always complicated by the fact
that, as with other facets of the Occupation, the nexus of culture and propaganda was handled not by one administrative agency but several. The predictable result was constant friction and rivalry. Turf disputes between the Hotel
Majestic and the Paris Embassy continued to center on the latter's claim to
control all matters political, a contention approved in principle by OKW in
Berlin. Yet Otto Abetz wanted more. Military officials should be confined
to censorship, while all "positive" activities, such as the planning of cultural

events in Paris, should be left to him and to the Embassy's German Institute.[1] Abetz's bald intention was not only to curtail the Stülpnagel administration but also to exclude interference from Josef Goebbels's propaganda ministry in Berlin in order to avoid useless duplication. Eventually, the Ambassador scored a notable victory in this regard when the Propaganda-Staffel Paris was disbanded in early November 1942. But in reality the altercation was never fully resolved, since the MBF's Propaganda-Abteilung continued to function and refused to abdicate its active, albeit weakened, role.[2]

Given this conflictive undertone, generalizations about the effectiveness of German propaganda in France do not come easily. It is striking that the Germans usually expressed a sober and often negative view about the possibility of persuading the French to adopt their vision of a New Europe under Nazi aegis. As one propaganda official put it, any efforts to promote Franco-German entente must always reckon with "the resentments, even the hate" engendered by the war and the Occupation.[3] Food and fuel shortages, by instilling a "fear of winter," tended to deepen "the old lethargy and indecisiveness" among Parisians, who remained obedient but "reserved." These were hardly terms that bubbled with enthusiasm for collaboration, and German records ordinarily contained few illusions that the Occupation was succeeding in winning hearts and minds in any abundance, especially since the future of France in case of an ultimate German triumph was "completely unclear."[4] Such uncertainty was only magnified after the United States entered the war. Memories of Yankee troops flooding French roads in 1918 were still fresh. However, the battle in the Pacific was far away, and, moreover, the Japanese seemed to be winning it after Pearl Harbor and the fall of Singapore. If the Allies might in the end emerge victorious, that prospect was still distant in 1942. The consensus among those Germans charged with propaganda was consequently that the French were hunkering down for a long Occupation that was generally to be characterized by "indecision and disorientation."[5]

In this dark tableau one may nonetheless detect a few patches of false optimism. Rapid German advances in Russia during October 1941, for example, misled one German propagandist to speculate that the French were bound to realize "that the military decision has been definitively attained."[6] Similarly, early successes by General Rommel in North Africa and the Japanese in Asia caused the MBF's Kommando-Stab to conclude that the French would gradually come to accept that Germany represented the only hope to oppose Bolshevism in the defense of Europe and that they must therefore join with the Reich.[7] Such gauzy optimism reappeared in the summer of 1942 when the *Relève*, allowing a return of several French POWs, initially produced a "somewhat friendlier" public disposition in Paris that could be interpreted as acceptance of "the necessity of a pro-German attitude."[8] Yet these remarks were exceptional, and the rule was better summarized in November 1942 by the office of the Commandant of Greater Paris, only a few hours before the first Allied landings in Morocco. Ever following the war closely, the report stated, the French tended to see Stalingrad as another Verdun. Thus, most of them refused to believe that Germany would finally prevail, and their comportment accordingly remained "cool, hesitant, and negative."[9]

Against this backdrop of fluctuating public opinion—for which no scientific polling existed—we may set the specific attempts by Occupation authorities to steer French attitudes. One of these was the control of publications, the daily press, and radio. Censorship of books and magazines was relatively easy. The "Liste Otto," originally released in 1940, was regularly updated but little changed. It largely determined which writings could be printed and also those that were to be removed from bookstores and library shelves. Incidentally, this included, for unstated reasons, Margaret Mitchell's *Gone with the Wind*, declared by the Gestapo to be "undesirable"—presumably because the story portrayed the liberation of an enslaved people by an invading army.[10] The newspaper press, now with a daily circulation in Paris of nearly 1.5 million, likewise remained under close military surveillance and could be controlled by increasing or decreasing allocations of paper. For this purpose, an organization called the Messageries de la Coopérative des Journaux Français was created. A front for German censorship, it allowed the French Office des Papiers de Presse to fuss over details of rationing so long as favorites of the military administration received their ample share of allotments.[11]

Still a new and untamed technology in the 1940s, radio was another matter. The Germans could neither confiscate all the radio sets in occupied France nor effectively disrupt their reception of broadcasts from Britain. In Germany it was possible to enforce a restriction on hearing foreign news by radio (*Abhörverbot*), because the sympathy and discipline of the home audience could be counted on. But as Chief of the Military Administration Jonathan Schmid remarked, in France "conditions are precisely the opposite." Indeed, Werner Best's staff determined that an attempt by the Germans to forbid Radio London was already "a lost battle" and that a decree to that effect by the military regime, if unenforceable, could only hurt its reputation. This was therefore a matter best left to the French.[12] After appropriate pressure was applied to Jacques Benoist-Méchin, one of Vichy's representatives in Paris, French legislation was passed on 29 October 1941 that imposed a broad range of fines (200 to 10,000 francs) or prison sentences (six days to two years) for illegal reception of radio broadcasts from abroad. This measure was considered insufficient in the Hotel Majestic, however, and the French were informed that harsher measures should be imposed, including the death penalty. To this imperative the Vichy government responded in January 1942 that it was unlikely to achieve the desired objective. In fact, there is no evidence that the Occupation obtained any satisfaction or that the reception of illicit radio programs was substantially impaired.[13]

Film was another medium that merited careful German attention. Of course, part of this propaganda was censorship. In some cases, only minor cuts in films were required. For instance, in the colonial epic *Brazza*, scenes involving Georges Clemenceau and a Jewish banker were excised. There would also be no display of the British Union Jack.[14] In addition, as with books, lists of forbidden films were compiled with a coded system of designations: "H" for the German word *Hetz*, meaning any films containing anti-German agitation; "D" for politically or ideologically unsuitable dogma; and "J" for those featuring Jewish actors or producers. By the beginning of 1942, these classifications had been applied to over 200 films, among them, for example, *La Grande Illusion* (D), which was deemed unduly pacifist.[15] Understandably, synchronized German films appeared much more frequently on Parisian screens than before the war, but German censors complained that the average Frenchman still preferred to see old French films with stars like Fernandel and Danielle Darrieux, "even when he has seen them two or three times."[16]

No less significant than censorship was the encouragement of film production. This effort was mounted under the broad umbrella organization of the Alliance Cinématographique Européenne, founded in 1926, which loosely bound both the German UFA and the French Continental Films. Objections were raised among French filmmakers that the Germans were using this arrangement to take over the industry, but Abetz countered that they should be delighted to receive German investments, now that Anglo-American capital had been banished.[17] Particular importance was attached to the propaganda value of newsreels. German reports noted the spontaneous applause in French cinemas at the showing of military action in Russia. Yet such documentaries should take French sensitivities into account: the graphic depiction of Soviets burning a church was preferable to scenes of German troops using flamethrowers.[18] The German Institute began the practice of showing newsreels at social occasions to which Laval, Fernand de Brinon, and other Vichy luminaries were invited, along with French artists, intellectuals, and professors. Except for the university types, they were, so Rudolf Schleier believed, "extremely impressed."[19] Once more, it was thought better for German propagandists to control the news whenever possible without appearing to do so. No doubt that explains the lengthy negotiations to form a single newsreel production company in Paris, which came to be called France Actualités and which was declared to be owned 60 percent by the French and 40 percent by the Germans. The actual balance of power, as everyone knew, was rather different.[20]

The promotion of cultural life in France—above all, in Paris—remained a high priority for the Occupation. The list of musical presentations was long and illustrious, including acclaimed pianists (Wilhelm Kempff and Walter Gieseking), operas (*Tristan und Isolde* and *Der Fliegende Holländer*), operettas (*Die Lustige Witwe* and *Die Fledermaus*), the Berlin Philharmonic and the Wiener Sängerknaben, a Mozart Week and a Richard Strauss Week, and so on.[21] Two aspects of this intense artistic activity are noteworthy. First, it reached a crescendo during the second phase of the Occupation at a time when France's own lyric theater "now finds itself moribund," as was admitted, with some exaggeration, by Vichy's official information office. The cost of producing an opera (about 50,000 francs) or operetta (at least half that amount) was becoming prohibitive for the French. By offering subsidies to mount these productions, the Germans thus enjoyed a growing monopoly on high culture, and they were proceeding with pride to exercise it.[22] Second, the same rivalries that plagued other sectors of the propaganda war also surfaced in the artistic sphere. Once again, the German Embassy was attempting to muscle the military administration aside. Concerts and other cultural events should never have a military face, so the argument ran in the Rue de Lille, because "even the mildest and fairest occupation, in a country like France, will be unable to prevent a negative stance of the population." Hence, all "positive" measures such as musical presentations should be left to civilians, that is, to the Embassy. And increasingly they were.[23]

Parenthetically, let it be added that far less attention was meanwhile lavished on public lectures and theater productions imported from Germany for the obvious reason that they could not avoid butting against the language barrier. Thus, there was little or no resonance when the noted Berlin historian Wilhelm Windelband appeared one evening in the Hotel George V to give a talk entitled "Bismarck und Frankreich 1870." The same response met a German-language production by Berlin's Lessing Theater of Shakespeare's *As You Like It*.[24]

Besides music, the most successful German propaganda efforts in the public realm were exhibitions. Few of these concerned the arts, simply because Germany had little to trump the international supremacy of French painting. An exception was a much ballyhooed show of sculpture by Arno Breker in the early summer of 1942, attendance at which was estimated (or exaggerated?) at 65,000. Privately, Abetz took full credit for it, although he insisted that in public the Breker exhibit should appear to be under French sponsorship.[25] For the most part, exhibitions created in Paris during the Occupation were dedicated to didactic purposes with the aim of encouraging acceptance of Nazi ideology, as a brief listing—"Le Bolshevisme contre l'Europe," "La Vie Nouvelle," "La France Européenne," "Le Juif et la France"—makes perfectly clear. The Embassy was particularly pleased with these well-attended events and gratified by the expanding role of its Information Section in sponsoring them, even though their impact was admittedly not measurable.[26]

The academic establishment proved to be rocky soil for the spores of German propaganda. The difficulties began in the Paris *lycées*, where the elite of French youth tested the limits of repression. The discovery of a revolver at the Lycée Charlemagne, for instance, brought a prompt investigation by agents of the Gestapo.[27] But the center of agitation, without a doubt, was the fabled Lycée Henri IV. In July 1941, three of its pupils were arrested on a charge of abetting a female spy and were sentenced to death. Only a timely intervention by Fernand de Brinon managed to have the penalty commuted to sixteen years of prison at Rheinbach near Cologne.[28] Intimidating as this was, it did not prevent a recurrence of "trouble" in the form of scuffles in the streets of the Latin Quarter between *lycée* students and uniformed proto-fascist youth groups such as the Jeunesse Nationale Populaire.[29] Inevitably, the teaching corps was implicated as well. One *lycée* professor of English was executed in April 1942 because of his "active sympathy" with Communism; in this instance, pleas on his behalf went unheeded. Another faculty member at Henri IV was arrested that September after an enemy propaganda tract was found in his mail. His whereabouts, the provost of Henri IV reported, were unknown.[30] Disorder and hard feelings were heightened throughout the Occupied Zone by German requisitions, which in some cases caused serious overcrowding. An estimated 40 percent of school buildings were seized for military barracks and office space—as many as two-thirds of those in Reims—although some were subsequently released for classroom use after standing empty. Because of the large number of vacant public buildings and available tourist hotels in Paris, the problem was less acute there than elsewhere.[31]

University life was in the meantime subjected to restrictions and close observation by the Occupation. French students did not need to fear military conscription, of course, but during vacations they were recruited for farm labor. In the summer of 1941, for example, 415 of 505 students at Sciences Po were dragooned by the Service Civique Rural.[32] Their professors came under scrutiny. Four of them were rounded up and subsequently released after an interrogation wrung from them the admission that they hoped for an Anglo-American victory in the war. But they maintained that such opinions had not been communicated to students in lectures, and the Abwehr was unable to prove the contrary. In general, the Germans concluded that strict censorship of lectures was in any event unfeasible, because it would create the impression that professors had been "bought."[33] On political or racial grounds, numerous instructors were nonetheless barred from the classroom, although ten eminent academic personalities in Paris, as well as four in the provinces, had this *Verbot* lifted in June 1942. Among them was France's most famous historian, Marc Bloch, whose reprieve, as we know, did not last.[34] Occupation authorities remained suspicious of French academicians even when they tolerated them. Frédéric Joliot, as noted, was permitted to continue his laboratory work in nuclear physics at the Collège de France under military "protection," even though both he and his wife Irène were considered to be "radical leftist and anti-collaborationist."[35] When a proposal was advanced in the summer of 1942 for the creation of a European association of university professors (*Dozentenbund*), it was immediately disparaged and rejected by the Paris Embassy with the explanation that the French professorate was the element of society currently least inclined toward collaboration. The project was therefore declared to be premature.[36]

Although a similar mistrust existed with regard to the Roman Catholic Church, the Church presented less of a problem for the Occupation—a fact that could be partly ascribed to its hierarchical structure and greater self-discipline. Closely monitored gatherings of French bishops in Paris during 1941 suggested to the Germans that the higher clergy was willing to accept collaboration. Paris Cardinals Suhard and Baudrillart were both rabid supporters of Marshal Pétain, and only Archbishop Gerlier of Lyon remained a strident critic of Vichy's religious policy. Indeed, on his deathbed in May 1942, according to Abetz, Baudrillart expressed his fondest hope to meet God soon and explain to Him why it was necessary to oppose General de Gaulle and support Pétain.[37] Yet, as before, lower clergymen were regarded by the Occupation with a different eye. Symptoms of anti-German agitation among them were not difficult to detect, as Abetz reported to his superiors in Berlin, and therefore "they must be viewed in the future as our most dangerous opponents."[38] At a meeting of regional prefects in February 1942, a spokesman for the French Ministry of the Interior claimed that the attitude of the clergy was "excellent"—by which he meant that they remained quiet and neutral—although he deplored their "reserve" when it came to collaboration. It would be the duty of the prefects to dissipate fears about the diminished role of the Church in a New Europe led by Nazi Germany. No one was heard to challenge the implied assumption that such fears still abounded.[39]

French politics remained in a mess, just as the Germans intended. The normal activities of a Western democracy—campaigns, candidates, elections, parliaments—were forbidden. What played out instead was a charade in which politics and propaganda were indistinguishable. With varying degrees of success, Occupation authorities pursued three objectives. The first was to prevent any sort of political monopoly. There should be no single unified movement—not even a pro-collaborationist one—that might eventually escape strict German control. Rather, the policy was to promote an "incredible flourishing of stillborn political splinter groups," each of which would be, in Abetz's words, "as independent as possible." In this effort, the Occupation largely succeeded, as evidenced by the inordinate number of bit players who crossed the political scene in Paris, usually leading a puny entourage of enthusiasts.[40] Second, in France there should be no fascist party aping the Nazi Party. Paramilitary and unpopular factions like the Parti National-Socialiste Français were seen as unruly street gangs that disrupted public order and thus soiled the reputation of the military administration. Admittedly, questions arose as to which organizations fit this description. For the time being, Jacques Doriot's Parti Populaire Français was so identified at the Majestic and therefore banned. But the German Embassy pointed out that Doriot's youth groups were "especially active" in the cause of collaboration and that it might be "necessary" to allow their participation. In December 1941 that decision was reached with the proviso that uniforms and parades would be prohibited, a stipulation more readily stated than realized.[41] Third, it was thought useful to cultivate one right-wing political force that would be completely dependent on German directions and constitute a counterweight to the Communists. Initially chosen to perform this task was Marcel Déat's Rassemblement National Populaire (RNP), founded in January 1941, which absorbed Eugène Deloncle's Mouvement Social Révolutionnaire. The RNP seemed a likely candidate in view of its top billing in a police report as an "arbitrary and monstrous creation" of the Paris Embassy. Yet this coalition, in the German perspective, failed to develop the desired coherence or dynamism, especially as the Deloncle wing contained too many "diverse elements" to be reliable. The result was an alphabet soup of contending factions that all too well corresponded to the original intention of the Occupation to avoid a political monopoly.[42]

What conclusions or lessons can be drawn from this *tour d'horizon*? At the risk of stating the obvious, the first and simplest is that defeated people do not generally appreciate being occupied by a foreign power. And there is precious little that clever propaganda or political manipulation can do to change that fundamental circumstance. This is especially true when public security and adequate provisioning are not assured. Such shortcomings are unavoidably compounded by deficiencies of the occupying force, whether in terms of inadequate personnel, internal conflicts, or self-contradictory policy. Finally, and particularly relevant in this case, the role of exterior events can be crucial in the drift and flow of public opinion, breeding uncertainty, indecision, and disinclination to accept the currently prevailing conditions of occupation as final.

Chapter 10

EICHMANN IN PARIS

D ecidedly, when discussing the Occupation, there is no way around that
grating word *Entjudung*, meaning an intention to eliminate all Jews—or
at least what was called "Jewish influence"—from French public life. The effort
to do so was slow to gather momentum, but gather it did once the Nazi war
machine crossed the Polish border into Soviet Russia and began to add mil-
lions to the population of the Greater German Reich. Although distant, those
events patently supplied a context for policies and actions in Paris that must
always be kept in view.

The indecision, hesitation, and confusion that were evident before late June
1941 continued into the second half of that year. Whereas the concept of a
"Final Solution" designated in a general way a commonly accepted ultimate
objective of the German administration in the French capital, the method
and pace of its implementation were still far from certain. That discordance
was clearly expressed in a conference at the beginning of July between the
Paris Embassy and representatives of the SS. Speaking for the former, Rudolf
Schleier made a case for gradualism. Measures against Jews that had been
realized in Germany only after years of Nazi agitation, he said, could not be
enforced overnight in France without suitable preparation. It would therefore
be well to begin with "energetic" steps to curb foreign Jews. The French themselves would then "one day" come around to applying the same standards to
those who were still "temporarily protected." Theodor Dannecker, the Gestapo's
specialist for Jewish affairs, had heard this argument before and was obviously

impatient. But he now professed to see some validity in it, although he stressed the need to reach an agreement about the proper tempo. Such agreement was in fact not achieved for months to come, so that one may observe—all the complexity notwithstanding—that a sweeping persecution and deportation of French Jews did not begin until 1942.[1]

As for complexities, a full account of them would fill several volumes. Here it must suffice to enumerate briefly a few of the major obstacles to the formulation and execution of a comprehensive policy. Under German decrees, for instance, banks and businesses were permitted to retain some Jewish employees as technical advisers in subaltern positions, so long as they did not come into direct contact with their customers. Violations were frequent and irrepressible. Lists of Paris firms under Jewish ownership or management ran into the hundreds, and large corporations such as Air France and the Galeries Lafayette were difficult, if not impossible, for the Germans to fathom.[2] Likewise, Jews were tolerated "consciously or unconsciously" within major publishing houses, including Hachette, Calmann-Lévy, Nathan, Ferenzi, and Cluny. Attempts to arrange the sale of these enterprises to "Ayrans" were repeatedly frustrated, German propaganda officials complained, by "interference" from the Embassy, which sided with the French Service du Contrôle in three-quarters of the cases and "hindered [or] sabotaged" effective action.[3] A related problem was to identify stockholders, often widely dispersed, and to determine when the number of shares held by Jews had been sufficiently reduced to eliminate their influence. The German liaison officer with the Service du Contrôle was so disgusted about delays in obtaining pertinent information that he drafted a form letter of inquiry, to which French bureaucrats might respond by merely filling in the blanks. Whether this was evidence of deliberate foot-dragging or of sheer incompetence, no one seemed quite sure.[4]

Another issue was mixed marriages. When was a firm to be considered Jewish? The short answer was gender. If the male Jewish owner of an enterprise was deceased and the management of it was taken over by his non-Jewish spouse, the firm would still be considered Jewish and should therefore be sold or liquidated. The possible resulting complications of settling ownership claims in extended mixed families are not difficult to imagine.[5] Even enterprises in which Jews were summarily dismissed from the directorate could also present confounding ambiguities. The large ship-building firm Penhoët, whose manufacturing facilities were in St. Nazaire and administrative offices in Paris, was a good example. The chief engineer was regarded as indispensable, although a Jew, because he was overseeing the construction of twelve heavy freight vessels under contract from the Reich. His removal would therefore cause "damage to German interests." Less certain was the fate of another Jewish engineer, who would be retained only if Penhoët agreed to build an aircraft carrier for Germany. Once that project was completed or canceled, he could be dismissed. In any event, it was imperative, as an official of the military administration's Economic Section cautioned, to avoid "a clash between the interest of armaments and the interest of a rapid Aryanization."[6]

In December 1941, a new telephone directory for Paris was published. This hefty volume, containing 280,000 names, was promptly analyzed by the *Pariser Zeitung*. True, there were fewer Jews than before. Whereas there had been 747 entries under "Lévy" or "Léwy" in 1939, there now remained 477; under "Bloch," there had been 270, and now there were only 170. Of "obviously" Jewish names, the newspaper commented, 1,400 were still to be found. Apparently, the Jewish question was far from resolved, and further evidence confirmed that fact. [7] The list of Jews who continued to exercise their profession in Paris under the German Occupation was long. Included were lawyers, government functionaries, physicians, surgeons, dentists and dental technicians, opticians, and so forth. For the most part, they were French citizens and long-time residents of the city whose services were essential to the quality of a civilized nation. Their expulsion would be no simple or painless task.[8]

Direct action against Jews in the summer and autumn of 1941 was so sporadic and so entangled with the seizure of hostages and other arrests that an accurate statistical accounting is precluded. On 7 July, for example, the Prefecture of Police reported the detention of 750 persons over a span of ten days, 110 of which were identified as Jews, nearly all of them foreigners.[9] Gradually, this kind of razzia involving Jews became a category unto itself—*Judenaktion*. On orders from Dannecker, as retaliation for sabotages, mass arrests were conducted by French police in Paris on 20–21 August. As a result, 2,894 Jews were sent to Drancy, and a month later the German Feldgendarmerie incarcerated another 3,477 Jews from the Paris region.[10] Besides those held at Drancy and at the camps of Pithiviers and Beaune-la-Rolande in the Loiret, more than a thousand Jews sat in Stalag 22 at Compiègne. The Propaganda-Staffel in Paris reported that anti-Semitic elements in the French population "frequently" asked why the Germans did not more severely punish those guilty of the attacks and assassinations, "namely, the Jews." Indeed, on occasion they did. On 14 December 1941, forty-three Jews were transferred from Drancy to Mont Valérien for execution.[11]

Yet despite the "positive cooperation" of French functionaries and police, the overriding reality for the Occupation authorities directly concerned was a frustratingly lethargic bureaucratic pace. They found reports and statistics of the Service du Contrôle too often incomplete, providing an insufficient basis for a decision about the Aryanization of French business firms. By mid-November 1941, of 3,185 dossiers gathered for that purpose, only 430 had been submitted for German approval, and even that number was suspect. As one Occupation official complained, many of those transactions were "purely for the form, whereas in actuality everything remains as before."[12]

Signs of strain became evident before the end of the year. One telltale symptom was increasing friction between Dannecker's SS detail and CGQJ chief Xavier Vallat, who stood accused of protecting rather than persecuting the Jews by making far too many exceptions for French veterans and others with special pleas. Dannecker consequently saw to it that a "specialist" from his office was attached to the CGQJ—over Vallat's objections and denials.[13] There was meanwhile growing German pressure for the French to pass additional anti-Jewish legislation, perhaps allowing the Germans thereby to withdraw some of their own decrees. To have a French façade on Aryanization was "a desirable circumstance" for the Occupation, it was thought, if only Vallat's subordinates would function with more alacrity. In any event, the mutual primary goal, as they were instructed in emphatic terms, must be "the expulsion of Jews from France."[14] These words were written just as the hostage crisis was reaching its peak. The guilt of "Jewish-Communist" terror gangs was not in doubt at the Hotel Majestic, and Otto von Stülpnagel did not shrink from drawing an appropriate conclusion, proclaiming "the necessity ... of severe and comprehensive measures against the Jews."[15]

The scene was now set for the tragic events that befell the Jewish population in France during 1942. That development, although of one piece, can best be divided into three main aspects: segregation, Aryanization, and deportation.

Who was to speak for the French Jews? The answer emerged in late January in the form of the Union Générale des Israélites de France (UGIF), which has been compared with some justification to the Jewish councils of elders (*Judenräte*) meanwhile created in Eastern Europe. To Marshal Pétain, the UGIF promised "with emotion" to serve in a representative capacity, while adding an unconditional caveat that "it is impossible for us to recognize the principle that the French of Jewish religion should be excluded from the national community."[16] Yet this was precisely the Nazis' objective: to separate the Jews from others. One may properly speak of a specifically Nazi initiative in this instance, because it clearly emanated from ideological hard-liners in Paris and Berlin. Occupation authorities in France generally remained quite reluctant to defy or humiliate the Vichy regime by moving directly against French Jews. Rather, their policy would continue to be—as Dr. Carltheo Zeitschel, the Paris Embassy's chief of Jewish affairs, indelicately put it—to concentrate on "especially detestable" persons, meaning the more than 200,000 Jews who had recently immigrated to France, at least since 1919, or who lacked French citizenship. The others should be largely spared from drastic actions until the French populace was better prepared by anti-Semitic propaganda to cope with them.[17]

This view was definitely not shared by Helmut Knochen, Theodor Dannecker, or their Sipo-SD staff in Paris. On 10 March 1942, Knochen and Dannecker participated in a conference in Berlin, attended by Adolf Eichmann representing Heinrich Himmler's Reichssicherheitshauptamt (RSHA), at which it was determined that all Jews in Holland, Belgium, and France would be required to wear a yellow Star of David, the very symbol of racial segregation.[18] The only difficulty was to gain the indulgence of Vichy. For the Paris Embassy, Zeitschel and Schleier argued that "in no case" should the Occupation simply override Pierre Laval's opposition but instead attempt "to harness the French regime." Only if that failed might the star be stipulated by German decree. Dannecker disagreed. There was no need for negotiation or a public explanation, he contended. Rather, the measure should just be announced by decree "in the framework of the Final Solution of the European Jewish question."[19]

A change of heart at the Embassy did not occur until early May. Three factors played a role. One of them was circumstantial: a violent shooting incident in Argenteuil, northwest of Paris, created, as Zeitschel had to concede, a "politically very favorable situation."[20] The second was Vallat's dismissal from the CGQJ and his replacement by Louis Darquier de Pellepoix, a veteran anti-Semite from whom a less mincing conduct in the matter could be expected.[21] The third was the simultaneous arrival in Paris of Carl Oberg. Already on 12 May, three weeks before officially taking command of all police operations in France, Oberg conferred with Zeitschel and Dannecker on the modalities of enforcement. Three stars would be handed out to each Jew in the Occupied Zone after they had been manufactured by a French firm in Paris. At Oberg's bidding, Heinrich von Stülpnagel then signed a decree—without any accompanying French legislation—that required all Jews, French and foreign, to wear a star as of 7 June. With his customary immodesty, Oberg thereupon proclaimed that he was hereafter in charge of preparing "the solution of the Jewish question in Europe."[22]

This brief narrative is sufficient to establish that the star was imposed over objections by the French (who still refused to allow it in the Unoccupied Zone) and despite serious reservations from within the Occupation. The decree marked a decisive turn toward the more radical means of segregating French Jews that henceforth came under consideration: isolating Jewish schoolchildren, excluding all Jewish teachers from the classroom, squeezing Jewish students out of higher education, declaring a special curfew for Jews, prohibiting Jews from being seated in restaurants, bistrots, theaters, cinemas, race tracks, bathhouses. In the Occupied Zone, there would be, as Oberg imperiously announced with another decree in mid-June 1942, no exceptions. Doubtless in fact there were some. But Jews were now more vulnerable, more conspicuous in the street, and more easily singled out for discrimination than ever before.[23]

The term "Aryanization" is not usually to be found in a standard English dictionary, nor does it appear in the index of many reputable histories of the Vichy period.[24] Yet it is indispensable for any description of the Occupation and its policy toward the Jews. Starting in 1941, "administrative commissars" were assigned to French firms identified by the CGQJ's Service du Contrôle— ever prompted, of course, by the Germans—as being under Jewish influence, that is, having Jewish owners, directors, or stockholders. Their number grew exponentially in 1942 from hundreds to thousands.[25] Once dossiers on these various businesses were prepared by the French and approved by their German supervisors, they could either be Ayranized by eliminating Jews or liquidated through sale to non-Jewish clients. All revenues were to be turned over to a German agency called the Treuhand for short.[26] If this procedure sounds complicated, it was. And it was often far from satisfactory. German officials repeatedly expressed criticism about "simulated Aryanization," about "straw men" who camouflaged residual Jewish influence, and about the "deplorable" performance of the CGQJ's bureaucracy.[27] A dilemma for the Occupation, especially as manpower needs in Eastern Europe began draining away its ranks, derived from the lack of personnel. Either the Germans themselves would need to take over Aryanization, or they must leave it to the French and suffer the misbegotten consequences. There was actually no choice but the latter, and the explicit policy became to pursue Aryanization "with approval but without participation" of the Germans, while the French were expected to act "independently and on their own responsibility." One complication for this policy was the desire of the Vichy regime to maintain property and funds, insofar as possible, in French rather than German hands.[28]

The end result was an immense bureaucratic apparatus that lurched on during the rest of the Occupation. If highly imperfect, this operation was not at all negligible. Whereas the rate of Aryanization declined slowly in early 1942, statistics rose again that autumn and averaged about 400 a month for the year.[29] Consequently, after gathering about 2.6 million francs in 1941, the Treuhand could claim to have collected more than 8 million francs from 3,951 firms by the end of September 1942. This record was achieved despite undeniable "organizational frictions" and the tendency of French functionaries to act "as if Aryanization were a measure solely introduced and executed" by the Germans.[30] On the contrary, unless one counts exhibitions and musical performances in Paris, it was probably the most elaborate and successful example of Franco-German collaboration during the war years.

A major reform of the Aryanization program was attempted in the autumn of 1942 as part of a general reorganization of the CGQJ under Darquier de Pellepoix, who vowed to effect a total elimination of Jewish influence from the French economy. The erratic Service du Contrôle was abolished and a new section (Aryanisation Économique) was installed in its stead at the CGQJ to alleviate the "incoherence" of months past. All of this activity occurred as usual under pressure from the Occupation. For the Germans, as French Minister of Finance Pierre Cathala remarked, it was important to "reinforce their pretensions."[31] Whether the administration thereby became any more efficient is difficult to measure but doubtful. In July 1942, Heinrich von Stülpnagel judged that economic *Entjudung* was progressing well enough in the Occupied Zone, except for Paris, where the staff of the CGQJ had nonetheless tripled from 170 to 543. In all, according to one German estimate, by early November dossiers had been started and commissars assigned to nearly 33,000 French enterprises. That round figure seems inflated. Yet if Aryanization still remained incoherent and incomplete, it was certainly not for lack of paperwork.[32]

In discussing the deportation of Jews from France, one might speculate about when the action was put into motion. Certainly no later, the answer must be, than early October 1941. Just before leaving Paris at that time for an appointment with Adolf Hitler in Berlin, Otto Abetz was approached by Zeitschel, his assistant for Jewish affairs, who recommended that Abetz urge the Führer to order the shipment of all Jews in French concentration camps "to the East" in order to relieve crowding. During his conversations with Hitler, Abetz raised the subject and gained approval for the action, provided adequate transportation could be arranged for it.[33] Before year's end, the details were specified. The plan was to gather 1,000 Jews (a figure later set at 1,100) in Compiègne by transferring a large number of them from Drancy. These "Jewish-Bolshevik elements" would be readied as a "work detail" and must therefore be able-bodied males.[34] It will be recalled that Otto von Stülpnagel, then mired in the hostage crisis, offered no objection to such arrangements and in fact assured his superiors in Berlin that sending "a certain number" of prisoners to Germany or to "the East" would be the most effective reprisal against attacks on German military personnel in Paris.[35] This development, it should be emphasized, originated in Paris and began well before the Wannsee Conference of January 1942, a date that is ordinarily regarded as the defining moment for the Final Solution.

In early 1942, Werner Best confirmed the Occupation's intentions and added more details. The contingent of Jews at Compiègne must be aged 18 to 55, "fit for labor" (*arbeitsfähig*), and French, stateless, or from an occupied country (thus no English or American Jews would be taken, in order to avoid retaliations abroad).[36] On 10 March, Dannecker attended a conference in Berlin—the same meeting where the Star of David was mandated for France—and there set out for Reich officials the urgency of deporting Jews from the overflowing quarters at Compiègne. Speaking for the RSHA, Eichmann concurred. Several agreements were struck between the two men. Spouses in mixed marriages would be exempted. The Jews selected should have good shoes and at least one blanket. Their names should be inscribed on a list, one copy of which was to be sent to Himmler's office in Berlin and another to Auschwitz. This casual bureaucratic mention of Auschwitz at the very least dissipated any lingering doubt about what was meant by the recurring and ritual phrase "to the East."[37]

Ten days later, back in Paris, Dannecker spelled out the consequences. The first deportation convoy, *Sonderzug 767*, would leave Paris on 28 March and arrive in Auschwitz at exactly 5:00 AM on the morning of 30 March (although actually the first train left on 27 March). The prisoners would be composed solely of French, Polish, and Russian Jews. Although the MBF declined to provide enough German guards, "contrary to [a] request" from Dannecker's office, third-class carriages, instead of freight cars, would be used for the first rail transport across Germany. Repeatedly, in German dispatches and reports, it was explicitly stated that this action was to provide labor for a camp that famously bore a jarring inscription above its main gate of entry: "ARBEIT MACHT FREI."[38]

That summer, shipments from France—now directly from Drancy—became routine. The shortage of guards remained a headache, and hence the deployment of freight cars also became routine. However, the problem of transportation was soon resolved. At a meeting in mid-May with Lt. General Otto Kohl, the head of the Eisenbahntransportabteilung (ETRA), Dannecker was delighted to find his interlocutor "an unmitigated opponent of Jews," who ardently favored "a Final Solution of the Jewish question with the objective of a total destruction of the enemy." Kohl promised to provide rolling stock to deport as many as 20,000 persons "to the East." He was prepared to be "radical," he said, even at the risk of seeming "crude." Dannecker had found his man.[39] The only issue now was to secure adequate space at camps in Eastern Europe that could be made available to accommodate all the Jews from France. Dannecker proudly reported his interview with Kohl to RSHA headquarters and inquired whether facilities were ready to receive steady detachments of Jews from Drancy. He would be "grateful," Dannecker wrote on 15 May, if a contingent of 5,000 able-bodied Jews (only 5 percent women and no children) could be accepted and located at once. Far from being prodded by Berlin, one can only conclude, SS men in Paris were seizing the initiative on their own.[40]

Eichmann was delighted. He, too, stressed that only the physically fit should be sent to Auschwitz, but he wanted the pace to be increased. Three thousand Jews a week was not enough. There was talk of sending 10,000 in late June and another 22,000 by mid-July. To encourage such a hastened tempo of "evacuation," as he called it, Eichmann paid a visit at the outset of July 1942 to Paris, where he conferred with Dannecker. Together they determined that "the Final Solution" was currently proceeding "smoothly and certainly" in the Occupied Zone, although the operation could be further accelerated.[41] It is worth noting that the Paris Embassy registered "no reservations" (*keine Bedenken*) about this policy and that Abetz personally approved a quota of 40,000 Jewish laborers for Auschwitz. His only stipulation, as a sop to Vichy, was that the deportations should begin with foreigners and not affect French Jews until later. Neither Eichmann nor Dannecker found reason to reject that principle so long as they controlled its practice.[42]

Eichmann's trip to Paris was crucial because it was shortly followed by detailed planning for the most sensational incident of the second phase of the Occupation. Within a fortnight, on 16 and 17 July 1942, that planning was converted into action. A massive round-up of Jews took place, not only in Paris, but also throughout the Occupied Zone and in some parts of the Unoccupied Zone. Thousands were caught in this net—12,884 to be exact (3,031 men, 5,802 women, and 4,051 children).[43] Of these, many hundreds of adults were sent to Drancy, where they were readied for immediate deportation. Another large contingent was consigned to camps in the Loiret. And the rest, mostly parents with their children, were huddled into the Vélodrome d'Hiver, a mammoth sports arena on the Seine near the Eiffel Tower that gave its name (Vel d'Hiv) to the entire affair. As Ernst Jünger dispassionately noted in his diary, one could hear "wailing in the streets" of Paris. No incident during the Occupation years has been so carefully documented and so closely studied. It would therefore be supererogatory to recount a lengthy narrative of events that occurred in July and in the months that followed. Suffice it to record here that in all about 40,000 Jews were deported from France before the end of 1942.[44]

From the standpoint of the Occupation, this decisive action was a stirring success (although admittedly below original expectations), which was made possible by the convergence of three salient factors. The first was the blinking green light in Berlin. After his return to the German capital, Eichmann remained in close contact with authorities in Paris, notably with the cluster of SS and Gestapo personnel. Meanwhile, with exquisite timing, Himmler reached Auschwitz on 17 July for a tour of inspection. While there, he also visited the adjacent camp of Birkenau in order to witness the selection and extermination of 449 Jews who had just arrived from Holland. Others were to be literally worked to death.[45] The fact that Jews in France would meet the same fate was certainly known to Himmler and Eichmann and, presumably, to some of those with whom they had direct dealings. What cannot be precisely determined is who or how many persons in Paris were at that time privy to the truth.

A second factor was the favorable alignment of planets in Paris. Oberg was now in place there, assuring a firm hand in police affairs that had hitherto been lacking. He was assisted by the savvy Knochen, who played a better second fiddle than first. Although he had been active in planning the Vel d'Hiv razzia, Dannecker was reassigned at this moment and replaced by the equally relentless Heinz Röthke, who was placed in command of distributing the prisoners. The machinations of this triumvirate could be conducted without interference from either Heinrich von Stülpnagel's military administration or Abetz's Paris Embassy. The only real impediment was Laval, who continued to insist that solely foreign Jews should be deported, offering no objection, for example, to the shipment of 3,100 Romanians and 1,100 Greeks. For the most part, that wish was initially respected by the Germans, especially after Himmler signaled his acquiescence.[46] Laval's other caveat, however, created surprise and consternation. He wanted the more than 4,000 Jewish children who had been captured to accompany their parents into exile on the dubious assumption that the Germans intended to organize a new state for them in Eastern Europe. This would avoid pathetic scenes of families being torn apart in Paris. Besides, Vichy had no desire to provide care for such a large number of orphans. The rub for Oberg and his underlings was that shipping children in freight cars might seem scarcely less humane, and it was likely to raise skepticism about the assiduously cultivated myth that Auschwitz was nothing more than a work camp. Consulted by Knochen from Paris, Eichmann gave his consent to Laval's request. The children would be deported—never to return.[47]

Third, Laval's two conditions aside, the French were on board. René Bousquet made all the difference. In Vichy's view, the entire purpose of his taking charge of the national police was to secure the independence of French law enforcement. But the price of that illusory autonomy was Bousquet's concession that the French police would fully collaborate with Oberg in quashing obstreperous and undesirable elements. And they did. Hundreds of Jewish residences were invaded by French officers, who then herded their captives into busses, guarded them in detention centers (including the Vel d'Hiv), and escorted them to the railway depot at Drancy-Le Bourget. This cooperation of French police and gendarmes, according to German military reports, was "extraordinarily good." Otherwise, the undermanned forces of the Gestapo and the German Feldgendarmerie could not have carried out an operation of such magnitude, and there would consequently have been no Vel d'Hiv. Even if German goals for deportation were, and remained, well short of stated objectives, Franco-German collaboration clearly made the implementation of Nazi racial policy far more feasible.[48]

We are confronted here with one of the most difficult and delicate questions of interpretation in history. It must be shocking to find the name of Auschwitz so early and so often mentioned in the German documentation of this period. But what did it mean then to those who freely used it? The notion—or perhaps the pretense—that Auschwitz was merely a labor camp, to which only the mature and able-bodied should be sent, invariably ran through German records in Paris from late 1941 onwards. There was in all of that evidence no reference whatever to the frightful reality that was taking shape: nothing about the triage at the railway terminal inside the camp—one line for work detail, the other for extermination—and nothing about the gas chambers and the ovens. Did those in charge of the Occupation know or suspect what was actually happening in Poland? Surely the answer varies in different cases, depending on how high or low one looks in the hierarchy. In the end, the point is that the Germans in Paris did not need to be aware of everything in order to perform the task of ridding France of Jews. After all, *Entjudung* was now the official policy of the Third Reich. Those who carried it out in the West only had to do their part. Others, in the East, would take care of the rest.[49]

Changing of the guard on the Rue de Rivoli

A drum and bugle corps in the Avenue Kléber near the Hotel Majestic

Café terraces are still packed—with German soldiers

Street scene at the Place du Tertre on Montmartre

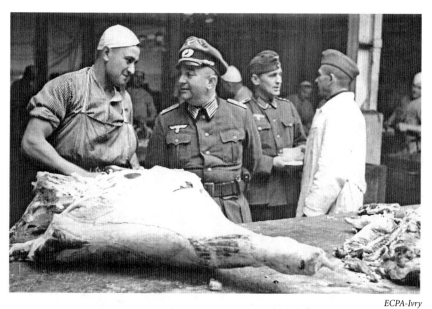

German meat inspectors confer with French butchers

A little black market operation on the street

German officers in an open limousine leaving the Place Vendôme

A first-class carriage in the Paris metro at rush hour

German soldiers gain directions from a local policeman

A daily parade passes in the center of Paris

Damage caused by Allied bombing of the Renault factory on 4 April 1943

A Franco-German funeral service for victims of the air raid

A German memorial service in the cemetery of Ivry-sur-Seine

An intimidating sight known to every Parisian during four years

PART III

Holding On

(November 1942–June 1944)

Chapter 11

A TURN OF FORTUNE

Operation Torch brought the war back to France. After the fall of Paris in the summer of 1940, the din of battle had receded to faraway places—to the islands of the Pacific and the steppes of Russia. During that time, the French capital lay in waiting, sullenly quiet, its population apathetic and its public life usually subdued despite sporadic outbursts of violence. The Anglo-American landing in North Africa abruptly changed that atmosphere and focused everyone's attention on the fact that Western Europe was once more destined to become a scene of combat. Now military action was just across the Mediterranean waters in the Maghreb, directly involving territory that was both technically and emotionally a part of the French nation. Thus, in November 1942, a third phase of the Occupation began.

The configuration of France and the nature of the Occupation were likewise suddenly altered. In personal letters to Marshal Pétain, Adolf Hitler explained why the Third Reich must take "necessary measures" of self-defense by crossing, and thereby erasing, the demarcation line.[1] German troops rushed to the southern coast and pointed their binoculars across the sea. In effect, they thereby annexed Vichy France to the Occupied Zone and assumed command everywhere from Roubaix to Marseille. For the military administration this move had daunting implications. It meant that an entirely new bureaucracy would need to be installed in the former Unoccupied Zone and, accordingly, that there would be a need for a batch of new *Feldkommandanten* with their offices and their staffs and their complex relations to local French prefects and mayors. The immense space between the demarcation line and the shores of the Midi would henceforth have to be supervised and administered, just at a time when manpower needs elsewhere had greatly reduced the MBF's staff in Paris. Heinrich von Stülpnagel and Carl Oberg agreed that to function effectively under the new circumstances, the German army and the police would require a simplification of procedures as well as a redistribution of all personnel. The status quo was no longer tenable.[2]

In Paris, German authorities attempted to evaluate the new situation in reports to their superiors back in Berlin. Although there was general agreement among them, it is useful to separate these sources into three main components. The first raft of messages emanated from security police and SS officers, often in the form of dispatches addressed directly to Heinrich Himmler. He was told that there was now increasing talk of a forthcoming liberation and that "many have changed their position." Operation Torch had created "a hitherto unknown Germanophobia" in France, with as many as 95 percent of the population now anticipating an ultimate Allied victory. But uncertainty about the immediate future was such that a "nervous climate" prevailed in Paris, even though the annual Armistice Day ceremonies on 11 November 1942 passed without any public incident.[3] When the Allied campaign bogged down in Tunisia in early December, the populace's initial enthusiasm was dampened, and a more realistic mood of "stolid resignation" settled in, as Helmut Knochen commented. Parisians began to understand that a military outcome was not near: instead of three months, liberation might have to wait five years. Still, by the beginning of 1943 there was no denying a "general rejection of all things German" and a widely shared hope among the French for "an imminent collapse of Germany and an Allied victory in this year."[4]

A second opinion originated from the hierarchy of military administration, percolating up from several *Kreiskommandanten* in the Paris region to their *Feldkommandant*, whence on to the Commandant of Greater Paris, then finally to MBF Stülpnagel. From the resulting dozens of memoranda between November 1942 and March 1943, it is possible to extrapolate a consistent pattern that largely corroborated the impressions gathered by Himmler's RSHA in Berlin. The French were reacting with a certain *Schadenfreude*, harboring few doubts about an eventual German defeat and adopting the attitude of a somewhat bemused bystander. There was plenty of negativism toward the Occupation but no sign of a "terrorist movement" or an open rebellion. An uprising would be likely only in the event of "a successful enemy invasion." Rather, the Germans would have to reckon with passive resistance and tantrums of rejection: delays, discourtesy in shops, and slowdowns in factories.[5] "Today Germany no longer has very many friends," lamented one *Kreiskommandant* in a Paris suburb, while another remarked, "The attitude toward Germany is altogether degraded." They estimated that a maximum of 10 percent of the population might be considered collaborationist. It was not surprising, then, that "there is talk of a decisive turn of fortune in the war."[6] These frank expressions following the North African landing were more than enough to reveal the hollowness of military celebrations in Paris at the end of January 1943 marking the tenth anniversary of the Nazi seizure of power. Notably, in the morning there was a solemn wreath-laying at the cemetery of Ivry, and in the evening a splendid gala at the Palais de Chaillot with the motto: "Wir werden siegen, weil uns Adolf Hitler führt" (We shall be victorious because Adolf Hitler leads us).[7] Such expansive German confidence was meanwhile belied by the unfavorable bulletins that continued to reach Paris as the battle of Stalingrad approached its disastrous conclusion. The consensus among military officials of the Occupation was that everything depended on the course of outside events. Only an impressive German triumph could alter the ambient gloom, and that was apparently not in the offing.[8]

Diplomatic channels did not present any more consolation. The Foreign Office in Berlin was informed that although Paris was outwardly calm, public opinion had in fact hardened. "A considerable worsening" of circumstances was the only conclusion to be drawn. Sponsored by the Paris Embassy and a frequent visitor to the French capital, Professor Friedrich Grimm was only slightly more sanguine. He detected a "general confusion" there and speculated that 10 percent of Parisians favored collaboration, 10 percent remained firmly opposed, and the other 80 percent still temporized. But he also confirmed that the drift of public perception under the Occupation would depend on military developments in the Mediterranean and Russian theaters. Whatever transpired, Grimm observed, there was nonetheless little danger of an insurrection in France simply because "the populace is tired."[9] All things considered, after the first week of November 1942, the prognosis of German authorities in Paris was neither uplifting nor reassuring. The optimism that had characterized the first two phases of the Occupation was rapidly dissipating, and the swagger was gone.

This evident decline of verve and self-confidence tended to exacerbate already existing internal conflicts. Upon closer examination, the entrails of the military administration were not a pretty sight. Truth to tell, Heinrich von Stülpnagel was scarcely more successful than his cousin Otto had been in containing the erosion of his authority. He seemed perpetually embattled on all sides. First, as before, the MBF was forced to fend off the diplomatic corps. At odds over policy with Joachim von Ribbentrop because of his zealous support of Pierre Laval, Otto Abetz was recalled in December 1942 to Berlin, where he languished as if in exile for a full year.[10] Yet the Paris Embassy remained active and, under Rudolf Schleier, managed to give Stülpnagel unrelenting grief, as the following two examples illustrate. Recently transferred from Wiesbaden and appointed in Paris as the Reich's diplomatic representative for economics and finance, Richard Hemmen conferred in January 1943 with Laval. Stülpnagel had not been informed about the meeting, and he was incensed to learn of it. Hemmen was summoned to the Hotel Majestic, where the general complained about being excluded and coldly advised him that the MBF alone held the power to negotiate directly with heads of the Vichy regime. Attempts by Schleier to soothe Stülpnagel's ruffled feelings were ineffective. He would be willing to talk further with a delegation from the Embassy, Stülpnagel huffed, but only after he had received a written explanation of Hemmen's action.[11]

Although this affair concerned a relatively minor matter, it was an indicative one. That was made clear by another festering dispute over the control of propaganda. Despite the Embassy's putative authority to regulate all matters political in France, the Propaganda Section of the military administration continued to issue bulletins and directives. The result was duplication and friction that prompted an appeal for arbitration to the OKW's chief of staff, Wilhelm Keitel, who chose to back the Embassy. He did so, however, without consulting Joseph Goebbels, whose propaganda ministry in Berlin had a stake in maintaining an open line to the MBF staff in Paris. They could all expect more trouble, one observer correctly remarked, when Goebbels found out and undertook a counterattack.[12] Again, nothing was settled. One of Abetz's first actions after returning to his post at the Rue de Lille in December 1943 was to draft and circulate a list of eight instances in which the Propaganda Section had interfered with the political initiatives of the Embassy. It was one against all and all against one.[13]

Stülpnagel's second worry was Fritz Sauckel. Whereas the German military administration ordinarily tried to spare public sentiment in Paris and to avoid overbearing demands, Sauckel's blustering determination to raise quotas for the recruitment of labor risked an unpopularity that complicated dealings with French officials there and in Vichy. Moreover, against Stülpnagel's express wishes, Sauckel appointed a personal envoy in Paris, Julius Ritter, who (like Hemmen) took it upon himself to confer privately with Laval. When Sauckel departed after a stay in the French capital in early August 1943, he profusely thanked the MBF for the "far-reaching agreement" they had attained on the labor question. To this, the well-informed Stülpnagel retorted with indignation that Ritter had already violated the "comradely spirit" of their accord and that the MBF alone was authorized to conduct direct negotiations in the name of the Occupation. He demanded that Ritter be so instructed. Otherwise, in light of their "mutual distrust," the military administration threatened to withdraw altogether its cooperation in the labor recruitment program, which would surely be a crippling blow.[14]

A third challenge came from the relatively new power base being created by Oberg. As the supreme German police commander, he had initially been successful in squeezing out competitors. On a visit to Paris in mid-November 1942, for instance, the head of the Abwehr, Admiral Wilhelm Canaris, agreed to turn over to Oberg all files concerning the chase after Communists, which had previously been managed in the Hotel Lutétia. Similarly, control of munitions stored at German depots in France, formerly the domain of military *Feldkommandanten*, was henceforth assumed by Oberg's police force.[15] There was yet another factor to be considered. Since France was once again a war zone, renewed importance was accorded to the military command post known as OB West under Field Marshal Gerd von Rundstedt, who demanded a free hand for law enforcement in the former Unoccupied Zone. This claim led to a conflict with Oberg, who insisted that "observations of anti-German actions" within the police everywhere in France must continue under his direction.[16] To back up his chief, in a report filed on 17 August 1943, Knochen deplored the "passive resistance" and lack of dedication in the ranks of the French police and bluntly proclaimed the need for a purge. The Gestapo should not hesitate, he declared, "to arrest certain [police] functionaries and to expel them to the Reich." This exclamation drew immediate objections from both the Paris Embassy and the German military administration. Knochen was accused of mixing fact with fiction, leading to "exaggerated conclusions." To the contrary, he was told, the French police bureaucracy, though sometimes acting with hesitation, was functioning perfectly well. Calling Knochen on the carpet at the Hotel Majestic, Stülpnagel demanded a reasoned explanation of the "contradictions" in his statement. Evidently it was not satisfactory. Knochen would soon be gone.[17]

This intensified in-fighting of the Occupation—often sharp, even when petty—undoubtedly betrayed a markedly heavier atmosphere in Paris during 1943. Another symptom of it was the open discussion and preparation for a "serious circumstance" (*Ernstfall*), a standard euphemism for an anticipated Allied invasion of the Continent.[18] This expression recurred intermittently during the spring and summer as bad news about the war accumulated. On the Eastern Front, after the surrender of Field Marshal Paulus at Stalingrad in February, the last major German counterattack was repulsed in July, and the Russians began their slow and inexorable push toward Berlin. By that time, the North African campaign had come to a close: Rommel had been defeated, and the Anglo-Americans reigned everywhere from Egypt to the Atlantic. Sicily was invaded and Mussolini deposed that July, bringing the enemy one step closer. Finally, on 2 September 1943, the Allies landed on the shores of Italy. Surely France would be next.

How did the Germans stationed in Paris respond to a truth that could be neither spoken nor hidden? A good starting point for an answer to that question is 19 August 1943. On that day, doing his duty to the end, Knochen drafted two memoranda shortly before his final departure from SS headquarters in the Avenue Foch. They presented, rather than a rhetorical farewell, a dry analysis of what to expect. In the first memo, he warned that the French police were "less than ever" to be counted on "in case of a crisis." Instead, it must be feared that, in the event of an invasion of France, they would conspire to stab German troops in the back—and that they would likely do so in spite of the fact that they were currently aiding the Occupation in tracking down Communists.[19] The second long memo from Knochen's office, on twenty-one single-spaced typed pages, expanded and explained the first. Since late 1942, there had been an evident shift of popular support from the Communist leadership to the "national resistance," meaning the Gaullists, and it was "beyond doubt that even in the upper echelons of the police there continues to be sympathy with that movement." Indeed, in support of it, the staff of the Paris Prefecture of Police had become "predominantly anti-German." An *Ernstfall* was therefore sure to present an acute danger if large, organized, and armed French police squads fell under the influence of invaders. Neither they nor the French people in general were likely to see a future in collaboration with Germany. Although Knochen thereupon disappeared, his parting shot enunciated the themes that were to resound again and again in German reports from Paris stretching into 1944.[20]

Besides these concerns about the reliability of the French police and other French officials, Occupation authorities had to protect their own forces. Air raid drills, already begun in 1942, became more frequent and strict. The administration made clear that this was not child's play. For failing to observe regulations promptly during one drill, sixty German soldiers were sentenced to a brief jail term at the Fresnes prison.[21] Meanwhile, gas masks were checked and rechecked. Blood types were gathered and recorded. And reams of documents were shredded to clean out office files, a practice begun in 1940 that was now expedited.[22] Most conspicuous of all, a large concrete bunker, to which access was determined by rank, was erected adjacent to the Hotel Majestic. Only officers with special passes were allowed on the upper floors of the bunker. Candles were distributed in case of an electric power outage. Military personnel at the Majestic were instructed to deposit one small piece of luggage with essentials in the bunker, ready to go.[23] All of this activity was devoted to a single objective—to keep the military administration functioning in Paris up to "the last possible point in time."[24] Yet no decisive military action was forthcoming in 1943, and the long period of waiting was wearing on everyone's nerves. Stülpnagel had to worry about defeatism, weakening discipline, and alcoholism among the troops.[25] Consequently, there was more than enough time to think the unthinkable. What, one officer at the Majestic wondered, would come of the Occupation "if the military situation should be definitively decided against us?" He was not alone in having no answer. His personal recommendation was not to waste time with military preparations to defend Paris at a moment (February 1944) when the war might still be won. It would be sufficient to devote one Sunday a month to practice grenade throwing and rifle shooting at a firing range.[26] Such an attitude well expressed a palpable sense of helplessness that overcame the Occupation as the spring of 1944 arrived.

An *Ernstfall* could not be averted; it could only be faced and dealt with by measures that were incapable of altering the outcome. For his part, Stülpnagel issued orders emphasizing that all papers to be destroyed should be *completely* burned. Paris was becoming a city of courtyard bonfires.[27]

Enter Joseph Darnand. Reorganization of the French police in the wake of the Oberg-Bousquet agreements in late 1942 was accompanied, on the fringes, by a shake-up of the Légion des combattants, a Pétainist veterans' organization agitating on behalf of the Vichy government. Dissatisfaction with this effort provoked the formation in January 1943 of a more highly motivated offspring, the Service d'Ordre Légionnaire (SOL), of which Laval anointed Darnand as leader. When René Bousquet then proved in Oberg's judgment to be inadequate to the task—and when German confidence in the loyalty of the French police began to evaporate in 1943—Darnand was asked in July to head the Milice Française, a cadre of paramilitary militia groups of several thousand men, fanatics all, who constituted the backbone of the so-called Maintien de l'Ordre (MO). By joining the Waffen-SS in August, hence donning a German uniform and swearing an oath of allegiance to Adolf Hitler, Darnand won German confidence and, as Secretary General of the MO, replaced Bousquet as the main law enforcement officer in all of France. As one Occupation official commented, "under German pressure" Darnand thereby became the most powerful French police chief since Joseph Fouché during the Napoleonic era.[28]

This maneuvering in high places requires mention here because it occurred at a time when, in Stülpnagel's opinion, the French regime in Vichy was displaying "practically no leadership" and administrative initiative was correspondingly declining. Darnand's Milice was called upon to fill that gap, and, despite German misgivings about allowing an unduly potent police presence in France, the military administration accepted it.[29] As Paris awaited a full-scale Allied assault on the European Continent, therefore, the question of collaboration was being sharpened to its finest point: would the French, as some had in North Africa, actually fight beside their German comrades to stave off an invasion of the mother country? Both sides were uncertain.

Chapter 12

A Police State

The shortage of personnel for policing France became a more pressing and acute problem for the Occupation once the Germans took charge of all the territory south of the demarcation line. Such insufficiency proved to be an intractable handicap that crippled the military administration to the end. The result was an increased pressure for the *Verstaatlichung* of the French police, that is, the creation of a united, more efficient national organization under a single command that could be held responsible for cooperation and discipline. This necessity, for that is what it was, explained the growing prominence of René Bousquet and then Joseph Darnand. However, despite their avowed willingness to collaborate, and notwithstanding repeatedly codified formal agreements, a satisfactory solution was not found. Ultimately, the tenure of Carl Oberg in managing police affairs—like that of Fritz Sauckel in recruiting French labor— must therefore be considered a disappointment for the German cause.

Stability in law enforcement was never achieved. Recurrent attempts to reform the existing French police structure were accompanied by a constant accumulation of ever more perplexing responsibilities that were assigned to it. In addition to the routine duties of keeping public order, the French were expected to perform tasks such as arresting those who evaded or shirked required labor service, breaking up strikes "by all available means," guarding utilities and railway installations, assisting in the roundup of Jews, and sealing off the porous Franco-Spanish frontier. These daunting German demands inevitably provoked tensions between occupiers and occupied, of which four were conspicuous.[1]

The independence of the French police was supposedly guaranteed by agreements between Oberg and Bousquet, in return for which the latter's minions would display greater alacrity in executing orders from the Germans. This arrangement, as Bousquet remarked, was intended to end the "paralysis" in the previous phases of the Occupation and to provide a new impulse for the French to manage their internal affairs. In reference to a bomb attack on the Canebière in Marseille in mid-April 1943, one of Bousquet's staff begged him to press Oberg for further assurances that "the autonomy of the French police will be respected." Meeting with Oberg on the following day, Bousquet did so and was rewarded with a positive response.[2] Yet in practice the principle of autonomous action by the French remained ambiguous and was frequently undercut. Some assigned tasks were frankly disagreeable and therefore reluctantly fulfilled. One of them, for example, was chasing down workers on furlough from their labor service in Germany who decided to disappear rather than return. Another was performing guard duty at isolated posts, especially for prolonged stretches at night. And, to be considered later, there was obvious reluctance by Paris police officials, prompted by the Vichy regime, to authorize the apprehension of French Jews for deportation, although the evidence is indisputable that they did so when closely supervised by the Gestapo. Such reservations were matched by the tendency of German security forces to seize the initiative whenever it suited them (or when the French were slow to comply) by conducting house searches, interrogations, arrests, and trial proceedings that could lead to internment or a death penalty.[3]

Closely related was the question of custody. It was first raised by rare instances when a parachutist—either a downed RAF pilot or possibly a clandestine Resistance fighter—was captured. The Germans regarded this as strictly a military matter properly left to them. But the French sometimes hesitated to cede custody with its potentially lethal consequences.[4] The issue proved to be much larger, a particularly juicy apple of discord. Generally compliant as he was, Bousquet was nonetheless keen to limit German jurisdiction. His policy was, for instance, not to turn over custody of any prisoners detained merely for spreading political propaganda. Oberg was willing to grant that those arrested by French police should ordinarily be tried in French courts, except when individuals were accused of perpetrating attacks on German civilian or military personnel.[5] Fine distinctions were not in vogue with the Gestapo, however, and disputes predictably arose. When Helmut Knochen insisted on taking custody of several suspects after an attack in August 1943, a French chief of police countered by criticizing the German practice of seizing French prisoners, trying, and executing them—with a "regrettable influence" on police morale.[6] Sharp disagreements of this sort came to a head in December 1943 after a German soldier was assassinated and six persons were promptly taken into custody by the French police. When the police refused to surrender the men to the Sicherheitsdienst, on the grounds that they were being held in a detention center outside of police control, Oberg personally intervened. The six were brought to the Gestapo.[7] This altercation was one of the reasons that Bousquet was replaced by Darnand, under whom the custody issue became less of an irritant, although he too did not escape an Oberg reprimand. On one occasion Darnand even suggested releasing 500 "terrorists" to the Germans in order to alleviate crowding in Lyon prisons, but he specified that they should be sent to labor details in Germany rather than being tried by German military tribunals.[8] This suggestion was exceptional; more usual, in cases of doubt, was procrastination. One official explained that "within the French police there exists hostility toward the Germans and against members of political parties that collaborate with them." Although hypothetically "inadmissible," the refusal to give up custody of elements of the opposition remained a vexing and unresolved aspect of the Occupation.[9]

A third sore point was a continuing lack of adequate armament. Bousquet's chief assistant in Paris, Jean Leguay, cited an immediate need—in view of the fact that French police were "practically disarmed"—for 6,000 revolvers in addition to some automatic weapons. The problem was that equipment and munitions depots remained "totally under German control" and that any such requests were "purposeless" without Oberg's prior approval.[10] In general, the Germans were notably unresponsive to inquiries about increasing the French police force and arming it. A few weapons were parceled out, but not many. For all of France, according to one official reckoning in September 1943, the police possessed 564 rifles, 291 submachine guns, and 66 machine guns. Paris police did receive generous allotments of pistols (but with only five or six cartridges each), yet no machine guns or "modern weapons," as the Prefect of Police complained, in spite of "more and more numerous" terrorist attacks in the capital city. Especially police stations were being assaulted "with an unbelievable audacity" by well-armed gangs. Consequently, unless they were better equipped to meet the rising tide of violence, the police were sure to face insurmountable difficulties in the maintenance of public order.[11]

Finally, as mentioned, the Germans agreed with Darnand to permit the creation of the Milice, a uniformed and armed paramilitary force that engendered further controversies. The painful strain on German tolerance began with the Milice's predecessors, the Légion des combattants and the even more unruly and militant Service d'Ordre Légionnaire (SOL). Considering themselves outside of and superior to the regular police, legionnaires repeatedly provoked scuffles with them in the streets of Paris. In these melees, the Germans often found themselves in an uncomfortable posture as arbiters, thereby risking the appearance of permissiveness regarding public disorder if they failed to clamp down on the Légion.[12] Embarrassment with this circumstance facilitated the emergence of Darnand, who promised to implement greater discipline as well as stricter repression in return for a strengthened and armed Milice. One potentially important result was a shake-up of French administration in January 1944, as a result of which seven new regional prefects and twenty new departmental prefects were appointed to serve under Darnand's aegis. These novitiate functionaries, with "sharp and constant" German supervision, were to help energize police cadres throughout France.[13] Whether such measures actually succeeded in that purpose is altogether dubious. By 1944, in the midst of a "crisis of recruitment," the reliability of the French police was seriously placed into question by the Occupation. Whereas police officials—notably, the so-called Brigades Spéciales—had usually been cooperative in tracking and apprehending Communists, they were far less willing to administer harsh treatment when it came to the "national resistance," essentially meaning the militant Gaullist cells that now became increasingly involved in overt anti-German activities. A lesser, albeit also troubling, development was a series of attacks by men impersonating police officers, whose uniforms could apparently be obtained on the black market.[14] Both Darnand and Heinrich von Stülpnagel spoke of a gathering "banditry" that must be repressed, but the Milice proved to be insufficient in halting the gradual erosion of public tranquility. Thus, Darnand's policy of law enforcement, *maintien de l'ordre*, scarcely merited that description by the summer of 1944.[15]

As the Occupation's confidence in the French police noticeably waned, the banner of the Gestapo was unfurled, and the aggressive behavior of German security forces markedly increased after the Allied invasion of North Africa. Although they cannot be tabulated without bothersome lacunae, statistics in Sipo-SD files showed a proliferation of arrests in Paris by German police agents: 79 from 26 November to 9 December 1942; 167 in the latter half of January 1943; 277 a month later in February; and 453 during a comparable period in July. Their French counterparts were greatly disturbed by what one police memo called "massive arrests in all classes of society," claiming in November 1943 that the Germans had apprehended 8,000 persons since the beginning of the year. Moreover, in all, the French estimated that 120,000 of their citizens had passed through German jails and camps since the onset of the Occupation. These round numbers do not inspire trust in their precision, but there is no doubt that the Gestapo was doing more than its part, as Bousquet observed, to meet "the wave of terrorism that is rolling over our country" with "cold and implacable determination."[16] Meanwhile, French police activity must have seemed rather modest by comparison. The Prefecture of Police boasted that it had detained more than 9,000 persons in the Paris region since the beginning of July 1940 (3,877 imprisonments plus 5,234 other arrests, to be exact).[17] But Gestapo records during the first four months of 1944 put the matter into better perspective, as the following calculations reveal.

Police Arrests in Early 1944

Period	German	French	Total
30 December 1943–14 January 1944	180	69	249
14–29 January 1944	332	85	417
29 February–14 March 1944	335	99	434
15–29 April 1944	268	152	420
30 April–13 May 1944	302	36	338
14–30 May 1944	237	50	287
Totals	1,654	491	2,145

Source: AN Paris, F[7], 15142

It may appear inadmissible to speak of a German gulag in France, but that term is neither anachronistic nor altogether inappropriate. Alone in Greater Paris there were six prisons (Fresnes, La Santé, La Roquette, Cherche-Midi, Les Tourelles, and Romainville) in full use, in addition to three prison camps (Drancy, Gare d'Austerlitz, and a *camp de la folie* for the mentally afflicted at Nanterre)—not to mention nearby Compiègne or the two accessible compounds, serving as reservoirs, at Pithiviers and Beaune-la-Rolande in the Loiret.[18] A definitive census of the ceaselessly shifting population incarcerated in those institutions is well out of reach. Records kept by French police officials were very incomplete, perhaps because they were particularly eager to deny their own excesses and to leave that reputation to the Germans. Besides, the French were more worried about procedures than numbers. At the beginning of 1944, one police memorandum (for internal consumption) castigated Gestapo officers for "the brutality of their methods," which seemed out of scale with the offenses committed. Furthermore, there was evidence of "arbitrary cruelty," doubtless an oblique reference to torture, a word no one dared to declare. Manifestly, it was the intention of the Occupation to intimidate the majority of the population, which, though obliged to bow before such force, was "separating itself definitively from any idea of collaboration."[19]

Yet in spite of the Occupation's muscle, terrorist attacks targeting railways, electric power lines, communications, and industrial plants continued and mounted. By one count they averaged about 3,600 in all of France during the first three months of 1944, then spiked to over 4,000 in April.[20] Although the center of Paris was relatively quiet, trouble was lapping up on all sides. A reported 300 arms and munitions depots had been raided (with the French blaming the pillage on the Occupation's "systematic refusal of all requests" to equip their police), thereby putting countless weapons into circulation. Correspondingly, personal assaults on police and the Milice increased, with 130 deaths among them recorded in the twelve months before April 1944.[21] Sabotage likewise spread, especially on the railroads, as indicated by the growing number of arrests of both bureaucratic personnel and *cheminots*. An average of

129 arrests a month was reported for May to September 1943 and 194 a month from that October to February 1944. The French National Railway Company (SNCF) had long been under suspicion by the Sipo-SD, which since April 1943 maintained lists of state railway officials who were to be immediately arrested in case of an Allied landing. In addition, orders were in place that strikes by railway workers should be "relentlessly suppressed."[22] But no matter what its methods, the Occupation was helpless to halt the deterioration of French administration, even in its highest places. In mid-May 1944, fourteen prefects were arrested by the Gestapo; a week later, forty prefects were appointed to fill vacancies. And for the purge, there was no end in view.[23]

In the meantime, after November 1942 the hostage issue dissipated but did not entirely disappear. Statistics in early 1943 indicated a perceptible decline in the number of persons arbitrarily arrested and executed in retaliation for attacks on German military personnel. Ironically, it was Otto von Stülpnagel's view that finally prevailed: rather than the massive shooting of French hostages *pour l'exemple*, it would be far better to deport suspected terrorists or funnel them through the military court system. The real difference was not that the killing of civilians decreased but that it henceforth became largely hidden from public sight.[24] This change in policy was adopted by the Sipo-SD in Paris and approved by the RSHA in Berlin. The shift in emphasis was embellished by Heinrich Himmler with six pages of new instructions about modes of execution. Some of these were familiar: a rifle squad should consist of at least six men firing from a distance of five paces. More original were explicit details about hanging, which was to be carried out by fellow prisoners rewarded with an allocation of three cigarettes per victim. Corpses, Himmler further specified, should be delivered to either a crematorium or the anatomy class of a university clinic. If neither was possible, they might be buried in a Jewish cemetery or in the section of other cemeteries usually reserved for suicides.[25]

Initially, of course, there was confusion in distinguishing between hostages and those convicted of alleged crimes. Yet some of the former, executed in late 1943, could be positively identified: eighty-eight on 11 August, forty-six on 21 September, and fifty on 2 December. For those unfortunates, the customary procedures were observed. They were gathered and escorted to Mont Valérien, where the death sentences were carried out followed by cremation at Père Lachaise. Subsequent investigations have confirmed that the total number of hostages shot at Mont Valérien was not 4,500, as announced by a plaque on display there, but precisely 1,007.[26]

Important as it is to gain a sense of magnitude, other statistics are unfortunately less secure. The Occupation's armed forces in France were dispersed after November 1942 into more than fifty regions, each under a *Feldkommandant* who presided over a military tribunal capable of pronouncing and executing death sentences. Reports of these proceedings were then sent to the Hotel

Majestic in Paris, where the MBF staff collated the results and forwarded them to Berlin. It was not an exact science. What of the Frenchman, after his conviction, who was killed while attempting to escape? Or the one who died of tuberculosis before he could be executed? Furthermore, many such records were deliberately scattered or destroyed in mid-1944 as Paris was being evacuated. Still, some statistics conveyed by one reporting channel, via the Paris Embassy to the Berlin Foreign Office, have been preserved, and other fragments remain. A meticulous scholar has calculated that from the Armistice of 1940 to the beginning of June 1942, German courts in the Occupied Zone issued death sentences to 655 persons, of whom 434 were executed.[27] If these numbers may be accepted as a baseline to that point, the picture thereafter is decidedly murkier because the extant documentation is always incomplete and sometimes contradictory. Only one thing is certain: without access to these records at the time, no one in France could possibly have realized the full extent of what was occurring in all of those widely distributed military tribunals.

Even if scantly informed, Vichy officials were understandably anxious about the mounting toll of French citizens. Again, their first estimates were well higher than the verifiable count of executions. According to the Direction des Services de l'Armistice (DSA) in the Hotel Thermal, besides more than 550 hostages killed by the Germans before the end of 1942, military courts had sent about 950 persons to their death, a total (it was said) of exactly 1,736.[28] While these figures do not correspond with other sources, they do suggest two valid conclusions: first, that the number of those silently condemned by German military tribunals during the Occupation greatly exceeded the hostage victims, whose fate had caused so much public emotion; and, second, that the effectiveness of French attempts to mitigate death sentences steadily diminished. In evidence one may cite DSA estimates that in all, 365 death sentences had been announced during 1940 and 1941, stirring 207 separate interventions by the French government and obtaining 145 commutations. Those figures for 1942 were, respectively, 1,015, 308, and only 55.[29] Matters grew worse. As the Occupation wore on, the Vichy regime, at the urging of Darnand, created its own system of courts-martial. Thereupon, Heinrich von Stülpnagel promptly ordered German courts not to be outdone by their French counterparts. They should instead strive to promote swift sentencing and execution of prisoners—often, as it turned out, without any prior notification to the French. As a consequence, requests for clemency became infrequent and ineffective.[30]

Of all the German military tribunals, that of Paris was by far the most active, with prisoners being routinely condemned in 1943 at a rate of two or three a week. In the event that the Gestapo succeeded in exposing a gang, as many as thirty death sentences might be pronounced in a single day. Probably the single court of the Commandant of Greater Paris accounted for a third or more of executions in France. Its daily or weekly reports established the relative frequency of the crimes with which prisoners were charged. Most prominent among them were espionage, abetting the enemy, possession of arms, and guerrilla activity. Obviously, these categories were not mutually exclusive, since an individual might be found simultaneously guilty of all four.[31] Examining the same raw data of reports, it is possible to confirm that 54 prisoners were executed in Paris after sentencing by German military tribunals between 23 October 1943 and 1 February 1944, and, as the pace quickened, another 84 in the fortnight from 30 March to 15 April 1944. In different terms, on average, nearly 150 (a minimum verifiable number) faced a firing squad or the gallows in Greater Paris during each of the first four months of 1944.[32]

Needless to emphasize, great caution is required here. One unfortunate statistical complication was created by the appearance in the French countryside of the *maquis*, an open and armed resistance force. It is virtually impossible to separate persons captured or killed in this essentially military struggle from those picked up and tried for other reasons, including various acts of sabotage, under the German police and court structure. One memo from the Majestic's military staff, for instance, listed 50 "terrorists" killed, 22 wounded, and 768 apprehended. Unclear was how many of these, if any, were among the also reported 123 death sentences handed down by military tribunals during November and December 1943.[33]

As is so often the case in modern and contemporary history, the investigator's headache is not too few data but too many. In this instance, the evidence that can be assembled comes mainly from three sources. The first, perhaps the least reliable yet nonetheless indicative, comprised the statistics adopted by the French government, which are best conveyed in a box score drafted in Vichy to illustrate the extent of German police action during the entire Occupation up to the end of February 1944.

Northern Zone	Arrests	Death Sentences	Executions
1940	354	211	9
1941	4,671	158	109
1942	12,229	1,009	716
1943	7,577	800	670
1944	443	84	207
Total	25,274	2,262	1,711
Southern Zone			
(1940–1944)	4,640	84	111
Italian Zone			
(1940–1944)	2,190	1	1
Totals	32,104	2,347	1,823

Source: "Statistique Générale," 27 February 1944, AN Paris, AJ[41], 329.

There is one glaring anomaly in these figures: a greater number of executions than death sentences in the later stages of the Occupation. If so, it could be explained only by an increasing tendency of the Germans to execute prisoners without trial, just as uncounted numbers of persons were at the same time being deported without notification to their family or news being made available as to their whereabouts. This troubling practice dates back to a December 1941 decree known as *Nacht und Nebel* (Night and Fog) that was directly inspired by Hitler.[34] It is apparent, in any event, that by far the most executions occurred in the former Occupied Zone, the least in the Italian Zone. The most intense period for executions through military tribunals was in 1942 and early 1943, when Paris was the epicenter of the Occupation, before attention of German authorities became distracted by the guerrilla war centered mostly in the South and in the Alps. Statistics released by the Hotel Majestic claimed that French losses during the Occupation's struggle against the *maquis* in the first three months of 1944 reached about 800 dead and over 6,500 captured.[35]

In addition, French officials compiled a composite record concerning the fate of French hostages from the Armistice to the beginning of 1944.

Northern Zone	Arrested	Executed	Deported
1940	7	—	—
1941	313	246	321
1942	941	502	351
1943	56	58	1,504
Total	1,317	806	2,176
Southern Zone	84	31	—
Italian Zone	24	—	—
Totals	1,425	837	2,176

Source: "Statistique Générale" 27 February 1944, AN Paris, AJ[41], 329.

Waiving the question of exactitude, these numbers confirm that the execution of hostages by the military administration was most frequent in the Occupied Zone until November 1942 and that their number decreased markedly thereafter. Instead, deportations became more common. Thus, the locale but not the outcome was changed for most individuals sentenced by military tribunals, even when they were not Jews, who were condemned to a nearly certain death and for whom a separate reckoning is necessary.[36]

The other two statistical sources were provided by German Occupation authorities: one from Heinrich von Stülpnagel's headquarters in the Majestic and a second from Otto Abetz's Embassy. Both ultimately depended on the reports of field officers stationed throughout France as well as the Commandant of Greater Paris. According to the MBF, 267 death sentences were executed in January and February 1944, plus another 153 in March. Although

Embassy records are more erratic, one may count a minimum of 160 executions in the period from 21 January to 29 March 1944 and 190 from that time until 25 April. Obviously, a discrepancy is created by incongruent chronologies: one record omits the first three weeks of January, whereas the other extends through most of April. There is consequently no way to choose between the totals of 420 and 350, and the generalization must do that in early 1944 at least 100 French civilians, probably far more, fell each month before German firing squads or on the gallows. Sobering enough, this estimate does not include those killed in distant pockets of resistance such as the Vercors or the Jews deported to Auschwitz.[37]

Through all of this turmoil the French capital remained remarkably passive. Paris was arguably the safest place in Europe, relatively unscathed in comparison with London, Rotterdam, Warsaw, or the major urban areas of Germany, such as Berlin, Hamburg, and Munich. Police records show that random attacks and explosions continued to occur in the twenty *arrondissements* and in the immediate suburbs. Yet most Parisians were unaware or scarcely informed of the reach and force of German repression throughout France. People lived day to day, trying to avoid hunger, cold, and trouble. It seemed that everyone was waiting for the great Allied armada that was certain to land someday on French shores.

Chapter 13

A DEEP CONTRADICTION

⌣

After November 1942, what difference did the approach of war make for the French economy? Although it was unanimously accepted that the Allied invasion of North Africa marked an important moment in the Occupation, German reactions naturally varied. "The situation in France is completely altered," observed one official in the Hotel Majestic. The French population was now overcome with "resignation, fatigue, and worry," wrote another. The opening of a southern front was simply "a turning point," added a third.[1] Why so?

First of all, cut off from its colonial possessions, France was bound to suffer even more severe food shortages. Vegetables, fruits, potatoes, grain, fish, wine, and olive oil counted among the products no longer available from the African continent—a reduction, according to one unverifiable source, of 40 percent in foodstuffs for the motherland. The French diet, in any event, was henceforth "extremely insufficient." Occupation authorities calculated that nutrition in France, on a par with Germany in pre-war years, had sunk drastically: the average daily intake of a Frenchman was 1,462 calories versus 2,352 in Germany, about 38 percent less. Already plagued by shortfalls in coal supplies and electrical current, Parisians in particular were adversely affected.[2]

In addition, with another winter approaching in December 1942, it was distressing that woolens could not be purchased in Paris shops and were available only on the black market. The existence of a thriving sub-economy of illicit goods had long been a disturbance for the Occupation, and it was an especially sensitive topic for Hermann Göring, the head of the Four Year Plan in Berlin, who was annoyed by French complaints that the Germans themselves were to blame—because they spent freely to obtain whatever they wanted—and that previous measures to control illegal sales had been "much too benign." The upshot was an order from Göring's office in January 1943 that an initiative, a Schwarzmarkt-Aktion, should be undertaken to quash the black market in Paris by the end of March. This edict specifically included German military personnel in France for whom the "ruthless repression" of forbidden commerce would be "without any exceptions." Regardless of rank, anyone found guilty was to face a court-martial. As usual, the Majestic meanwhile enlisted cooperation from the French police, who claimed to make 1,859 arrests of civilians in a "crushing effort" to respect Göring's wishes.[3] Subsequent German documents made clear, however, that all manner of shortages still persisted in the marketplace and that the black market did not disappear. The result was that rations were further limited in 1943 and that "strong tensions" were thereby created between a disenchanted populace and the Occupation.[4]

A global reckoning of France's economic decline during the war years can only be quite approximate. A German staff report estimated that coal shipments to Paris from various mining regions met 50 percent of normal requirements in October 1943, 39 percent in November, and 25 percent in December. This progressive slump was attributed mainly to transportation problems, which also explained the shortage of wood and therefore paper supplies, thought to be diminished by 30 percent.[5] The SNCF submitted figures comparing food deliveries to Paris in November 1942 with November 1943: in one year, meat was down 50 percent, salt 25 percent, wine 24 percent, milk 17 percent, and so forth. In early 1944, as another memo stated, transportation was "stretched to the limit." Constrictions of food and fuel stocks usually affected non-essential industrial firms at first, whereas those directly engaged in the manufacture of arms (the so-called Rü-Betriebe) were spared. But, unavoidably, they also became squeezed and were forced in mid-February 1944 to report a diminution in production of 9 percent. Later that spring, in the wake of Allied bombing and local sabotage, there was an almost complete cessation of coal shipments from northern mining fields. Worse, the Majestic admitted, no improvement was foreseeable.[6]

These circumstances were exacerbated by ever rising quotas for the delivery of French goods and foods to the Reich. The amount of such requisitions was personally set and insisted upon by Göring, who left no doubt that their objective was "the best possible result for Germany." Directions from the Four Year Plan were binding, as the French were instructed at a conference in August 1943. Their only part in the discussions would concern the proper means to fulfill the required quotas.[7] Increased shipments of grain and meat from France were special objects of German attention, although it was obvious that the dietary gap was sure to widen as a consequence. Complaints from Vichy about the "extraordinary difficulties" of compliance were generally acknowledged but ignored. They included the reluctance of French farmers to cooperate, repeated sabotages of equipment such as threshing machines, inroads of enemy radio propaganda throughout agricultural areas, and even some incidents of "open rebellion."[8] The MBF's Economic Section conceded that German demands were not only difficult but "in some cases impossible." Moreover, it was evident that the Occupation lacked adequate means to impose its will or completely satisfy the demands from Berlin. With the menace of an Allied invasion hovering overhead, the Wehrmacht's field commanders could not disperse their troops throughout all of rural France. Yet without such a broad deployment of force, there was no assurance that the assigned quotas would be reached. In short, the allegedly almighty Militärbefehlshaber in Frankreich possessed "completely insufficient instruments of power."[9]

The current wisdom was that French wages were 20 to 25 percent lower than the German average, whereas French prices were 10 to 15 percent higher—a circumstance, if remotely accurate, that Pierre Laval called "unbearable."[10] But Laval's campaign to raise wages was beaten back by Fritz Sauckel, who insisted that inflation, along with the black market, must be strangled in its Paris cradle. Initially, his sole concession was to allow a modest 10 percent raise for skilled workers in the metal trades essential for the German war effort. This measure only provoked hard feelings, as well as absenteeism "bordering on sabotage," in other branches of industry. To ease that tension, in turn, Sauckel finally agreed to allow textiles and mining to join metallurgy, and, near the bottom of the scale, he also granted Laval's urgent request to boost salaries above the subsistence level for employees in electricity, chemicals, and insurance.[11] But there he drew the line. He reminded the French that he exercised full authority granted directly by Hitler to control the price and wage structure in all of Western Europe and that it would be "positively absurd" to permit an exception for them. Not only did he demand stricter enforcement of price controls, he proposed that prices actually be rolled back to their 1939 level.[12] This announcement was greeted with consternation even within Sauckel's own administrative team in Paris, where the practicality of such a drastic reduction was questioned in light of estimates that French prices had increased 130 percent since the beginning of the war. Sauckel's response was somewhat vague on whether he would press the matter, but he admonished his subordinates that they must be "tough and unyielding" in the fight against inflation. There were to be no more wage increases that did not promote armament production by lengthening the workday.[13] That directive was in fact followed, as some skilled laborers began to elevate their income by putting in more than fifty hours a week. Yet Sauckel was far from placated. After meeting with French cabinet ministers Cathala and Bichelonne on 4 February 1944 and agreeing to certain wage adjustments, he gathered the next day in the Hotel Ritz with members of the MBF staff and rescinded them, as the transcript noted, "to be sure without the knowledge of the French." In principle, the Vichy regime was amenable to "the stabilization and eventual reduction of prices," but only if some "wage corrections" were admitted by the Occupation and it was recognized that a return to pre-war levels was "not possible."[14] Sauckel's *volte face* on wages brought confusion to these attempts to sort out negotiation of salary limits and, ordinarily withdrawn to Bavaria or Berlin, his presence in Paris became more infrequent. Thus out of touch, his dominance over regulations waned in 1944 as the French economy approached the brink of disintegration.

A word must be said here about the constantly unnerving threat of labor strikes. In Paris, as in other French industrial centers, a general strike never materialized. Yet work stoppages were common and sometimes ominous. In late November 1942, for instance, over 4,000 Citroën workers (more than half of the factory's labor force) went out on strike for higher wages, and a few weeks later two armament plants in Paris briefly closed in protest over labor recruitment, resulting in eighteen arrests.[15] Although it did not reach an eruption, such agitation never ceased, and the Gestapo was not alone in warning of "significant unrest." Indeed, the Germans hesitated to carry out inspections of industrial facilities for fear of further stirring hostility among the workers.[16] Carl Oberg was among those who expressed concerns about the strike threat. In a December 1943 memo to Heinrich Himmler, he cautioned his chief about the "extraordinary confusion" of German labor policy in France, especially since his Sicherheitspolizei would "under no circumstances" be capable of suppressing serious trouble in the work force, given that the French police were "increasingly unreliable."[17] One can only conclude from this that the Occupation was extremely fortunate that no concerted strike movement developed. In May 1944, the French information service reported thirty-eight strikes that month nationwide. Yet from extant records it is impossible to reconstruct an accurate statistical account of them over time. Besides, that became gradually less relevant as labor disruptions, as well as attempts to contain them, blended into a confused and splotchy overall picture of resistance and repression.[18]

There were other worries for the Occupation. In early December 1942, the Commandant of Greater Paris compiled a list of fifty-one recent sabotages in his jurisdiction.[19] Like strikes, sabotages were difficult to measure in size or number. But if the urge to quantify could not be fully requited, the anecdotal evidence was voluminous and convincing. Acts of sabotage could never be stopped, and reference to them littered administrative records. Without question, they became more and more frequent as the months passed and reached a climax near the time of the Normandy invasion. Railway installations and electric power lines were particularly vulnerable. One comment by the MBF's Economic Section in May 1944 might stand here for all the rest: sabotage to

France's electricity grid, it said, was being conducted "systematically and with continually rising effectiveness."[20]

The same was true of Allied bombing raids in French territory, for which, thanks to the SNCF, better numbers became available. Although scattered and imperfect, they offer a consistent image of unrelenting havoc inflicted on the French transportation system. For the period from 1 July 1942 to 28 February 1943, a total of 451 air raids on railway installations was recorded, in which 77 persons were killed and 348 wounded. Moreover, 176 locomotives were destroyed, with 61 being damaged.[21] During 1943, "a serious increase" occurred, and a pattern became discernible. Allied pilots concentrated at first on pounding repair facilities (*ateliers*) and railroad junctions before turning to attack stations and individual trains. These forays became "more and more intense," so that rail traffic in western France was "seriously paralyzed." From 12 to 24 May 1943, there were a reported eighty-five bombing raids on railroads, that is, more than a dozen each day. On two days in mid-September, bombers struck sixteen freight trains, five passenger trains, three German military convoys, and eight railway terminals. Nineteen locomotives were destroyed or damaged, five persons were killed, and twenty-two were wounded. In view of this devastation, the head of the MBF's Economic Section, Dr. Elmar Michel, was forced to conclude that the transportation infrastructure in France had become "extremely strained" and that shipments to Paris were consequently encountering "the greatest difficulties."[22]

In addition to the railways, French industrial firms were also taking a beating. Large manufacturing plants in the Paris region, such as Renault, Citroën, and Dunlop, were repeatedly bombed. In late November 1943, the Majestic received a list of thirty-one damaged factories that required some repair. To deal with this problem, a "catastrophe corps" (*Katastropheneinsatz*) was organized to move engineers and workmen from site to site.[23] The Allied air campaign was meanwhile complemented by clandestine sabotage. During the first half of March 1944 alone, the MBF staff recorded 177 locomotives struck by air raids, 68 disabled on the tracks by explosive devices, and 48 derailments. The count for the month of April was higher: in all 788 locomotives were damaged, of which 178 were totaled. With most of the SNCF's workshops out of commission, these were literally irreparable losses.[24] Little wonder that Heinrich von Stülpnagel announced a month before the Allied invasion of the Continent that the Occupation was facing "a very grave crisis." With France's transportation network crippled, coal supplies had dwindled, several industrial plants had been forced to close, and total production had diminished by 30 percent.[25]

Throughout it all, Occupation officials in Paris repeated tirelessly that their goal was to render the French economy as useful as possible for the German war effort. And after Operation Torch and President Franklin D. Roosevelt's proclamation of the Allied policy of "unconditional surrender" at the Casablanca conference in January 1943, Dr. Michel specified for the Majestic that the effort should be "total." One must therefore wonder to what extent the stated goal was achieved. What, in other words, did occupied France actually contribute to the Nazi war economy? One indication may be gained from information provided by the Renault factory in the Paris suburb of Billancourt. Despite the bombings and some loss of skilled labor to the Reich, this plant's production of trucks rose through most of 1942, reaching about 1,500 vehicles a month by that autumn. A peak was attained in October at 67 units daily, after which the level dropped slightly to an average of about 50. Output then leveled off during 1943 before it began to decline once more in 1944. According to contemporary German accounts, that trend was altogether typical of French industry as a whole.[26]

Aggregate figures available for the first two years of the Occupation detail the enormous quantity of raw materials and manufactured goods transported from France to Germany by the summer of 1943.

Iron, ore, scrap metal	8,000,000 tons
Other metals and ores	
Copper	240,580 tons
Aluminum	247,678 tons
Bauxite	679,080 tons
Machines	
Locomotives	283 units
Freight cars	834 units
Automobiles	424 units
Trucks	31,340 units
Watches	66,000 monthly
Alarm clocks	200,000 monthly
Chemicals: soda	126,000 tons
Leather	
Work shoes	3,180,000 pairs
Other shoes	5,210,000 pairs
Rubber	12,381 tons
Textiles	287,000 tons

Source: "Leistungen der französischen gewerblichen Wirtschaft für Deutschland," 31 July 1943, AN Paris, AJ[40], 779.

To these statistics must be added the "crucial importance" of French agricultural products for the Reich. For the year 1943, for instance, they included 1.4 million tons of grain, 270,000 tons of meat, 24,000 tons of butter, and 4,200,000 hectoliters of wine. By early 1944, according to the MBF's Economic Section, gathering reliable statistics on the chaotic French economy was "totally excluded." Yet one of its staff reports included estimates that 65 percent of the French labor force was engaged in the German war effort, which was consuming 72 percent of France's total production and 93 percent of its industrial goods. However approximate they were, viewed by the Occupation these calculations certainly spoke of successful exploitation on a grand scale.[27]

The foregoing panorama of the French economy during 1943 and early 1944 provides the setting for a thick description of the most serious political crisis of the Occupation since the hostage issue erupted in August 1941. This primarily concerned demands by the insatiable Sauckel for a vastly increased recruitment of French labor for the Reich. The first "Sauckel Initiative" had limped to the finish line by the end of 1942, filling its quota of 250,000 workers to be transferred to Germany, of which 150,000 were classified as skilled, mostly in metallurgy.[28] Supposedly, it was to be a one-time action. But even before January 1943, Sauckel disclosed plans for a second initiative, that is, the transfer of another 250,000 laborers in the first four months of the year. Complaints from the French, who naturally felt betrayed, as well as some negative rumbles within the MBF's own military administration about a likely reduction of French productivity, did not deter him. Flaunting telegrams of support from the Führer and from Albert Speer, Sauckel responded that recruitment would be curbed only if huge gaps might thereby be created in the French arms industry. Hitler's orders allowed no contradiction and "absolutely must be kept."[29] Reports from both the Commandant of Greater Paris and the Gestapo about the "significant unrest" in the French work force left Sauckel unruffled. Although labor recruitment was still legally voluntary, the German procedures actually resembled a labor draft. When, to Sauckel's annoyance, Vichy officials referred to these roundups as "deportation," he dismissed his French critics as "procrastination artists" (*Hinhaltekünstler*).[30]

It is worthwhile here to eavesdrop on one of several personal confrontations between Sauckel and Laval at the Paris Embassy in the Rue de Lille. There, on 12 January 1943, Sauckel laid out the terms of the next recruitment effort: another 250,000 French workers were to be transferred to Germany, of which again 150,000 were to be skilled. The *Relève* would remain in effect at a ratio of one POW returned to France for every three skilled workers. They would need to move fast, however, by transporting 4,500 a day across the Rhine. Laval was incredulous. Sauckel did not seem to understand that "I represent a country having no army, no fleet, no colonial empire, and no more treasure." To be sure, "I am doing everything to expedite a German victory," Laval boasted, but whereas Sauckel could assure German workers that they were supporting the Reich, he could not tell the French that they were working for France. "My task is made harder every day," Laval pleaded, faced as he was with "the impossibility of continuing in this way." Sauckel did not flinch. The French were responsible for the war, he claimed, because their politicians sided with English plutocrats and American Jews. Furthermore, whatever France contributed to the war effort, the German sacrifice was greater. "You must know one thing," he barked, "the German people will win this war. They will fight on, even if in Europe one stone does not remain on top of another."[31]

It would be difficult to invent a dramatic scene that more perfectly captures the essence of these two protagonists, one an abject supplicant, the other a fanatic. The outcome was swift and predictable. To avoid excessive bullying by German recruiters, the French agreed on 10 February to implement a formal labor draft, the Service du Travail Obligatoire (STO), which recalled the Bousquet-Oberg deal on the police, trading French servility for a modicum of independence from German control. It was a decidedly unpopular measure, as the Gestapo observed, meeting the "sharpest rejection" and stirring increasing enmity toward Germany among the population, including a "massive flight" of young Frenchmen to the *maquis*.[32] Yet judged solely by statistics, it succeeded. Like the first "Sauckel Initiative," the second reached and indeed slightly exceeded its quota. The rub was that Laval expected Sauckel, as a reward, to grant an extended pause. Instead, he immediately presented the French with yet another quota of 50,000 recruits for the month of April 1943.[33] Laval balked. Moreover, vigorous objections circulated from both the Hotel Majestic and the French Embassy. But Sauckel summoned Laval once more and revealed his determination to mount a third recruitment campaign: 120,000 workers to the Reich by the end of May and another 100,000 in June. With a pathetic whimper, Laval protested that such an effort was "materially possible but morally impossible," suggesting that Sauckel would succeed only in arousing further opposition among French workers and thereby unintentionally make himself Charles de Gaulle's closest accomplice. Of course, Sauckel insisted and Laval conceded.[34]

The third "Sauckel Initiative" was a failure. From the beginning it was plagued by three enervating conflicts. The first was a personal friction between Sauckel and Heinrich von Stülpnagel. Ever keen to protect his frayed prerogatives, the MBF objected to Sauckel's presumption of unrestrained authority over the French economy, which had led to "mutual distrust and reservations." His staff members in the Majestic found that excessive demands imposed on the STO were proving "very disruptive." In addition, Stülpnagel's military field commanders showed little enthusiasm for the repeated bouts of recruitment, as one of them reported, especially since the French displayed "absolutely no inclination to take up work in Germany."[35] The second conflict involved labor needs within France. After November 1942, the imminence of a possible Allied invasion created a renewed urgency for the Organisation Todt (OT) to complete the construction of the Atlantic Wall. OT's own labor requirements accordingly grew, for which the third "Sauckel Initiative" created "a conflict with our purposes." The shortfall of OT's quotas became painfully evident: a goal set for mid-July 1943 was to settle 23,000 new workers in the coastal regions, of which but 5,000 appeared.[36] The third, and most fundamental, conflict was the still unclarified contradiction between the goal of increasing French production while siphoning off skilled labor for Germany. Latent since Sauckel first set foot in Paris, this problem grew exponentially with every new round of recruitment quotas delivered by him from Berlin. Here was the festering root of resentment within the MBF's Rü staff, that is, among those Occupation officials assigned to expedite the output of the French arms industry. They therefore indicated no regret whatever while reporting at the end of June that the third initiative was "an obvious failure." The numbers bore them out. By the end of July, Sauckel's latest quota was barely half-filled, and his program was encountering "steadily growing difficulties."[37] Yet remarkably, he was already plotting a fourth initiative for 1944. When informed of this, the Minister of Industrial Production, Jean Bichelonne remarked in a classic bit of French understatement: "It is perhaps too much."[38]

Bichelonne brought these matters front and center. In an uncharacteristic (for a Vichy cabinet member) move, he took the initiative and expressed to Stülpnagel a wish to increase French productivity for "the European war economy." He wondered if direct talks with Speer might advance that cause. Several weeks later he received a cordial personal reply from Speer himself, who invited the astonished Frenchman to be his guest in Berlin. On the morning of 17 September 1943, the two met in Speer's office, where they agreed on the desirability of developing France's economic contribution. However, such an objective could be realized only by raising French production of coal. That subject was a principal item on the agenda of an afternoon session at the Wannsee—the site of a more notorious conference many months earlier—at which both sides concurred that a significant boost of French coal supplies (200,000 tons a month) would require the introduction of 15,000 new miners. This task might take four to five months, during which Germany agreed temporarily to provide the needed fuel. Yet all was not harmony. A summary of the two meetings disclosed a mutual incomprehension because the Germans "absolutely do not understand the passionate opposition of the French people to work in Germany." But the key sentence was this: "Minister Speer and his staff do not foresee an increase in the number of French laborers working in Germany."[39]

The full implications of that remark did not become apparent until late November. By then Sauckel had revealed his incredibly ambitious projections for Aktion 44, a conscription in the next year of one million workers to meet the needs of French industry and the Organisation Todt, as well as another million for transfer to Germany. Not alone, Speer was skeptical. His already wavering support for Sauckel had tipped into frank negativity with the failure of the third labor recruitment effort in France. In the process, he became convinced that it made more sense to award further contracts to French industrial firms, thus keeping the bulk of their labor force in France and avoiding the unpopular shift of workers to the Reich, at least until all requirements set by the military administration in Paris were satisfied. If Hitler still hesitated to abandon Sauckel, Speer's personal access to the Führer and his broad influence in Berlin would weigh heavily on the outcome. Sauckel was overmatched.[40]

Simple in its basic outlines, this story brought to an inglorious close one of the most controversial and emotionally trying aspects of the Occupation. That Sauckel's labor recruitment program was to be canceled altogether right after the Normandy landing would be no surprise. Its demise was already assured. For the record, it is worthwhile to tabulate here the final returns.

First Initiative (1 June–31 December 1942): French workers to the Reich	239,750
Second Initiative (1 January–31 March 1943):	250,259
Third Initiative (1 May–31 December 1943):	169,357
Total	659,366

For Greater Paris, those figures were respectively 84,142, 69,756, and 28,278 for a total of 182,176. It is striking that the participation of Paris in Sauckel's programs steadily declined from a third to a fourth, then to a fifth. Finally, as Paris went, so went France.[41]

Chapter 14

A WANING HOPE

The war news went from bad to worse, and there was very little that German propaganda could do about it. Whatever the official message of military bulletins, this was the assessment of Occupation authorities in Paris. As for the French, rumors of the fierce battle raging at Stalingrad in late 1942 raised "great expectations" of an Allied triumph, as one district field commander reported from the suburbs, a theme constantly being discussed in bread lines and over an *apéritif* or two at neighborhood bars. Observations of the Sicherheitspolizei went ever further: many Parisians were expecting an imminent German collapse, an Anglo-American landing in the spring of 1943, and a complete Allied victory by the end of that year. If such spirited optimism was unjustified, the trend of public opinion was undeniable and could only be confirmed by Adolf Hitler's communiqué to the Paris Embassy on 3 February 1943 that "the battle of Stalingrad has ended."[1]

As Friedrich Grimm rather weakly suggested, maybe the verdict at Stalingrad would actually be beneficial, at least from the standpoint of propaganda, because it was sure to magnify the French fear of Bolshevism. But this notion found little echo in either the military administration or the Gestapo. In fact, one memo related that the Bolshevik bogey, little heeded any more, was generally greeted with "a condescending smile." Ernst Kaltenbrunner, Nazi head of the Sipo-SD in Berlin, detected "an ever widening anti-German attitude among French workers." His underlings in Paris concurred. True, there was some anxiety about Soviet expansion, but that was easily trumped by the desire for a German defeat.[2]

In the hallways of the Hotel Majestic, the opinion hardened that French dispositions were "mostly determined by military events." Of course, other factors, such as food shortages, German requisitions, labor recruitment, deportations, and air raids, also mattered. Yet as a propaganda officer at the Paris Embassy loquaciously noted, it was "doubtful that the possibility still exists to influence the basic attitude of the greatest part of the population until the beginning of a more favorable military situation." By the summer of 1943, that was unquestionably the consensus within the Occupation.[3]

Longstanding differences nonetheless reappeared. As support for collaboration began to crumble, some Germans became openly contemptuous of the wobbly French. Fritz Sauckel wrote back to Hitler's crony Martin Bormann in Berlin that the public in Paris just did not grasp the hard facts of the war. Whereas the Reich was straining to the utmost, "here everything peacefully takes its accustomed course." He was especially caustic about Parisian women, some of whom were still cavorting in "unimaginable luxury."[4] Helmut Knochen expressed himself in a similar fashion, deploring the passivity of most French bureaucrats, "the considerable difficulties" among workers with regard to Sauckel's labor recruitment program, and the general "lack of understanding" for Nazi policy toward Jews—all evidence, as he saw it, of "insufficient volition."[5] These remarks provoked complaints at the German Embassy. Knochen's report on the remaining possibilities for effective propaganda were "tendentious and one-sided," wrote Rudolf Schleier. It was simply not true, as Knochen insisted, that the French now treated Germans with "arrogance and disdain." Nor did they regard the approach of Allied armies with satisfaction; rather, with anxiety. And there was no evidence that the French administration was encouraging "open resistance." Such disclaimers and rebuttals became common currency while the Occupation attempted to salvage whatever it could of that elusive entity—favorable public opinion.[6]

It would not be easy. "Today we must confess," Schleier admitted at a meeting of German officers in late August 1943, "the majority no longer believes in a German victory." Yet Carl Oberg tried to reassure all concerned. He had recently visited Hitler and found him "gleaming with the assurance of victory." There were unconfirmed rumors of a plot to unseat him, a villainous threat that could only plunge Germany into a civil war. "The German people do not want peace," Oberg thundered. "The German people want victory, cost what it will." He concluded with an emphatic "Long live the Führer!"[7] But such declamations no longer had much, if any, positive effect. Diplomatic and administrative correspondence during the following months registered the nearly unanimous opinion that the drift of things was decidedly negative and that German propaganda lacked the means to deter it.[8]

The usual instruments of propaganda were consequently somewhat compromised. Most severely curtailed was the cinema. Restrictions on electricity required limiting the number of film presentations per week and closing some theaters, production facilities, and technical laboratories. By the summer of 1943, French film production had fallen by half. Furthermore, for a simple reason, one key element of earlier propaganda efforts lost much of its effectiveness. The Germans were no longer able to supply newsreels with heroic scenes of their military advances. Now, at best, they could feature only episodes of stubborn defense in Italy and Russia, accounts of heavy casualties inflicted on enemy troops, or lamentations about Allied bombings that were destroying cathedrals and other cultural treasures in Germany. Live by the sword, die by the sword.[9] One noteworthy exception was a documentary made about Marshal Pétain's visit to Paris in the spring of 1944. Pleased by the assembled footage, Otto Abetz seized the opportunity to refute allegations of Anglo-American propaganda that Pétain was merely a prisoner of the Germans and hence bereft of broad popular support. Otherwise, in the late stages of the Occupation, there was not much to show except a few frothy German film hits like Zarah Leander's *Die grosse Liebe* and Marika Rökk's *Der Tanz mit dem Kaiser*, as well as the fresh spectacle of a feature in color, *Die goldene Stadt*.[10]

The main problem for the newspaper press and other publications was paper. After the Operation Torch landings, a few dailies, including notably the *Figaro*, were shut down for political reasons because of their "quite hostile and anti-collaborationist position." Others were restricted by the German manipulation of paper supplies, especially in provincial cities like Lyon, where it was thought better to circulate the more easily and tightly controlled Parisian press. Particularly favored by the Occupation were *Le Petit Parisien*, *Paris Soir*, and *Le Matin*.[11] In Paris in late February 1943, 120 French journalists were instructed that three propaganda themes were to be emphasized: the recovery of national unity, exemplified by the erasure of the demarcation line and the administrative reintegration of the departments of the Nord and Pas-de-Calais; the necessity, like it or not, for the French to participate actively in the German war effort, thus abandoning their passivity; and, inevitably, the peril of Bolshevism, against which the Reich was magnificently defending all of Europe, including France.[12] Censorship was meanwhile continued with lists of banned writings and frequent directives of dos and don'ts to newspaper editors. They were told, for instance, to print fewer reports of damage caused by Allied air raids and, when covering such events, always to stress that the attacks were conducted by Anglo-American bombers, not by "unknown" assailants. Also, it was thereafter forbidden to refer to rescues by a "catastrophe corps" (*Katastropheneinsatz*); rather, the terminology to be used was an "air war corps" (*Luftkriegseinsatz*).[13] During Pétain's appearance in Paris in April 1944, he gave an improvised speech at the Hôtel de Ville that contained some inappropriate and ambiguous phrases, or so the German Embassy thought. A "correct text" was therefore provided by German propaganda experts to

French radio and press. To ensure adequate coverage of the occasion, Paris newspapers were offered a temporary 50 percent increase of paper allotments, which several of them refused.[14] By this time the paper shortage was becoming acute, so that most dailies were limited to four pages three days a week and two pages three days a week. This pittance was further constricted by an across-the-board 25 percent reduction of paper for the press in November 1943. The estimated pre-war allotment had been 1,500 tons of paper a week. In 1942, it was down to 600 tons, and the approximate weekly ration for 1943 was 300. Accordingly, circulation of the newspaper press was condemned to a drastic decline by 1944.[15]

Radio was a different matter. As before, the air waves were ruled by Britannia, much to the chagrin of German propaganda personnel in Paris. Radio Paris, they had to concede, was no match for Radio London, and the Vichy-sponsored French national radio network (Radio nationale), still disorganized after its headquarters had been recently moved back to Paris, promised no improvement.[16] A remedy was not in sight. The Germans faced the fact that there were nearly ten million private radio sets in France, 83 percent of them with shortwave reception. As Joseph Goebbels himself admitted, a total confiscation was beyond the pale. An effort to do so, it was calculated, would require a full-time staff of 3,000 to work for three years or 12,000 for three months—a sheer impossibility.[17] Irregular cuts in electrical current posed another problem, upsetting the schedule of essential propaganda broadcasts like the *Voix du Reich*, as well as a controversial talk show hosted in fluent French by a noted German personality known as "Dr. Friedrich."[18] In the confusion, some attempt was made in the spring of 1944 to confiscate all radios in Normandy and other French coastal areas on the Channel. But this uncompleted action only served to underscore the futility of fully regulating the irrepressible advance of modern communications technology.[19]

In Paris, the Occupation made a considerable effort to maintain an air of normalcy, as if to pretend that things were well in hand and the Germans comfortably in charge. This meant staging handball tournaments, soccer matches, and rowing regattas on the Seine. Especially popular was a Ping-Pong contest, held at an auto club on the Place de la Concorde, between the Paris All-Stars and Slovakia. In addition, innumerable language and Bible classes were made available to the public, and many outdoor concerts continued to attract sizable crowds.[20] A special event in March 1944 was a boxing exhibition to celebrate the fiftieth birthday of the former French champion Georges Carpentier, famously once a foe of Jack Dempsey. At ringside, his German counterpart Max Schmeling was introduced and "lustily received," according to the delighted Abetz. Schmeling was also given huge applause when he entered the ring at the conclusion. Perhaps in sports and music, at least, it may be permissible to speak of successful German propaganda.[21]

Kultur (with a capital K) was also not neglected. At the beginning of 1943, forty-four theaters were operating in Paris. Piano concerts, with such international celebrities as Wilhelm Kempff and Walter Gieseking, were frequent. The Berlin Philharmonic appeared again at the Paris Opéra, and all nine of Beethoven's symphonies were presented in five concerts at the Palais de Chaillot. The Comédie Française even staged a production in German of Gerhard Hauptmann's *Iphigenia in Delphi.*[22] Was it excessive? That question was raised by propaganda officials in Berlin, who feared that too many events, especially German poetry readings, might be poorly attended and that eager Occupation authorities in Paris could be overestimating the cultural appetite of the French public. Thus, "a considerable reduction" was perhaps in order. Another obvious concern, once more, was the shrinking supply of electricity. In December 1943, it became necessary to order a curfew of 10:00 PM for all Parisian theaters, concert halls, cinemas, restaurants, and nightclubs. Exceptions were made for weekends.[23]

Yet the torrent of high culture continued unabated. Alone during the month of March 1944, barely ten weeks before D-Day, the Paris Opéra managed to mount six ballets, in addition to operatic works by Gluck, Wagner, Verdi, Gounod, Berlioz, and Richard Strauss. Not to be outdone, the Opéra Comique presented two operas each by Puccini (*Tosca* and *La Bohème*), Bizet (*Carmen* and *Les Pêcheurs de Perles*), and Massenet (*Manon* and *Werther*), plus Debussy's *Pelléas et Mélisande.* All were presumably subsidized by appreciative Occupation authorities.[24] The Gruppe Kultur in the MBF's Propaganda Section was in the meantime preparing a final flourish by making arrangements for 113 concerts in the summer. Likewise, Karl Epting's German Institute composed a wish list of coming attractions for the 1944–1945 season that included, besides the ubiquitous Kempff and Gieseking, Elisabeth Schwarzkopf, the Munich Philharmonic, and a return engagement by the Wiener Sängerknaben. Public lectures in Paris were announced that included a galaxy of academic stars like Carl Schmitt, Martin Heidegger, Werner Heisenberg, Erich Wolff, and the distinguished historians Rudolf Stadelmann and Gerd Tellenbach.[25] Foreseen originally for the end of May 1944 but moved to the second day of June, one gala evening featuring Herbert von Karajan and the Berlin Philharmonic had to be postponed again when the conductor failed to appear in time. The problem, it seems, was that Karajan's second wife, Anita Gütermann (whom he married in 1942), had one Jewish grandparent. When her application for a visa to France was initially rejected "for military reasons [*sic*]," the concert was rescheduled for 9 June 1944. This date, falling three days after the Normandy invasion, turned out to be inconveniently late.[26]

Frequent public ceremonies of celebration by the Germans, mostly for their own edification, were a related and notable aspect of the Occupation. Given the seriousness of the military situation, observance in 1943 of the tenth anniversary of the Nazi seizure of power on 30 January was declared to be a "memorial day" (*Gedenktag*) rather than a "holiday" (*Feiertag*). Members of the High Command and the diplomatic corps dutifully assembled at the Palais de Chaillot in solemn commemoration, which, remarked Schleier, demonstrated "how much the Germans in Paris are vicariously participating in the struggles" on the Russian front.[27] When the news spread a few days later that the battle of Stalingrad had ended in defeat, Foreign Minister Joachim von Ribbentrop promptly ordered the organization of another memorial service for the Reich's fallen heroes, adding some instructions: "Especially, as always, the absolute confidence in victory by the entire German people and its leadership is to be emphasized." But where should these ceremonies be held? One suggestion was to create a memorial plot for German soldiers in the Bois de Boulogne. The Embassy observed, however, that there was too much traffic (and, one may add, danger of desecration) because of strollers and racetrack patrons. The site was therefore "neither desirable nor feasible." The distant cemetery at Ivry-sur-Seine was surely more suitable.[28] In such ceremonies it was striking during the third phase of the Occupation that the Nazi Party played a much more prominent role than before, as Abetz remarked in regard to proceedings at Ivry in March 1944. Presided over by the Commandant of Greater Paris and attended as usual by staff members from both the military administration and the Paris Embassy, this *Heldengedenkfeier* was conspicuously populated as well, in a show of unity, by uniformed members of the Nazi Party. The same was evident in preparations to celebrate the Führer's birthday on 20 April 1944, which was to be marked by a gigantic gathering in the Gaumont movie palace at the Place de Clichy. The theme of that splendid occasion, announced by the Nazi propaganda chief in Paris, was "Solidarity between Army and Party."[29] Similar attempts at public display by the French were generally discouraged. A small and quiet observance for Jeanne d'Arc in May 1943 was permitted, but only with the proviso that she be praised not as the freedom-loving maid of Orléans but as the victim of English aggression at Rouen: just as RAF bombers destroyed that city, so Jeanne had forfeited her life there in fire at the stake. The Germans also found no reason to forbid a subdued gathering at the Palais de Chaillot in April 1944 to mark the hundredth birthday of France's most notorious anti-Semite, Édouard Drumont. But they were far less pleased when Pétain laid a ceremonial wreath at the grave of General Joseph Joffre, the hero of the 1914 battle at the Marne. The Embassy saw to it that initial newspaper reports of the act were repressed and that no further mention of it was made in the press or on the radio.[30]

Control of religious ceremonies was less strict and hardly necessary. Yet distrust of the clergy and suspicion of the Church hierarchy in France became more evident. The most contentious issue by far was Sauckel's labor recruitment program with its French offspring, the STO, regarded by Church leaders as a Draconian measure designed to kidnap French youth away from their families. When pastoral letters from various French archbishops registered a protest, the Gestapo prompted the Paris Embassy to contact Pierre Laval, who agreed to clamp down on such public utterances. Schleier also requested Pétain to lodge a criticism against the episcopate for the disturbance of Franco-German relations.[31] The effect was negligible. Heretofore a convinced supporter of collaboration, Cardinal Suhard now broke ranks to reassure the faithful that opposition to the *Relève* was appropriate. In general, Suhard remained loyal to the Occupation, Schleier explained to Berlin, but he could not support the "Sauckel Initiatives" without turning popular opinion against the Church. Still, in a direct confrontation with the Cardinal, Schleier vigorously promoted the Nazi creed. In every country where the Nazis and their cohorts had taken over, he said, a result had been the banishment of "the children of the Revolution"—meaning liberals, Marxists, Communists, Freemasons, and anarchists. Not coincidentally, all of them were sworn enemies of the Church, Schleier continued, and it was therefore imperative that Catholics support the common cause, especially against "the leader of the dissidence," General de Gaulle.[32] Reported back to Berlin, this outburst received an enthusiastic second from Sipo-SD commander Kaltenbrunner, who tended to blame "dangerous activities" within the French Church on the "particularly hateful" anti-German agitation by Archbishop Gerlier of Lyon (a former Paris barrister before entering the priesthood). Given Suhard's recalcitrance and the passivity of Laval and Pétain, it seemed likely that the clergy would now "take the side of the national resistance and other opponents of National Socialism."[33] The situation, in other words, was that most of the French clergy were at one with the populace in the expectation of an Allied victory. Cardinal Suhard's reassurances about "the good relationship" between the Church and the Occupation failed to persuade German officials in Paris that Catholic priests and laymen could any longer be counted on to stay the course.[34]

Still less did the Germans evince confidence in French intellectuals, university professors, and *lycée* students. In addition to "cleansing" faculties, as well as the staff of the Bibliothèque Nationale, the Sipo-SD made a practice of investigating various reprehensible individuals. The journalist Alfred Fabre-Luce, to name one, was considered "completely anti-German" and therefore "dangerous"—he was "an intellectual in the worst sense of the term." Likewise, the historian Georges Bourgin was castigated for his "temporizing, not to say negative, attitude that most representatives of the French intelligentsia take vis-à-vis Germany."[35] Close watch was continued on schoolbooks, especially history texts, which were routinely expurgated or altogether forbidden.[36] Yet the Gestapo in Paris was careful not to stir resentment by indiscreet displays of force, preferring undercover methods to keep the calm. In March 1943, the military administration approved a return from Lyon to the capital by the displaced École Polytechnique in order to separate its students from "irksome political influences" in the provinces and accustom them to "another climate" in Paris.[37]

But the generally degraded circumstances of the Occupation were such that a gradual deterioration in the education system became noticeable. One sore point, as noted, was the STO and the question of whether students could be conscripted for labor duties. The danger of bombings in the coastal regions required moving pupils to other areas, resulting in empty schools here, overcrowded classrooms there. Air raids caused a delay in opening schools in the autumn of 1943. Looking for a silver lining, the German Embassy remarked that scenes of aimless pupils loitering in the streets of Paris made good propaganda against Allied barbarism.[38] At the beginning of 1944, the French Minister of Public Education prepared detailed lists of students and teachers arrested by the Germans. Because of sheer size, Paris naturally took the lead with a total of 141 since June 1940, but several other cities, such as Rennes (117), Poitiers (91), Bordeaux (87), and Besançon (84), had relatively significant numbers. A substantial percentage were soon released, while others were sentenced to only brief prison terms. In any event, all were subjected to Gestapo interrogation techniques that were bound, at the very least, to be unsettling.[39] The accumulation of these factors—personal dislocations, air raids, censorship and surveillance, police arrests—created what French cabinet members called "particularly painful conditions," which in May 1944 were serious enough to necessitate the cancellation of many *concours*, the terminal examinations that ordinarily climaxed the school calendar.[40] By then the Paris education system was in the last throes of disintegration, as the following statistics demonstrate. During the 1938–1939 academic year, primary schools in Paris enrolled nearly 200,000 pupils. By December 1943, that total was down by half. On 20 May 1944, attendance was recorded for exactly 52,189, and on 5 June that figure was further reduced to 36,246. As the Allied invasion of France neared, *sauve qui peut*, nearly four-fifths of the city's schoolchildren had already been evacuated. In the meantime, students at the Occupation's own German school were being transferred to Berlin.[41]

Finally, as for politics, little activity in Paris during 1943 and early 1944 merited that term. Two parties, Jacques Doriot's PPF and Marcel Déat's RNP, were the Tweedledum and Tweedledee of the Occupation. Both were marginally useful for the Germans, but neither really enjoyed much popularity. The PPF was more overtly fascist, its paramilitary units clad in marine-blue uniforms, standing at attention with arms outstretched, shouting "Doriot, Doriot" and "Doriot au pouvoir." But Doriot kept his distance from the Vichy government, refused open support for the Milice, and seemed mostly intent on remaining the uncontested leader of an isolated movement. Although rejecting overtures to join a unified political organization under government aegis, Déat's faction was closer to Joseph Darnand and actively recruited for the Milice, while Déat himself became Minister of Labor in the Vichy cabinet. None of this mattered greatly to the Occupation, except when party rallies led to "regrettable incidents," as the Prefecture of Police complained, and resulted in "the most violent attacks" on French police.[42] Otherwise, the landscape in Paris was populated by an odd assortment of quasi-political organizations, of which three deserve mention. The Groupe Collaboration was still in existence and indeed claimed to have 100,000 members in France, 10,000 of them in Paris, both dubiously round numbers. This group, led by Jean Weiland, was confined mostly to sponsoring lectures and concerts, for which it received modest subsidies in the name of propaganda. But the obvious problem was that its cause grew distinctly more unpopular as time passed, and it came under constant menace from a growing armed resistance. After being threatened that he would be "slaughtered like a dog," Weiland requested weapons and was personally provided with a pistol. Still alarmed by "anarchy" in the provinces, he retreated to Paris, wondering what the use might be of his group's efforts if its cadres were "followed, threatened, and murdered."[43] Mention should also be made here of the Comité Ouvrier du Secours Immédiat (COSI), originally promoted by the military administration to distribute funds, collected from Paris Jews in the wake of the hostage crisis, in order to aid victims of Allied bombing attacks. This public beneficence was regarded by the Occupation as salutary propaganda, and Heinrich von Stülpnagel was persuaded in February 1943 to award an additional million francs to COSI to continue its charitable donations.[44] To this uninspiring list may be added the Cercle Européen, essentially a high-minded and mostly honorary club encouraged by the Paris Embassy to jawbone Germany's defense of Western culture against the encroachment of Bolshevism. Its membership included 200 Germans, of which 33 were military officers, roiling yet another controversy between the Embassy (pro) and the MBF (con) about the appropriateness of the army's participation in "politics."[45]

By 1944, only two political formations actually counted. One was the mutually wary alliance between Gaullists and Communists in what was now often identified as the "national resistance." In propaganda leaflets and posters, General de Gaulle was effusively described as "the future leader and savior of France." If they were hardly charmed by this notion, Communists in Paris nonetheless remained mostly quiet in the confidence, as the Prefect of Police observed, that they would soon be contributing to "a national insurrection and the German defeat."[46] The major opposing protagonist was represented by Darnand's *miliciens*. It was their purpose, no less, to pursue "the political, social, economic, intellectual, and moral recovery of France." This daunting task would of course be accomplished within the context of Nazi Germany's New Order, "at an hour when everyone questions and doubts."[47] That hour struck at dawn on 6 June 1944 when the first Allied landing craft touched the shores of Normandy.

Chapter 15

A WRETCHED CONCLUSION

The Final Solution was underway in France well before the Allied invasion of North Africa, but it took a long while to evolve and did so erratically. Because of German personnel shortages, the fate of French Jews depended importantly on the collaboration of the French police with the armed forces of the Occupation. A police reform in late 1942 essentially returned oversight of Jewish affairs to the Prefecture of Police at the Quai des Orfèvres by abolishing a separate unit that had been detached for that purpose. Now a new Service des Questions Juives there was directed by Commissar Permilleux, who reported to the Prefect of Police in Paris, to the Ministry of the Interior in Vichy, and ultimately to the German Gestapo. Theodor Dannecker's successor, Heinz Röthke, was the man primarily in charge, and he repeatedly made clear that he would "very closely" monitor the implementation of Nazi racial policies. Thus, if the grudging complicity of the French police was beyond question, so too was the attentiveness of the Gestapo in supervising it.[1]

During the immediate post–Operation Torch phase of the Occupation, there was little friction between French and German law enforcement authorities for the simple reason that the police generally did as they were told. They continued to participate in razzias and to conduct routine interrogations, house searches, and arrests of Jews. But which Jews? Given the Vichy policy of protecting those with French citizenship, that issue was bound to create a complication in the chain of command. The first sand thrown into the machinery of deportation was a refusal by French police on 12 February 1943 to assist in the transfer of

French Jewish inmates from Drancy to the nearby railway station at Le Bourget. The Gestapo was thereby obliged to request that a commando of thirty to forty men from the Ordnungspolizei appear the next morning at 5:00 AM to perform that task. Charged with keeping the trains rolling, Röthke was incensed, but he could not promptly obtain the willing obedience he required. "It is to be expected," he wrote in March, "that henceforth the French police will no longer cooperate in the transportation." In fact, this conclusion was unduly pessimistic, as later statistics on deportation were tragically to demonstrate. More often than not, the French police complied.[2]

Yet the result was German impatience and a renewed determination of the Occupation to get on with the evacuation of all Jews from France. Agents of the Sipo-SD themselves therefore began in 1943 to make frequent arrests of Jews, and they did so under explicit orders to act without regard to nationality or other circumstances. They should take care always to apprehend entire families. Parents would be held responsible for their offspring, so that a misdemeanor committed by their children might send adults with them to Drancy.[3] There was meanwhile a basic shift in tactics. The original intention after Operation Torch was for the French police to herd all Jews in the former Occupied Zone into the Paris region, the departments of the Seine and Seine-et-Oise, where they could be more readily observed and controlled. As it became more obvious, however, that the Germans would need to take direct command in order to expedite the mass deportation of all Jews, the plan was altered to ship them straight to the transit camp at Drancy and then on "to the East." Hence, the German policy gradually changed from relocation to removal, and the *Endlösung* became the undisputed order of the day.[4]

Policy was one thing, execution of it another. While the Germans were debating about procedures and making arrangements to implement them, daily life for the Jewish population in Paris was being degraded. The step from discrimination to persecution was short. Although many studies exist on this aspect of the Occupation, it is worthwhile to indicate briefly the kind of harsh and humiliating measures that fell on those Jews who escaped arrest and remained in the city. The tone was set by four recommendations from Louis Darquier de Pellepoix, now chief of the Commissariat Général aux Questions Juives (CGQJ): (l) in addition to wearing a yellow star, Jews should always carry an identification card stamped with "JUIF"; (2) Jews would be forbidden to change their address; (3) all Jewish organizations (except the compliant Union Générale des Israélites de France) were to be dissolved; and (4) any persons caught assisting Jews might be severely punished.[5] German decrees did the rest. Jews were permitted to frequent only certain designated restaurants and cafés. Separate "Jews only" shops were also identified; otherwise, in department stores and markets, Jews were allowed to make purchases only during the morning hour from 11 to 12. Jews could not use public phone booths. Jews had to declare their property (making confiscation of it easier), and so forth in a swelling program of segregation.[6]

If such stipulations were relatively easy to enforce, far more troublesome was the Occupation's ambition to purge Jews from public administration, higher education, and the liberal professions. Again, the Germans were theoretically willing to leave this process in the hands of the French, but progress was aggravatingly slow. In July 1943, Darquier reported to Röthke that there were thirty-two Jewish pharmacies still operating in the Paris region. The *Journal Officiel* published lists of dozens of Jewish physicians who were also practicing—many of them, Röthke complained, with obviously Jewish names like Blumenfeld and Cohen. What was being done by the CGQJ to end this "intolerable condition"? If satisfaction was not soon forthcoming, he admonished, the Gestapo would be required to act "in a drastic manner."[7] Individual cases of German intervention are of course too numerous to classify. One instance is illustrative. In spite of regulations for a complete blackout of Paris by night, light was emanating from the Hotel Ritz onto the Place Vendôme, illuminating the Ministry of Justice on the opposite side of the square. Investigation revealed that the director of the Ritz was married to a Jew, who was arrested one evening at Maxim's for repeatedly demanding aloud that the orchestra play "God Save the King." The Gestapo was not amused, and the woman was sentenced to three months in prison.[8]

An isolated case may inadvertently raise a general question. Why did the Hotel Ritz still have Jews in management? What had come of the much vaunted effort to "Aryanize" the French economy? For once, the problem was not lack of staffing. Located behind the Bibliothèque Nationale on the Place des Petits Pères, the CGQJ had opened in early 1941 with a bureaucratic corps in Paris of 170 (among 228 in all of the Occupied Zone). Another 179 were added in October 1941, and 102 a year later. A decree in November 1942 proposed 177 more. By the beginning of 1943, the Paris staff devoted to Aryanization numbered 543 members housed in three buildings, and they needed more space. If anything, Aryanization was eventually to drown in a bureaucratic swamp.[9]

Big Brother was never far. The Economic Section of the MBF had several specialists devoted to the issue, one of whom was permanently detached to CGQJ headquarters, and they could always call on the assistance of the Sipo-SD. Appointments and dismissals of "administrative commissars" (*Administrateurs provisoires* or *Kommissarische Verwalter*), those directly supervising the liquidation or sale of Jewish business firms, were subject to German approval. And it was the German Treuhand that kept account of the proceeds. All of these scattered and fragmentary records testify that Aryanization had become big business, and a messy one.[10]

Tempo mattered. Slowness was likely to be seen as weakness, it was thought at the Majestic. After early November 1942, the Germans would therefore need to kick the program up to a higher gear in the Occupied Zone and extend it swiftly into the former Unoccupied Zone as well.[11] Yet the difficulties of doing so were legion. Both German administrators and French functionaries were forever struggling to determine whether a certain firm was Jewish or not. How could they rid France of "Jewish influence" if they could not even define it? There were endless problems with incompetent commissars, incomplete or incoherent files, overlapping laws and decrees, and legalities that produced constant friction between French and German bureaucrats. As a rule, the Germans preferred to remain in the background and leave individual transactions to the CGQJ. Just "do what is necessary," Darquier was enigmatically instructed when a sale of Jewish property was suspected to have been obtained under false pretenses by a culpable straw man covering for the Jewish owners.[12]

Hardly surprising, then, was the judgment of the MBF's administrative staff that economic *Entjudung* was faltering while growing increasingly unpopular. Most of the blame fell on Vichy. Darquier had drafted plans to hasten the process, but they were not promptly adopted. Because of "the persistently hesitant attitude of the French regime," Aryanization was making "no noteworthy progress," despite Darquier's good intentions. Little amelioration would occur, Stülpnagel's staff was forced to concede, "without German supervision and constant prodding." By the summer of 1943, as a result, the entire program was stumbling in a state of oscillation.[13]

How much was actually accomplished? The statistics were confused by French claims and German challenges. By July 1943, Darquier reported, over 10,000 Jewish firms and properties had been either liquidated or sold for a profit of slightly more than 300 million francs, of which at least three-quarters had changed hands in Greater Paris. Officials in the Majestic were skeptical, suspecting both dubious bookkeeping practices and possible corruption. Surely there should be much more revenue, given that the total value of Jewish possessions in France was alleged to be 22 billion francs. But a new statistical report in September was not more encouraging, causing Darquier to opine that at this rate complete Aryanization would take another ten years.[14] The rest was disarray. Records of the CGQJ became kaleidoscopic, without summaries to collect or collate them. Numbers from the Treuhand were not much better. One report listed the income until the end of 1942 at exactly 34,277,920.20 francs and at 46,457,955.35 francs for the year 1943. Adding to the confusion, another document attempted to separate seized enemy property (after the United States' entry into the war), a profit estimated at about 60 million francs in 1943, from funds collected by the ongoing Aryanization program. No wonder contemporaries and historians alike have responded to these approximations with some bewilderment. Decidedly, in any event, the great losers were Jews.[15]

In these developments, the first half of 1944 was already prefigured. With a staff of only seven, the group at the Majestic specifically charged with supervising economic *Entjudung* was incapable of keeping track of the hundreds of

French drones at the Place des Petits Pères. After an inspection of the CGQJ's accounting procedures, a member of the Treuhand office reported back that the bookkeeping was so chaotic, an overview of it was impossible. In view of the "numerous and grave difficulties" and "a general instability," there was an evident need to regroup. But the administrative stress was structural and morale was low, the Germans concluded, because in a sense the CGQJ was working to eliminate its own raison d'être (once all Jewish property was confiscated), which was "a permanent invitation to inertia."[16] An air of inevitability hence surrounded the dismissal of Darquier de Pellepoix in the spring of 1944. His fanatical anti-Semitism was no substitute for administrative skill. Yet his replacement, Charles du Paty de Clam, was no improvement. It was especially dismaying when he announced that his major interest, rather than Aryanization, would be the "spiritual struggle" against Judaism. The Germans could only comment that their worst fears had been realized: the CGQJ was paralyzed, and there was little prospect of anything beyond "French bureaucratic routine."[17] The closer D-Day approached, the more disheveled the Aryanization program became. Appropriately, a conspicuous number of memoranda passing between the Hotel Majestic and the CGQJ were stamped simply "no response." Thus, economic *Entjudung* remained virtually as incomplete as it was unjust.[18]

The same generalizations did not quite apply to deportations. By 1943, the modalities of mass transportation of Jews to the East had been "considerably modified" and regularized. The Germans assumed complete control for administration in the interior of the prison facility at Drancy, relegating French gendarmes to guard duty on the camp's exterior perimeter. The inmates thus became "a floating population," not to be detained there for an indefinite period but prepared for immediate shipment by rail at an irregular but frequent rate of 3,000 per week.[19] Directly commanding this vast operation of displacement were Helmut Knochen and Heinz Röthke, who instructed Sipo-SD officers at other camps to channel all available Jews henceforth through Drancy. As the number of locomotives made available by the SNCF was adequate, their only problem was to secure enough freight cars to contain the steady flow of prisoners, now including entire families with their children and the elderly. Talk of Auschwitz as a labor camp was no longer to be heard. Alas, Röthke wrote to the RSHA in Berlin, "transport in passenger cars is unfeasible because of the lack of guards." He wondered whether freight cars could be deployed even during the months of severe frost. In essence, the answer to that question had been settled long ago and was reiterated in a message from Heinrich Himmler to Martin Bormann: whatever it took, all French Jews were to be deported.[20]

One incident provided an experimental dry run. After an attack by partisans on German personnel at Rouen in January 1943, the Gestapo issued orders that all Jews were to be vacated from the Department of Seine-Inférieure and sent at once to Drancy. This operation, with the assistance of the French police, was declared by the Sipo-SD to be "a complete success"—despite the fact that "the overwhelming majority of the population" deplored it.[21] Admittedly, as ever, there were other problems of a more practical sort. In addition to the "stiffening political situation," meaning Vichy's reluctance to approve the detention and deportation of French Jews, there was still confusion about segregating Jews from hostages and other prisoners. The sheer amount of paperwork was immense, more than administrators could manage. Furthermore, Drancy was chaotic and overcrowded, its contingent of condemned cellmates numbering over 4,000 in mid-February 1943. Sanitary conditions there correspondingly worsened, resulting in increased illness, epidemics, and deaths among the captives.[22]

Perhaps Vichy's objections had some effect, but not enough to alter significantly the sordid events in progress. Pleas by Marshal Pétain and Pierre Laval were always couched in a fawning rhetoric of loyalty, as when they registered stubborn opposition to German arrests of French Jews on humanitarian grounds "without wanting thereby to express a philo-Semitism." Carl Oberg responded to this disclaimer by declaring that henceforth the deportations "will be accomplished with the exclusive participation of German police forces." Knochen confessed more realistically to Adolf Eichmann that in light of French recalcitrance and the Paris Gestapo's shortage of personnel, a total *Entjudung* of France could "scarcely be accomplished" within the near future. And by 1944, that was the only future that mattered.[23]

Nevertheless, "it should and must be achieved," said Röthke. By "it" he unambiguously meant the export of all Jews, foreign and French, to concentration camps in the East or to their country of origin. He had little use for Laval's incessant whining, as he saw it, because "the order of the Führer about the Final Solution of the Jewish question in all of Europe is clearly established." Earlier, the Germans had agreed that the entire operation would be gradual, beginning with enemy and alien Jews. But now the time had come to put Nazi racial theory into practice. The trains must continue to roll.[24] And so they did. How nearly was the Gestapo's ambition realized? By Röthke's count, 52,000 Jews had departed from Drancy by August 1943, leaving 70,000 in the former Occupied Zone (of which 60,000 resided in Greater Paris) and 200,000 in the rest of France. Contemporary French statistics (probably somewhat inflated) set the number of deported Jews at 57,000 by the outset of 1944, 72,000 by 1 May, and 81,000 before late July. Whatever the exact count of deportations, the German Occupation will forever stand accused of sharing a major responsibility for the slaughter of innocent humanity on a large scale.[25]

It seems altogether fitting to conclude this analysis of the third phase of the Occupation by offering a comment here on one of the most controversial issues arising from this period—the role of the French. It is perfectly clear, first of all, that the once fashionable view that virtually the entire nation embraced resistance, in body or spirit, will no longer do. That self-serving concept was laid to rest decades ago. Yet the opposite proposition—that most of the French were cowardly and collaborationist until the last moment of their liberation—also does not accord well with the evidence. It is more than an obvious exercise in triangulation to conclude that the complicated reality lay somewhere in between. True, the great bulk of the population, particularly in Paris, remained passive and stoic throughout the Occupation. Also true, the French police usually complied with German objectives, including the programs of forced labor and Aryanization, roundups and razzias, the detention of Communists, and the deportation of Jews. The stated rationale was always the same: if nothing was done by the French, matters would be left open to far more outrageous action by German military authorities and the Gestapo. The same was true of the bureaucracy. Cooperation with the Occupation could plausibly be seen as a prophylactic measure, a way to protect the populace from the worst consequences of the French defeat in 1940 and the long agony of living under the domination of a foreign power. This attitude was sanctioned and indeed encouraged by Pétain, Laval, and the entire Vichy regime. Responsibility for the death of tens of thousands of Jews deported from France cannot therefore be ascribed to a few rotten apples at the Prefecture of Police. It must be traced to the top.

If these observations verge on the self-evident, they need to be plainly stated, just as it has been necessary to cite in detail the documentation on which they are based. Less patent are some of the nuances and questions that must be added and that can gain a clear profile only from a careful study of administrative records left from the Occupation. One such consideration, often too little appreciated by those who have most harshly condemned French collaboration, was the constant and close supervision maintained by German authorities over their counterparts in Paris. If a relatively moderate stance characterized the military correctness of Otto and Heinrich von Stülpnagel, Werner Best, Elmar Michel, Hans Speidel, and others in the Hotel Majestic, the tone of the Occupation was nonetheless increasingly determined by Nazi zealots like Carl Oberg, Fritz Sauckel, Theodor Dannecker, and Heinz Röthke. Under these circumstances, there was precious little that French functionaries in Paris could do to defend their autonomy. In most instances, the sole possible course for them was delay, and delay they frequently did. It is only fair to judge that the tepid attitude of many bureaucrats and ordinary citizens—aside from the heroic resistance of a few—was one of the reasons why many French Jews had their lives and their property saved. Consequently, the Final Solution in France fell far short of the Third Reich's worst intentions.

That being said, two further observations require a place here. First, one must ask whether political and popular reluctance to do German bidding was the single explanation for the survival of a majority of French Jews. The answer is certainly no. In an important sense, time simply ran out for the Occupation. Nazi Germany's ultimate aspiration to remove every last Jew from France was beyond doubt. But the approaching military struggle on the Continent presented endless complications. In addition to the effects of Allied bombing and local acts of sabotage, the French infrastructure of industry and energy was badly overstretched. Bureaucratic confusion was endemic, and, as this study has amply demonstrated, the turf wars and internal conflicts among German administrative bodies never ceased. One must also include the small and often short-lived resistance groups, usually headquartered in Paris during the final phase of the Occupation, and the covert assistance offered to Jews by ordinary French citizens (many of them not Jewish) throughout the war years. These factors cannot be precisely weighed, of course, but the cumulative debilitating result was undoubtedly to create more and more physical difficulties for the hectic effort to apprehend, assemble, and transport Jews from France across the European heartland. By 1944, the killing machine was broken and beyond repair.[26]

Finally, a hypothetical question is in order. What if Pétain and his entourage in Vichy, as well as lesser lights in Paris like René Bousquet and Joseph Darnand, had simply refused to cooperate with the Germans? Would the consequences actually have been far worse, as they claimed? This investigation suggests the contrary. From the beginning of the Occupation, and ever more acutely toward its end, both the military administration and the Gestapo suffered from a shortage of personnel in France. They themselves recognized that without the active and willing collaboration of French functionaries and police, it would have been impossible to approach even remotely the goals and quotas that were demanded from Berlin. This problem visibly worsened following the Operation Torch landing, once the Germans were obliged to occupy all of France and no relief from manpower shortages could be expected after the fall of Stalingrad and the invasion of Italy. That the Nazis were able to sustain some remnant of their racial program under such trying conditions was possible only because others were induced or compelled to remain their helpers.[27]

PART IV

PULLING OUT
(June–August 1944)

Chapter 16

THE TWILIGHT WEEKS

Once the Allied armies had secured a foothold on the French mainland, the days of the Occupation were clearly numbered. Everyone knew it, although few Germans stationed in Paris were as yet prepared to admit openly the obvious and painful truth. Nevertheless, as the final weeks passed—especially after the Allied military breakout from the Normandy peninsula at the end of July 1944—pressing realities had to be met and necessary consequences faced.

At first, little changed outwardly in Paris. Whatever the surface appearance, however, within the Hotel Majestic a heightened tension was palpable. MBF headquarters there was immediately placed on high alert. Orders from Heinrich von Stülpnagel were that all members of his military administration were to be at the ready, day and night, "with weapon in hand." Officers at every rank were to obey instructions with strictness and to assure "ruthless execution" of them in contacts with the French population.[1] Freiherr von Boineburg-Lengsfeld, Ernst Schaumburg's replacement as the Commandant of Greater Paris, grandly announced that the struggle for Europe had begun in earnest and that "the fate of Greater Germany" now hung in the balance. It would be the German objective to defend the capital city and thus to sustain Occupation authorities in their function "as long as possible."[2] Yet at the same time, Stülpnagel's emissaries were scouting eastern France for a suitable site for withdrawal in the event of a "special case" (*Sonderfall*), a typical euphemism for the fall of Paris to invading forces. By mid-July, contingency plans had been drafted, and the decision had been made to fall back to St. Dié and the nearby village of Fraize in the Vosges. When need be, the Occupation stood ready to depart.[3]

Such was the setting for the often recounted events of 20 July 1944, when the failure of a plot against Hitler's life trumped a successful military coup in Paris. Shortly after the event, Carl Oberg wrote an account of how his office was invaded that evening by ten armed men, led by Major General Walther Brehmer, and he was whisked away to the Hotel Continental. There, along with other SS officers and Nazi Party leaders, he was informed by Commandant Boineburg of the plot and confined under armed guard. Oberg was then taken to the Hotel Raphael (next to the Majestic), where a confrontation took place with Stülpnagel and his adjutant Caesar von Hofacker, a cousin of Hitler's putative assassin, Claus Schenk von Stauffenberg, who had earlier phoned from Berlin with the mistaken report that Hitler was dead.[4] By now the news was out: the Führer lived. After a stiff meeting at the bar of the Raphael, in the presence of Ambassador Otto Abetz, Stülpnagel was led off and bundled into the backseat of a limousine heading toward Berlin. On the way, at Verdun, he attempted suicide by a pistol shot to the head, succeeding only in blinding himself. Suffering and helpless, he was transported to Berlin where he was mercilessly hanged on a meat hook. Writing about this gruesome episode in retrospect, Werner Best could not find high words of praise for the part of his martyred former chief, suggesting that Stülpnagel had not actually been among the true and persistent resisters against Nazi rule in Paris and that he had taken sides with them only when that seemed the sole way to maintain his command. If so, one can only say that he paid dearly for his wavering allegiance to the Third Reich.[5]

These internal affairs of the German military regime, however dramatic, had little impact on public life in Paris. The capital remained eerily quiet, like a crocodile sunning on a rock, ready to snap. The calm can partly be explained by admonitions against a premature uprising from both American General Eisenhower and, speaking via Radio London to his growing legion of followers, General de Gaulle. The Communists also observed a prudent silence, preparing for an insurrection without the widespread popular support to provoke one. June and July saw a few wildcat strikes but no general movement of revolt among the ranks of labor. While rail traffic was severely disrupted in surrounding areas, Parisian metros continued to circulate within the city, albeit with reduced schedules. The entire civic transport system had to be closed by 10:20 PM, meaning that the last metro left its end station at 9:45.[6]

Strangely, even as Allied armies began to besiege all of western France, the Germans made a strenuous effort to nourish the cultural life of Paris. The Propaganda Section proudly announced ninety-one concerts in June. State theaters were still operating throughout the week, with smaller private theaters presenting events on weekends. During the fierce battle in Normandy, for the edification of arms workers, the Palais de Chaillot managed to mount a Labiche comedy and a production of *La Traviata*. Art auctions went on at the Hôtel Drouot, where a Matisse painting sold for 428,000 francs and a Bonnard canvas for 305,000 francs. Painting exhibits, such as the "Salon des Tuileries" at the Palais de Tokyo, were displayed to large crowds. As late as the last day of July, a new show of watercolors opened at the Paris Orangerie. Meanwhile, although reduced from four to two a week, daily programs continued at Paris racetracks. One would scarcely have guessed that a liberating army would enter the city within barely a fortnight.[7]

At the same time, under "the necessary pressure" by German authorities to meet their demands, the French bureaucracy carried on. Contrary to expectations, as the MBF's administrative staff commented in mid-July, since the invasion there had been no spike in resistance activity in Paris, and therefore harsher measures of repression were not required. Those measures seemed rigid enough as things were. Sipo-SD statistics recorded hundreds of arrests in the Paris region: nearly 400 by the Germans from 30 June to 14 July (of which 51 were identified as "terrorists"), plus another 46 apprehended by French police. It is worth noting that, throughout this period, the action of French law enforcement was far more restrained than that of the Gestapo. Although personnel checks in the street and neighborhood sweeps, under German supervision, were conducted by French officers, it was indicative that police recruitment had fallen off and that frequent reports of defections among rural gendarmes were reaching Paris.[8]

Acts of sabotage and aerial bombardments were unrelenting in the Paris region without touching the inner city. One count in mid-June listed altogether more than 8,000 casualties in the northern zone of Occupation, whereas the toll for central Paris was 16. The western suburbs fared less well. One June attack resulted in 18 dead and 30 wounded in the vicinity of Versailles, Saint Cyr, and Orsay.[9] Sabotage, besides cutting rail connections, particularly affected phone services and electrical power cables. These, in turn, restricted factories and business firms and thereby created—for the first time since 1940—unemployment. One striking difference from the beginning of the Occupation, however, was the absence of a mass exodus from the capital. Instead, refugees were "streaming" into Paris in search of a safe haven.[10]

Not before the end of July did Paris begin to shut down. Because of the electricity shortage, cinemas were forced to close. To the consternation of the Communists, there was nevertheless no uprising or general strike, despite production slowdowns and increasing attacks on German military personnel, usually followed by retaliation in the form of hostage-taking and executions. It was also hunting season for *miliciens* and other members of the MO, who suffered losses by assassination, of which Joseph Darnand's propaganda head, Philippe Henriot, was the most prominent victim. Unsurprisingly, this round of random violence and repression, spinning out of control, produced serious friction among the French. More than once, street clashes broke out between the Milice and police. If it is too much to speak of an incipient civil war, by early August the steaming cauldron of conflict between those willing to preserve a semblance of public order and those seeking to destroy it had reached a boiling point. Paris, as one German military report compellingly described it, had become a scene of "complete confusion."[11]

Before shifting the focus, another matter must be mentioned. As conditions worsened, the gloves of repression came off. Fed by rumors of armed conspiracies and planned terrorist attacks, cases of torture became more common. Too unbearable to be recounted but too alarming to leave aside, this hidden chapter of the Occupation has been preserved by classified photographs now housed in the French Archives Nationales. It was also briefly but graphically revealed years later during the 1954 trial of Carl Oberg, when the presiding judge quietly read aloud terse charges of "eyes and genital parts ripped out, fingers cut off with a kitchen knife and a hammer, etc." In the courtroom, the transcript reads, "women cry, even among journalists." Enough said.[12]

Parisians noticed particularly the simultaneous collapse of the French economy, for it was they who suffered most from it. Because of continuous bombings, "virtually without pause," Paris became isolated. Besides the growing scarcity of foodstuffs, the lagging availability of coal and therefore electricity meant ineluctable cutbacks and layoffs. Even the arms industry was hindered "to the greatest extent."[13] Precisely how much loss of productivity occurred was difficult to determine. Estimates depended on the location and perspective of observers as well as the object or objects of their attention. The post-invasion deficit of industry was variously indicated as 25 percent, 33 percent, 45 percent, 50 percent, or 70 percent—as so often, not an exact science. By mid-July, the conclusion within the German military administration was unambiguously depressing. According to the MBF's Administrative Section, the entire French economy was "badly crippled." Reports from the Economic Section were still more negative: the economic trajectory of France was downward, and "the curve is steeply declining."[14]

One confirmation of distress was a redistribution of the labor market. Within a week after the Normandy incursion, work on the Atlantic Wall ceased. Since the system of coastal fortifications had already been breached at a central point, there was no sense in further reinforcing the flanks. Instead, units of the Organisation Todt were to be redeployed to assist in repairing bombing damage.[15] Otherwise, labor was now generally underutilized as more businesses and factories closed or operated on reduced schedules in order to conserve energy. Those considered essential for the war effort, thus classified as *Rüstungs-Betriebe*, were functioning at most on a five-day week, others but two or three days; and many of them stayed open only three hours per day.[16] Closings, as noted, created unemployment for the first time in four years, yet the movement of labor to the Reich was halted. Even if workers could be recruited, they could not be efficiently transported. On 6 July 1944, Fritz Sauckel finally confessed the full extent of his failure to the Führer. During the first half of the year, out of a quota of a half million, barely 40,000 French laborers had actually signed up for transfer to Germany, most of them coerced into doing so. All but disintegrated, the STO was therefore abruptly disbanded.[17] Ten days later, a conference on the European labor situation was convened at the Wartburg in southern Germany, where Sauckel emitted his last hurrah. In a passionate speech he warned that a Bolshevik victory would bring "the destruction of our culture and the elimination of the white race." He conceded that the shortfall of his most recent recruitment effort was "a huge slap" to the face of the Third Reich, but he nonetheless expressed supreme confidence that "we can win the war, and we will win the war." In a more subdued tone, another speaker remarked simply that there had been "virtually no results" from France.[18]

For obvious reasons, the best criterion for assessing the deteriorating economic circumstances was the fate of the French National Railway Company, which found itself in dire straits. With its installations and rolling stock the target of incessant Allied air raids, the SNCF was meanwhile harassed daily by Occupation authorities to ensure both the provisioning of Paris and the swift flow of men and materiel necessary for the military campaign in progress. Whereas the main concern of French officials was the former, the Haupt-Verkehrs-Direktion (HVD) headquartered in Paris made it clear that all military requirements must have absolute priority and be enforced "even with a certain brutality." That did not bode well for Paris.[19] Moreover, negotiations over the daily operation of railroads were complicated by an undisguised mutual distrust between SNCF and HVD. Immediately after D-Day, just as they had long foreseen, Gestapo forces arrested a number of SNCF managers, including Pierre-Eugène Fournier, the president of its Administrative Council, and (not for the first time) several lower employees and workers. This rapid pre-emptory move gave the Germans a heavy club with which to thwart any possible strike attempts by French *cheminots*. After some hard bargaining, an accommodation was reached. In return for promises to keep the trains running with "the same energy and courage" as before, Fournier and fifty members of the SNCF staff were released.[20]

Such deals did nothing to offset the "disastrous consequences" of aerial bombardments and acts of sabotage that were reducing French railways to a shambles. Minister of Industrial Production and Communications Jean Bichelonne admitted that "a very bad situation" was developing despite the strenuous effort of 60,000 French and foreign laborers consigned to transportation repairs. By the beginning of July, the SNCF reported, only one-third of its rolling stock was still available. At the same time, so Berlin was told, over 600 locomotives, damaged or destroyed, were currently out of service in the race between Allied bombers and

French repair crews. By the middle of the month, outside the already clogged war zone, the only main rail lines still open to Paris were connections from Lille and Reims. Cut off were the cities of Dijon, Metz, Strasbourg, Lyon, Marseille, Toulouse, and Bordeaux. Even if some of these routes could be temporarily reopened, it was evident to all that Paris was being strangled—"at the mercy of the slightest incident"—and that sending food and fuel by rail had become impossible. Henceforth, once again as in 1940, trucks would have to do.[21]

At the beginning of August, one survey for the preceding month counted 724 separate air attacks against French railways, of which 158 were on stations, 130 on other installations, and 73 on trains. Furthermore, sabotage activity had undergone an "extraordinary increase." For Paris, one particularly critical problem as a result was the damage to tracks leading to the city's northeastern section of La Villette, hindering the arrival of livestock from rural France and thus severely restricting the supply of meat available from the slaughterhouses located there.[22]

In the month of August, for the first time, a serious wave of strikes took place. French workers were becoming nervous and less willing to sweat for a lost cause and its masters. The first major break in ranks occurred on 9 August at an SNCF repair facility in St. Denis, where a thousand skilled technicians briefly halted work. Two days later, a similar strike erupted in another *atelier* at La Villette. This time the Gestapo promptly intervened and threatened immediate reprisals if the insubordination were not ended by afternoon. Although most workers reappeared by 5:00 PM, the trouble there sputtered on for several days. Also, after a work stoppage at Noisy-le-Sec, the Germans again made a show of force and arrested fifteen SNCF employees. Yet the strike reports continued to accumulate at the Majestic: from Montrouge, Ivry, and La Chapelle. At a meeting of SNCF officials on 13 August, it was agreed to avert a general strike in return for the release of more imprisoned *cheminots*. But in truth the dyke was cracking.[23]

The economic result of all this destruction and agitation was in part measurable. Statistics were gathered on coal shipments to Paris from the departments of the Nord and Pas-de-Calais. During the three months of February through April 1944, before the invasion, they had averaged forty trainloads of about 800 tons each, that is, about 32,000 tons a month. The total for May was seven trains and for June two. Thereafter, the capital city was running on reserves and fumes.[24]

Remarkably, industrial plants in the Paris region continued to produce armaments for the German war effort until 17 August, even as Allied tanks were arriving at the city's gates. In the eyes of the Occupation, that phenomenal performance could largely be attributed to the steady loyalty and cooperation of French business managers "about whose personal attitude [there was] scarcely ever reason to complain." The same, despite scattered strikes, was true of the SNCF bureaucracy, whose obedience to German orders endured "to the last moment." Likewise, such a positive evaluation applied to most French workers, whose usual comportment was summarized in a word by a retrospective

German evaluation as "impeccable" (*einwandfrei*).[25] Such comments tend to undercut later attempts by SNCF apologists to claim that their company had been animated by a "spirit of resistance" at all levels throughout the Occupation. Individual resisters there unquestionably were. Many *cheminots* were involved in passive or active opposition to German military rule. But the record speaks more certainly of institutional collaboration than of anything that could legitimately be characterized as Resistance.[26]

Another activity of the Occupation also lasted until its final day. In both of its principal aspects, deportation and Aryanization, the program of *Entjudung* continued. Arrests of Jews and their deportation via Drancy did not end with the Normandy invasion. In three respects, however, these matters were thereafter somewhat different. First, in addition to apprehending Jews, the Gestapo had its hands full with tracking down others: Resistance fighters, priests, functionaries, academics, and intellectuals. No certain tabulation of this increasingly frantic repression is possible, but it is likely that the resulting chaotic circumstances of this period enabled some Jews to escape detection and hence extinction.[27] Second, as material conditions worsened, the German gulag itself began to crumble. Because the SNCF could no longer supply sufficient locomotives, moving prisoners from outlying camps to the Paris region was not as feasible as before. A preliminary plan, never realized, was consequently developed to relocate the entire penal system at Besançon in eastern France. Third, tragically, the Gestapo displayed a belated special interest in Jewish children, perhaps because they provided the most available targets. On 21 July, 240 of them were taken from Paris orphanages, and another 400—protected heretofore by the Union Générale des Israélites de France—were deported on 31 July. A supremely irrational waste of effort in the midst of a military crisis, this relentless and ruthless campaign did not cease until the day before Allied forces reached Paris, 17 August, when a last shipment of fifty-one Jews left Drancy by rail.[28] Although a final reckoning can only be approximate, there is now a consensus that the total number of Jews deported from France reached slightly more than 75,000. About one-third of them were French, the rest foreign. This means that nearly 88 percent of French Jews survived the Holocaust, but barely half of the foreign Jews who had been resident in France before the Occupation did so. Of the nearly 59,000 shipped from Drancy, at most 2,500 returned. It is ironic, although all too appropriate, that a monument to the deported rests today behind the cathedral of Notre Dame on the eastern tip of the Île de la Cité, the former site of the Paris morgue.[29]

Aryanization likewise continued apace. Always a jumble, statistics became even more fragmentary in the final weeks. One report listed 126 liquidations or sales of Jewish firms in the second half of June, right after the Normandy invasion, but the compilation of reliable numbers was already in doubt and could no longer be provided. Like so many industrial plants in Paris, the CGQJ began shutting down. Since the Paris metro service was gradually curtailed for lack of electricity, the staff of the so-called Aryanisation Économique began working on a reduced schedule and spent much of its time in tidying up files or sending them, finished or not, to the Germans. A final report by the MBF's Economic Section on 15 August did little to dissipate the confusion.[30] Undated estimates of the Treuhand, probably post-war, set the number of Aryanization transactions completed during the Occupation since 1940 somewhere between 16,000 and 18,000. It was the Economic Section's conclusion that the entire process of Aryanization thereby reached 43 percent of completion.[31]

This contemporary evaluation by German authorities stands in contrast to the findings of a later French investigative commission that Aryanization was in fact virtually complete and the economy of northern France had effectively been cleared of Jewish "influence" by the end of the Occupation.[32]

Disposition of Jewish Holdings in the Occupied Zone
According to Estimates of the Mission Mattéoli

Transactions	Percentage
Sale	26.7
Liquidation	24.6
Other	5.0
Not disposed	26.1
Unknown	12.1
Without object	5.5
Total	100.0

One hundred percent? For three reasons, the complete eradication of Jewish holdings in Paris and the rest of the former Occupied Zone is unlikely. First, there are all those unspecified categories—"other," "unknown," etc.—that accounted for nearly half of the recorded transactions. Only sales and liquidations were certain. Second, this paper trail became conspicuously cluttered and confused as the end of the Occupation neared. The statistical picture was blurred by repeated bureaucratic failings of the CGQJ resulting from irregular office hours, incomplete files, and unanswered memos. Third, as the correspondence of German supervisors made clear from the beginning, many of the recorded transactions were far from perfect. French functionaries were constantly being prodded to make more thorough investigations, correct faulty reporting, and provide further proof that Jewish personnel and stockholders had actually been eliminated and not hidden behind false claims and financial straw men. After all, we must recall that nearly three-quarters of the Jews in France survived, and it is doubtful that they had been entirely deprived of business connections and private wealth. Rather, it would seem that the Aryanization program, like deportation, had finally become bogged down in the morass of German military defeat. Nonetheless, estimates of the total amount confiscated from French Jews during the Occupation range as high as five billion francs.[33]

A disturbing question remains. Why was it so important, under such adverse conditions, to pursue the programs of *Entjudung* to the Occupation's last breath? The answer can probably be found in a final report of the MBF's administrative staff. Continuation of these efforts, it stated, was a sign of German strength. Hesitation to deprive Jews of property or to transport them to Auschwitz would be interpreted as weakness. At all costs, German authorities in Paris needed to demonstrate that they were still in command and that they retained the right and the power to impose their will on the French. This "success," as the report concluded, would require alert surveillance and a determination to carry on. So they did.[34]

As was true from the beginning of the Occupation, repression of undesirables and dissidents could not function effectively without the collaboration of French police forces. The Germans were counting on Darnand's Milice, and they apparently had good reason to do so. Immediately after the Allied landing, Darnand announced the full mobilization of his elite corps. It was not a popular measure, however, since many had become *miliciens* by joining what they thought were to be reserve units offering attractive stipends but little action. Now they were being called upon to hunt and fight the *maquis*, who were daily carrying out sabotages, armed attacks on German military personnel (averaging well over fifty a day), and the seizure of weapons and munitions. The unavoidable results were unrest in the ranks and a notable reluctance of reservists to answer Darnand's summons to duty.[35]

As if these reports reaching Paris were not enough, horrific accounts meanwhile began to circulate of the most dreadful single incident of the Occupation, the slaughter at Oradour-sur-Glane, a small town near Limoges, where on 10 June 1944 villagers became victims of a reprisal by the SS: 642 men, women, and children were machine-gunned or burned to death. Within days, this heinous action was publicly condemned by the Bishop of Limoges "in the name of simple natural morality," and relations between the Occupation and the Church sank out of sight. That deterioration was sealed by the arrest of six Catholic bishops and several other clergymen during the weeks that followed.[36] Unable to ward off either attacks by partisans or excesses by the Germans, Darnand came under heavy criticism from Jacques Doriot's party, the PPF, as a "completely failed" leader. He faced charges that his mobilization of the Milice had only hastened recruitment for the *maquis* and that his Maintien de l'Ordre had become no more than an instrument of German repression. These recriminations soon translated into repeated street clashes in Paris that pitted *miliciens* alternatively against "terrorists" or the French police. Like everything else, it appeared, the Milice was contributing to disorder in the capital. In an attempt to squelch such trouble and to regain control of law enforcement in Paris, Darnand returned to the capital from Vichy in early August. He did so in vain, however, and was forced to flee in haste to Sigmaringen in southern Germany before the end of the month.[37]

One might imagine that the Nazi propaganda machine in France would be silenced by the successful Allied landing. Not so. Throughout June and July, the Germans kept up a steady drumbeat of news flashes about the slow advance and heavy losses of Anglo-American forces, bottled up as they were within the Normandy peninsula, and rumors were spread about the mounting devastation rained on Britain by Germany's secret weapons. The mood was thus ostentatiously upbeat at a huge anti-Bolshevik ceremony at the Palais de Chaillot on 22 June to celebrate the third anniversary of Nazi Germany's crusade against Soviet Russia. This theatrical exuberance was followed by a press conference at the German Embassy, where it was solemnly announced that the war had at last entered a "decisive phase." Lacking enough space to maneuver on the coast, so the argument ran, enemy troops would be "obliged" to progress toward the interior of France and therefore away from their naval protection. This would enable the Germans to throw military reserves into combat in massive counterattacks inflicting more severe casualties. Translation: German defenses on the Normandy front were collapsing.[38] Another propaganda release went further. The German army now had the Allies in a trap, since they must either achieve total victory or admit that Germany was invincible. True, in armament the Americans held a material advantage, but the Third Reich would meet it with "moral superiority."[39] There were just two problems. The Normandy breakout occurred on the last day of July, and, as the Embassy sheepishly conceded, "there are very few French any more who are really convinced of a German victory." The best propaganda, it seemed, was the populace's fear of air raids. Accordingly, German press officials in Paris released bogus statistics that 80,000 French civilians had recently been killed by Allied bombers, a figure soon revised upward to 118,000.[40]

Meanwhile, the Embassy made much of a message from Joseph Goebbels expressing his hope and expectations for a positive contribution by France to an "ultimate victory."[41] But what were the prospects at a moment when enemy forces were moving to encircle Paris? An attempted answer to that question was contained in a later Abwehr report reviewing the events of that August. At the month's beginning, following the optimistic statements by Goebbels and also Heinrich Himmler, morale among the Occupation authorities was "still rather good." But rapid Allied advances brought "strong discouragement." Germans in Paris were impatiently awaiting the deployment of new weapons "on which all hopes are pinned." Then, revealingly, the memorandum added a sentence that said it all: "Everyone hopes for a miracle through the new weapons, since only through them can the war be concluded with success for us."[42] Unfortunately for them, there was only one miracle weapon that could now have saved the Third Reich, and Germany did not possess it. Undeterred, the Propaganda Section duly repeated the official gospel by claiming, barely one week before the Allies stormed Paris, that "signs are already visible of an impending change of the war in favor of Germany."[43]

Cooler heads prevailed. On 9 August 1944, the MBF staff began preparations for the long anticipated *Sonderfall* of evacuating the capital. Three days later, the Abwehr commenced "destructive measures" by shredding and burning its secret files.[44] On the following morning, 13 August, instructions were issued to the entire MBF staff for a pullout from the Hotel Majestic to St. Dié and Fraize. The Hotel Ritz was emptied of personnel on the next day. Simultaneously, an incident occurred at the Place de la République where German female staff workers were being evacuated from the Hotel Moderne. Crowds gathered to witness the event, and as the women mounted into trucks, they were showered with catcalls and whistles. By then, after confiscating twenty Paris busses, several trucks, and automobiles, the entire military administration had departed.[45]

On 15 August 1944, Adolf Hitler gave orders to destroy Paris factories, bridges, and public buildings, which had been mined for the purpose. The current military commander in France, General Karl Kitzinger, had arrived from Ukraine in late July to replace Stülpnagel, a week after the abortive coup attempt that ended the latter's tenure as MBF. Unfamiliar with circumstances in Paris or with the elaborate bureaucracy he was supposed to direct, Kitzinger was completely ineffectual in the post to which he had been hastily assigned. His flight from Paris was scarcely noticed. Instead, another figure appeared in the person of General Dietrich von Choltitz, who had been awarded the grandiose title Commanding General and Military Commander of Greater Paris (Kommandierender General und Wehrmachtsbefehlshaber von Gross-Paris). He was, in short, not the successor of the cousins Stülpnagel but of Ernst Schaumburg. Choltitz promptly announced that since Paris had become part of the war zone, his assignment would be to defend the capital city and to maintain law and order there. As is long and well-known, however, Choltitz hesitated to execute Hitler's wishes for the city's destruction, although the matter was pending and the outcome still uncertain. In the meantime, the municipal police of Paris went on strike, and outbursts of violence erupted on the streets. Because German intentions were unclear, barricades were erected overnight, arms were distributed, and calls for insurrection brought many Parisians into the streets. As a result, the ensuing ferocious melee understandably but perhaps needlessly cost the lives of those excited French patriots whose names are now commemorated on dozens of small plaques throughout the capital. Doubtless they wanted to do something to save the honor of France, or their own, but the liberation of the city was already assured. Paris was not burning. On 25 August 1944, Choltitz was admonished that his garrison must surrender or face "total extermination." He met that afternoon with French General Leclerc and other Allied officers at the Gare Montparnasse and issued orders that hostilities should cease.[46] The Occupation of Paris was terminated.

EPILOGUE
The Long Handshake

The Germans were great record-keepers. During the four years and two months of the Occupation of Paris, they managed to produce tens of thousands of documents that recorded in minute detail every conceivable aspect of their military administration. Even though a substantial portion of those papers was either scattered or deliberately destroyed as the Occupation came to a close, huge quantities of them remain—vastly more than a single scholar could digest in a lifetime. From that surfeit of evidence it is necessary to select, and on that selection the historical record must be based. Of all the documents written near the Occupation's end or shortly thereafter, one stands out. Although this memorandum was undated and unsigned, it was clearly composed by an officer within the military administration at the Hotel Majestic, one who witnessed the final days and then sat down to describe the Occupation's evolution and dénouement.[1]

According to this extraordinarily perceptive account, the Allied invasion came as no surprise. Planning for the eventuality of an evacuation of Paris had proceeded for months before the June 1944 landing, and few in the Majestic harbored any illusions that such an outcome could be averted. By the beginning of August, with the news that the Allied surge from Normandy could no longer be contained, that assumption became a certainty. Yet the capital seemed quieter than ever. Because of the shortage of electricity, city lights burned only for one hour at dawn and another before midnight. Theaters, cinemas, bars, and restaurants were closed. Meanwhile, German military staff members in the Majestic worked on, and they continued every day to receive visits from the same French officials who had come to their offices during the past months and years. If not friends, they had come to know one another and had developed a close personal relationship. All of them, French and German, knew that the end was approaching, but no one dared to express that reality in words. As a rule, there was no jesting or hinting, no clever remark or strained parting salutation. Instead, the only indication of a farewell was an unusually lengthy silent clasp of hands.[2]

To understand the significance of that gesture, one must keep a firm grasp of chronological sequence. The German Occupation had evolved over time, and with it so had the meaning of collaboration. No doubt, that term has become a dirty word in the lexicon of French history, but only gradually did it acquire the thoroughly pejorative connotations that we now associate with it.

During the first phase of the Occupation, before the German invasion of Russia, nothing seemed more natural than, in a literal sense, "working together." That was immediately apparent, for instance, when German soldiers joined French farmers in the harvest of early autumn 1940. Everyone had an interest in the gathering, distribution, and sale of foodstuffs that, as a result, initially remained in abundant supply. In central Paris, commerce thus resumed quickly after the fall of France, and the cooperation of French and German functionaries to promote it was taken for granted. Meanwhile, in Paris the Germans were to be seen everywhere: in the metro, on the streets, in restaurants and shops, at the theater, and also in bars and brothels. Each personal encounter implicated the French ever deeper in approval or acceptance of the unavoidable circumstances of Occupation. Collaboration assumed a multiplicity of forms, and complicity became a commonplace of daily life. The persistence of a black market provided a perfect example. Attempts to suppress it proved to be of little avail, since French and Germans alike benefited from it. The geographic division of France, the existence of a Vichy regime, and the nimbus of glorification that surrounded Marshal Pétain also gave collaboration an aura of respectability. Even the Communist Party, at first restrained by the Nazi-Soviet Pact, adopted a stance that verged on acquiescence. Raucous political activity was all but eliminated from the public sphere, and with rare exceptions the Church hierarchy meekly complied with admonitions to maintain a low profile. Before June 1941, in short, collaboration seemed an eminently sensible arrangement between victors and vanquished.

Germany's assault on the Soviet Union changed that ambiance by setting off a wave of terrorism and repression in the Occupied Zone. Assassinations and attacks on German military personnel brought on prompt retributions by Occupation authorities, who hoped thereby to master the situation and restore order. They largely failed to do so, however, and a hostage crisis became the big stinking albatross of the Occupation. These developments not only caused a change in the military command in Paris, they cleared the way for the arrival of the two most unsavory characters in the entire German cadre of administration, Carl Oberg and Fritz Sauckel. By seizing control respectively of the police and the economy, this pair of officers contributed significantly to altering the atmosphere in 1942 and consequently to redefining collaboration. Previously held in abeyance, an unapologetic brutality now reached the surface. In effect, the Occupation thereby underwent a process of Nazification, for which the police razzias and roundups of Jews—notably that of the Vel d'Hiv—were the signature events. This context explains the pivotal figure of René Bousquet, whose pact with the devil, by supposedly trading alacrity for autonomy, gave collaboration a new and more sinister meaning. There could be no scientific measurement of the response of the French population, but analyses by German propaganda officials were unanimous on two points: that the majority of Parisians had adopted a more tentative attitude toward their nation's cooperation in a Nazi-dominated Europe, and that public opinion depended entirely on the military progress of the war.

The verdict was rendered at the outset of the third phase of the Occupation by the Allied invasion of North Africa and the crushing defeat of the Wehrmacht at Stalingrad. Now entirely occupied, France had already slipped far down the slope of collaboration. When Pierre Laval, speaking for Vichy, announced that he wished for a German victory, he was doing no more than drawing the ultimate logical conclusion from his regime's prior actions and policies. It was altogether appropriate, therefore, that Laval increasingly leaned on Joseph Darnard and his Milice, a vigilante force representing a desperate attempt to maintain law and order. But after early 1943, it was clear that Germany was losing the struggle for hegemony in Europe. It was also obvious that the collaborationists had long since crossed a line, and there was no turning back. Their options were limited to victory or defeat. Laval desired the first, to which he and his followers were irrevocably attached, but he would soon have to accept the other. The same was true of German authorities in Paris. Some of them still talked a good game, but the encroaching military reality now dictated that preparations be made to abandon their post. Many tasks of the Occupation were thus left unfinished, due in part to the half-hearted cooperation of French functionaries during the last phase of its existence and to the increasingly open hostility of the French population, but also to the unresolved internal conflicts of the German regime and the ever more acute shortage of its administrative manpower. Amply documented in this study, these factors proved in the end to have far-reaching ramifications for the Occupation's lagging attempts to exploit the French economy, repress the mounting waves of public violence, and complete the planned expulsion of all Jews from France.

A perceptible sense of inevitability enveloped the capital city after the Allied invasion of Normandy. The period from that time until the final days in August 1944 could constitute for the Occupation only a postscript that was bound to culminate in the liberation of Paris. That event, we must recall, had by no means appeared predestined in the summer of 1940. It did not seem so until the summer of 1944. In the interval, Parisians had endured the trying, humiliating, and essentially absurd experience of a German Occupation. It ended, without a word, with a long handshake at the Hotel Majestic.

It is always unwise to put too much weight on a metaphor. Yet, without any wish to add a faux happy ending to what was surely one of the cruelest and saddest chapters in European history, it is permissible to observe here that the remarkable reconciliation of France and Germany since the Second World War cannot properly be detached from the trauma mutually shared at close quarters by the two nations for more than four years. This wrenching experience should not simply be counted as an unfortunate interlude to be placed within parentheses, as if the Fourth Republic followed directly from the Third. Rather, disturbing as that might seem, the Occupation must be seen as an integral prelude to the years thereafter. In a certain sense, the long handshake endures to this day. Could this be because the Occupation had a salutary effect of demystifying both sides and dispelling tired myths about being hereditary enemies? Otherwise, there may be no adequate explanation for the emergence of a united post-war Europe.

If so, of course, that would constitute only half of the story. The rest, frequently and ably recounted elsewhere, concerns the complex interaction of the clandestine French Resistance and the exiled Free French, who together participated in the liberation of Paris and the nation—not to mention the largely unrecorded and often costly acts of individual citizens who resented collaboration and in their fashion opposed it at every opportunity. One finds relatively few references to these matters in this text, for which there are several explanations. First is the fact that the two branches of German military administration most directly involved with repressing insurgent activity in Paris, the Abwehr and the Gestapo, were also the most scrupulous in destroying self-incriminating records before departing from the capital in August 1944. The resulting paucity of such hard evidence therefore necessarily precludes a close examination of German attempts to thwart potential insurrectionary organizations in Paris. Secondly, the Germans soon learned that the delicate assignment of singling out genuine French "terrorists" from the civilian population (as they tried to do during the hostage crisis) was often better left to the French police—in particular, the Brigades Spéciales, whose repeated dragnets were highly effective in rounding up Parisians suspected of direct responsibility for acts of violence. Traditional police methods, in other words, were sometimes more efficacious than the more clumsy and brutal tactics of the Occupation's own forces. The Germans, in truth, were often ignorant of the nature of the Resistance, and what they did not know, they usually did not record. Furthermore, as noted, until the very last days of the Occupation, Paris was remarkably quiet, occasional bomb attacks and assassinations notwithstanding. The heavily patrolled boulevards and streets of the inner city provided scant protection for incipient movements of armed resistance. From the beginning, Paris was literally swarming with German military personnel, Gestapo agents, and police officials of all sorts. If the French capital can in some regard be said to have become the headquarters of the Resistance by 1944, it was unquestionably also the pith of repression. It was therefore grimly appropriate that the capture and severe torture of Jean Moulin occurred not in Paris but in Lyon. Those distressing events, as well as the entire history of Resistance fighters in the *maquis*, transpired well beyond the purview of this volume, and as a consequence they have found little place here.

To strike a final and fair balance is accordingly difficult. It would doubtless be too much of a stretch, and perhaps even a bit perverse, to ascribe the character of today's Europe solely to its antecedents in Franco-German collaboration during the war years. Yet the opposite pole, uncomfortably seated in a sweeping definition of the French Resistance, also has its share of ambiguities. The latter properly features such distinguished names as Jean Monnet, Robert Schuman, and especially Charles de Gaulle. No one can forget the image of that other long clasp of hands, as de Gaulle and Konrad Adenauer stood side by side in the cathedral of Reims. We must recall, however, that it was a defeated, divided, and morally weakened Germany to which de Gaulle became reconciled. He made his peace with Bonn, not with Berlin. It appears, in fact, that he is more likely to be remembered not as a deeply committed European but as the last great champion of conservative French nationalism, whose efforts to refurbish the grandeur of France were embodied by the *force de frappe* and the atomic bomb, the two vetoes of British entry into the Common Market in 1963 and 1967, France's ostentatious withdrawal from NATO, and the curt eviction of NATO's headquarters from Paris.

Whatever the ultimate reckoning of history, if such there should ever be, it is certain that the restoration of a peaceful Franco-German relationship—the double helix of post-war Europe—will stand as a supreme achievement of the late twentieth century. Under vastly different circumstances from those of the wartime Occupation in Paris, collaboration has prevailed after all. It is a great story, still waiting to be written.

Appendix

Classified French Police Files at the
Archives Nationales in Paris

A fter some initial discouragement and considerable delay, I was finally able to obtain special authorizations (*dérogations*) to consult several restricted cartons housed in the series F[7] (Police Générale) of the Archives Nationales (AN).

It goes without saying that the period of the Occupation produced raw feelings and deep animosities during as well as following the war years. Although the number of persons involved is still in dispute, there was unquestionably a significant purge of French collaborationists after the Liberation. We have those unforgettable photos of women with their heads shaved, Pierre Laval on trial, and the pathetic figure of Marshal Pétain at the end—eclipsed only by the indelible image of General de Gaulle and other Resistance leaders triumphantly descending the Champs-Élysées. Winners and losers were caught up together in this emotional maelstrom, and it is not surprising that some public officials and professional archivists felt a need thereafter to allow justice to take its course without undue public exposure beyond the courtroom. That, presumably, explains the existence of the classified files and the lengths to which a researcher must go to obtain access to them.

But what do they actually contain? Only a partial answer to that question is currently possible, pending an overdue blanket declassification of the documents at issue. Fortunately, the present administrative regime of the AN has of late been increasingly forthcoming, and I especially want to thank Mme. la Directrice Martine de Boisdeffre, M. Christian Oppetit, and Mlle. Emilie Charrier for their cooperation in allowing me to examine some of the material that appeared relevant for the preparation of this study.[1]

Most of the contents of these cartons, let it be said at once, date from the post-war years, making it all the more appropriate to comment on them in the appendix of a work that is otherwise based almost entirely on evidence contemporary with the Occupation period itself. Only a sparse few original documents, or copies of them, are to be found that can be securely dated before August 1944—and they, virtually without exception, can only confirm data and observations already available in unclassified police reports. There is consequently no obvious reason to maintain restrictions on these records.

A few examples may suffice to make the point. One memorandum dated 12 February 1943 removes doubt (but was there any?) regarding the attitude of the SS in Paris about the so-called Jewish question. Writing to the Reichssicherheitshauptamt (RSHA) in Berlin, Helmut Knochen reiterates his intention, on orders from Adolf Eichmann, to "evacuate" all Jews in France to the East. More than a year after the infamous Wannsee Conference had adopted the Final Solution, this directive could hardly have occasioned a surprise in the RSHA. Yet two of Knochen's comments are worth noting for the record. He confirms Pétain's stubborn opposition to the deportation of French Jews, and he pointedly criticizes René Bousquet's attempts to hinder German efforts. We see laid out here, in other words, the context of Bousquet's replacement by Joseph Darnand, in his role as commander of the Milice, to be head of the Maintien de l'Ordre (MO). Knochen also emphasizes to his superiors the acute shortage of German administrative personnel in France after the Allied landing of November 1942 in North Africa. To ensure the enforcement of Nazi racial policy in all of the occupied territory after the disappearance of the demarcation line, therefore, "the deployment of French police is imperative." The collaboration of the MO with the Gestapo, in short, had clearly become an urgent necessity for the Germans.[2]

Another memo from January 1944 attempts to tabulate the results of that collaboration. Therewith Ambassador Otto Abetz sends to Berlin four lists of "preventive" arrests in Paris. Among them one finds the names of various French administrators, prefects, *inspecteurs des finances*, professors, and assorted intellectuals who had become persons of interest "for Gaullist, Marxist, and other activity hostile to the Reich." According to Abetz, during 1943 alone, such apprehensions by the Germans totaled nearly 35,000 French citizens, while the French police had rounded up more than 9,000. Among these "dissidents," who were "justifiably suspected," appeared the names of celebrities such as Louis Aragon, Bernard Faÿ (curiously), Robert d'Harcourt, Louis Madelin, Jean Monnet, and Pierre Renouvin. The memo continues: "Whenever any concrete elements of suspicion existed, even of minor importance," it was standard procedure to make an immediate arrest. No wonder that the prisons became filled to overflowing and that the fear of disappearing into *Nacht und Nebel* correspondingly grew.[3]

Otherwise, these files reveal little from contemporary sources beyond routine police reports and records. Some clusters of documents concern French political leaders and organizations, such as, for example, Colonel François de la Rocque and the Parti Social Français. Another lesser figure who emerges here is Roland Krug von Nidda, the German diplomatic representative at Vichy, whose daily contacts with Pétain's government there provided much fodder for the mills of collaboration. A curiosity item is the large dossier on Winston Churchill, whose movements were closely followed by French police starting in the war years. Not only his visit to Paris in 1945 was documented, but also his stays in the late 1940s at French spas like Aix-les-Bains, Aix-en-Provence, and Antibes, as well as Monte Carlo. Particular attention was devoted to his repeated vacations in the early 1950s at Cap d'Ail on the estate of Lord Beaverbrook (alternately misspelled "Beaverbrock" or "Baeverbrook"). Perhaps some future biographer of Churchill may find this trivia noteworthy.[4]

The real interest of the classified police files of the AN lies not in any of the above but in the post-war investigations of prominent German officials of the Occupation who were eventually brought to trial. Three stand out: Otto Abetz, Helmut Knochen, and Carl Oberg. After being arrested, each was brought back to Paris and interrogated at length by officers of the French Sûreté Nationale in preparation for an appearance before a court of law. Transcripts of these closed sessions have all the interest of an autopsy being performed before our eyes. Obviously, they must be treated with the utmost caution by historians, who cannot fail to detect a common denominator of attempted self-exculpation by the Germans.[5]

It is difficult to determine which of the three testimonies is the most disingenuous. The statements made by Abetz cover a wide range of topics, including his activity between the wars with the Comité Franco-Allemand, associations with the Nazi Party, propaganda and press actions by the Paris Embassy, confiscation of art treasures, deportations and labor conscription, and relations with political personalities, such as Édouard Herriot, Paul Reynaud, and Jean Luchaire. None is more revealing, however, than Abetz's declarations about the Jewish question, regarding which he denies any direct activity—even when confronted with accusations by one of his underlings at the Paris Embassy, Carltheo Zeitschel, that he was instrumental in the formulation and execution of German racial policy. That charge was "completely false," Abetz categorically states: "I never transmitted any suggestion whatever on the Jewish question to Ribbentrop, to Himmler, or to anyone whomever." Zeitschel's allegations were therefore "absurd," Abetz claims, since as Ambassador he had "no competence at all concerning the regulation of Jewish questions in France." Abetz thus presents himself as an innocent bystander, a faithful supporter of Franco-German cooperation, and a calm voice of reason in the face of Nazi fanaticism. Anyone who has carefully read the account in this volume, among many others, must respond to Abetz's auto-justification with frank skepticism. The contemporary evidence of the Occupation patently contradicts his version of events, leaving no doubt about his deep involvement with the persecution and elimination of thousands of Jews.[6]

The case of Oberg was of a different sort. Arrested by the Americans in the Tyrol after the war, incarcerated at Baden Baden, and then transferred to Paris (whence he had fled on 18 August 1944), Oberg was widely and publicly condemned from the outset as the "butcher of Paris," directly responsible as he was for mass deportations, massacres like Oradour-sur-Glane, destruction with heavy casualties of the Old Port at Marseille, and countless expeditions against the *maquis* throughout France. As chief of the SS in Paris and head of the Gestapo there, Oberg could scarcely deny the counts against him. But he could attempt to mitigate their impact by shifting a large portion of malfeasance onto the French. With an undeniable shortage of personnel, he claimed, it was manifestly impossible for the Germans to do more than oversee from afar police actions that were of necessity conducted mainly by the French. This was the entire sense of his agreements with René Bousquet, and only Bousquet's failure to maintain sufficient initiative by the French police led Oberg to propose replacing him at the end of 1943 with Joseph Darnand, "who inspired my complete confidence." And so on. Oberg's depiction of his own ineffectuality because of the sheer lack of numbers did not represent much of a defense, and, when tried in post-war years, it did nothing to quiet the clamor for his head in the French press.[7]

More problematic was the interrogation of Knochen. Also arrested by the Americans in January 1946, he was initially confined at Dachau before being brought back that November to Paris, where he was interviewed by the Sûreté and then held at the prison of Cherche-Midi pending further investigation. When questioned about his responsibilities as second-in-command of the Gestapo in Paris, specifically regarding the treatment of prisoners, Knochen replied flatly: "I knew nothing of tortures." Of course, it was known that there were some instances of "enhanced interrogation" (*verschärfte Vernehmung*) of a captive, which meant that "one could strike him, reduce his rations." But Knochen denied that he had ever witnessed such a procedure and assumed that it remained within proper bounds. He did admit that he had heard about sessions of "waterboarding" (*baignoires*), but he was unaware that any deaths resulted from them. "For the first time, I heard mention of torture at the Nuremberg trials, and I was very astonished by it." To this statement Knochen added: "I cannot understand how my services could employ such procedures of torture without my being informed." Historians may be excused for sharing Knochen's lack of comprehension, since the notion that a Gestapo chief in Paris during more than three years of the Nazi Occupation had no knowledge whatever of torture inflicted by his own men strains credulity beyond the breaking point. If there is a semantic problem at issue—is simulated drowning not a torture and is "enhanced interrogation" not a euphemism?—it pales before the awful reality that took place night after night in the cellars of Paris detention centers.[8]

One question received extensive and yet inconclusive treatment in the immediate post-war period. How many civilians were executed by the Germans in France? A department-by-department survey of that issue was conducted by the Sûreté in the spring of 1947. The statistical findings were as follows:

French civilians summarily executed	9,729
French civilians executed after arrest and detention	10,500
Members of the Forces Françaises de l'Intérieur executed	5,251
Total	25,480

These figures were reviewed by a second survey in 1952, which concluded that the most recent estimates reached about 5,000 greater than the earlier figure, that is, more than 30,000 in total. The truth, naturally, is that we shall never know the precise number and that historians will forever puzzle over the many contingencies and contradictions.[9]

Finally, several references to General Dietrich von Choltitz deserve our attention. Because he was in some sense a hero of the Liberation, his declarations were far less controversial than the others and were openly reported in the public forum, for instance, in a 1949 article in *Le Figaro*, "Why I Did Not Destroy Paris in 1944." Comfortably retired in Freiburg-im-Breisgau at the time, Choltitz could reflect on the tumultuous events of August 1944 and recall that at a critical moment he conferred with Abetz, who was fully in agreement that the beautiful French capital city, where he had so long resided, should not be damaged. Make of this testimony what we will, it serves as a useful reminder that guilt and blame come in degrees, and that the historian is always on the side of complexity.[10]

ABBREVIATIONS

AA	Auswärtiges Amt, Berlin
Abt.	Abteilung
AN	Archives Nationales, Paris
BA	Bundesarchiv, Berlin and Koblenz
BA-MA	Bundesarchiv-Militärarchiv, Freiburg
BdS	Befehlshaber der Sicherheitspolizei
CDJC	Centre de Documentation Juive Contemporaine
CGQJ	Commissariat Général aux Questions Juives
COSI	Comité Ouvrier de Secours Immédiat
DB	Deutsche Botschaft
DSA	Direction des Services de l'Armistice
ETRA	Eisenbahntransportabteilung
FK	Feldkommandantur
GBA	Generalbevollmächtigter für den Arbeitseinsatz
GFP	Geheime Feldpolizei
HVD	Haupt-Verkehrs-Direktion
KK	Kreiskommandantur
MBF	Militärbefehlshaber in Frankreich
MO	Maintien de l'Ordre
MVB	Militärverwaltungsbezirk
NSDAP	Nationalsozialistische Deutsche Arbeiterpartei
OBH	Oberbefehlshaber
OKH	Oberkommando des Heeres
OKW	Oberkommando der Wehrmacht
OT	Organisation Todt
PA-AA	Politisches Archiv-Auswärtiges Amt, Berlin

PPF	Parti Populaire Français
Prop.-Abt.	Propaganda-Abteilung
RNP	Rassemblement National Populaire
RAF	Royal Air Force
RSHA	Reichssicherheitshauptamt
Rü	Rüstungs-Abteilung
SCAP	Service du Contrôle des Administrateurs Provisoires
SD	Sicherheitsdienst
Sipo	Sicherheitspolizei
SOL	Service d'Ordre Légionnaire
SNCF	Société Nationale des Chemins de Fer
SPAC	Service de Police Anti-Communiste
SS	Schutzstaffel
STO	Service du Travail Obligatoire
UGIF	Union Générale des Israélites de France
Wi	Wirtschafts-Abteilung
Wwi	Wehrwirtschafts-Abteilung
WWSF	Wehrwirtschaftsstab Frankreich
WWSW	Wehrwirtschaftsstab West

NOTES

Introduction

1. Guy Beaujouan et al. (eds.), *La France et la Belgique sous l'occupation allemande 1940–1944. Les fonds allemands conservés au Centre historique des Archives nationales* (Paris, 2002). Stefan Martens (ed.), *Frankreich und Belgien unter deutscher Besatzung 1940–1944. Die Bestände des Bundesarchiv-Militärarchivs Freiburg* (Stuttgart, 2002).
   2. Robert Aron, *Histoire de Vichy* (Paris, 1954).
   3. Robert O. Paxton, *Vichy France: Old Guard and New Order, 1940–1944* (New York, 1972).
   4. Jean-Pierre Azéma, *De Munich à la Libération (1938–1944)* (Paris, 1979; rev. ed., 2002). Jean-Louis Crémieux-Brilhac, *La France libre. De l'appel du 18 juin à la libération*, 2 vols. (Paris, 1996; rev. ed., 2001). Philippe Burrin, *La France à l'heure allemande 1940–1944* (Paris, 1995).
   5. Serge Klarsfeld, *Vichy-Auschwitz. Le rôle de Vichy dans la solution finale de la question juive en France*. 2 vols. (Paris, 1983–1985).
   6. Eberhard Jäckel, *Frankreich in Hitlers Europa. Die deutsche Frankreichpolitik im Zweiten Weltkrieg* (Stuttgart, 1966).
   7. Hans Umbreit, *Der Militärbefehlshaber in Frankreich 1940–1944* (Boppard, 1968).
   8. Bernd Kasten, *"Gute Franzosen." Die französische Polizei und die deutsche Besatzungsmacht im besetzten Frankreich 1940–1944* (Sigmaringen, 1993).
   9. Julian Jackson, *France: The Dark Years, 1940–1944* (Oxford, 2001).

Chapter 1: Law and Order

1. On the German entrance into Paris, see the older narratives of Henri Amouroux, *La vie des français sous l'occupation*, 2 vols. (Paris, 1961), pp. 16–20; Henri Michel, *Paris allemand* (Paris, 1981), pp. 15–51; David Pryce-Jones, *Paris in the Third Reich: A History of the German Occupation, 1940–1944* (London, 1981), pp. 3–18; and Herbert R. Lottmann, *The Fall of Paris: June 1940* (New York, 1992), pp. 341–70. More recent accounts notably include Azéma, *De Munich à la Libération*, pp. 147–56; Burrin, *La*

France à l'heure allemande, pp. 24–38; and Adam Tooze, *The Wages of Destruction: The Making and Breaking of the Nazi Economy* (London, 2006), pp. 368–95. The French exodus from Paris is neatly summarized by Hanna Diamond, *Fleeing Hitler: France 1940* (Oxford, 2007). For a brief sketch of the background to these events, see Allan Mitchell, *A Stranger in Paris: Germany's Role in Republican France, 1870–1940* (New York and Oxford, 2006).

2. See the standard treatment of the German military administration in Paris by Umbreit, *Der Militärbefehlshaber*, pp. 1–52. In a much later overview, he emphasizes the improvised character of the Occupation. Hans Umbreit, "Die Verantwortlichkeit der Wehrmacht als Okkupationsarmee," in Rolf-Dieter Müller and Hans-Erich Volkmann (eds.), *Die Wehrmacht als Mythos und Realität* (Munich, 1999), pp. 743–53.

3. See Jäckel, *Frankreich in Hitlers Europa*, pp. 59–74.

4. See Ian Kershaw, *Hitler 1936–45: Nemesis* (New York, 2000), pp. 51–60, 87–104, 299–300 (and note 99 on p. 922). Several authors identify the date of Hitler's stop in Paris as 23 June 1940, including Jäckel, *Frankreich in Hitlers Europa*, p. 46; Pryce-Jones, *Paris in the Third Reich*, p. 13; and Diamond, *Fleeing Hitler*, p. 51.

5. Brauchitsch to O. von Stülpnagel, 20 October 1940, BA-MA Freiburg, RW 35/1.

6. See Ahlrich Meyer, *Die deutsche Besatzung in Frankreich 1940–1944. Widerstandsbekämpfung und Judenverfolgung* (Darmstadt, 2000), pp. 13–33; and Ulrich Herbert, *Best. Biographische Studien über Radikalismus, Weltanschauung und Vernunft, 1903–1989* (Bonn, 1996), pp. 251–322.

7. On Schaumburg, see Umbreit, *Der Militärbefehlshaber*, pp. 38–40. He is not mentioned by Paxton, *Vichy France*, Burrin, *La France à l'heure allemande*, or Jackson, *France: The Dark Years*. On the area detached from Schaumburg's command, see the excellent monograph by Thibault Richard, *Vivre en région parisienne sous l'Occupation. La Seine-et-Oise dans la guerre (1940–1944)* (Condé-sur-Noireau, 2004).

8. Abetz to Speidel, 22 June 1940, PA-AA Berlin, Paris 1313. Achenbach to Speidel, 22 June 1940, ibid., 1275. Streccius to Leiter der GFP, 28 June 1940, AN Paris, AJ⁴⁰, 885. See Kasten, "*Gute Franzosen*"; and Jens Banach, "Heydrichs Vertreter im Feld. Die Inspekteure, Kommandeure und Befehlshaber der Sicherheitspolizei und des SD," in Gerhard Paul and Klaus-Michael Mallmann (eds.), *Die Gestapo im Zweiten Weltkrieg. "Heimatfront" und besetztes Europa* (Darmstadt, 2000), pp. 82–99.

9. Chef der Militärverwaltung in Frankreich, Verwaltungsstab to the Vertreter der französischen Regierung, 23 September 1940, AN Paris, AJ⁴⁰, 880. "Polizeilicher Schutz für Paris," 21 October 1940, ibid. The figure of 5,000 is set by Grégory Auda, *Les Belles Années du "milieu," 1940–1944. Le grand banditisme dans la machine répressive allemande en France* (Paris, 2002), pp. 97–204. But it was only 2,400, according to Pryce-Jones, *Paris in the Third Reich*, p. 127, and 2,220 in the final phase of the Occupation, says Rita Thalmann, *La mise au pas. Idéologie et stratégie sécuritaire dans la France occupée* (Paris, 1991), p. 294. In any event, on the consequences of the shortage of German manpower in Paris, see Kasten, "*Gute Franzosen*," pp. 55–63.

10. Chef des MVB Paris, Verwaltungsstab, "Vermerk," 20 August 1940, AN Paris, AJ⁴⁰, 879. Langeron to Platzkommandanten der Stadt Paris, 21 August 1940, ibid., 880. German troops were instructed to insist on a proper salute but to do so without "excessive pettiness." Chef des Militärverwaltungsbezirks Paris, Kommandostab, "Stabsbefehl," 24 August 1940, ibid., 879. Schmid to Streccius, 2 October 1940, BA-MA Freiburg, RW 35/284. "Lagebericht des Militärbefehlshabers in Frankreich—Kommandostab—für den Monat Oktober 1940," 1 November 1940, ibid., 4.

11. Major Prinz von Ratibor, "Meldung," 12 November 1940, AN Paris, AJ⁴⁰, 876. 72. Infantrie-Division, Abt. Ic to Kommandant von Paris, Abt. Ic, 29 November 1940, ibid., 877. See Jackson, *France: The Dark Years*, p. 287.

12. Reports by Prefect of Police Langeron, 5 and 26 May 1941, AN Paris, AJ⁴⁰, 553.

13. Leitender Feldpolizeidirektor to Chef der Militärverwaltung in Frankreich, Verwaltung Paris, 2 August 1940, ibid., 885.

14. Knochen to Abetz, 12 October 1940, PA-AA Berlin, Paris 1275. Knochen to Wagner (German Quartermaster General in Fontainebleau), 15 October 1940, ibid. Schmid, "Lagebericht für den Monat Oktober 1940," 1 November 1940, BA-MA Freiburg, RW 35/285.

15. Reports by the Prefect of Police, 1 December 1940, 24 February and 23 June 1941, AN Paris, AJ⁴⁰, 553.

16. This personnel shortage led to the formulation by Werner Best that it would be German policy to develop a "supervisory administration" (*Aufsichtsverwaltung*) that left much initiative to the French. See Meyer, *Die deutsche Besatzung in Frankreich*, pp. 13–33.

17. "Bericht über einen Feuerüberfall auf die Posten vor dem Stabsgebäude des Marinegruppenkommandos West in der 43, Avenue Maréchal Fayolle am Bois de Boulogne," 13 August 1940, AN Paris, AJ⁴⁰, 888. OBH, Kommandostab, Abt. IIa, "Stabsbefehl Nr. 28/40," 16 August 1940, ibid., 439. Streccius to Bezirkschefs A, B, C, D, and Paris, 12 September 1940, ibid., 444.

18. Telegram from Abetz to AA Berlin, 30 October 1940, PA-AA Berlin, Paris 1319.

19. SD to Abetz, 11 February 1941, ibid., 1276. The same expression appeared in a simultaneous report to Berlin: Sipo-SD to Heydrich, 11 February 1941, AN Paris, AJ⁴⁰, 550. Later, "the development of the Resistance movement" was also discussed in MBF, Kommandostab, "Lagebericht für die Monate April/Mai 1941," 31 May 1941, BA-MA Freiburg, RW 35/6.

20. On Knochen, see Simon Kitson, *The Hunt for Nazi Spies: Fighting Espionage in Vichy France* (Chicago and London, 2008), pp. 16–22; Jacques Delarue, *Histoire de la Gestapo* (Paris, 1962), pp. 260–74; and Ahlrich Meyer, *Täter im Verhör. Die "Endlösung der Judenfrage" in Frankreich 1940–1944* (Darmstadt, 2005), pp. 34–43.

21. FK Paris-Ost, Abt. Ia to Chef des MVB Paris, Verwaltungsstab, 3 March 1941, AN Paris, AJ⁴⁰, 880. Kommandant von Gross-Paris, Militärverwaltungsstab to FK 528 (Tours), 13 March 1941, ibid., 888. From the vast literature treating the French police in this unfavorable light, one may well choose Maurice Rajsfus, *La police de Vichy. Les forces de l'ordre françaises au service de la Gestapo 1940/1944* (Paris, 1995); and Jean-Marc Berlière, *Les policiers français sous l'Occupation* (Paris, 2001).

22. Large clusters of such messages from police informants for the periods 8–18 November and 3–7 December 1940 may be found, for example, in AN Paris, AJ⁴⁰, 869. Many more are printed in André Halimi, *La délation sous l'Occupation*, 2nd ed. (Paris, 2003).

23. "Aktenvormerkung," 5 December 1940, CDJC Paris, LXXIX-13. See Paxton, *Vichy France*, p. 41; and Denis Peschanski, *La France des camps. L'internement, 1938–1946* (Paris, 2002), pp. 202–7.

24. Best to the Leitender Feldpolizeidirektor, 15 February 1941, AN Paris, AJ⁴⁰, 891.

25. Schaumburg to the Prefect of Police, 5 June 1941, ibid., 871.

26. Stülpnagel, "Richtlinien für die Zusammenarbeit zwischen dem Militärbefehlshaber und dem Beauftragten des Chefs der Sicherheitspolizei und des SD in Frankreich," 25 March 1941, BA-MA Freiburg, RW 35/32. See Willy Jasper, *Hotel Lutétia. Ein deutsches Exil in Paris* (Munich and Vienna, 1994), pp. 293–306.

27. Stülpnagel to Chefs der MVB A, B, C, Bordeaux, and Kommandant von Gross-Paris, 26 March 1941, BA-MA Freiburg, RW 35/548.

28. *Führererlass* (memo by Hitler), 20 November 1940, BA Koblenz, R 43/II 1440a. Stülpnagel to Abetz, 26 March 1941, PA-AA Berlin, Paris 2467. Abetz to Stülpnagel, 31 March 1941, ibid. Stülpnagel to Abetz, 3 April 1941, ibid. Abetz to Stülpnagel, 4 April 1941, ibid. See the full-length biography by Barbara Lambauer, *Otto Abetz et les Français ou l'invers de la collaboration* (Paris, 2001); and the briefer commentaries by Jäckel, *Frankreich in Hitlers Europa*, pp. 59–74; and Pascal Ory, *Les collaborateurs 1940–1945*, 2nd ed. (Paris, 1980), pp. 11–20, 36–40.

29. Stülpnagel to Abetz, 20 April 1941, PA-AA Berlin, Paris 2467. Abetz to Stülpnagel, 5 May 1941, ibid. See the self-serving depiction of these circumstances by Otto Abetz, *Das offene Problem. Ein Rückblick auf zwei Jahrzehnte deutscher Frankreichpolitik* (Cologne, 1951), pp. 132–44.

30. Stülpnagel, "Abhören nichtdeutscher Rundfunksender," 9 June 1941, PA-AA Berlin, Paris 2467.

31. "Lagebericht des Militärbefehlshabers in Frankreich—Chef des Verwaltungsstabes," 7 March and 5 April 1941, BA-MA Freiburg, RW 35/5. See Jäckel, *Frankreich in Hitlers Europa*, p. 186.

32. Kommandant von Paris, "Kommandantur-Befehl Nr. 1," 19 June 1940, AN Paris, AJ[40], 868. "Interniertenlager Drancy" to the Kommandant von Gross-Paris, Verwaltungs-Stab, 16 June 1941, ibid., 885. See Maurice Rajsfus, *Drancy. Un camp de concentration très ordinaire* (Paris, 1996), pp. 44–76; and Adam Rayski, *Le choix des juifs sous Vichy. Entre soumission et résistance* (Paris, 1992), pp. 143–64.

Chapter 2: Rules and Regulations

1. Speidel to the Prefect of the Seine, 17 June 1940, BA-MA Freiburg, RH 36/548. See Gilbert Badia, "Vivre à Paris (1939–1944). Impressions d'un témoin," in Wolfgang Drost et al. (eds.), *Paris sous l'Occupation. Paris unter deutscher Besatzung* (Heidelberg, 1995), pp. 11–22.

2. Schmid to Streccius, 2 October 1940, BA-MA Freiburg, RW 35/284.

3. Kommandant von Paris, "Kommandantur-Befehl Nr. 32," 26 July 1940, AN Paris, AJ[40], 868; "Kommandantur-Befehl Nr. 64," 2 September 1940, ibid.; and "Kommandantur-Befehl Nr. 98," 24 October 1940, BA-MA Freiburg, RH 36/31. See Eric Alary, *Les Français au quotidien 1939–1949* (Paris, 2006), pp. 147–76.

4. Kommandant der Stadt Paris, "Wichtige Anschlüsse in Paris," 21 June 1940, AN Paris, AJ[40], 879. The Hotel Ritz on the Place Vendôme was specially designated for visiting military officers from Fontainebleau and Berlin. Kommandant von Paris, Abt. Ic to Heeresgruppenkommando D, 24 October 1940, ibid., 870. See Michel, *Paris allemand*, pp. 35–42; Dominique Venner, *Histoire de la Collaboration* (Paris, 2000), pp. 130–31; and Jackson, *France: The Dark Years*, p. 169.

5. "Befehl für die Gliederung, Organisation und Sicherung im Bereich des Militärbefehlshabers Paris," 18 June 1940, AN Paris, AJ[40], 868. Brauchitsch to MBF, 19 June 1940, BA-MA Freiburg, RH 36/548.

6. Kommandant von Paris, "Kommandantur-Befehl Nr. 1," 19 June 1940, AN Paris, AJ[40], 868; "Kommandantur-Befehl Nr. 3," 21 June 1940, ibid.; and "Kommandantur-Befehl Nr. 58," 24 August 1940, ibid. Chef des MVB Paris, Verwaltungsstab, "Vermerk," 17 August 1940, ibid., 879. MBF, Verwaltungsstab to Chef des MVB Paris, 16 November

1940, ibid., 892. The smoking ban was relaxed in early 1941. Kommandant von Paris, "Kommandantur-Befehl Nr. 170," 24 February 1941, ibid., 868.

7. Kommandant von Paris, "Kokainübermittlung an dt. Offiziere und uniformierte Mädchen," 28 October 1940, ibid., 872. "Armee Tagesbefehl," 8 August 1940, ibid., 868. These scattered orders were reinforced by an edict from Hitler to all German troops in France, dated 7 July 1940, stressing that the excessive consumption of alcohol would undermine strict military discipline. Martin Moll (ed.), *Führer-Erlasse 1939–1945* (Stuttgart, 1997), p. 130.

8. Kommandant von Paris, Platzmajor, "Zur Beachtung," (?) June 1940, AN Paris, AJ⁴⁰, 868. Kommandant von Paris, "Kommandantur-Befehl Nr. 7," 25 June 1940, ibid.; and "Kommandantur-Befehl Nr. 56," 22 August 1940, ibid. Kommandant von Gross-Paris, "Kommandantur-Befehl Nr. 33," 25 April 1941, BA-MA Freiburg, RH 36/33. After assuming his new title, Schaumburg began to renumber these bulletins.

9. Keitel, "Beschlagnahmtes feindliches Staats- und Privateigentum," 9 November 1940, AN Paris, AJ⁴⁰, 879.

10. Heeresgruppendkommando B to Chef der Militärverwaltung, Kommandostab Paris, 13 August 1940, ibid., 872. Schaumburg, "Besichtigung von Paris," 30 August 1940, ibid. By September 1940, there were four *Soldatenheime* in Paris: at the Champs-Élysées, Boulevard de Sébastopol, Place Blanche (opposite the Moulin Rouge), and Boulevard St.-Michel (near the Panthéon). A fifth was soon opened beside the Eiffel Tower. Kommandant von Paris, "Kommandantur-Befehl Nr. 79," 20 September 1940, BA-MA Freiburg, RH 36/31. Later, another was added at the grand brasserie Wepler near the Place de Clichy. Kommandant von Paris, "Kommandantur-Befehl Nr. 171," 25 February 1941, AN Paris, AJ⁴⁰, 868.

11. Kommandant von Paris, Abt. Ic, "Zwischenfall in der Metro," 6 November 1940, AN Paris, AJ⁴⁰, 872. Kommandant von Paris, "Kommandantur-Befehl Nr. 122," 29 November 1940, ibid., 868.

12. Schaumburg, "Kommandantur-Befehl Nr. 8," 26 June 1940, ibid. MBF, Kommandostab, Abt. Ic, "Tagesbericht Nr. 10," 15 July 1940, BA-MA Freiburg, RH 36/562. Schaumburg, "Kommandantur-Befehl Nr. 35," 1 August 1940, AN Paris, AJ⁴⁰, 868. "Liste der in Paris für Wehrmachtsangehörige zugelassenen öffentlichen Häuser," 5 November 1940, ibid. See Insa Meinen, *Wehrmacht et prostitution sous l'Occupation (1940–1945)* (Paris, 2006), pp. 21–51, 301–14.

13. GFP 610 to Kommandant von Paris, 13 November 1940, AN Paris, AJ⁴⁰, 872. Kommandant von Paris, "Anzeige, dass deutsche Soldaten im Fairyland absteigen," 25 November 1940, ibid., 869. Schaumburg, "Kommandantur-Befehl Nr. 134," 18 December 1940, ibid., 868. See Alary, *Les Français au quotidien*, pp. 414–19; Patrick Buisson, *1940–1945 Années érotiques. Vichy ou les infortunes de la vertu* (Paris, 2008), pp. 77–108.

14. Feldpolizeikommissar to GFP, Sittenkommissariat Paris, 18 September 1940, AN Paris, AJ⁴⁰, 871.

15. Kommandant von Paris, Gruppe Heeresstreifendienst to Kommandant von Paris, Abt. Ic, 10 February 1941, ibid., 873.

16. MBF, Verwaltungs-Stab, Abt. Verwaltung, V pol, "Bekämpfung der Geschlechtskrankheiten," 1 May 1941, BA-MA Freiburg, RW 35/564. See Insa Meinen, "'Dass der Geschlechtsverkehr mit nicht kontrollierten weiblichen Personen unterbunden wird.' Zur Reglementierung der Prostitution durch die Wehrmacht in Frankreich 1940–1944," in Stefan Martens and Maurice Vaïsse (eds.), *Frankreich und Deutschland im Krieg*

(*November 1942–Herbst 1944*). *Okkupation, Kollaboration, Résistance* (Bonn, 2000), pp. 235–50; and Meinen, *Wehrmacht et prostitution*, pp. 53–114.

17. Oberquartiermeister Frankreich to MBF, Kommandostab, 23 July 1940, AN Paris, AJ⁴⁰, 549. MBF, Wirtschaftsabteilung, "Verlegung der Sperrstunde," 25 September 1940, ibid. Kommandant von Paris, "Sperrstunde für Zivilbevölkerung," 4 October 1940, ibid., 872.

18. MBF, "Abbrennen offener Feuer während der Dunkelheit," 21 October 1940, ibid., 891. Kommandant von Paris to Chef des MVB Paris, 31 December 1940, ibid., 871. Kommandant von Paris, Gruppe Heeresstreifendienst, "Aufenthalt der franz. Zivilbevölkerung in den Lokalen nach Polizeistunde," 28 January 1941, ibid., 873. MBF, "Sperrstunde für die Zivilbevölkerung und Polizeistunde im besetzten Gebiet Frankreichs," 8 February 1941, ibid., 549.

19. Memo by Lt. Dietsch, 10 November 1940, ibid., 870.

20. Feldpolizeikommissar Gierham, "Bericht: Antideutsche Kundgebungen in einem französischen Kino," 23 September 1940, ibid., 890. Leitender Feldpolizeidirektor to Chef des MVB Paris, 28 September 1940, ibid. Eugen Schwer, "Protokoll," 8 October 1940, ibid.

21. Chef des MVB Paris, "Aktenvermerk," 8 October 1940, ibid., 879. Knochen to Abetz, 12 October 1940, PA-AA Berlin, Paris 1275. Chef der Militärverwaltung, Kommandostab to Chef des MVB Paris, 17 October 1940, AN Paris, AJ⁴⁰, 889. MBF, Propaganda-Abteilung, Referat Film, "Tagesbericht für die Zeit vom 12. Juni–18. Juni 1941," 19 June 1941, BA-MA Freiburg, RW 35/221.

22. MBF, Kommandostab to Kommandant von Paris, 26 November 1940, AN Paris, AJ⁴⁰, 891. Kommandant von Paris to MBF, 16 December 1940, ibid. "Rapport sur le Service de Dératisation à Paris," 20 December 1940, ibid.

23. Bard to Kommandant von Gross-Paris, Militärverwaltungsstab, 20 May 1941, ibid. Bard replaced Langeron as Prefect of Police on 14 May 1941. See Richard Cobb, *French and Germans, Germans and French: A Personal Evaluation of Two Occupations, 1914–1918/1940–1944* (Hanover, NH, and London, 1983), pp. 128–29.

24. MBF, Kommando-Stab, Abt. Ia, "Tagesbericht Nr. 20," 25 July 1940, BA-MA Freiburg, RH 36/562; and "Tagesbericht Nr. 21," 26 July 1940, ibid. Chef des MVB Paris to Kommandant von Paris, 12 August 1940, AN Paris, AJ⁴⁰, 879. Chef der Militärverwaltung in Paris, Kommandostab, Abt. Ic, "Lagebericht für die Zeit vom 1. bis 10.8.40," 15 August 1940, BA-MA Freiburg, RW 35/302. Schwarz, "Bericht über Frankreich," 24 September 1940, ibid., RW 24/15. See Dominique Veillon, *Vivre et survivre en France, 1939–1947* (Paris, 1995), pp. 127–32; and Alary, *Les Français au quotidien*, pp. 266–71.

25. Schmid to Streccius, 2 October 1940, BA-MA Freiburg, RW 35/284.

26. OKW to AA, 5 November 1940, ibid., RW 5/358.

27. III. Infantrie-Regiment 81, Abt. Ic, "Stimmungsbericht," 24 March 1941, AN Paris, AJ⁴⁰, 874. II. Infantrie-Regiment 81, Abt. Ia, "Stimmungsbericht," 25 March 1941, ibid. I. Infantrie-Regiment 81, Abt. Ia, "Stimmungsbericht," 26 March 1941, ibid.

28. "Lagebericht des Militärbefehlshabers in Frankreich—Chef des Verwaltungsstabes—März 1941," 5 April 1941, BA-MA Freiburg, RW 35/5; and "Stimmungsbericht der Propaganda-Staffel Paris für die Zeit vom 28. März bis 5. April 1941," 5 April 1941, AN Paris, AJ⁴⁰, 873.

29. Leitender Feldpolizeidirektor (Greiner) to Kommandant der Stadt Paris, 22 July 1940, AN Paris, AJ⁴⁰, 876. Greiner to Kommandant der Stadt Paris, 21 August 1940, ibid., 877. SS-Sonderkommando Paris to Best, 27 August 1940, ibid., 550. Knochen

to Best, 7 September 1940, ibid. MBF, Verwaltungs-Stab, "Lagebericht für den Monat September 1940," 30 September 1940, ibid., 444. Knochen to Best, 8 October 1940, PA-AA Berlin, Paris 1275. Kommandant von Paris, Platzmajor to Abt. Ic, 12 January 1941, AN Paris, AJ⁴⁰, 870.

30. Knochen to Best, 21 August 1940, AN Paris, AJ⁴⁰, 550. "Lagebericht des Chefs der Militärverwaltung in Frankreich, Verwaltungsstab, für den Monat August 1940," 31 August 1940, ibid., 444. Knochen to Abetz, 24 October 1940, PA-AA Berlin, Paris 1275.

31. Greiner to Kommandant der Stadt Paris, 22 July and 21 August 1940, AN Paris, AJ⁴⁰, 876, 877.

32. Knochen to Best, 21 August and 4 September 1940, ibid., 550. "Lagebericht des Chefs der Militärverwaltung in Frankreich, Verwaltungsstab, für den Monat August 1940," 8 September 1940, PA-AA Berlin, Paris 1275.

33. Abetz, "Telephonat mit Leg. Sekr. von Grote am 18. September 1940," 19 September 1940, PA-AA Berlin, Paris 1290. Grimm, "Bericht über meine Reise nach Paris vom 15.–24. Oktober 1940," 30 October 1940, ibid., 1328.

34. "Lagebericht des Militärbefehlshabers in Frankreich—Chef des Verwaltungsstabes (für Februar 1941)," 7 March 1941, BA-MA Freiburg, RW 35/5. MBF, Kommando-Stab, Abt. Ia, "Lagebericht für die Monate April/Mai 1941," 31 May 1941, AN Paris, AJ⁴⁰, 443.

35. Schaumburg to Propaganda-Staffel Paris, 21 June 1941, AN Paris, AJ⁴⁰, 874. See Azéma, *De Munich à la Libération*, pp. 147–64.

Chapter 3: Economy and Armament

1. MBF, Wirtschaftsabteilung, "Tagesmeldung Nr. 1," 17 June 1940, AN Paris, AJ⁴⁰, 578. "Bericht über die ersten Ermittlungen betreffend die Organisation der Arbeitsverwaltung und Arbeitslosenhilfe im Départment de la Seine," 19 June 1940, ibid., 853. MBF, Wehrwirtschafts- und Rüstungsstab Frankreich, "Kriegstagebuch," 23 June 1940, BA-MA Freiburg, RW 24/1. MBF, Abt. Wi, "Tagesmeldung Nr. 17," 6 July 1940, AN Paris, AJ⁴⁰, 578. The best general study of this topic is still Alan S. Milward, *The New Order and the French Economy* (Oxford, 1970), although he is accused of reaching "exaggerated and schematic judgments" by Gregor Janssen, *Das Ministerium Speer. Deutschlands Rüstung im Krieg* (Berlin, 1968), p. 349.

2. OKW, "Wehrwirtschaftsorganisation in Frankreich," 20 June 1940, AN Paris, AJ⁴⁰, 879. MBF, Wehrwirtschafts- und Rüstungsstab Frankreich, "Kriegstagebuch. Bericht der Ereignisse," 18–22 June 1940, BA-MA Freiburg, RW 24/2. MBF, Abt. Wi, "Tagesmeldung Nr. 2–10," 20–28 June 1940, AN Paris, AJ⁴⁰, 578. MBF, Abt. Rü, "Bericht der Ereignisse," 2–3 July 1940, BA-MA Freiburg, RW 24/2.

3. "Wirtschaftsbericht über die Tätigkeit der Wirtschaftsabteilung," 1 July 1940, BA-MA Freiburg, RW 35/303. Brauchitsch, "Zusammenarbeit im Dienste der Militärverwaltung," 11 July 1940, AN Paris, AJ⁴⁰, 879. Streccius, "Zusammenarbeit im Dienste der Militärverwaltung," 11 July 1940, ibid., 449. For background, see Christian Bachelier, *La SNCF sous l'Occupation allemande, 1940–1944, Rapport documentaire*, 2 vols. (Paris, 1996).

4. MBF, Abt. Wi, "Tagesmeldung Nr. 19–23," 8–12 July 1940, AN Paris, AJ⁴⁰, 578.

5. MBF, Abt. Wi soz., "Tagesmeldung," 17 July 1940, ibid., 853. MBF, Abt. Arbeitseinsatz und Sozialwesen, "Zehntages-Meldung für die Zeit vom 1.–10.8.1940," 10 August 1940, ibid.

6. "Wirtschaftsbericht über die Tätigkeit der Wirtschaftsabteilung im Militärverwaltungsstabe des Militärbefehlshabers in Frankreich," 1 July 1940, BA-MA Freiburg, RW 35/303. MBF, Verwaltungs-Stab, Abt. Ic, "Tagesbericht Nr. 16," 21 July 1940, ibid., RH 36/562.

7. MBF, Abt. Wi, "Wirtschaftsbericht für die Zeit vom 21. bis 31. Juli 1940," 1 August 1940, ibid., RW 35/303. On the black market, see Amouroux, *La vie des français sous l'occupation*, pp. 157–84; Ian Oustry, *Occupation: The Ordeal of France 1940–1944* (London, 1997), pp. 128–32; and in general Paul Sanders, *Histoire du marché noir 1940–1946* (Paris, 2001); and Fabrice Grenard, *La France du marché noir (1940–1949)* (Paris, 2008).

8. Beauftragter für den Vierjahresplan to MBF, 16 July 1940, AN Paris, AJ⁴⁰, 835. "Erfahrungsbericht über die Anwerbearbeit in der Zeit vom 3. bis 6.8.40," 7 August 1940, ibid., 855.

9. "Vermerk über den ersten Abtransport von Landesarbeitern aus Frankreich nach Deutschland am 15.8.40," 22 August 1940, BA-MA Freiburg, RW 35/1148. "Vermerk über die Abfertigung des zweiten Transports von ausländischen Arbeitskräften von Frankreich nach Deutschland am 22.8.40," 26 August 1940, ibid. "Vermerk. Betr.: Abfertigung des dritten Transports von Ausländern nach Deutschland (aus Frankreich) am 28.8.40," 28 August 1940, ibid. "Vermerk über den 3. Abtransport," 31 August 1940, ibid. These shipments had become a daily routine by the next month: "Vermerk über die Abtransporte am Dienstag, den 3.9. und Mittwoch, den 4.9.40 von ausländischen Arbeitskräften aus Frankreich nach Deutschland," 6 September 1940, ibid.

10. MBF, Abt. Rü, "Bericht der Ereignisse," 3, 17, and 18 August 1940, ibid., RW 24/2.

11. MBF, Kommando-Stab (Speidel), "Lagebericht für den Monat September 1940," 29 September 1940, ibid., RW 35/4.

12. MBF, Abt. Rü, "Bericht der Ereignisse," 20 August 1940, ibid., RW 24/2.

13. Göring to Chef der Militärverwaltung in Frankreich, 12 September 1940, AN Paris, AJ⁴⁰, 855. Michel to MVB Chefs A, B, C, Paris, and Bordeaux, 13 September 1940, ibid., 779. MBF, Abt. Rü, "Bericht der Ereignisse," 25 September 1940, BA-MA Freiburg, RW 24/2.

14. MBF, Abt. Wi I, "Wirtschaftsbericht für September 1940," 2 October 1940, BA-MA Freiburg, RW 35/303. On Michel and the beginning of Germany's economic exploitation of France, see Fabrizio Calvi and Marc J. Masurovsky, *Le Festin du Reich. Le pillage de la France occupée 1940–1945* (Paris, 2006), pp. 241–65.

15. MBF, Wi Rü Stab Frankreich, "Bericht der Ereignisse," 11 October 1940, BA-MA Freiburg, RW 24/2.

16. Knochen to Abetz, 8 October 1940, PA-AA Berlin, Paris 1275.

17. MBF, Abt. Wi I, "Wirtschaftsbericht für September 1940," 2 October 1940; and "Wirtschaftsbericht über die Lage im Bereich des Militärbefehlshabers in Frankreich, Oktober 1940," 1 November 1940, BA-MA Freiburg, RW 35/303. MBF, Abt. Wi, "Lagebericht für den Monat November 1940," 1 December 1940; and "Wirtschaftsbericht über die Lage im Bereich des Militärbefehlshabers in Frankreich. Dezember 1940, Januar 1941," 1 February 1941, ibid.

18. Schmid to Streccius, 2 October 1940, ibid., 284. Knochen to Wagner, 17 October 1940, PA-AA Berlin, Paris 1275. MBF, Abt. Wi, "Wirtschaftsbericht über die Lage im Bereich des Militärbefehlshabers in Frankreich, Dezember 1940, Januar 1941," 1 February 1941, BA-MA Freiburg, RW 35/303.

19. Thielen, "Bericht," 31 October 1940, AN Paris, AJ⁴⁰, 859.

20. "Bericht: Werbung in Orléans," 5 December 1940, ibid. It should be recalled, moreover, that nearly a million French prisoners of war were still being held in Germany, a theme emphasized by Richard Vinen, *The Unfree French: Life under the Occupation* (New Haven, 2006), pp. 183–213.

21. Chef des Wehrwirtschafts- und Rüstungsstabes Frankreich (Barckhausen), "Einsatz ausländischer Arbeitskräfte," 31 December 1940, BA-MA Freiburg, Wi IA3/3. Telegram from the Generalquartiermeister to MBF, Wirtschaftsabteilung, 18 January 1941, AN Paris, AJ⁴⁰, 848. Michel to Lehideux, 17 February 1941, ibid., AJ⁴¹, 83. Commissariat à la lutte contre le chômage, "Compte-rendu sommaire des relations du Commissariat … avec les autorités d'occupation," 16 April 1941, ibid.

22. Michel, "Wirtschaftsbericht für September 1940," 2 October 1940, BA-MA Freiburg, RW 35/303. Schmid, "Lagebericht für den Monat September 1940," 2 October 1940, ibid., 284. MBF, Abt. Wi I, "Wirtschaftsbericht über die Lage im Bereich des Militärbefehlshabers in Frankreich. Oktober 1940," 1 November 1940, ibid., 303.

23. "Kriegstagebuch des Wirtschafts- und Rüstungsstabes Frankreich: Bericht der Ereignisse," 6 and 9 January 1941, ibid., RW 24/3. MBF, Abt. Rü, "Bericht der Ereignisse," 20 January 1940, ibid. MBF, Kommando-Stab, "Lagebericht für die Monate Dezember 1940 und Januar 1941," 31 January 1941, AN Paris, AJ⁴⁰, 443.

24. Lierau to OKW, 26 January 1941, PA-AA Berlin, Paris 1328. Lierau to AA, 7 February 1941, ibid., 1298.

25. Schaumburg, "Kommandantur-Befehl Nr. 104," 2 November 1940, AN Paris, AJ⁴⁰, 868. See Alary, *Les Français au quotidien*, pp. 209–15.

26. Chef des MVB Paris, Verwaltungs-Stab pol, "Vermerk," 19 February 1941, AN Paris, AJ⁴⁰, 890.

27. MBF, Abt. Rü, "Bericht der Ereignisse," 21 January 1941, BA-MA Freiburg, RW 24/3.

28. MBF, Abt. Rü, "Bericht der Ereignisse," 3 February and 26 March 1941, ibid.

29. MBF, Abt. Wi VII, "Richtlinien für die Anwerbung von Arbeitskräften im Bereich des Militärbefehlshabers in Frankreich," 15 April 1941, ibid., RW 35/1352.

30. Kommandant von Gross-Paris, Militärverwaltungsstab to MBF, Abt. Arbeitseinsatz und Sozialwesen, 25 April 1941 and *passim*, AN Paris, AJ⁴⁰, 857. AGO Flugzeugwerke to MBF, Abt. Wi VII, 9 May 1941, ibid.

31. MBF, Kommando-Stab, Abt. Ia, "Lagebericht für die Monate April/Mai 1941," Anlage 11, 31 May 1941, ibid., 443.

32. "Kraftfahrzeug-Erzeugung in den französischen Kraftfahrzeug-Fabriken. Verteilung auf Wehrmacht und ziviler Sektor. Juli 1940 bis 31. März 1941," 31 March 1941, PA-AA Berlin, Paris 2404.

33. Göring to Brauchitsch, 29 March 1941, AN Paris, AJ⁴⁰, 874.

34. MBF, Abt. Rü, "Bericht der Ereignisse," 28 and 31 May, 2 June 1941, BA-MA Freiburg, RW 24/3. Telegram from Abetz to AA, 5 June 1941, PA-AA Berlin, Paris 1315.

Chapter 4: Culture and Propaganda

1. On "glittering Paris" of the Occupation years, see Michel, *Paris allemand*, pp. 315–46; Jackson, *France: The Dark Years*, pp. 310–16; and Serge Added, "L'euphorie théâtrale dans Paris occupé," in Jean-Pierre Rioux (ed.), *La vie culturelle sous Vichy* (Paris, 1990), pp. 315–48.

2. MBF, Kommando-Stab, Abt. Ic, "Tagesbericht Nr. 1," 6 July 1940, BA-MA Freiburg, RH 36/562. MBF, Propaganda-Abteilung, Untergruppe Theater, "Tätigkeitsbericht für die Zeit vom 14.–19. November 1940," 19 November 1940, AN Paris, AJ⁴⁰, 1001. Kommandant von Paris, "Kommandantur-Befehl Nr. 131," 12 December 1940, ibid., 868.

3. Epting to AA, 21 December 1940, PA-AA Berlin, Paris 1380. See Eckard Michels, *Das Deutsche Institut in Paris 1940–1944* (Stuttgart, 1993), pp. 18–43; Frank-Rutger Haussmann, *"Auch im Krieg schweigen die Musen nicht." Die deutschen wissenschaftlichen Institute im Zweiten Weltkrieg* (Göttingen, 2001), pp. 100–30; and Barbara Lambauer, "Otto Abetz, inspirateur et catalyseur de la collaboration culturelle," in Albrecht Betz and Stefan Martens (eds.), *Les intellectuals et l'Occupation 1940–1944. Collaborer, partir, résister* (Paris, 2004), pp. 64–89.

4. Kommandant von Paris, "Kommandantur-Befehl Nr. 139," 30 December 1940; and "Kommandantur-Befehl Nr. 171," 25 February 1941, AN Paris, AJ⁴⁰, 868. See Kathrin Engel, *Deutsche Kulturpolitik im besetzten Paris 1940–1944. Film und Theater* (Munich, 2003), pp. 240–325.

5. Kommandant von Paris, "Kommandantur-Befehl Nr. 112," 13 November 1940; and "Kommandantur-Befehl Nr. 136," 21 December 1940, AN Paris, AJ⁴⁰, 868.

6. Kommandant von Paris, "Kommandantur-Befehl Nr. 63," 30 August 1940; "Kommandantur-Befehl Nr. 67," 5 September 1940; "Kommandantur-Befehl Nr. 68," 6 September 1940; and "Kommandantur-Befehl Nr. 76," 16 September 1940, BA-MA Freiburg, RH 36/31. Kommandant von Paris, "Kommandantur-Befehl Nr. 123," 30 November 1940, AN Paris, AJ⁴⁰, 868.

7. MBF, Propaganda-Abteilung to Propaganda-Staffel Paris, 19 November 1940, AN Paris, AJ⁴⁰, 1002. "Aufstellung über Variétés, Music-Halls usw.," 1941, ibid., 1004. Kommandant von Paris, Abt. Ia to Propaganda-Staffel Paris, 27 February 1941, ibid., 879.

8. DB (Rahn) to Kommandant von Paris, 31 August 1940, PA-AA Berlin, Paris 1339. Rahn and Abetz to AA, 15 October 1940, ibid., 1319. Knochen to Abetz, 22 October 1940, ibid., 1275. "Bericht über die Freimaurerei in Paris," sent by DB to AA, 8 December 1940, ibid., 2497.

9. Epting to AA, 9 April 1941, ibid., 1380. See Michels, *Das Deutsche Institut*, p. 90.

10. Minutes kept by Achenbach (DB), "Unterredung am 13.8.40 mit Major Schmidtke," 13 August 1940, CDJC Paris, LXXI-30. Abetz to Ribbentrop, 14 August 1940, ibid., 31.

11. Telegram from Abetz to Ribbentrop, 22 August 1940, ibid., 36. Kolb to Abetz, 29 August 1940, PA-AA Berlin, Paris 1294. Memorandum by Hitler, 20 November 1940, BA Koblenz, R 43/II 1440a.

12. Keitel to Heydrich, 5 July 1940, AN Paris, AJ⁴⁰, 569. Keitel to Brauchitsch, 17 September 1940, ibid., 459. Memo by Göring, 5 November 1940, ibid. See Michel Rayssac, *L'exode des musées. Histoire des oeuvres d'art sous l'Occupation* (Paris, 2007), pp. 188–89, 208–13, 239–42.

13. Abetz to Stülpnagel, 9 March 1941, PA-AA Berlin, Paris 1321. Schmid to DB, 17 March 1941, ibid. Walter Bargatsky, *Hotel Majestic. Ein Deutscher im besetzten Frankreich* (Freiburg, 1987), pp. 64–80. See Pryce-Jones, *Paris in the Third Reich*, pp. 88–93; Engel, *Deutsche Kulturpolitik im besetzten Paris*, pp. 111–38; and the chapter entitled "Vols de guerre. Les Nazis et les archives françaises (1940–1944)," in Sophie Coeuré, *La mémoire spoliée. Les archives des Français, butin de guerre nazi puis soviétique* (Paris, 2007), pp. 12–58.

14. GFP (Greiner) to Kommandant der Stadt Paris, 21 August 1940, AN Paris, AJ⁴⁰, 877. Best, "Verbot des Abhörens ausländischer Sender," 13 September 1940, BA-MA Freiburg, RW 35/537. "Lagebericht des Militärbefehlshabers in Frankreich—Kommandostab—für den Monat Oktober 1940," 1 November 1940, ibid., 4. "Tätigkeitsbericht der Prop. Abt. Frankreich für die Zeit vom 16.–22.12.1940," 23 December 1940, AN Paris, AJ⁴⁰, 1001. See Aurélie Luneau, *Radio Londres. Les voix de la liberté (1940–1944)* (Paris, 2005), pp. 106–23.

15. "Tätigkeitsbericht der Prop. Abt. Frankreich für die Zeit vom 7.–13.10.1940," 14 October 1940, AN Paris, AJ⁴⁰, 1001. MBF, Verwaltungs-Stab, Wirtschaftsabteilung, 5 November 1940, ibid., 891. Office des Papiers de Presse et d'Éditions, "Mars 1941: État des livraisons faites aux quotidiens," 7 April 1941, ibid., 1013. See Venner, *Histoire de la Collaboration*, pp. 168–72.

16. These lists are contained in AN Paris, AJ⁴⁰, 1006.

17. "Liste Otto: ouvrages retirés de la vente par les éditeurs ou interdits par les autorités allemandes," (?) September 1940, PA-AA Berlin, Paris 1211. MBF, Verwaltungs-Stab, Gruppe Schrifttum, "T[ätigkeits]-Bericht über die Zeit vom 29.8.–5.9.1940 einschliesslich," 5 September 1940, AN Paris, AJ⁴⁰, 1005. Gruppe Schrifttum, "T-Bericht über die Zeit vom 6.9.–12.9.1940 einschliesslich," 12 September 1940, ibid. Gruppe Schrifttum, "T-Bericht für die Zeit vom 13.9.–18.9.," 18 September 1940, ibid. Feldpolizeikommissar to the MBF, Verwaltungs-Stab, 23 September 1940, ibid., 569. See Pascal Fouché, *L'édition française sous l'Occupation*, 2 vols. (Paris, 1987), 1:19–37; and Venner, *Histoire de la Collaboration*, pp. 178–86.

18. Epting, "Aufzeichnung" (for Abetz), 6 November 1940, PA-AA Berlin, Paris 1374.

19. MBF, Verwaltungs-Stab, Gruppe Schrifttum, "Tätigkeitsbericht für die Zeit vom 31.10.–6.11.40," 7 November 1940, AN Paris, AJ⁴⁰, 1005. "Die Massnahmen der deutschen Militärverwaltung zur Bereinigung der französischen Lehrbücher von deutschfeindlichem Inhalt," (?) December 1940, ibid., 558. MBF, Verwaltungs-Stab, Abt.V to Best, 9 December 1940, ibid., 559.

20. Telegram from Abetz to AA, 3 January 1941, PA-AA Berlin, Paris 1276. Abetz to AA, 15 January 1941, CDJC Paris, LXXI-50.

21. "Tätigkeitsbericht der Prop. Abtg. Frankreich für die Zeit vom 8.1.–25.1.1941," 27 January 1941, CDJC Paris, LXXV-97.

22. "Statistique des étudiants au 31 juillet 1939," 31 July 1939, AN Paris, F¹⁷, 13380. "Différence entre le pourcentage du nombre des étudiants au 31 décembre 1940 et celui du nombre des étudiants au 31 décembre 1939," 31 December 1940, ibid., AJ⁴⁰, 566.

23. Memo by MBF, Verwaltungs-Stab, Abt. Verwaltung, V Kult 426 (Dahnke), 23 August 1940, ibid., AJ⁴⁰, 566. Epting to Südhoff, 20 September 1940, ibid. Dahnke to Referat Schule und Kultur, 30 September 1940, ibid.

24. Fanal to Roy, 31 October 1940, ibid., F¹⁷, 13385. MBF, Verwaltungs-Stab, Abt. Verwaltung, Referat V Kult to the Délégué du gouvernement français (Boissieu), 31 October 1940, ibid. Roy to MBF, 9 November 1940, ibid. Roy to Best, 31 January 1941, ibid. The three professors were Paul Langevin, Ernest Tonnelat, and Henri Wallon. Only Langevin, a close family friend and personal mentor of Frédéric Joliot, was imprisoned. On Joliot, see note 29, this chapter.

25. Dahnke to Boissieu, (?) October 1940, AN Paris, AJ⁴⁰, 566.

26. Memo from MBF, Verwaltungs-Stab, Abt. Verwaltung, Referat V Kult, "École libre des sciences politiques," 3 October 1940, ibid. Knochen to Dahnke, 7 December

1940, ibid., 567. NSDAP, Leiter des Einsatzstabes (Rosenberg) von Behr to the Chef der Militärverwaltung, 5 March 1941, CDJC Paris, LXXVII-2.

27. Memo by OBH, Verwaltungs-Stab (Fuchs), 24 October 1940, AN Paris, AJ⁴⁰, 556. Memo by Schmid (V Kult), "Behandlung des deutschfeindlichen Schrifttums in den öffentlichen wissenschaftlichen Bibliotheken," 9 December 1940, ibid., 569. See Jackson, *France: The Dark Years*, p. 190.

28. Epting to Südhoff, 20 September 1940, AN Paris, AJ⁴⁰, 566. "Lagebericht der Gruppe 4 (Schule und Kultur) für den Monat März 1941," 29 March 1941, ibid., 556. Knochen to MBF, Kommando-Stab, Abt. Ic, 15 April 1941, ibid., 566. Carcopino to the Recteurs des Académies, 7 June 1941, ibid., F¹⁷, 13384. Memo by Dahnke, 14 June 1941, ibid., AJ⁴⁰, 556.

29. "Rapport de M. Joliot Curie," 17 (or 18?) August 1940, ibid., F¹⁷, 13385. Ministère de l'Instruction Publique et des Beaux-Arts, "Message téléphonique," 19 August 1940, ibid. Best to the Collège de France, 16 September 1940, ibid. For an appraisal rather favorable to Joliot, see Nicolas Chevassus-au-Louis, *Savants sous l'Occupation. Enquête sur la vie scientifique française entre 1940 et 1944* (Paris, 2004), pp. 97–113; and for a more critical version of the story, see Burrin, *La France à l'heure allemande*, pp. 315–22. Also see the biography by Michel Pinault, *Frédéric Joliot-Curie* (Paris, 2001); and the balanced commentary by Gabriele Metzler, "Wissenschaft im Krieg. Frédéric Joliot-Curie und die deutschen Besatzer am Collège de France," in Martens and Vaïsse (eds.), *Frankreich und Deutschland im Krieg*, pp. 685–700.

30. Boissieu to the Ministère de l'Instruction Publique, 23 September 1940, AN Paris, F¹⁷, 13385. Ministère de l'Instruction Publique, "Note sur l'occupation des laboratoires de M. Joliot," 11 October 1940, ibid. Boissieu to MBF, 17 October 1940, ibid. Boissieu to Chef der MVF, 19 October 1940, ibid., AJ⁴⁰, 558. Boissieu, "Note verbale," 19 October 1940, ibid. MBF, Verwaltungs-Stab, Abt. V to OBH, Generalquartiermeister, 5 November 1940, ibid.

31. OBH to MBF, Verwaltungs-Stab, 11 November 1940, ibid., AJ⁴⁰, 558. OBH to Rüst (Forschungsabteilung), 13 November 1940, ibid. Schmid to Boissieu, 18 January 1941, ibid., F¹⁷, 13385.

32. Professor Kienle, "Bericht über eine Reise nach Paris," 7 May 1941, sent from Berlin by the Reichsminister für Wissenschaft, Erziehung und Volksbildung to MBF, Verwaltungs-Stab (Dahnke), 10 June 1941, ibid., AJ⁴⁰, 567.

33. Chef der Militärverwaltung in Frankreich, Kommando-Stab, Abt. Ic, "Lagebericht für die Zeit vom 1. bis 10.8.40," 15 August 1940, BA-MA Freiburg, RW 35/302. "Lagebericht des Militärbefehlshabers in Frankreich—Kommando-Stab—für den Monat Oktober 1940," 1 November 1940, ibid., 4. OKW to AA, 14 November 1940, ibid., 358.

34. "Lagebericht für den Monat November 1940," 3 December 1940, ibid., 4. Telegram from Abetz to AA, 13 December 1940, PA-AA Berlin, Paris 1372. Speidel, "Politische Lage in Frankreich," 25 January 1941, BA-MA Freiburg, RW 35/238. SD to Abetz, 11 February 1941, PA-AA Berlin, Paris 1276. See Jacques Duquesne, *Les catholiques français sous l'occupation*, 2nd ed. (Paris, 1996), pp. 180–84.

35. Memo by the Chef der Militärverwaltung, Kommando-Stab, Abt. Ic, 6 October 1940, AN Paris, AJ⁴⁰, 891. Stülpnagel, "Jugendorganisationen und Vereinspolizei," 18 November 1940, BA-MA Freiburg, RW 49/110. Best to Boissieu, 14 June 1941, AN Paris, F¹⁷, 13374.

36. MBF, Kommando-Stab, "Lagebericht Februar 1941," 7 March 1941, AN Paris, AJ⁴⁰, 443. "Lagebericht des Militärbefehlshabers in Frankreich—Chef des Verwaltungsstabes

(für Februar 1941)," 7 March 1941, BA-MA Freiburg, RW 35/5. MBF, Kommando-Stab, "Lagebericht für die Monate April/Mai 1941," 31 May 1941, ibid., 6.

37. Abetz, "Politische Arbeit in Frankreich," 30 July 1940, CDJC Paris, LXXI-28.

38. DB to AA, 11 October 1940, PA-AA Berlin, Paris 1125 A. Schleier (DB) to Speidel, 30 October 1940, ibid., 1275. Memo from Braeckow (Ministry of Propaganda, Berlin) to Major Schmidtke, 14 November 1940, sent by Schleier to Luther (AA), 28 November 1940, ibid. See Albert Betz, "Die 'geistige Führung in Europa' erringen? Selbstinszenierungen des Dritten Reichs im Paris der Okkupation," in Martens and Vaïsse (eds.), *Frankreich und Deutschland im Krieg*, pp. 649–57; Thalmann, *La mise au pas*, pp. 129–95; and the chapter entitled "La haute couture à l'heure allemande" in Dominique Veillon, *La Mode sous l'Occupation*, 2nd ed. (Paris, 2001), pp. 141–75.

39. Schmid (Verwaltungs-Stab), "Lagebericht für den Monat Oktober 1940," 1 November 1940, BA-MA Freiburg, RW 35/285. Lierau to AA, (?) May 1941, PA-AA Berlin, Paris 1144 Z.

40. "Wochenbericht der Filmprüfstelle. Verbotene Filme vom 27. Februar bis zum 5. März 1941," 5 March 1941, AN Paris, AJ[40], 871. MBF, Propaganda-Abteilung, Referat Film, "Tätigkeitsbericht für die Zeit vom 5. März–12.März 1941," 12 March 1941, BA-MA Freiburg, RW 35/220. Telegram from Epting to AA, 25 March 1941, PA-AA Berlin, Paris 1381. MBF, Propaganda-Abteilung, Referat Film, "Tätigkeitsbericht für die Zeit vom 1. Mai–7. Mai 1941," 7 May 1941, BA-MA Freiburg, RW 35/221. See David Welch (ed.), *Nazi Propaganda: The Power and the Limitations* (London, 1983), pp. 284–92; Venner, *Histoire de la Collaboration*, pp. 188–91; Engel, *Deutsche Kulturpolitik im besetzten Paris*, pp. 337–401; and Jackson, *France: The Dark Years*, pp. 318–26.

41. Sipo-SD to Best, 29 August 1940, AN Paris, AJ[40], 550.

42. "Besprechung in der Deutschen Botschaft," 7 January 1941, ibid., 551.

43. Prefect of Police Langeron to Dr. Kiessel, 14 December 1940, CDJC Paris, LXXIX-14/15. MBF, Kommando-Stab, Abt. Ic to Verwaltungs-Stab, 13 January 1941, AN Paris, AJ[40], 551. AA to Abetz, 6 February 1941, PA-AA Berlin, Paris 1301. Schleier to AA, 27 May 1941, ibid.

44. MBF, Verwaltungs-Stab to Chefs der MVB A, B, C, and Bordeaux, 29 March 1941, AN Paris, AJ[40], 876. Schleier to AA, 18 June 1941, PA-AA Berlin, Paris 1273.

45. "Aktennotiz über die Besprechung bei Generalfeldmarschall von Brauchitsch im Hotel Ritz in Paris am 16. Oktober 1940, 15.30 Uhr," 16 October 1940, AN Paris, AJ[40], 459. Kommandant von Gross-Paris, Militärverwaltungsstab to DB, 7 March 1941, PA-AA Berlin, Paris 1313. Schleier to AA, 23 April 1941, ibid., 1315. Best to DB, 23 April 1941, ibid.

46. Knochen, "Ereignismeldung," 16 November 1940, PA-AA Berlin, Paris 1328. OKW, Amt Ausland/Abwehr, "Aussen- und militärpolitische Nachrichten," 7 January 1941, BA-MA Freiburg, RW 5/354. II. Infantrie Regiment 81, Abt. Ia, "Stimmungs-bericht," 27 January 1941, AN Paris, AJ[40], 873. "Tätigkeitsbericht der Prop. Abtg. Frankreich für die Zeit vom 8.1.–25.1.1941," 27 January 1941, ibid., 1001. Report of the Prefecture of Police, 3 February 1941, ibid., 553.

47. "Lagebericht vom 16. August 1940," 20 August 1940, AN Paris, AJ[40], 550. SD to Abetz, 26 October, 2 November, and 24 December 1940, 11 February 1941, PA-AA Berlin, Paris 1275–1276.

48. Prefecture of Police to the Kommandant von Gross-Paris, 28 April and 1 May 1941, AN Paris, AJ[40], 882. Kommandant von Gross-Paris, Militärverwaltungsstab to MBF, Kommando-Stab, Abt. Ic, 29 May 1941, ibid., 877. Prefecture of Police, "Die kommunistische Propaganda," 3 June 1941, ibid., 553.

Chapter 5: Germans and Jews

1. See Peschanski, *La France des camps*, pp. 164–70.

2. "Aktennotiz über Aussprache mit dem Einsatzstab Rosenberg," 28 August 1940, AN Paris, AJ[40], 569. "Aktion der Deutschen Botschaft zur Sicherung von Kunstschätzen," 9 September 1940, BA-MA Freiburg, RW 35/698. "Vermerk" (initialed by Stülpnagel), 13 September 1940, ibid. Best, "Vorstellung der französischen Regierung gegen die Erfassung des jüdischen Kunstbesitzes," 15 January 1941, ibid. Stülpnagel to Brauchitsch, 31 January 1941, ibid., 1. See Anne Grynberg, *Les camps de la honte. Les internés juifs des camps français, 1939–1944* (Paris, 1991), pp. 141–45.

3. Bremer, "Aufzeichnung für den Herrn Botschafter," 7 March 1941, PA-AA Berlin, Paris 1321. Scheid to Schleier, 17 March 1941, ibid., 1283. Utikal, "Bericht über die Tätigkeit des Einsatzstabes der Dienststellen des Reichsleiters Rosenberg für die westlichen besetzten Gebiete und die Niederlande in Frankreich," 20 March 1941, BA-MA Freiburg, RW 35/705.

4. Chef der Militärverwaltung in Frankreich, Verwaltungs-Stab to Bezirkschefs, Feldkommandanten, and Kreiskommandanten, 27 September and 7 October 1940, AN Paris, AJ[40], 536. Chef der Militärverwaltung, Verwaltungs-Stab, Abt. V (Albrecht), "Identitätskarten für Juden," 7 October 1940, ibid., 548. Armee-Kommando 2, Abt. Ic, "Massnahmen gegen jüdische Geschäfte," 14 October 1940, ibid., 872. Langeron to Chef des MVB Paris, 26 October 1940, CDJC Paris, LXXIX-10. Chef des MVB Paris to MBF, Verwaltungs-Stab, 14 November 1940, ibid. Schleier to AA, 23 November 1940, PA-AA Berlin, Paris 1318. On Vichy's anti-Semitic legislation, see Venner, *Histoire de la Collaboration*, pp. 122–23. It appears likely that there were about 300,000 Jews in France, of whom two-thirds resided in Paris. See Peschanski, *La France des camps*, pp. 21–33.

5. See Philippe Verheyde, "L'aryanisation économique. Le cas des grandes entreprises," in Georges Bensoussan, (ed.), *Aryanisation. Le vol légalisé* (Paris, 2000), pp. 7–30 (published in the *Revue d'Histoire de la Shoah*, N°. 168), based on Verheyde's doctoral dissertation, *Les mauvais comptes de Vichy. L'aryanisation des entreprises juives* (Paris, 1999).

6. Prefect of Police to Chef des MVB Paris, Verwaltungs-Stab, 20 December 1940, AN Paris, AJ[40], 890. "Aufzeichnung betr. Zentrales Judenamt in Paris," 28 February 1941, PA-AA Berlin, Nachlass Schleier, II. See the comprehensive parliamentary report by René Rémond, *Le "Fichier Juif"* (Paris, 1996); Peschanski, *La France des camps*, pp. 175–83; Delarue, *Histoire de la Gestapo*, pp. 276–78; and Claudia Steur, *Theodor Dannecker. Ein Funktionär der Endlösung* (Essen, 1997), pp. 45–91. On the "twisted road" of French anti-Semitic tendencies before 1940 and of self-motivated later initiatives by Vichy against Jews in France, sometimes without German prodding, see the chapter entitled "The Path to Vichy" in Vicki Caron, *Uneasy Asylum: France and the Jewish Refugee Crisis, 1933–1942* (Stanford, 1999), pp. 321–53.

7. Chef der Militärverwaltung in Frankreich, Militärverwaltung Paris to the Prefecture of Police, 24 July 1940, AN Paris, AJ[40], 885.

8. MBF, Kommando-Stab, Abt. Ia, "Auszugsweise Abschrift aus dem Lagebericht ... für den Monat Februar 1941," 7 March 1941, ibid., 553.

9. "Lagebericht des Militärbefehlshabers in Frankreich—Chef des Verwaltungsstabes (für Februar 1941)," 7 March 1941, BA-MA Freiburg, RW 35/5.

10. "Israëlites envoyés le 14 mai 1941 dans des camps de concentration du départment du Loiret," 14 May 1941, CDJC Paris, LXXVII-12. MBF, Kommando-Stab, "Lagebericht

für die Monate April/Mai 1941," 31 May 1941, BA-MA Freiburg, RW 35/6. GFP to the Chef der Militärverwaltung, 6 June 1941, AN Paris, AJ⁴⁰, 885. Memo entitled "Israëlites étrangers internés au Centre des Tourelles," sent by François (Prefecture of Police) to the Kommandant von Gross-Paris, 17 June 1941, CDJC Paris, LXXVII-19. Later memos from François gave additional statistics for July 1941, ibid.

11. Best, "Die Behandlung der Juden im besetzten Gebiet," 19 August 1940, AN Paris, AJ⁴⁰, 548. On the role of Abetz and the German Embassy in the Jewish question, see Meyer, *Täter im Verhör*, pp. 23–34.

12. MBF, Abt. Wi, quoted in a memo by the Verwaltungsabteilung, 8 August 1940, AN Paris, AJ⁴⁰, 890.

13. MBF, Verwaltungs-Stab, Abt. V (Mahnke), "Die Behandlung von Juden im besetzten Gebiet," 22 August 1940, ibid., 548. MBF, Verwaltungs-Stab, Abt. V (Bardenheuer), "Behandlung der Juden im besetzten Gebiet," 27 August 1940, ibid.

14. Storz, "Massnahmen gegen Juden im besetzten Gebiet," (?) September 1940, CDJC Paris, XXIV-5a.

15. Best, "Die Verordnung über die Behandlung der Juden im besetzten Frankreich," 18 September 1940, AN Paris, AJ⁴⁰, 548. Heydrich to Luther, 24 September 1940, PA-AA Berlin, Nachlass Schleier, II.

16. Dannecker, "Zentrales Judenamt in Paris," 21 January 1941, CDJC Paris, V-59. Knochen to Best, 28 January 1941, ibid., 63. On the post-war testimony of these two personalities, see Meyer, *Täter im Verhör*, pp. 34–66.

17. Sipo-SD, Dienststelle Paris to Heydrich, 11 February 1941, AN Paris, AJ⁴⁰, 550.

18. MBF, Verwaltungs-Stab, Abt. V (Mahnke), "Weitere Behandlung der Judenfrage in Frankreich," 3 February 1941, ibid., 548.

19. Telegram from Schleier to AA, 24 March 1941, PA-AA Berlin, Paris 1318.

20. Telegram from Abetz to AA, 3 April 1941, ibid.

21. Best to Stülpnagel, 4 April 1941, AN Paris, AJ⁴⁰, 548.

22. MBF, Verwaltungs-Stab, Abt. Wi I, "Wirtschaftsbericht für September 1940," 2 October 1940, BA-MA Freiburg, RW 35/303. "Aktennotiz der Besprechung bei Generalfeldmarschall von Brauchitsch im Hotel Ritz in Paris," 16 October 1940, AN Paris, AJ⁴⁰, 459. Brauchitsch to Stülpnagel, 12 November 1940, BA-MA Freiburg, RW 35/2.

23. Stülpnagel, "Instruktion für die Kommissarischen Verwalter jüdischer Unternehmen," 12 November 1940, AN Paris, AJ⁴⁰, 614.

24. Blanke, "Explication … au sujet de la note concernant le projet de nouvelles ordonnances concernant les juifs," (?) December 1940, AN Paris, AJ³⁸, 592. MBF, Verwaltungs-Stab, "Lagebericht für den Monat November 1940," 3 December 1940, BA-MA Freiburg, RW 35/4.

25. Blanke to Service du Contrôle, 8 February 1941, AN Paris, AJ³⁸, 338.

26. This history was later outlined in "Mémoire sur la situation des agents du Commissariat Général aux Questions Juives," 6 March 1944, ibid., 1. See Aurélie Audeval et al., "Arisierungsnetzwerke'. Akteurskonstellationen, Arbeitsteilung und Interessenkonflikte bei der 'Arisierung' grösserer Unternehmen in Frankreich 1940-1944," *Francia* 32, no. 3 (2005): 101–38.

27. Best, "Betreff.: den französischen Generalkommissar für Judenfragen Xavier Vallat," 5 April 1941, CDJC Paris, XXIV-15. Blanke to Villoutreys de Brignse, 18 April 1941, AN Paris, AJ³⁸, 339. On Vallat, see Michael Marrus and Robert O. Paxton, *Vichy France and the Jews* (New York, 1981), pp. 75–119; and Caron, *Uneasy Asylum*, pp. 328–30.

28. Directeur Général de la Police Municipale (Paris) to the Prefecture of Police, 20 August 1940, CDJC Paris, LXXIX-5. Knochen to Best, 21 August 1940, AN Paris, AJ⁴⁰, 550.

29. Chef des MVB Paris, Verwaltungs-Stab, "Vermerkung," 1 September 1940, CDJC Paris, LXXIXa-4.

Chapter 6: The Hostage Crisis

1. Prefect of Police, "Bericht über die Auswirkung des Kriegsbeginns gegen Russland auf die Pariser Bevölkerung," 24 June 1941, sent by the Kommandant von Gross-Paris to MBF, Kommando-Stab, Abt. Ic, 26 June 1941, AN Paris, AJ⁴⁰, 871. Reports from the Prefect of Police to the Kommandant von Gross-Paris, 30 June and 15 July 1941, ibid., 882.

2. Commissaire de Police de la circonscription d'Ivry-sur-Seine to Chef de la Feldkommandantur, 4 July 1941, ibid., 874. Prefect of Police, circonscription d'Aubervilliers to Kreiskommandant of St. Denis, 6 July 1941, ibid. Direction des renseignments généraux et des jeux, "Die kommunistische Propaganda," 7 July 1941, ibid., 877. Prefect of Police, "Die kommunistische Propaganda," 8 July 1941, ibid., 553. See Meyer, *Die deutsche Besatzung*, pp. 54–82.

3. Keitel, "Aussetzung der Vollstreckung von Todesurteilen gegen franz. Staatsangehörige," 30 June 1941, BA-MA Freiburg, RW 35/1.

4. Report by the Prefect of Police, "Die Gaullistische Propaganda," 21 July 1941, sent by Kommandant von Gross-Paris to MBF, Kommando-Stab, Abt. Ic, 22 July 1941, AN Paris, AJ⁴⁰, 871. MBF, Kommando-Stab, "Lagebericht für die Monate Juni/Juli 1941," 31 July 1941, BA-MA Freiburg, RW 35/7.

5. Reports by the Prefect of Police, "Die kommunistischen Umtriebe," 11, 18, and 25 August 1941, AN Paris, AJ⁴⁰, 553.

6. Sipo-SD, Dienststelle Paris, "Kommunistische Demonstrationen am 13.8.1941 in Paris," 14 August 1941, ibid., 875. Schleier to AA, 16 August 1941, PA-AA Berlin, Paris 1314. Bard to Schaumburg, 6 September 1941, AN Paris, AJ⁴⁰, 881.

7. Stülpnagel to Abetz, 4 August 1941, PA-AA Berlin, Paris 2467. MBF, Verwaltungs-Stab, "Einleitung schärferer Massnahmen zur Bekämpfung des Kommunismus durch die franz. Regierung," 11 August 1941, AN Paris, AJ⁴⁰, 553. Stülpnagel, "Bekämpfung des Kommunismus," 15 August 1941, CDJC Paris, VIII-2.

8. Memo by Schaumburg, 18 August 1941, BA-MA Freiburg, RW 36/34.

9. Stülpnagel, "Tagesbefehl Nr. 18/41," 18 August 1941, AN Paris, AJ⁴⁰, 871. Schaumburg to MBH Paris, Verwaltungs-Stab, 21 August 1941, ibid. "Bekanntmachung," 22 August 1941, BA-MA Freiburg, RW 35/539.

10. Telegram from Schaumburg to Wagner, 22 August 1941, BA-MA Freiburg, RW 35/539.

11. MBF, Kommando-Stab, Abt. Ic, "Fernmündlich von VOVF, 17.8., 18.45 Uhr," 27 August 1941, AN Paris, AJ⁴⁰, 553.

12. "Drei Kommunisten hingerichtet," *Pariser Zeitung*, 28 August 1941, ibid., 444. "3 agitateurs communistes condamnés à mort," *Le Matin*, 29 August 1941, ibid., 553.

13. Best, "Kommunistenbekämpfung," 30 August 1941, BA-MA Freiburg, RW 35/539. Speidel and Schmid to Brinon, 3 September 1941, ibid.

14. "Lagebericht des Beauftragten des Chefs der Sicherheitspolizei und des SD," 4 September 1941, AN Paris, AJ⁴⁰, 553. "Avis," *Le Matin*, 6 September 1941, ibid., 550. List

of executions sent by MBF, Kommando-Stab, Abt. Ic to the Militärverwaltungsstab, 21 October 1941, ibid., 871. See Sven Olaf Berggötz, "Ernst Jünger und die Geiseln. Die Denkschrift von Ernst Jünger über die Geiselerschiessungen in Frankreich 1941/42," *Vierteljahrsheft für Zeitgeschichte* 51 (2003): 404–72.

15. MBF, Verwaltungs-Stab, Abt. Verwaltung, "Sühnemassnahmen anlässlich der Ermordung eines Wehrmachtsangehörigens (Fall Moser)," 11 September 1941, BA-MA Freiburg, RW 35/539.

16. Keitel, "Kommunistische Aufstandsbewegung in den besetzten Gebieten," 16 September 1941, ibid., 536. Kommandant von Gross-Paris, "Kommandantur-Befehl Nr. 129," 19 September 1941, AN Paris, AJ[40], 868. MBF, Verwaltungs-Stab, Abt. Verwaltung (Bälz), "Staatsgerichtshof: Aburteilung von Kommunisten," 23 September 1941, BA-MA Freiburg, RW 35/539. Kommandant von Gross-Paris, Kommando-Stab, Abt. Ia, "Lage- und Tätigkeitsbericht für die Zeit vom 14.9.–12.11.41," 17 November 1941, AN Paris, AJ[40], 875.

17. Speidel, "Note des franz. Polizeipräfekten, Admiral Bard, über die Tätigkeit der Polizei," 25 September 1941, AN Paris, AJ[40], 444.

18. "Noms de 27 otages fusillés le 22 octobre 1941," 22 October 1941, ibid., AJ[72], 260. Stülpnagel, "Aufzeichnung über meine telephonische Rücksprache mit Generalmajor Wagner am 22.10.," 23 October 1941, BA-MA Freiburg, RW 35/1.

19. Bälz to Best, 24 October 1941, BA-MA Freiburg, RW 35/308.

20. Abetz, "Attentate gegen deutsche Wehrmachtsangehörige," 25 October 1941, PA-AA Berlin, Nachlass Schleier, II. On Hitler's meeting with Pétain and Laval at Montoire, a village near Tours, see Fred Kupferman, *Laval*, 2nd ed. (Paris, 2006), pp. 300–309; and Burrin, *France à l'heure allemande*, pp. 105–19.

21. Stülpnagel, "An die französische Bevölkerung," *Pariser Zeitung*, 29 October 1941, BA-MA Freiburg, RW 35/11.

22. Speidel, "Die politische Lage," 30 October 1941, ibid.

23. Reports from the Prefect of Police, 3 and 10 November 1941, AN Paris, AJ[40], 553. FK 757 to Kommandant von Gross-Paris, Abt. Ia, 18 November 1941, ibid., 897.

24. MBF, Kommando-Stab, Abt. Ia, "Lagebericht für die Monate Oktober/November 1941," 30 November 1941, BA-MA Freiburg, RW 35/10. Chef des MVB A (St. Germain), "Überprüfung der Geiselliste," 22 December 1941, CDJC Paris, XLIV-18.

25. Report by the Prefect of Police, (?) January 1942, AN Paris, AJ[40], 887. "Conférence du 3 janvier avec le Docteur adjoint pour la justice militaire Bälz," 3 January 1942, ibid., F[7], 14886. Reports by the Prefect of Police, 5 and 19 January 1942, ibid., AJ[40], 553. Stülpnagel, "Sicherheit der deutschen Wehrmacht in Frankreich," 6 January 1942, ibid., 451.

26. GPD, V pol 2, "Vermerk," 6 January 1942, AN Paris, AJ[40], 887. See Umbreit, *Der Militärbefehlshaber*, pp. 124–35.

27. Stülpnagel to Wagner, 15 January 1942, BA-MA Freiburg, RW 35/536.

28. Stülpnagel to Schmid, 14 January 1942, ibid., 1.

29. Stülpnagel to Keitel, 15 February 1942, ibid. His farewell to the army of Occupation was simply entitled "Tagesbefehl Nr. 4/42," which loyally closed with a rather pathetic "Sieg Heil unserem Führer!" on 20 February 1941, AN Paris, AJ[40], 441. A perceptive evaluation of Stülpnagel and his successor is contained in the unpublished memoirs of Werner Best, "Erinnerungen aus dem besetzten Frankreich 1940 bis 1942," BA Koblenz, N/1023 12. Stülpnagel's nervous breakdown, recorded by Best, is confirmed by Ernst Jünger, "Das erste Pariser Tagebuch," in *Sämtliche Werke. Tagebücher*

(Stuttgart, 1979), 2:308–9. See also Lucien Steinberg, *Les allemands en France, 1940–1944* (Paris, 1980), pp. 92–108; and Umbreit, *Der Militärbefehlshaber*, pp. 135–40.

30. Heinrich von Stülpnagel to MVB A, B, C, and Kommandant von Gross-Paris, 6 March 1942, CDJC Paris, XLVa-23. Chef des MVB A (St. Germain) to all Feld- und Kreiskommandanten, 14 March 1942, ibid., XLV-5. MBF, Kommando-Stab, Abt. Ic (Kossmann) to MVB A, B, C, and Kommandant von Gross-Paris, 12 May 1942, ibid., VIII-4. On the transition from Otto to Heinrich von Stülpnagel, see Bargatzky, *Hotel Majestic*, pp. 82–92.

31. Schaumburg to Schleier, 12 March 1942, PA-AA Berlin, Paris 1309. "Notiz," 12 March 1942, ibid., 2467. Schleier to Schaumburg, 31 March 1942, ibid., 1309. Schaumburg to Schleier, 14 April 1942, ibid. Schleier to Schaumburg, 24 April 1942, ibid.

32. Schleier to Abetz, 9 March 1942, ibid., R 27780. Schaumburg, "Avis," 10 March and 13 April 1942, AN Paris, F⁷, 15312. MBF, Verwaltungs-Stab (Kübler), "Veröffentlichung der Pariser Polizeipräfektur," 22 March 1942, ibid., AJ⁴⁰, 553.

33. Darlan to the Direction de la Police du Territoire et des Étrangers, 15 April 1942, AN Paris, F⁷, 14887.

34. Kommandant von Gross-Paris, "Avis," 9 May 1942, ibid., 15312.

35. Kommandant von Gross-Paris, "Avis," 31 May 1942, ibid.

36. "Anzahl der bisher erschossenen Geiseln," 30 May 1942, BA-MA Freiburg, RW 35/308. MBF, Kommando-Stab, Abt. Ia, "Lagebericht für die Monate April/Mai 1942," 31 May 1942, AN Paris, AJ⁴⁰, 444. "Erschossene Geiseln in der Zeit vom September 1941 bis Mai 1942," (?) June 1942, CDJC Paris, VII-3. During Otto von Stülpnagel's tenure as MBF, a total of 471 hostages were shot, according to Regina Delacor (ed.), *Attentate und Repressionen. Ausgewählte Dokumente zur zyklischen Eskalation des NS-Terrors im besetzten Frankreich 1941/42* (Stuttgart, 2000), pp. 55–56.

Chapter 7: A Dangerous Place

1. Reports by the Prefecture of Police, 30 June and 8 July 1941, AN Paris, AJ⁴⁰, 553. Hufnagel, "Besprechung mit Herrn Simon von der Polizeipräfektur Paris (Renseignements Généraux)," 7 July 1941, ibid. "Note des franz. Polizeipräfekten, Admiral Bard, über die Tätigkeit der Polizei," 25 September 1941, ibid., 444.

2. Kommandant von Gross-Paris to the Prefecture of Police, 5 July 1941, ibid., 870. Kommandant von Gross-Paris, "Kommandantur-Befehl Nr. 129," 19 September 1941, ibid., 868.

3. Memo by MBF, Verwaltungs-Stab (Hufnagel), 29 June 1941, ibid., 551. Stülpnagel to Brinon, 3 July 1941, ibid. MBF (Storz) to MVB A, B, C, and Bordeaux, 10 July 1941, ibid. Kommandant von Gross-Paris, Verwaltungs-Stab (Rademacher) to Prefect of Police, 18 July 1941, ibid., 892.

4. Memo by Best, 23 June 1941, BA-MA Freiburg, RW 49/110. The authorized parties were Le Feu (Delaunay), La Ligue Française (Costantini), Le Rassemblement National Populaire (Déat), Le Front Franc (Boissel), Le Francisme (Bucard), and Groupe Collaboration (Chateaubriant). Provisionally tolerated were Parti Français National-Collectiviste (Clémenti), Parti Populaire Français (Doriot), Le Parti Français (Ours), Mouvement Social Révolutionnaire (Deloncle), Amis du Maréchal (in Rouen), and Parti National Breton (in Rennes). The three forbidden parties were Parti National-Socialiste Français (Message), Croix de Feu (de la Rocque), and the CDAPH (Devoir).

5. Kommandant von Gross-Paris, Verwaltungs-Stab to MBF, Verwaltungs-Stab, 25 June 1941, AN Paris, AJ[40], 552. MBF, Propaganda-Abteilung Frankreich, "Protokoll über die Propagandabesprechung vom 27. Juni 1941 in der Botschaft," 27 June 1941, ibid., 874. "Note verbale pour Monsieur le Général Commandant des Forces Militaires d'Occupation en France," 9 July 1941, ibid., 552. Memo by MBF, Verwaltungs-Stab, 9 July 1941, ibid. MBF, Kommando-Stab, Abt. Ic, "Aufzeichnung," 10 July 1941, ibid. Stülpnagel to DB, 11 July 1941, ibid. Stülpnagel to the Zentralkomité der französischen Freiwilligenlegion gegen den Bolschewismus, 16 July 1941, ibid., 871.

6. Kommandant von Gross-Paris, Verwaltungs-Stab to MBF, Verwaltungs-Stab, 19 July 1941, ibid., 552. MBF, Propaganda-Staffel Paris to Propaganda-Abteilung Frankreich, 19 July 1941, ibid. MBF, Kommando-Stab, "Lagebericht für die Monate Juni/Juli 1941," 31 July 1941, ibid., 443.

7. Kommandant von Gross-Paris, Verwaltungs-Stab to *Paris Soir*, 8 July 1941, ibid., 870. Kommandant von Gross-Paris, "Kommandantur-Befehl Nr. 86," 15 July 1941; and "Kommandantur-Befehl Nr. 99," 4 August 1941, BA-MA Freiburg, RH 36/34.

8. Kommandant von Gross-Paris, Kommando-Stab to MBF, 17 July 1941, AN Paris, AJ[40], 549. Kommandant von Gross-Paris to MBF, Kommando- und Verwaltungs-Stab, 17 July 1941, ibid. Kommandant von Gross-Paris, "Kommandantur-Befehl Nr. 100," 7 August 1941, BA-MA Freiburg, RH 38/34.

9. Kommandant von Gross-Paris, "Kommandantur-Befehl Nr. 97," 31 July 1941; and "Kommandantur-Befehl Nr. 164," 8 November 1941, AN Paris, AJ[40], 868. Torpedo-Vorkommando to Kommandant von Gross-Paris, Kommandostab, 12 September 1941, ibid., 874. Kommandant von Gross-Paris, "Kommandantur-Befehl Nr. 55," 11 April 1942, BA-MA Freiburg, RH 36/35.

10. "Polizeiliche Ereignismeldung," 18 August 1941, AN Paris, AJ[40], 550. Feldgendarmerie-Trupp Paris to Kommandant von Gross-Paris, Kommando-Stab, 29 August 1941, ibid., 874. MBF, Verwaltungs-Stab to Stülpnagel, 21 November 1941, ibid., 553. GFP, "Ereignismeldung," 21 November 1941, ibid., 869.

11. Schaumburg to the Prefect of the Seine and the Prefect of Police, 26 November 1941, ibid., 871. Schaumburg, "Bekanntmachung," 28 November 1941, ibid., 887. Kommandant von Gross-Paris, "Kommandantur-Befehl Nr. 176," 29 November 1941, ibid., 868. MBF, Kommando-Stab, Abt. Ia, "Lagebericht für die Monate Dezember 1941/Januar 1942," 31 January 1942, BA-MA Freiburg, RW 35/12.

12. Knochen to Sipo-SD, Abt. IV J, 3 October 1941, CDJC Paris, I-17. Knochen to Sipo-SD, Abt. IV J, 4 October 1941, ibid., 20. Stülpnagel to OKW, 6 October 1941, ibid., 24. Stülpnagel to OKW, 8 October 1941, ibid., 25. Telegram from Stülpnagel to OKW, 21 October 1941, ibid., 29. "Aufzeichnung für den Herrn Botschafter Abetz," 31 October 1941, PA-AA Berlin, Paris 1277.

13. MBF, Kommando-Stab, "Lagebericht für die Monate Juni/Juli 1941," 31 July 1941, BA-MA Freiburg, RW 35/7. "Notiz. Besprechung mit dem Militärbefehlshaber am Sonnabend," 2 August 1941, PA-AA Berlin, Paris 2467. Stülpnagel to Brinon, 4 August 1941, CDJC Paris, IV-29. Feldgendarmerie-Trupp St. Denis, "Bericht," 16 August 1941, AN Paris, AJ[40], 874. Kommandant von Gross-Paris, Verwaltungs-Stab to Kommando-Stab, Abt. Ic, 15 September 1941, ibid., 870.

14. Wehrmachtsverkehrsdirektion Paris, Abt. Eisenbahnen to GFP 610, Sonderkommando Paris, 17 August 1941, CDJC Paris, VIII-3. MBF, Verwaltungs-Stab, Abt. IIb, "Vermerk," 18 August 1941, ibid. FK 758 to MVB A (St. Germain), 23 August 1941, ibid. MVB A to MBF, Verwaltungs-Stab, Abt. Verwaltung, 30 August 1941, ibid. Lt.

General von Lippe to FK 589, 17 December 1941, ibid. FK 758 to MVB A, 24 January 1942, ibid. MBF, Verwaltungs-Stab, Abt. Verwaltung, V pol to MVB A, B, C, and Kommandant von Gross-Paris, 17 March 1942, ibid.

15. Kommandant von Gross-Paris, Kommando-Stab to Schaumburg, 18 July 1941, AN Paris, AJ[40], 897. GFP, "Bericht über englischen Bombenabwurf in Paris," 1 October 1941, ibid., 869.

16. "Bericht über den Luftangriff auf Paris," 3 March 1942, BA-MA Freiburg, Wi IA3/187. MBF, Kommando-Stab, Abt. Ic to OB West, 6 March 1942, AN Paris, AJ[40], 550. Memo by MBF, Verwaltungs-Stab, Abt. Verwaltung, 9 March 1942, ibid.

17. MBF, Kommando-Stab, Abt. Ia, "Lagebericht für die Monate Februar/März 1942," 31 March 1942, BA-MA Freiburg, RW 35/14. MBF, Wi Rü Stab Frankreich, "Bericht der Ereignisse," 30 April 1942, ibid., RW 24/4. Kommandant von Gross-Paris, Verwaltungs-Stab to MBF, Verwaltungs-Stab, 1 May 1942, AN Paris, AJ[40], 872.

18. FK 757, Abt. Ia to Kommandant von Gross-Paris, 6 October 1942, AN Paris, AJ[40], 897. A similar memo listed ten such incidents in the period from 11 August to 17 September 1942: "Sabotageakte oder Anschläge bei denen Wehrmachtsangehörige oder Reichsdeutsche getötet oder verletzt wurden," 17 September 1942, CDJC Paris, XLV-92.

19. Bard, "Verfügung, welche die Bezirke der Stadt Paris und der Bannmeile des Seine-Departements ... gruppiert und die Befugnisse der Divisionskommissare festlegt," 22 July 1941, AN Paris, AJ[40], 871. Bard to Kommandant von Gross-Paris, Verwaltungs-Stab, 4 September 1941, ibid., 870.

20. Kommandant von Gross-Paris, Verwaltungs-Stab to Kommando-Stab, Abt. Ic, 9 September 1941, ibid., 871. Kommandant von Gross-Paris, Kommando-Stab, Abt. Ia to Abt. Ic, 17 September 1941, ibid., 875.

21. Schmid to Brinon, 19 September 1941, AN Paris, F[7], 14895. Pucheu, "Arrêté," 6 October 1941, ibid., 14900. SPAC, Direction Générale de la Police Nationale, "Note concernant la defense anti-Communiste de la France," 15 November 1941, ibid., 14881.

22. "État faisant connaître le nombre et le siège des brigades régionales de police judiciaire en Zone occupée," 23 September 1941, ibid., 14899. Ministère de l'Intérieur, Direction Générale de la Police Nationale to Best, 25 November 1941, ibid., 14895. On the effectiveness of French police actions, see Stephane Courtois, Denis Peschanski, and Adam Rayski, Le Sang de l'Étranger. Les immigrés de la M.O.I. dans la Résistance (Paris, 1989).

23. MBF, Kommando-Stab, Abt. Ia to Kommandant von Gross-Paris, 1 October 1941, AN Paris, AJ[40], 871. "Liste der am 23.8.1941 anl. der Waffensuche bei Waffenhändlern im Kommandanturbereich von Gross-Paris festgenommenen Personen," 14 October 1941, ibid., 875. Kommandant von Gross-Paris, Verwaltungs-Stab to Prefect of Police, 20 October 1941, ibid., 871. Prefect of Police to Kommandant von Gross-Paris, Verwaltungs-Stab, 12 November 1941, ibid., 890. Kommandant von Gross-Paris, Verwaltungs-Stab to MBF, Kommando-Stab, Abt. Ic, 13 November 1941, ibid., 875.

24. Best to Kommandant von Gross-Paris, 19 November 1941, ibid., 881. MBF, Verwaltungs-Stab, "Aufsicht über die franz. Polizei im besetzten Gebiet," 19 November 1941, ibid., 871. Heinrich von Stülpnagel, "Ausübung der Aufsicht über die franz. Polizei," 10 April 1942, BA-MA Freiburg, RW 35/340.

25. Kommandant von Gross-Paris, Kommando-Stab, Abt. Ia to Abt. Ic, 18 December 1941, AN Paris, AJ[40], 875. Best to Brinon, 22 January 1942, ibid., F[7], 14895.

26. MBF, Verwaltungs-Stab to Kommandant von Gross-Paris, Verwaltungs-Stab, 23 February and 3 March 1942, ibid., AJ[40], 883. MBF, Verwaltungs-Stab to DB, 24 March 1942, PA-AA Berlin, Paris 1314.

27. Schmid to Brinon, 17 December 1941, CDJC Paris, IV-86.

28. On Oberg, see Delarue, *Histoire de la Gestapo*, pp. 286–94, 371–76; and Umbreit, *Der Militärbefehlshaber*, pp. 107–17.

29. Hitler to Stülpnagel, 9 March 1942, AN Paris, AJ[40], 549. Stülpnagel, "Zusammenarbeit mit dem Höheren SS- und Polizeiführer in Frankreich," 22 May 1942, BA-MA Freiburg, RW 35/353. MBF to Brinon, 27 May 1942, AN Paris, AJ[40], 549.

30. Telegram from Abetz to Krug, 1 May 1942, PA-AA Berlin, Paris 2468. Prefect of Police to Kommandant von Gross-Paris, 18 May 1942, AN Paris, AJ[40], 882. MBF, "Zusammenarbeit mit dem Höheren SS- und Polizeiführer; hier: Übergang der polizeilichen Exekutive," 29 May 1942, BA-MA Freiburg, RW 35/32. MBF, Kommando-Stab, Abt. IIa, "Auflösung des Stabes des Leitenden Feldpolizeidirektors beim Militärbefehlshabers in Frankreich," 1 June 1942, AN Paris, AJ[40], 440. See Kasten, *"Gute Franzosen,"* pp. 29–37; and Ulrich Lappenküper, "Der 'Schlächter von Paris': Carl-Albrecht Oberg als Höherer SS- und Polizeiführer in Frankreich 1942–1944," in Martens and Vaïsse (eds.), *Frankreich und Deutschland im Krieg*, pp. 129–43.

31. Stülpnagel, "Personelle Veränderung und Umorganisation des Verwaltungsstabes," 31 May 1942, AN Paris, AJ[40], 450. MBF, "Stabsbefehl Nr. 1/42," 10 June 1942, ibid., 410.

32. Ministère de l'Intérieur, Direction Générale de la Police Nationale, "Note," 2 July 1942, ibid., F[7], 14900. "Note de Monsieur le Général Oberg (texte définitif)," 23 July 1942, ibid., 14886. See Steinberg, *Les allemands en France*, pp. 126–30, 152–56; Burrin, *La France à l'heure allemande*, pp. 158–64; Kasten, *"Gute Franzosen,"* pp. 69–73; and Jackson, *France: The Dark Years*, pp. 215–17.

33. Braunstumm to DB, 16 July 1942, PA-AA Berlin, Paris 2468. Bousquet to all prefects in the Occupied Zone, 17 July 1942, AN Paris, F[7], 14898. Telegram from DB (Schwendemann) to AA, 18 July 1942, PA-AA Berlin, Paris 2468. Bargatzky, *Hotel Majestic*, pp. 93–95. Two further such shipments occurred on 24 January 1943 and 27 April 1944. See Claudine Cardon-Hamet, *Mille otages pour Auschwitz. Le convoi du 6 juillet 1942* (Paris, 1997), pp. 187–95.

34. Telegram from Abetz to AA, 8 August 1942, PA-AA Berlin, R 27781. Oberg, "Bekanntmachung," 11 August 1942, CDJC Paris, XLV-44. "Liste der am 11.8.1942 auf dem Mont Valérien erschossenen 88 kom. Terroristen," 11 August 1942, ibid. Oberg to Himmler, 18 September 1942, ibid., 83. Knochen to Sipo-SD in Bordeaux, 18 September 1942, ibid., 82. "Liste der am 21. September 1942 in Paris auf dem Mont Valérien zu erschiessenden 46 Sühnenpersonen," 18 September 1942, ibid.

35. Oberg to Sipo-SD, Abt. II ju, 24 June 1942, CDJC Paris, VII-2. MVB A to MBF, Verwaltungs-Stab, 26 June 1942, AN Paris, AJ[40], 549.

36. DB to MBF (Humm), 7 July 1942, PA-AA Berlin, Paris 2447. MBF (Holzmann) to DB, 7 August 1942, ibid.

37. Sipo-SD, S pol II, "Vermerk" and "Notiz," 13 August 1942, CDJC Paris, VII-2.

38. Sipo-SD, S pol II/3 to Prefect of Police, 14 August 1942, ibid., XLV-44. "Zum Lagebericht," 20 August 1942, ibid.

39. "Abschrift aus der Kriegsstrafverfahrensordnung vom 17.8.1938," (?) August 1942, ibid., VII-2. Sipo-SD, S pol II/3, "Vermerk. Betr.: Exekution," 13 October 1942, ibid.

40. Sipo-SD, S pol II/3 to BdS, 16 September 1942, ibid., XLV-78. Sipo-SD, S pol II to BdS, 16 September 1942, ibid., 79.

41. Knochen, "Unter deutscher Leitung stehende politische Haftlager und Zivilinterniertenlager im besetzten Gebiet Frankreichs," 10 October 1942, PA-AA Berlin, Paris 2487.

42. Schleier to AA, 13 October 1942, ibid., 1329. Between June 1940 and July 1941, 162 death sentences were pronounced by MBF tribunals, of which 42 were carried out, according to Gaël Eismann, "L'escalade d'une répression à visage légal. Les pratiques judiciaires des tribunaux du Militärbefehlshaber in Frankreich, 1940–1944," in Gaël Eismann and Stefan Martens (eds.), *Occupation et répression militaire allemandes. La politique de "maintien de l'ordre" en Europe occupée 1939–1945* (Paris, 2007), p. 135.

43. MBF, Verwaltungs-Stab, "Lagebericht über Verwaltung und Wirtschaft, Juni/September 1942," 1 October 1942, BA-MA Freiburg, RW 35/287. Memo by the Kommandant von Gross-Paris, 8 October 1942, AN Paris, AJ⁴⁰, 441. See Mathieu Flonneau, "'Roulez quand même ...'. La circulation et les services de transport à Paris entre 1939 et 1945," in Marie-Noëlle Polino (ed.), *Transports dans la France en guerre 1939–1945* (Rouen, 2007), pp. 21–48.

44. Memo by MBF, Kommando-Stab, Abt. Ic (Kossmann), 22 October 1942, AN Paris, AJ⁴⁰, 441. Abetz to Humm, 28 October 1942, PA-AA Berlin, Paris 1279. Humm, "Vortragsnotiz für Herrn Botschafter Abetz," 30 October 1942, ibid.

45. MBF, Verwaltungs-Stab, "Lagebericht über Verwaltung und Wirtschaft, Juni/September 1942," 1 October 1942, BA-MA Freiburg, RW 35/287. Kommandant von Gross-Paris, Kommando-Stab, Abt. Ic, "Lagebericht der Abt. Ic, Berichtszeit Oktober 1942," 5 November 1942, AN Paris, AJ⁴⁰, 897.

Chapter 8: Strict Controls and Stringent Quotas

1. "Stimmungsbericht der Propagandastaffel Paris," 31 October 1941, AN Paris, AJ⁴⁰, 873. MBF, Kommando-Stab, Abt. Ia, "Lagebericht für die Monate Oktober/November 1941," 30 November 1941, BA-MA Freiburg, RW 35/10.

2. "Vermerk," 28 May 1942, AN Paris, AJ⁴⁰, 796. Stülpnagel to Backe (Reichsminister für Ernährung und Landwirtschaft), 10 June 1942, ibid.

3. MBF, Verwaltungs-Stab to Reichsministerium für Ernährung und Landwirtschaft, 28 July 1942, PA-AA Berlin, Paris 1292.

4. "Protokoll über die Unterredung zwischen Kriegsverwaltungschef Dr. Michel und Herrn Ministerpräsident Laval," 3 August 1942, AN Paris, AJ⁴⁰, 796.

5. Stülpnagel to Backe, 10 June 1942, ibid. Göring to Stülpnagel, 15 August 1942, ibid.

6. "Aktenvermerk," 28 August 1942, ibid. Stülpnagel to Brauchitsch, 3 September 1942, ibid. Brauchitsch to OKW, 4 September 1942, ibid. "According to Goering's secretary Paul Koerner, the German military commander in France thought Goering's quotas so outrageous that he refused to pass them on to the authorities in Paris," notes Tooze, *The Wages of Destruction*, p. 547.

7. "Sitzung des Handelpolitischen Ausschusses vom 7. September 1942," 18 September 1942, AN Paris, AJ⁴⁰, 796. "Fernschreiben. Betreff.: Aufbringung des landw. Ablieferungssolls aus Frankreich," 22 and 23 September 1942, ibid.

8. MBF, Verwaltungs-Stab, Abt. Wi Ic, "Entwicklung und Lage der französischen Wirtschaft im Bereich des Militärbefehlshabers Frankreich im Jahre 1941," 26 September 1942, BA-MA Freiburg, Wi IA3/7. "Kriegstagebuch des WWSF," 26 September–2 October 1942, ibid., RW 24/5.

9. "Bericht über Verhandlungen mit dem Militärbefehlshaber in Frankreich vom 23.–25. September 1942," 29 September 1942, AN Paris, AJ⁴⁰, 796. Abetz, "Lieferung landwirtschaftlicher Erzeugnisse aus Frankreich an das Reich," 29 September 1942, ibid.

10. Barnaud, "Circulaire," 14 August 1941, ibid., F^{1a}, 3668. Kuehllewein, "Das Verhältnis der Feldgendarmerie zur Preisüberwachung," 15 September 1941, ibid., AJ^{40}, 880. Armeeoberkommando 1, Oberquartiermeister, "Besondere Anordnung für die Versorgung Nr. 249," 9 February 1942, ibid., 872. MBF, Verwaltungs-Stab, Abt. Verwaltung, W ju to Gruppe Wi X im Hause, 16 April 1942, BA-MA Freiburg, RW 35/570. MBF, Verwaltungs-Stab, Abt. Wi, "Lohnpolitik in Frankreich," 28 August 1942, AN Paris, AJ^{40}, 591.

11. MBF, Verwaltungs-Stab, Abt. Wi VI, "Zur Aufstellung Monats-Indexziffern der Lebenshaltungskosten in Paris," 17 October 1942, AN Paris, AJ^{40}, 409.

12. MBF, Verwaltungs-Stab, Abt. Wi X, "Preise für die wichtigsten landw. Erzeugnisse," 10 February 1942, ibid.

13. "Contrôle des restaurants fait en liaison avec la police et le contrôle des prix," 20 October 1941, ibid., 784. See Alary, *Les Français au quotidien*, pp. 259–64; and Sanders, *Histoire du marché noir*, pp. 125–43.

14. "La suppression des restaurants hors classe," *Le Petit Parisien*, 17 July 1942, AN Paris, AJ^{40}, 785. Michel to MBF, 31 July 1942, ibid., 784.

15. Stülpnagel to DB, 30 October 1942, PA-AA Berlin, Paris 1279.

16. MBF, Verwaltungs-Stab, Abt. Verwaltung, V pol to Gruppe V ju im Hause, 15 and 19 September 1941, BA-MA Freiburg, RW 35/581. Memo by MBF, Verwaltungs-Stab, Abt. Verwaltung, V pol, 29 September 1941, ibid.

17. MBF, Wi Rü Stab Frankreich, "Bericht der Ereignisse," 18 December 1941, ibid., RW 24/3. MBF, Kommando-Stab, Abt. Ia, "Lagebericht für die Monate Februar 1942/ März 1942," 31 March 1942, ibid., RW 35/14.

18. Kommandant von Gross-Paris, "Kommandantur-Befehl Nr. 146," 13 October 1941, ibid., RW 36/34. MBF, Wi Rü Stab Frankreich, "Bericht der Ereignisse," 12 December 1941, ibid., RW 24/3.

19. MBF, Wi Rü Stab Frankreich, "Bericht der Ereignisse," 22 December 1941, ibid., RW 24/3. MBF, Wi Rü Stab Frankreich, "Bericht der Ereignisse," 30 January, 5 and 28 February, 2 and 14 March 1942, ibid., 4.

20. MBF, Wi Rü Stab Frankreich, "Bericht der Ereignisse," 1 April 1942, ibid. MBF, Verwaltungs-Stab, Abt. Wi I, "Wirtschaftsbericht für die Monate Februar/März 1942," 1 April 1942, ibid., RW 35/305. MBF, Wi Rü Stab Frankreich, "Bericht der Ereignisse," 20 April and 16 June 1942, ibid., RW 24/4. Kommandant von Gross-Paris, "Kommandantur-Befehl Nr. 129," 3 October 1942, ibid., RH 36/36.

21. Kommandant von Gross-Paris to MBF, Verwaltungs-Stab, Gruppe Arbeitseinsatz und Sozialfragen, 11 July and 11 October 1941, AN Paris, AJ^{40}, 858. OKW to Reichsarbeitsministerium, 12 September 1941, BA-MA Freiburg, Wi IA3/156. MBF, Verwaltungs-Stab, Abt. Wi VIII, "Vermerk über die Besprechung beim Wi Rü Stab Frankreich am 18.9.1941," 19 September 1941, AN Paris, AJ^{40}, 859. Michel, "Einsatz französischer Arbeitskräfte in Deutschland; hier: Einsatz geschlossener Arbeitergruppen," 25 November 1941, BA-MA Freiburg, RW 35/1352.

22. Der Beauftragte für den Vierjahresplan, der Generalbevollmächtigte für das Kraftfahrwesen to OKW, Wi Rü Amt (in Berlin), Abt. Rü 2, 5 August 1941, BA-MA Freiburg, Wi IA3/132. MBF, Verwaltungs-Stab, Abt. Wi VII to Firma Kurbelwellenwerk, 12 August 1941, AN Paris, AJ^{40}, 858. MBF, Verwaltungs-Stab, Abt. Wi, "Anwerbung von Ausländern nach Deutschland; hier: Vertragsdauer und Urlaubsanspruch," 13 January 1942, ibid., 896.

23. "Compte-rendu de la réunion tenue à l'Hôtel Thermal … au sujet du recrutement de la main-d'oeuvre française pour l'Allemagne," 3 October 1941, AN Paris, AJ^{41},

83. Darlan to Abetz, 20 October 1941, PA-AA Berlin, Paris 2453. MBF, Verwaltungs-Stab, Abt. Wi VII, "Vermerk," 5 and 14 January 1942, AN Paris, AJ[40], 846. See Vinen, *The Unfree French*, pp. 116–23, 281–312.

24. "Réunion à l'Hôtel Majestic le 18 mars 1942 à 16 heures 30," 18 March 1942, AN Paris, AJ[41], 83. Timm to OKW, Wi Rü Amt, 25 March 1942, BA-MA Freiburg, Wi IA3/132. See Jean-Pierre Harbulot, "L'administration française et le STO," in Bernard Garnier and Jean Quellien (eds.), *La main-d'oeuvre française exploitée par le IIIe Reich* (Caen, 2003), pp. 47–65.

25. Sauckel to OKW, 7 April 1942, PA-AA Berlin, Paris 2453. Sauckel to AA, 24 April 1942, ibid. For a sketch of Sauckel, see Tooze, *The Wages of Destruction*, pp. 515–19.

26. AA (Luther) to Abetz, 8 May 1942, PA-AA Berlin, Paris 2453. Luther to Abetz, 10 May 1942, ibid., 2445. Sauckel to Abetz, 11 May 1942, ibid. See Peter W. Becker, "Fritz Sauckel, Generalbevollmächtigter für den Arbeitseinsatz," in Ronald Smelser and Rainer Zitelmann (eds.), *Die Braune Elite*, 2 vols. (Darmstadt, 1993–1994), 1:236–45; and Bernd Zielinski, "L'exploitation de la main-d'oeuvre française par l'Allemagne et la politique de collaboration (1940–1944)," in Garnier and Quellien (eds.), *La main-d'oeuvre française*, pp. 47–65.

27. Abetz to AA, 10 June 1942, PA-AA Berlin, Paris 1453. Luther, "Aktennotiz," 14 June 1942, ibid., R 27780. MBF, Kommando-Stab, Abt. Ic to Sipo-SD, 17 June 1942, CDJC Paris, VII-1. MBF, Verwaltungs-Stab, Gruppe Arbeitseinsatz und Sozialfragen to Referat "Inneres" im Hause, 7 August 1942, ibid. See Jackson, *France: The Dark Years*, pp. 219–21.

28. Abetz to AA, 16 June 1942, PA-AA Berlin, Paris 2445. "Aktenvermerk über die Besprechung am 8.9.42, 17⁰⁰ bei Herrn General Barckhausen," 8 September 1942, BA-MA Freiburg, RW 24/38. On Speer, see Tooze, *The Wages of Destruction*, pp. 552–89.

29. Henning, "Kriegstagebuch des Deutschen Beschaffungsamts in Frankreich für die Zeit 10.6.42–30.9.42," 30 September 1942, BA-MA Freiburg, RW 24/37. Stülpnagel to Barnaud, 7 October 1942, PA-AA Berlin, Paris 2446.

30. Telegram from Stülpnagel to Sauckel and Speer, 8 October 1942, BA-MA Freiburg, RW 24/39. Telegram from Speer to Stülpnagel, 8 October 1942, ibid. See Tooze, *The Wages of Destruction*, pp. 515–19.

31. MBF, Wi Rü Stab Frankreich, "Bericht der Ereignisse," 29 December 1941, 3 and 16 January 1942, BA-MA Freiburg, RW 24/4. MBF, Kommando-Stab, Abt. Ia, "Lagebericht für die Monate Februar 1942/März 1942," 31 March 1942, ibid., RW 35/14.

32. MBF, Wi Rü Stab Frankreich, "Bericht der Ereignisse," 23 April, 4 and 16 June 1942, ibid., RW 24/4. Abetz to AA, 16 June 1942, PA-AA Berlin, Paris 2445. "Niederschrift der Besprechung in Paris am 15.6.1942 nachmittags unter Leitung des Ministers für Bewaffnung und Munition Reichsminister Speer," 18 June 1942, BA-MA Freiburg, RW 24/38. "Aufzeichnung über Äusserungen Präsidenten Lavals in einer privaten Unterhaltung mit Reichsminister Speer im Anschluss an ein Mittagessen in der Botschaft Paris am 15. Juni 1942," 19 June 1942, PA-AA Berlin, Paris 2445.

33. Keitel, "Organisation der Wehrwirtschafts- und Rüstungsdienststellen in Frankreich," 26 June 1942, BA-MA Freiburg, Wi IA3/2. "Kriegstagebuch des Wehrwirtschaftsstabes Frankreich," 1–7 August 1942, ibid., RW 24/5. MBF, Verwaltungs-Stab, "Anlagen zum Bericht über Verwaltung und Wirtschaft: Juni/September 1942," 1 October 1942, ibid., RW 35/288.

34. "Aktenvermerk über die Besprechung im Wi Rü Amt," 12 October 1942, ibid., RW 24/40.

35. Abetz to Krug, 15 October 1942, PA-AA Berlin, Paris 2446. Sauckel to Stülpnagel, 25 and 29 October 1942, AN Paris, AJ⁴⁰, 846. Sauckel to Ritter, 29 October 1942, ibid.

36. "Tagung des GBA," 2 November 1942, AN Paris, AJ⁴⁰, 846.

Chapter 9: A Lost Battle

1. Abetz to Wagner, 29 April 1942, PA-AA Berlin, Paris 1206. OKW to MBF, 5 July 1942, ibid., 1136 A. DB (Rahn) to AA, 21 September 1942, ibid.

2. Telegram from DB (Krüger) to AA, 18 July 1942, ibid., 1115 A. Abetz to AA, 23 July 1942, ibid., 1367. NSDAP (Schultz) to DB (Krüger), 5 August 1942, ibid., 1115 A. AA (Luther) to DB, 16 October 1942, ibid. MBF, Propaganda-Abteilung, "Stabsbefehl," 5 November 1942, AN Paris, AJ⁴⁰, 1001. See Umbreit, *Der Militärbefehlshaber*, pp. 150–55.

3. Lucht, "Note relative à la visite par M. Roy le 2 septembre à la Propagandastaffel," 2 September 1941, AN Paris, F¹⁷, 13391.

4. MBF, Kommando-Stab, "Lagebericht für die Monate Juni/Juli 1941," 31 July 1941, ibid., AJ⁴⁰, 443. Kommandant von Gross-Paris, Kommando-Stab, "Lage- und Tätigkeitsbericht für die Zeit vom 13.7–13.9.41," 17 September 1941, ibid., 875. MBF, Kommando-Stab, "Lagebericht für die Monate August/September 1941," (?) September 1941, BA-MA Freiburg, RW 35/8. Propaganda-Staffel Paris, "Kurzbericht über die Tätigkeit der Gruppen in der Zeit vom 1.11.41 bis 8.11.41," 8 November 1941, AN Paris, AJ⁴⁰, 873.

5. Propaganda-Staffel Paris, "Stimmungsbericht," 13 December 1941, AN Paris, AJ⁴⁰, 873. Propaganda-Staffel Bordeaux to MBF, Propaganda-Abteilung Frankreich, 13 February 1942, PA-AA Berlin, Paris 2402. MBF, Kommando-Stab, "Lagebericht für die Monate Februar 1942/März 1942," 31 March 1942, BA-MA Freiburg, RW 35/14.

6. Propaganda-Staffel Paris, "Lagebericht," 11 October 1941, AN Paris, AJ⁴⁰, 873.

7. MBF, Kommando-Stab, "Lagebericht für die Monate Dezember 1941/Januar 1942," 31 January 1942, BA-MA Freiburg, RW 35/12.

8. FK 757 (Paris region), "Lagebericht," 12 and 14 July 1942, AN Paris, AJ⁴⁰, 897.

9. Kommandant von Gross-Paris, Kommando-Stab, "Lagebericht der Abt. Ic, Berichtzeit Monat Oktober 1942," 5 November 1942, ibid.

10. MBF, Propaganda-Abteilung, Referat Schrifttum, "Complément à la liste des ouvrages dont la vente est interdite (Liste Otto)," 18 July 1941, ibid., 559; and "Liste der unerwünschten französischen Literatur," 29 May 1942, PA-AA Berlin, Paris 1211. Sipo-SD to DB, Referat Kultur, 20 August 1942, ibid., 1112 A.

11. MBF, Propaganda-Abteilung, Referat Schrifttum, "Tageszeitungen," 1 August 1941, ibid., 1012. Propaganda-Staffel Paris, Gruppe Presse, "Memorandum," 28 August 1941, ibid., 1013. Messageries de la Coopérative des Journaux Français, "Rapport de la semaine," 23 February 1942, ibid., 1014. Comité des Papiers de Presse to Klecker, 24 July 1942, ibid., 1010. Propaganda-Staffel Paris, Gruppe Presse to Lt. Schulz, 28 August 1942, ibid., 1013. See Fouché, *L'édition française sous l'Occupation*, 2:9–37; and Umbreit, *Der Militärbefehlshaber*, pp. 155–58.

12. Schmid to MBF, Propaganda-Abteilung, 13 October 1941, BA-MA Freiburg, RW 35/537. MBF, Kommando-Stab, Abt. Ic to Verwaltungs-Stab, Gruppe V ju, 15 October 1941, ibid. MBF, Verwaltungs-Stab, Abt. Verwaltung, V pol 259 to Leiter der Abt. Verwaltung (initialed by Best), 25 October 1941, ibid.

13. MBF, Verwaltungs-Stab, Abt. Verwaltung, "Französische Verordnung über das Abhören ausländischer Sender," 31 October 1941, ibid. Stülpnagel to Brinon, 17

December 1941, ibid. Darlan to Brinon, 5 January 1942, ibid. See Umbreit, *Der Militär-befehlshaber*, pp. 158–63.

14. Distribution Parisienne des Films to Filmprüfstelle Paris, 31 July 1941, AN Paris, AJ⁴⁰, 1005.

15. AA to DB, 9 December 1941, PA-AA Berlin, Paris 1114. Le Délégué général en Zone occupée au Secrétaire général de l'information et de la propagande to Abetz, 13 February 1942, ibid.

16. MBF, Propaganda-Abteilung, Referat Film, "Tätigkeitsbericht für die Zeit vom 14. Oktober–31. Oktober 1941," 31 October 1941, BA-MA Freiburg, RW 35/224.

17. Abetz, "Aufzeichnung für den Militärbefehlshaber in Frankreich General der Inf. von Stülpnagel," 6 November 1941, PA-AA Berlin, Paris 1381. Inspecteur général des Services des Renseignements Généraux, "La situation du cinéma à Paris," 8 November 1941, AN Paris, F⁷, 15293.

18. MBF, Propaganda-Abteilung, Referat Film, "Tätigkeitsbericht für die Zeit vom 10. Juli–17. Juli 1941," 17 July 1941, BA-MA Freiburg, RW 35/222; and "Tätigkeitsbericht für die Zeit vom 12. September bis 19. September 1941," 19 September 1941, ibid., 223.

19. Schleier to AA, 25 July and 8 December 1941, 3 March 1942, PA-AA Berlin, Paris 1381.

20. Telegram from Abetz to AA, 18 August 1941, PA-AA Berlin, Paris 1381. Brinon to Schleier, 29 April 1942, ibid., 1144 Z. DB to Henri Clerc, 28 May 1942, ibid. Abetz to Brinon, 30 June 1942, ibid. MBF, Propaganda-Abteilung, Gruppe Film to DB (Knothe), 28 July 1942, ibid., 1143 B. See Welch, *Propaganda*, pp. 191–203.

21. Epting to AA, 4 July 1941, PA-AA Berlin, Paris 1142 Y. Schleier to AA, 18 July 1941, ibid. Telegram from Epting to AA, 23 July 1941, ibid., 1380. Reichsminist-erium für Volksaufklärung und Propaganda (Lang) to MBF, Propaganda-Abteilung, 22 August 1941, AN Paris, AJ⁴⁰, 1002. Propaganda-Staffel Paris, "Lagebericht," 29 January 1942, ibid., 1001. Telegram from Epting to AA, 25 March 1942, PA-AA Berlin, Paris 1380. Kommandant von Gross-Paris, "Kommandantur-Befehl Nr. 90," 24 June 1942, BA-MA Freiburg, RH 36/35.

22. Inspecteur Général des Services des Renseignements Généraux, "Note de Ren-seignement N° 7945/Z," 22 October 1941, AN Paris, F⁷, 15298.

23. Schleier to AA, 9 September 1941, PA-AA Berlin, Paris 1367. AA, Dienststelle Ribbentrop to Abetz, 27 October 1941, ibid., 1136 A.

24. Kommandant von Gross-Paris, "Kommandantur-Befehl Nr. 163," 7 November 1941, AN Paris, AJ⁴⁰, 868. MBF, Kommando-Stab, Abt. IIa, "Stabsbefehl Nr. 23/42," 1 March 1942, ibid., 439.

25. Abetz to Epting, 21 October 1941, PA-AA Berlin, Paris 1376. Knothe, "Aktennotiz" (for Abetz), 8 July 1942, ibid., 1111 B. See Rayssac, *L'exode des musées*, pp. 360–63.

26. Gidel to Bonnard, 16 July 1942, AN Paris, F¹⁷, 13360. Valtier, "Aufzeichnung für Herrn Legationsrat Berscher," 8 August 1942, PA-AA Berlin, Paris 1203. Schleier, "Aufzeichnung," 15 August 1942, ibid., 1111 B. "Aufzeichnung für Herrn Gesandten Schleier," 26 August 1942, ibid. Valtier to Rahn, 22 September 1942, ibid., 1125 B/2. Berscher (DB), "Bericht über die Arbeit der Informations-Abteilung der Deutschen Botschaft Paris vom September 1940–September 1942," 15 October 1942, ibid., 1124. See Burrin, *La France à l'heure allemande*, pp. 299–301.

27. Georgin (Proviseur du Lycée Charlemagne) to Roy, 4 July 1941, AN Paris, F¹⁷, 13385.

28. Maurrain (Doyen de la Faculté des Sciences) to Roy, 19 July 1941, ibid. Memo by Brinon, 24 July 1941, ibid.

29. Gidel to Bonnard, 17 June 1942, ibid., 13360.

30. Gidel to Roy, 4 May 1942, ibid., 13385. Jolibois (Proviseur du Lycée Henri IV) to Gidel, 26 September 1942, ibid.

31. Maurrain to MBF, Verwaltungs-Stab, Abt. Schule und Kultur, 30 July 1941, ibid., 13373. "Note pour Monsieur le Directeur de l'enseignement primaire," 25 August 1941, ibid. "Locaux non occupés mais réquisitionnés par les Autorités allemandes," 29 January 1942, ibid. "Note sur les réquisitions de locaux scolaires," 3 November 1942, ibid., 13379.

32. Sous-directeur de l'École libre des Sciences Politques to the Ministère de l'Agriculture, Service Civique Rural, 17 July 1941, ibid., 13380.

33. MBF, Verwaltungs-Stab, Abt. Verwaltung, V Kult 468 (Dahnke), "Die freimaurischen und bolschewistischen Kreise an der Sorbonne und im Akademiebezirk Paris," 25 November 1941, AN Paris, AJ[40], 567. Ewers (Gruppe AP/IV) to MBF, Verwaltungs-Stab, Abt. Verwaltung, V pol, 10 April 1942, ibid., 1008.

34. "Fonctionnaires relevés de l'interdiction d'enseigner," 1 June 1942, ibid., F[17], 13381.

35. MBF, Verwaltungs-Stab, Abt. Verwaltung, V Kult 463 (Dahnke) to Abwehrstelle (Hôtel Lutétia), 1 November 1941, ibid., AJ[40], 566; and V Kult 468 (Dahnke), "Die freimaurischen und bolschewistischen Kreise an der Sorbonne und im Akademiekreis Paris," 1 November 1941, ibid., 567.

36. DB (Krüger) to AA, 8 July 1942, PA-AA Berlin, Paris 1115 Z.

37. Knochen to Kommandant von Gross-Paris, 31 July 1941, AN Paris, AN[40], 875. Knochen to Abetz, 31 July 1941, PA-AA Berlin, Paris 1372. Schleier to AA, 6 August 1941, ibid. Abetz to AA, 6 November 1941, ibid., 2481. Abetz, "Notiz für den Herrn Generalkonsul Wüster," 4 June 1942, ibid.

38. Abetz to AA, 6 November 1941, PA-AA Berlin, Paris 1372.

39. "Procès-verbal de la conférence des Préfets Régionaux," 20 February 1942, AN Paris, F[1a], 3670. See Burrin, *La France à l'heure allemande*, pp. 222–32.

40. MBF, Verwaltungs-Stab (Ernst), "Comité de la Propagande Sociale du Maréchal," 28 August 1941, AN Paris, AJ[40], 552. "Observations des Autorités occupantes sur les divisions politiques de la France," 29 December 1941, ibid., F[7], 14897. Abetz to NSDAP (Landesgruppenleiter Neuendorf), 2 June 1942, PA-AA Berlin, Paris 1307.

41. Best to DB, 2 October 1941, PA-AA Berlin, Paris 1302. MBF, Verwaltungs-Stab to DB, 19 November 1941, ibid., 1310. DB (Schmidt) to MBF, Verwaltungs-Stab, 28 November 1941, ibid. MBF, Verwaltungs-Stab to DB, 18 December 1941, ibid.

42. "Observations des Autorités occupantes sur les divisions politiques de la France," 29 December 1941, AN Paris, F[7], 14897. DB (Achenbach) to NSDAP, Auslands-Organisation, Landesgruppe Frankreich, 2 March 1942, PA-AA Berlin, Paris 1305.

Chapter 10: Eichmann in Paris

1. Schleier, "Besprechung mit SS-Obersturmführer Dannecker am 1.7.41," 1 July 1941, PA-AA Berlin, Paris 1318. Among the numerous historical treatments of this subject, see especially Klarsfeld, *Vichy-Auschwitz*; Marrus and Paxton, *Vichy France and the Jews*; André Kaspi, *Les Juifs pendant l'Occupation*, 2nd ed. (Paris, 1997); Susan Zuccotti, *The Holocaust, the French, and the Jews* (New York, 1993); Renée Poznanski,

Les Juifs en France pendant la Seconde Guerre mondiale (Paris, 1994); and Florent Brayard, *La "solution finale de la question juive." La technique, le temps et les catégories de la décision* (Paris, 2004).

2. Blanke to the Italian Consulate in Paris, 26 June 1941, AN Paris, AJ⁴⁰, 612. Blanke to Service du Contrôle, 26 June 1941, ibid., AJ³⁸, 342. Stenger to Service du Contrôle, 18 and 31 July, 19 September 1941, ibid., 343–45. Michel to Service du Contrôle, 17 December 1941, ibid., 349.

3. Inspecteur Général des Services de Police Administrative, "Messageries Hachette," 1 July 1941, ibid., AJ⁴¹, 175. MBF, Propaganda-Abteilung, Referat Schrifttum, "Aktenvermerk über die Judenfrage in Paris," 17 July 1941, ibid., AJ⁴⁰, 1006; and "Le trust de la pensée aux mains de la judeo-maçonnerie par le monopole des messageries Hachette," 8 September 1941, ibid. See Fouché, *L'édition française sous l'Occupation*, 1:108–53.

4. Stenger to Service du Contrôle, 22 July 1941, AN Paris, AJ³⁸, 343.

5. "Contentieux Documentation. Mari (influence du ... dans l'aryanisation)," 24 July 1941, ibid., 592.

6. Kommandierender Admiral in Frankreich, Werftbeauftragter (Künzel) to MBF, Treuhand- und Revisionsstelle, 4 October 1941, ibid., AJ⁴⁰, 613. Der Beauftragter des Reichsministers—Seeschiffahrtsamt—für Frankreich to MBF, Treuhand- und Revisionsstelle, 17 October 1941, ibid. Blanke to Service du Contrôle, 18 October 1941, ibid., AJ³⁸, 346. MBF, Treuhand- und Revisionsstelle to Stenger, 22 October 1941, ibid., AJ⁴⁰, 613.

7. "La nouvelle annuaire téléphonique" (translation), *Pariser Zeitung*, 5 December 1941, ibid., AJ³⁸, 7.

8. Vallat to MBF, Verwaltungs-Stab, 16 January 1942, ibid., 9. Knochen to MBF, Verwaltungs-Stab, 20 January 1942, ibid., AJ⁴⁰, 548. Stenger to Service du Contrôle, 6 March 1942, ibid., AJ³⁸, 352.

9. Hufnagel, "Besprechung mit Herrn Simon von der Polizeipräfektur Paris (Renseignements Généraux)," 7 July 1941, ibid., AJ⁴⁰, 553. See Rajsfus, *La police de Vichy*, pp. 33–42; and Peschanski, *La France des camps*, pp. 198–204.

10. "Réunion du 22 août 1941 à l'Hôtel Majestic," 22 August 1941, AN Paris, F¹ᵃ, 3663. Kommandant von Gross-Paris, Chef des Verwaltungs-Stabs to MBF, Verwaltungs-Stab, 23 September 1941, ibid., AJ⁴⁰, 881. "Note des franz. Polizeipräfekten, Admiral Bard, über die Tätigkeit der Polizei," 25 September 1941, ibid., 444. See Grynberg, *Les camps de la honte*, pp. 310–18.

11. Propaganda-Staffel Paris, "Stimmungsbericht," 13 December 1941, AN Paris, AJ⁴⁰, 873. Entries for 12 and 14 December 1941, "À Paris," 31 July 1944, ibid., AJ⁷², 288.

12. MBF, Kommando-Stab, Abt. Ia, "Lagebericht für die Monate August/September 1941," 30 September 1941, ibid., AJ⁴⁰, 443. "État d'avancement d'aryanisation," 13 November 1941, ibid., AJ³⁸, 655. Blanke, "Note relative aux donations des juifs," 20 November 1941, ibid., 75.

13. Dannecker, "Überwachung der Entscheidungen des französischen Judenkommissariats über Nichtzugehörigkeit zur jüdischen Rasse," 4 November 1941, BA Berlin, F 70 Frankreich/31. "Gegnerisch-weltanschauliche Einflüsse in Frankreich," 10 November 1941, AN Paris, AJ⁴⁰, 413. Verbindungsstelle Frankreich der Organisation der Deutschen Wirtschaft to Blanke, 17 November 1941, ibid., 612. Vallat to Blanke, 3 December 1941, ibid., AJ³⁸, 9.

14. MBF, Verwaltungs-Stab to Vallat, 25 November 1941, ibid., AJ⁴⁰, 612. MBF, Kommando-Stab, Abt. Ia, "Lagebericht für die Monate Oktober/November 1941," 30 November 1941, BA-MA Freiburg, RW 35/10.

15. Stülpnagel to Brinon, 15 December 1941, AN Paris, F⁷, 14895. Stülpnagel, "Sicherheit der Deutschen Wehrmacht in Frankreich," 6 January 1942, CDJC Paris, VIII-2.

16. Union Générale des Israélites de France to Pétain, 20 January 1942, AN Paris, F⁷, 15310. See Richard I. Cohen, *The Burden of Conscience: French Jewish Leadership during the Holocaust* (Bloomington, 1987), pp. 48–69; and Rayski, *Le choix des juifs sous Vichy*, pp. 68–85.

17. Zeitschel to Achenbach, 3 March 1942, PA-AA Berlin, Paris 1318.

18. Knochen to Dienststelle Sturmbannführer Uhlers (in Brussels), 10 March 1942, CDJC Paris, XLIXa-1.

19. "Aktennotiz über die Unterredung zwischen SS-Obersturmführer Dannecker … und dem französischen Generalkommissar für Judenfragen, Vallat," 17 February 1942, ibid., XXIV-21. Dannecker, "Kennzeichnung der Juden," 15 March 1942, ibid., XLIXa-2. SD, "Absprache mit der Deutschen Botschaft. Kennzeichnung der Juden," 17 April 1942, ibid., 5.

20. Zeitschel to Best, 5 May 1942, PA-AA Berlin, Paris 1125 A.

21. Best to Sipo-SD, 31 March 1942, CDJC Paris, XLIXa-4. MBF, Verwaltungs-Stab, Abt. Verwaltung, "Sabotierung deutscher Anordnungen durch das Generalkommissariat für Judenfragen," 6 May 1942, BA Berlin, R 70 Frankreich/32. See Laurent Joly, *Vichy dans la "Solution Finale." Histoire du Commissariat général aux Questions juives (1941–1944)* (Paris, 2006), pp. 14–17. A quirky biography of Darquier (the "de Pellepoix" was invented), appropriate to the subject, is by Carmen Callil, *Bad Faith: A Forgotten History of Family, Fatherland, and Vichy France* (New York, 2006).

22. SD to RSHA, 23 May 1942, CDJC Paris, XLIXa-16. MBF to Brinon, 27 May 1942, AN Paris, AJ⁴⁰, 549. Oberg, "Kennzeichnung der Juden," 1 June 1942, CDJC Paris, XLIXa-18. Memo by Oberg, 3 June 1942, AN Paris, AJ⁴⁰, 1188.

23. MBF, Verwaltungs-Stab, Abt. Verwaltung, Gruppe 4 (Schule und Kultur) to Gruppe 5 im Hause, 18 May 1942, CDJC Paris, XLI-34. Propaganda-Staffel Paris to Knochen, 10 June 1942, ibid., XLIXa-32. Oberg, "Entwurf. 9. Verordnung über Massnahmen gegen Juden," 18 June 1942, ibid., XLI-3. On the yellow star, see Rajsfus, *La police de Vichy*, pp. 99–110; Poznanski, *Les Juifs en France*, pp. 290–305; and François Bédarida and Renée Bédarida, "La persécution des Juifs," in Jean-Pierre Azéma and François Bédarida (eds.), *La France des années noires*, 2nd ed., 2 vols. (Paris, 2000), 2:149–82.

24. Both Paxton and Jackson, for instance, mention Aryanization briefly in their text but omit it from the index. See Paxton, *Vichy France*, pp. 177–79; and Jackson, *France: The Dark Years*, p. 357. But see Antoine Prost et al. (eds.), *Ayranisation économique et restitutions. Mission d'étude sur la spoliation des Juifs en France* (Paris, 2000); Verheyde, *Les mauvais comptes de Vichy*; Marrus and Paxton, *Vichy France and the Jews*, pp. 152–60; Kaspi, *Les Juifs pendant l'Occupation*, pp. 112–29; Joly, *Vichy dans la "Solution Finale,"* pp. 596–609; and the chapter entitled "L'aryanisation économique. Vichy, l'occupant et la spoliation des juifs," in Henry Rousso, *Vichy. L'événement, la mémoire, l'histoire* (Paris, 2001), pp. 110–47.

25. Statistics may be gathered from dossiers of the Service du Contrôle, 17 December 1941 to 24 July 1942, AN Paris, AJ³⁸, 537.

26. "Abschlussbericht … über die Tätigkeit der Treuhand- und Revisionsstelle im Bereich des Militärbefehlshabers in Frankreich im Geschäftsjahr 1941," 31 December 1941, ibid., AJ⁴⁰, 591.

27. Memo from MBF, Abt. Wi I, 31 December 1941, ibid., AJ³⁸, 76. Stenger to Service du Contrôle, 21 and 26 January, 25 February, and 24 March 1942, ibid., 350–53.

28. Blanke to Sussdorf, 4 February 1942, ibid., AJ[40], 612. "Vermerk. Besprechung zwischen OKVR Rinke, Dr. Blanke und KR Stenger," 31 March 1942, ibid., 591. Stenger to Service du Contrôle, 2 April 1942, ibid., AJ[38], 78.

29. "Statistique des dossiers remis aux autorités allemandes pendant le mois du mars 1942," 1 April 1942, ibid., AJ[38], 654. The same file contains similar statistics for the balance of 1942.

30. "Vermerk. Bericht der Treuhand- und Revisionsstelle im Bereich des Militärbefehlshabers in Frankreich—Geschäftsjahr 1941," 26 May 1942, ibid., AJ[40], 615. "Vermerk. Einsetzungsgebühr für Judenvermögen," 2 October 1942, ibid.

31. Stenger to CGQJ, Direction de l'Aryanisation économique, 4 June 1942, ibid., AJ[38], 357. Blanke to CGQJ, 22 June 1942, ibid., 358. Darquier de Pellepoix, "Note pour MM. les Chefs de Section," 26 June 1942, ibid., 1. Roger Bourgeois, "Essai de réorganisation du Commissariat général aux questions juives," 30 June 1942, ibid. Cathala, "Patrimoines séquestrés et biens juifs. Incidents avec les autorités d'occupation," 17 July 1942, ibid., F[17], 13391.

32. MBF, Abt. Wi I/1 (signed by Stülpnagel) to MVB A, B, C, and Kommandant von Gross-Paris, 21 July 1942, ibid., AJ[40], 615; and "Wirtschaftsbericht über die Monate Juni/September 1942," 1 November 1942, BA-MA Freiburg, RW 35/305.

33. Zeitschel to Dannecker, 8 October 1941, CDJC Paris, V-11.

34. Schmid to Kommandant des Internierungslagers Compiègne, 19 December 1941, AN Paris, AJ[40], 871. Schmid to Kommandant von Gross-Paris, 30 December 1941, ibid.

35. Stülpnagel to Generalquartiermeister Wagner, 15 January 1942, BA-MA Freiburg, RW 35/536.

36. Best, "Behandlung jüdischer Häftlinge im Polizeilager Compiègne," 10 February 1942, CDJC Paris, IV-180.

37. Dannecker, "Deportierung von 1000 Juden nach dem Osten," 10 March 1942, ibid., XXVb-13. See Brayard, La "solution finale de la question juive," pp. 81–86.

38. Dannecker, "Abtransport der 1000 Juden aus Compiègne bzw. Drancy," 20 March 1942, CDJC Paris, XXVb-17. MBF, Kommando-Stab, Abt.Ia, "Lagebericht für die Monate Februar 1942/März 1942," 31 March 1942, BA-MA Freiburg, RW 35/14. MBF, Verwaltungs-Stab, Abt. Verwaltung, V pol, "Deportation asozialer Elemente nach dem Osten," 9 April 1942, AN Paris, F[7], 15142. See Steur, Theodor Dannecker, pp. 72–73.

39. Dannecker to Sipo-SD, Abt. IV J, 13 May 1942, CDJC Paris, XXVb-29. See Brayard, La "solution finale de la question juive," pp. 109–15.

40. Dannecker to RSHA, 15 May 1942, CDJC Paris, XXVb-29. SD Berlin to Dienststelle Paris, 16 May 1942, ibid. See Rajsfus, Drancy, pp. 44–76; and Cohen, The Burden of Conscience, pp. 88–94.

41. Eichmann to AA (Rademacher), 22 June 1942, PA-AA Berlin, Nachlass Schleier, II. Dannecker, "Weitere Judentransporte aus Frankreich," 29 June 1942, CDJC Paris, XXVb-44. Memo to RSHA by Eichmann, "Dienstbesprechung im Hinblick auf die bevorstehende Evakuierung aus Frankreich mit SS-Hauptsturmführer Dannecker, Paris," 1 July 1942, ibid., 45. See Klarsfeld, Vichy-Auschwitz, 1:83–87; and Peschanski, La France des camps, pp. 348–52.

42. Schleier to AA, 13 March 1942, CDJC Paris, XXVb-13. Abetz to AA, 2 July 1942, PA-AA Berlin, Nachlass Schleier, II. Dannecker to RSHA, 6 July 1942, CDJC Paris, XLIX-35. See Steur, Theodor Dannecker, pp. 82–83.

43. Röthke, "Abtransport staatloser Juden," 18 July 1942, CDJC Paris, XLIX-67.

44. Jünger, "Das erste Pariser Tagebuch," in *Sämtliche Werke. Tagebücher*, 2:347. See Heimo Schwilk, *Ernst Jünger. Ein Jahrhundertleben* (Munich, 2007), pp. 379–87. See also Marrus and Paxton, *Vichy France and the Jews*, pp. 217–78; Klarsfeld, *Vichy-Auschwitz*, 1:8, 55–87, 191; Poznanski, *Les Juifs en France*, pp. 316–19; Rayski, *Le choix des juifs sous Vichy*, pp. 99–117; and Jackson, *France. The Dark Years*, pp. 217–19.

45. See Claude Lévy and Paul Tillard, *La grande rafle du Vel d'Hiv (16 juillet 1942)*, 2nd ed. (Paris, 1992), pp. 92–95.

46. Unsigned memo from the SS in Paris to RSHA, "Abtransport von Juden aus Frankreich," 25 September 1942, CDJC Paris, XXVc-177. Dannecker's dismissal by Knochen was "very surprising," says Steur, *Theodor Dannecker*, pp. 85–86.

47. See Lévy and Tillard, *La grande rafle*, pp. 105–12; Marrus and Paxton, *Vichy France and the Jews*, pp. 228–34; Peschanski, *La France des camps*, pp. 345–48; and Brayard, *La "solution finale de la question juive,"* pp. 121–24, 141–45.

48. FK 757 to Kommandant von Gross-Paris, Kommando-Stab, 26 September 1942, AN Paris, AJ⁴⁰, 897. See Rajsfus, *La police de Vichy*, pp. 75–97; Peschanski, *La France des camps*, pp. 323–32; and Berlière, *Les policiers français sous l'Occupation*, pp. 29–35.

49. Some military personnel, transferred from the Russian front to Paris in late 1941, brought with them stories of mass executions in the East. "From then on there was no more incertitude at the Majestic," writes Bartgatzky, *Hotel Majestic*, pp. 101–3. See the chapter entitled "Das Wissen um Auschwitz," by Meyer, *Täter im Verhör*, pp. 270–98.

Chapter 11: A Turn of Fortune

1. Hitler to Pétain, 11 and 26 November 1942, AN Paris, AJ⁴¹, 87. See Robert O. Paxton, "La coupure décisive pour Vichy (novembre 1942). L'État français vassalisé," in Azéma and Bédarida (eds.), *La France des années noires*, 2:11–39.

2. MBF, Abt. WWSF, "Kriegstagebuch," 14–20 November 1942, BA-MA Freiburg, RW 24/5. MVB B (Angers) to MBF, Verwaltungs-Stab, 5 December 1942, AN Paris, AJ⁴⁰, 541. Oberg to Wolff (at the Wolfsschanze), 16 December 1942, BA Berlin, NS 19/2755. MBF, Kommando-Stab, Abt. Ia, "Monatsbericht für Dezember 1942," 6 January 1943, BA-MA Freiburg, RW 35/289. Stülpnagel to MBF, Kommando-Stab and Verwaltungs-Stab, 10 January 1943, AN Paris, AJ⁴⁰, 450.

3. Knochen to Himmler, 9 November 1942, BA Berlin, NS 19/3947. Telegram from Knochen to Himmler, 12 November 1942, ibid., 1927. Lischka to Himmler, 1 December 1942, ibid., 2542.

4. Knochen to RSHA, 11 December 1942, ibid., 1929. Sipo-SD, "Lagebericht für die Zeit vom 26. Nov. bis 9. Dez. 1942," 16 December 1942, ibid., R 58/ZR 945 A.01. Sipo-SD, "Lagebericht für die Zeit vom 10. bis 31. Dezember 1942," 6 January 1943, ibid. Sipo-SD, "Lagebericht für die Zeit vom 14. bis 25. Januar 1943," 30 January 1943, ibid., R 58/7742.

5. FK 757 (Neuilly) to Kommandant von Gross-Paris, 28 November 1942, AN Paris, AJ⁴⁰, 897. Kommandant von Gross-Paris to MBF, 4 December 1942, ibid. KK 896 (Asnières) to FK 757, 28 December 1942 and 28 January 1943, ibid. FK 757 to Kommandant von Gross-Paris, 28 January 1943, ibid.

6. KK 896 to FK 757, Abt. Ic, 28 November 1942, ibid. KK 786 (Montrouge) to FK 757, Abt. Ic, 28 November 1942, ibid.

7. Kommandant von Gross-Paris, "Kommandantur-Befehl Nr. 11," 28 January 1943, BA-MA Freiburg, RH 36/37.

8. Kommandant von Gross-Paris to MBF, 4 February 1943, AN Paris, AJ⁴⁰, 897. KK 786 to FK 757, Abt. Ic, 25 February 1943, ibid. FK 757, Abt. VI (Courbevoie) to FK 757, Abt. Ic, 27 February 1943, ibid. KK 896 to FK 757, Abt. Ic, 29 March 1943, ibid.

9. Telegram from Rahn to Ribbentrop, 25 November 1942, PA-AA Berlin, R 27782. Grosse, "Aufzeichnung" (for Schleier), 27 November 1942, ibid., Paris 1329. DB to Sipo-SD, 24 December 1942, ibid., 2479. Grimm, "Bericht über meine Reise nach Paris vom 14.12.–24.12.1942," 29 December 1942, ibid., 1330.

10. For background on the Ambassador's absence from Paris, see Lambauer, *Otto Abetz*, pp. 568–87.

11. Hemmen to AA, 23 January 1943, PA-AA Berlin, Paris 2472. Stülpnagel to Schleier, 30 January 1943, ibid.

12. General von Unruh to Keitel, Lammers, and Bormann, 27 July 1943, BA Berlin, NS 19/342. SS-Standartenführer Wirt to Himmler, 28 July 1943, ibid.

13. Abetz to AA, 18 December 1943, PA-AA Berlin, Paris 1106 X. See the comments on "Meine neue Mission in Paris" by Abetz, *Das offene Problem*, pp. 267–76.

14. Stülpnagel to Sauckel, 23 April 1943, AN Paris, AJ⁴⁰, 846. Sauckel to Stülpnagel, 10 August 1943, ibid. Stülpnagel to Sauckel, 12 and 21 August 1943, ibid.

15. Telegram from Oberg to Himmler, 16 November 1942, BA Berlin, NS 19/1928. MBF, Abt. WWSF, "Kriegstagebuch," 26–31 December 1942, BA-MA Freiburg, RW 24/5.

16. Blumentritt (signing for Rundstedt), "Aufgaben und Befugnisse des Höheren SS- und Polizeiführers und der ihm untergestellten Dienststellen im neubesetzten Gebiet," 6 March 1943, BA Berlin, R 70 Frankreich/12. Oberg, "Aufgaben und Befugnisse des Höheren SS- und Polizeiführers im neubesetzten Gebiet," 15 April 1943, ibid.

17. Kommandant von Gross-Paris, Militärverwaltung (Eckelmann) to Lt. General von Boinenburg-Lengsfeld, 23 August 1943, AN Paris, AJ⁴⁰, 539. Medicus, "Vermerk," 25 August 1943, ibid.

18. Medicus, "Verhalten der Militärverwaltung im Ernstfall," 4 March 1943, ibid.

19. Knochen, "Haltung der französischen Polizei," 19 August 1943, BA Berlin, R 70 Frankreich/13.

20. Sipo-SD, S pol II, "Bericht über die gegenwärtige Haltung der französischen Polizei," 19 August 1943, ibid. MBF, Verwaltungs-Stab, Abt. MVZ, "Lagebericht über Verwaltung und Wirtschaft. Juli/September 1943 mit Beitrag des Wehrwirtschaftsstabs West," 6 November 1943, BA-MA Freiburg, RW 35/292.

21. MBF, "Stabsbefehl Nr. 46," 31 August 1943, AN Paris, AJ⁴⁰, 410. Kommand- ant von Gross-Paris, Abt. Ia, "Bestrafungen wegen Nichtbefolgerung der Befehle bei Fliegeralarm," 25 September 1943, PA-AA Berlin, Paris 1123 A.

22. "Vernichtungsverhandlung," 20 March 1943, BA-MA Freiburg, RW 49/92. MBF, "Stabsbefehl Nr. 48" and "Stabsbefehl Nr. 49," 11 and 17 September 1943, AN Paris, AJ⁴⁰, 410. MBF, Verwaltungs-Stab, Abt. MVZ, "Abgabe von Akten und Vorbereitung für ein Ausweichen," 7 March 1944, BA-MA Freiburg, RW 35/317.

23. Oberstleutnant Besser, "Regimentsbefehl Nr. 58/43," 17 November 1943, BA- MA Freiburg, RW 35/317. MBF, Verwaltungs-Stab, "Merkblatt zur Benutzung des Bunkers bei Fliegeralarm," 1 March 1944, AN Paris, AJ⁴⁰, 852. MBF, "Stabsbefehl Nr. 21/44," 30 March 1944, ibid., 410.

24. MBF, Verwaltungs-Stab, Abt. Wi II to Fachreferat Wi II, 6 March 1944, BA-MA Freiburg, RW 35/1420.

25. Stülpnagel, "Mangel an Haltung," 16 October 1943, AN Paris, AJ⁴⁰, 451.

26. MBF, Verwaltungs-Stab (Hofacker), "Regiment Majestic," 23 February 1944, ibid.

27. MBF, "Stabsbefehl Nr. 30/44," 25 May 1944, ibid., 410.

28. Darnand to Laval, 14 July 1943, BA-MA Freiburg, RW 49/112. MBF, Abt. WWSW West, Gruppe Ic, "Monatsbericht Januar 1944," 15 February 1944, ibid., RW 24/11. The maximum strength of French Milice forces has been estimated between 15,000 and 25,000. For sketches of Darnand's role in leading them, see Pierre Giolitto, *Histoire de la Milice*, 2nd ed. (Paris, 2002), pp. 102–24, 191–227; Burrin, *La France à l'heure allemande*, pp. 174–79; and Jackson, *France: The Dark Years*, pp. 230–32, 530–31.

29. MBF, Verwaltungs-Stab, Abt. MVZ, "Lagebericht über Verwaltung und Wirtschaft Oktober/Dezember 1943," 27 January 1944, BA-MA Freiburg, RW 35/292.

Chapter 12: A Police State

1. Permilleux, "Résumé de mon entretien avec M. le Lieutenant Rötke [*sic*] et M. Schweblin, 31 avenue Foch, le 23 novembre," sent by Prefect of Police Bard to Bousquet, 26 November 1942, AN Paris, F[7], 14895. DB (Bode) to Zweigstelle Vichy, 5 January 1943, PA-AA Berlin, Paris 2454. Stülpnagel to DB, 6 January 1943, ibid., 1279. Schleier to AA, 29 January 1943, ibid., 2474.

2. Bousquet to Oberg, 13 April 1943, AN Paris, F[7], 14886. Humm to Leguay, 15 April 1943, ibid. Oberg to DB, 16 April 1943, PA-AA Berlin, Paris 1120 B.

3. "Procès-verbal. Conférence du 2 juin à 12 h," 2 June 1943, AN Paris, F[7], 14886. Bousquet to all regional and departmental prefects, 25 September 1943, ibid., 14897. The Gestapo "would have been impotent without the assistance and, most often, the initiative of the French police," comment Courtois, Peschanski, and Rayski, *Le sang de l'étranger*, p. 221.

4. MBF, Abt. WWSW, "Bekämpfung von Fallschirmjägern und Luftlandetruppen im Bereich des Militärbefehlshabers in Frankreich," 12 February 1943, BA-MA Freiburg, RW 24/9. Prefect of the Loir-et-Cher to Sipo (at Blois), 14 February 1943, AN Paris, F[7], 14886. Knochen to Leguay, 26 February 1943, ibid., 14889. Knochen to Bousquet, 13 September 1943, ibid.

5. Bousquet, "Note pour Monsieur Leguay," 26 February 1943, AN Paris, F[7], 14886. "Note pour Monsieur Bousquet," 14 May 1943, ibid.

6. Knochen to Bousquet, 31 August 1943, ibid., 14887. Regional Prefect of the Aisne-Ardennes-Oise-Somme to Bousquet, 2 September 1943, ibid., 14886.

7. Oberg to Bousquet, 9 December 1943, ibid., 14898. See Kasten, *"Gute Franzosen,"* pp. 107–20.

8. Oberg to Darnand, 2 February 1944, AN Paris, F[7], 14887. Darnand, "Note pour Monsieur le Délégué en Zône Nord du Secrétaire Général au Maintien de l'Ordre," 11 May 1944, ibid.

9. Brune (Commissaire de la Voie Publique) to Directeur Général de la Police Municipale, 16 May 1944, ibid., 14886.

10. "Conférence du samedi 20 mars 1943 aux services de la Police allemande, 74 avenue Foch, Paris," 20 March 1943, ibid. Laube (Sipo-SD) to Leguay, 26 June 1943, ibid., 14890.

11. Directeur Général de la Police Nationale, "Note pour Monsieur Leguay," 21 September 1943, ibid., 14890. Bard to Hagen, 25 September 1943, ibid.

12. Commissaire Divisionnaire des Gares Paris-Est et Paris-Bastille to Préfet Délégué du Secrétaire Général à la Police, 5 October 1943, ibid., 14897. Bousquet to Oberg,

14 October 1943, ibid. Commissaire de Police de la Gare St. Lazare to Commissaire Divisionnaire, 23 October 1943, ibid.

13. Prefect of Police to Minister of the Interior, 4 January 1944, ibid., 14904. MBF, Verwaltungs-Stab, Abt. MVZ, "Lagebericht über Verwaltung und Wirtschaft Oktober/ Dezember 1943," 27 January 1944, BA-MA Freiburg, RW 35/292. See Kasten, "Gute Franzosen," pp. 124–25.

14. Knipping to Prefect of Police, 31 January 1944, AN Paris, F⁷, 14900. Ministry of Justice to Ministry of the Interior, 11 February 1944, ibid., 14880. Oberg to Darnand, 25 March 1944, ibid., 14886. Clamoz to all regional and departmental prefects, 2 May 1944, ibid. See Courtois, Peschanski, and Rayski, Le sang de l'étranger, p. 10.

15. Stülpnagel, "Banden- und Sabotagebekämpfung," 12 February 1944, BA-MA Freiburg, RW 35/551. Darnand to Oberg, 16 March 1944, AN Paris, F⁷, 14898.

16. Sipo-SD, "Lagebericht," 16 December 1942, 30 January, 5 March, and 2 August 1943, BA Berlin, R 58/ZR 945 A.01 and 7742. Memo from DB (Krug), 31 October 1943, PA-AA Berlin, Paris 2479. DSA, "Étude sur la question des arrestations en France," 8 November 1943, AN Paris, AJ⁴¹, 257. See statistics on mounting violence in 1943 in Hans Luther, Der französische Widerstand gegen die deutsche Besatzungsmacht und seine Bekämpfung (Tübingen, 1957), p. 49.

17. Prefecture of Police to Ministry of the Interior, 4 January 1944, AN Paris, F⁷, 14904.

18. List of prisons contained in a police memo, "Seine," 1944, ibid., AJ⁷², 288.

19. Police report entitled "Rigueurs policières exagérées," 8 January 1944, ibid., AJ⁴¹, 60.

20. "Statistique des attentats terroristes—mois d'avril," (?) April 1944, ibid., F⁷, 15312.

21. Ministry of the Interior, Sous-Direction Technique, "Note pour Monsieur le Secrétaire Général au Maintien de l'Ordre," 3 April 1944, ibid., 14894. "Liste des miliciens et franc-gardes assassinés," 13 April 1944, ibid., 14896.

22. "Liste der französischen Eisenbahner, die im Ernstfalle sofort verhaftet werden sollen," 25 April 1944, BA Berlin, R 124/86. "Mémento de la conférence avec le Président Witgen tenue à la H.V.D.," 2 May 1944, AN Paris, AJ⁷², 1927. "Eisenbahnbetrieb im Kampffall," 11 May 1944, BA Berlin, R 124/86.

23. Oberg to Stülpnagel, 13 May 1944, AN Paris, AJ⁴⁰, 541. "Conférence de presse tenue à l'Ambassade d'Allemagne," 16 May 1944, ibid., F⁷, 14886. Abetz to MBF (Humm), 20 May 1944, ibid., AJ⁴⁰, 541. Knochen to Stülpnagel, 1 June 1944, ibid.

24. DSA, "État des personnes condamnées à mort et exécutées par les Autorités allemandes," (?) November 1942, ibid., AJ⁴¹, 257. MBF, Kommando-Stab, Abt. Ia (Kossmann), "Monatsbericht für Dezember 1942," 6 January 1943, BA-MA Freiburg, RW 35/289. DSA, "État des personnes condamnées à mort et exécutées par les Autorités allemandes," 27 January 1943, AN Paris, AJ⁴¹, 325. BdS, II pol to Sipo-SD, Abt. IV, 10 February 1943, CDJC Paris, XLV-62ᵈ. After mid-1942, the execution of hostages played "a lesser role," confirms Umbreit, Der Militärbefehlshaber, pp. 141–42.

25. Himmler, "Durchführungsbestimmungen für Exekutionen," 6 January 1943, CDJC Paris, VII-8.

26. BdS, II pol, "Aktenvermerk. Abtransport von Häftlingen," 10 February 1943, ibid., XLV-65. "Liste des otages fusillés et incinérés," 11 August, 21 September, and 2 December 1943, AN Paris, AJ⁷², 260. See Serge Klarsfeld and Léon Tsevery, Les 1007 fusillés du Mont Valérien parmi lesquels 174 juifs (Paris, 1995), p. 5; and Berlière, Les policiers français, pp. 202–19.

27. Umbreit, Der Militärbefehlshaber, p. 123.

28. DSA, "Compte rendu hebdomadaire pour la Zône Nord (occupée)," 4 March 1943, AN Paris, AJ[41], 325.

29. Ibid.

30. Stülpnagel, "Strafverfahren gegen Terroristen," 25 January 1944, BA-MA Freiburg, RW 35/551. "Tableau des condamnations à mort prononcées par les Autorités allemandes," memo forwarded by Brinon to Guerard, 13 April 1944, AN Paris, AJ[41], 325. Darnand to regional and departmental prefects of the Seine, Seine-et-Oise, and Seine-et-Marne, 16 April 1944, ibid., F[7], 14900.

31. Kommandant von Gross-Paris, "Kommandantur-Befehl Nr. 63," 17 May 1943, BA-MA Freiburg, RH 36/39. Peters to DB, 15 June 1943, PA-AA Berlin, Paris 2456. MBF, Kommando-Stab, Abt. Ic to Legationssekretär von Nostitz, 11 October 1943, ibid.

32. One Foreign Office file—PA-AA Berlin, Paris 2487—contains long lists of criminal charges and death sentences (*zum Tode*) throughout 1943.

33. MBF, Kommando-Stab, Abt. Ia, "Einsatzbericht für die Monate November und Dezember 1943," 15 January 1944, BA-MA Freiburg, RW 35/26.

34. See Joseph de La Martinière, *Le décret et la procédure Nacht und Nebel (Nuit et brouillard)* (Orléans, 1981), pp. 4–5; and Gaël Eismann, "L'escalade d'une répression à visage légal. Les pratiques judiciaires des tribunaux du Militärbefehlshaber in Frankreich, 1940–1944," in Eismann and Martens (eds.), *Occupation et répression*, pp. 127–68.

35. MBF, Kommando-Stab, Abt. Ia, "Einsatzbericht für die Monate Januar und Februar 1944," 15 March 1944, BA-MA Freiburg, RW 35/30. Stülpnagel, "Rapport mois de mars 1944 concernant constitution et mise en ligne des troupes de sûreté," 12 May 1944, AN Paris, AJ[72], 260.

36. See chapter 15.

37. MBF, Kommando-Stab, Abt. Ia, "Einsatzbericht für die Monate Januar und Februar 1944," 15 March 1944, BA-MA Freiburg, RW 35/30. DB to AA, 12 April and 16 May 1944, PA-AA Berlin, Paris 2487. Stülpnagel, "Rapport mois de mars 1944 concernant constitution et mise en ligne des troupes de sûreté," 12 May 1944, AN Paris, AJ[72], 260. A recent study, based on an entirely separate cache of military court records housed in the Bundes-Zentrale Nachweisstelle at Aachen, has concluded that MBF tribunals rendered in all nearly 4,000 death sentences between February 1941 and May 1944, of which about half were executed. This study also confirms that the rate of fatality steadily increased: from June 1940 to July 1941, only 25 percent of death sentences were executed, whereas from August 1941 to May 1942, the rate was 80 percent. See Eismann, "L'escalade d'une répression à visage légal," in Eismann and Martens (eds.), *Occupation et répression*, pp. 127–68.

Chapter 13: A Deep Contradiction

1. MBF, Abt.WWSF, "Kriegstagebuch," 7–13 November 1942, BA-MA Freiburg, RW 24/5. MBF, Verwaltungs-Stab, "Lagebericht über Verwaltung und Wirtschaft, Oktober bis Dezember 1942," (?) January 1943, ibid., RW 35/324. "Fünfter Tätigkeitsbericht der Deutschen Waffenstillstands-Delegation für Wirtschaft," 30 June 1943, AN Paris, AJ[40], 414.

2. Kommandant von Gross-Paris, "Lagebericht. Berichtszeit Monat November 1942," 4 December 1942, AN Paris, AJ[40], 897. MBF, Verwaltungs-Stab to Reichsminister für Ernährung und Landwirtschaft (Backe), 18 December 1942, ibid., 796. MBF,

Verwaltungs-Stab, "Lagebericht über Verwaltung und Wirtschaft, Oktober-Dezember 1942," 27 January 1943, ibid., 444. MBF, Verwaltungs-Stab, Abt.Wi, "Wirtschaftsbericht über die Monate Oktober–Dezember 1942," 28 January 1943, PA-AA Berlin, Paris 2462.

3. Göring, "Schwarzmarkt-Aktion," 15 January 1943, PA-AA Berlin, Paris 2462. OKW to AA, 19 February 1943, ibid. Göring to OKW, 17 March 1943, ibid. "Note au sujet de la position des Services français du Contrôle en ce qui concerne la lutte contre le marché noir," 30 March 1943, AN Paris, F[7], 14895.

4. MBF, Abt. Wi I, "Wirtschaftsbericht über die Monate Januar/März 1943," 22 April 1943, BA-MA Freiburg, RW 35/305. MBF, Verwaltungs-Stab, Abt. MVZ, Gruppe 3, "Lagebericht über Verwaltung und Wirtschaft Januar/März 1943," 22 April 1943, ibid., 288. Knoll, "Aufzeichnung für Herrn … Schwendemann," 14 May 1943, PA-AA Berlin, Paris 1124. See Alary, *Les Français au quotidien*, pp. 278–91; and Sanders, *Histoire du marché noir*, pp. 163–227, 263–72.

5. Memo by the Beauftragter des Militärbefehlshabers für Pressepapier, 18 and 28 December 1943, AN Paris, AJ[40], 1014. Rü-Kommando Paris-Est, "Kriegstagebuch," 31 December 1943, BA-MA Freiburg, RW 24/93.

6. Ministère de la Production Industrielle et des Communications, Direction des Chemins de Fer, "Note pour le Ministre," 5 January 1944, AN Paris, AJ[72], 1927. MBF, Abt. Wwi West, Gruppe Ic, "Monatsbericht Januar 1944," 15 February 1944, BA-MA Freiburg, RW 24/11. "Rapport pour le mois d'avril du Militärbefehlshaber en France," 17 June 1944, AN Paris, AJ[72], 260.

7. MBF, Abt.Wi III to Moritz, 14 December 1942, AN Paris, AJ[40], 796. Müller to MBF, Abt. Ernährung und Landwirtschaft (Reinhardt), 14 August 1943, ibid. "Vermerk," 19 August 1943, ibid., 856. "The formidable fact, however, is that in 1943 Germany was directly utilizing for her own purposes at the very least 40 percent of French resources, and probably more," says Milward, *The New Order*, p. 110.

8. Backe to MBF, Abt. Wi, 20 February 1943, PA-AA Berlin, Paris 2462. MBF, Verwaltungs-Stab, Geschäftsgruppe Ernährung, "Vermerk," 4 March 1943, AN Paris, AJ[40], 796. Reinhardt to Backe, 1 September 1943, ibid.

9. Reinhardt to Gramsch, 15 September 1943, AN Paris, AJ[40], 796.

10. "Auszug aus dem Sitzungsprotokoll anlässlich der Besprechung zwischen Gauleiter Sauckel und Regierungschef Laval," 5 March 1943, ibid., 847. "Ergebnis der Pariser Besprechungen vom 8.4. bis 13.4.1943 über die Durchführung lohnordender Massnahmen in Frankreich," 13 April 1943, ibid. "Fünfter Tätigkeitsbericht der Deutschen Stillstands-Delegation für Wirtschaft," 30 June 1943, ibid., 414.

11. Rü-Kommando Paris-Mitte, "Kriegstagebuch," 15 July 1943, BA-MA Freiburg, RW 24/100. "Vermerk," 26 October 1943, AN Paris, AJ[40], 847.

12. "Vermerk," 27 November 1943, AN Paris, AJ[40], 847. MBF, Abt. Wi VII to Glatzel, 30 November 1943, ibid.

13. Glatzel to Sauckel, 6 December 1943, ibid. Telegram from Sauckel to Glatzel, 19 January 1944, ibid. MBF, Verwaltungs-Stab, Hauptabteilung Arbeit, "Vermerk," 25 January 1944, ibid.

14. "Vermerk über die Besprechung beim Chef der Militärverwaltung über die Durchführung der lohnordenden Massnahmen am 7. Februar 1944," 9 February 1944, ibid.

15. Kommandant von Gross-Paris, "Lagebericht. Berichtszeit Monat November 1942," 4 December 1942, ibid., 897. MBF, Abt. WWSF, "Kriegstagebuch," 12–18 December 1942, BA-MA Freiburg, RW 24/5.

16. Sipo-SD, "Lagebericht für die Zeit vom 10. bis 31. Dezember 1942," 6 January 1943, BA Berlin, R 58/ZR 945 A.01. Stud to List, 15 November 1943, AN Paris, AJ⁴⁰, 852.

17. Oberg to Himmler, 4 December 1943, AN Paris, AJ⁴⁰, 846.

18. Memo by the Direction des Renseignements Généraux, 1 June 1944, ibid., F⁷, 15299.

19. Kommandant von Gross-Paris, "Lagebericht. Berichtszeit Monat November 1942," 4 December 1942, ibid., AJ⁴⁰, 897.

20. Memo by MBF, Abt. Wi II (Bach), 2 May 1944, BA-MA Freiburg, RW 35/233.

21. "Note pour la direction de la SNCF," 25 March 1943, AN Paris, AJ⁴¹, 356.

22. "Extrait. Compte-rendu de la réunion des secrétaires généraux ... de la délégation générale du Gouvernement Français dans les territoires occupés," 1 April 1943, ibid. Laporte, "Note pour la Direction des Services de l'Armistice. Objet: Attaques aériennes contre le réseau ferré," 27 May 1943, ibid. "Extrait de la note pour Monsieur l'Ambassadeur de France," 1 October 1943, ibid. MBF, Abt. Wi I, "Wirtschaftsbericht über die Monate Juli/September 1943," 6 November 1943, ibid., AJ⁴⁰, 444. See Georges Ribeill, "Trafics sous contraintes et performances exceptionnelles: un bilan ambigu," in Polino (ed.), *Transports dans la France en guerre*, pp. 153–74.

23. Berger to Friedrich, 2 November 1943, BA-MA Freiburg, RW 35/720. Deutsche Waffenstillstands-Delegation für Wirtschaft to MBF, Abt. Wi, 2 December 1943, ibid. Rüstungs- und Beschaffungsstab Frankreich to MBF, Verwaltungs-Stab, Hauptabteilung Arbeit, 15 March 1944, AN Paris, AJ⁴⁰, 849.

24. MBF, Abt. Wwi West, Gruppe Ic, "Monatsbericht März 1944," 15 April 1944; and "Monatsbericht April 1944," 13 May 1944, BA-MA Freiburg, RW 24/11.

25. Stülpnagel, "Rapport mois de mars 1944 concernant constitution et mise en ligne des troupes de sûreté," 12 May 1944, AN Paris, AJ⁷², 260.

26. Rü-Kommando Paris-Mitte, "Renault," 19 January 1943, BA-MA Freiburg, RW 24/99. Michel, "Grundsätze für die Warenbewirtschaftung," 2 April 1943, AN Paris, AJ⁴⁰, 1188.

27. Backhaus to Brandt, 12 January 1944, BA Berlin, NS 19/2190. MBF, Abt. Wi I/3, "Die französische Industrieproduktion und ihr Absatz für deutsche Rechnung seit 1942," 24 April 1944, CDJC Paris, IV-136. An attempt to represent the statistics with charts and graphs was made by Michel, "Der Beitrag des französischen Raumes zur Kriegswirtschaft," (?) April 1944, BA-MA Freiburg, RW 35/234. See "German Booty from France 1940–1944" by Milward, *The New Order*, p. 81, in which the author sets an astounding aggregate of 155 billion francs.

28. Schleier to AA, 21 and 24 November 1942, PA-AA Berlin, Paris 2446. Ritter to Sauckel, 4 December 1942, AN Paris, AJ⁴⁰, 846.

29. Schleier to AA, 3 December 1942, PA-AA Berlin, Paris 2454. "Aktennotiz über die am 22.12.1942, 16 Uhr, beim G.B.A. Paris stattgefundene Sitzung," 22 December 1942, BA-MA Freiburg, RW 24/39. "Aktennotiz über the Sitzung beim G.B.A. am 27.12.42, 10–12 Uhr," 27 December 1942, ibid. Ministère de la Production (Industrielle) et des Communications, "2ème opération d'envoi des ouvriers en Allemagne," 8 January 1943, AN Paris, F¹², 9968. "Niederschrift über die Besprechung mit Gauleiter Sauckel im Hotel Ritz," 11 January 1943, ibid., AJ⁴⁰, 846. "Vermerk über die Besprechung am 11.1.1943 des Gauleiter Sauckel mit den Rüstungsdienststellen," 11 January 1943, ibid.

30. Kommandant von Gross-Paris, "Lagebericht. Berichtszeit Monat Dezember 1942," 4 January 1943, AN Paris, AJ⁴⁰, 897. Sipo-SD, "Lagebericht für die Zeit vom 10.

bis 31. Dezember 1942," 6 January 1943, BA Berlin, R 58/ZR 945 A.01. "Aktenvermerk betr. II. Sauckelaktion," 13 January 1943, BA-MA Freiburg, RW 24/42.

31. "Aufzeichnung über die Besprechung zwischen Gauleiter Sauckel und Regierungschef Laval am 12.1.43 in der Deutschen Botschaft Paris," 12 January 1943, PA-AA Berlin, Paris 2454. See Kupferman, *Laval*, pp. 388–90.

32. Kaltenbrunner to AA, 2 March 1943, PA-AA Berlin, Paris 2454. Sipo-SD, "Lagebericht für die Zeit vom 16. bis 28. Februar 1943," 5 March 1943, BA Berlin, R 58/ZR 945 A.01. Lischka to RSHA, 18 March 1943, PA-AA Berlin, Paris 2454. Michel to the Beauftragter für den Vierjahresplan, 3 April 1943, AN Paris, AJ[40], 846. See Jacqueline Sainclivier, "La résistance et le STO," in Garnier and Quellien (eds.), *La main-d'oeuvre française*, pp. 517–34.

33. Schleier to AA, 29 March and 1 April 1943, PA-AA Berlin, Paris 2454. Grosse, "Aufzeichnung für Herrn Gesandten Schleier," 1 April 1943, ibid.

34. Schleier to AA, 9 April 1943, ibid.

35. Stülpnagel to Sauckel, 23 April 1943, AN Paris, AJ[40], 846. Rü-Kommando Paris-Mitte, "Kriegstagebuch," 28 April 1943, BA-MA Freiburg, RW 24/99. Bode (FK 517 at Rouen), "Wochenbericht für die Zeit vom 3.–8.5.43," 8 May 1943, AN Paris, AJ[40], 852. Bode to Ritter, 16 May 1943, ibid.

36. Bode to Ritter, 16 May 1943, AN Paris, AJ[40], 852. MBF, Abt. Wi VII, "Vermerk. Betr.: Gestellung von Arbeitskräften für die OT," 17 June 1943; and "Vermerk über die Besprechung mit Generalkommissar Weinmann," 14 July 1943, ibid., 856. See Christian Bougeard, "Les chantiers allemands du mur de l'Atlantique," in Garnier and Quellien (eds.), *La main-d'oeuvre française*, pp. 185–204.

37. Thoennissen, "Überblick des Amtchefs über die in der Zeit vom 1.1.43 bis 30.4.43 beim Deutschen Beschaffungsamt in Frankreich aufgetretenen wesentlichen Probleme, deren Entwicklung und Lösung," 30 April 1943, BA-MA Freiburg, RW 24/41. Rü-Kommando Paris-Ost, "Vierteljährlicher Überblick," 30 June 1943, ibid., 91. Rü-Kommando Paris-West, "Kriegstagebuch," 30 June 1943, ibid., 108. "Résultats des opérations du S.T.O. de l'origine au 1° juillet 1943," 1 July 1943, AN Paris, F[7], 14889. MBF, Abt. Wi VII to Körner, 27 July 1943, ibid., AJ[40], 846.

38. "Compte-rendu sommaire de la réunion du 27 juillet 1943 à 18h au Ministère de la Communication," 27 July 1943, AN Paris, F[12], 9968. On Bichelonne, see Jackson, *France: The Dark Years*, pp. 162–65.

39. Bichelonne to Stülpnagel, 26 July 1943, AN Paris, AJ[72], 1926. Speer to Bichelonne, 9 September 1943, ibid. "Procès-verbal de la conférence tenue à Berlin le vendredi 17 septembre dans le bureau de Monsieur le Ministre Speer," 17 September 1943, ibid. "Procès-verbal de la conférence tenue à Berlin (Wannsee) le vendredi 17 septembre 1943 après-midi," 17 Septembre 1943, ibid. "Compte-rendu sommaire des entretiens de Berlin entre M. Bichelonne et M. le Ministre Speer," 20 September 1943, ibid. See Tooze, *The Wages of Destruction*, p. 640.

40. Dorsch, "Niederschrift über die Besprechung beim Führer am 21. November 1943," 22 November 1943, BA Berlin, NS 19/2354. Speer to Sauckel, 22 November 1943, ibid. Oberg to Himmler, 4 December 1943, AN Paris, AJ[40], 846. On the conflict between Sauckel and Speer, see Janssen, *Das Ministerium Speer*, pp. 76–87, 121–32; and Arne Radtke-Delacor, "Verlängerte Werkbank im Westen. Deutsche Produktionsaufträge als Trumpfkarte der industriellen Kollaboration in Frankreich (1942–1944)," in Martens and Vaïsse (eds.), *Frankreich und Deutschland im Krieg*, pp. 327–50.

41. "Übersicht. Abtransportierte Kräfte—I., II. und III. Frankreich Aktion," 31 December 1943, AN Paris, AJ[40], 851.

Chapter 14: A Waning Hope

1. KK 786 (Montrouge) to FK 757 (Neuilly), 28 November 1942, AN Paris, AJ⁴⁰, 897. Sipo-SD, "Lagebericht für die Zeit vom 14. bis 25. Januar 1943," 30 January 1943, BA Berlin, R 58/7742. Schleier, "Umlauf an alle Botschaftsangehörigen," 3 February 1943, PA-AA Berlin, Paris 1123 A.

2. KK 786 to FK 757, 25 February 1943, AN Paris, AJ⁴⁰, 897. Kaltenbrunner to AA, 2 March 1943, PA-AA Berlin, Paris 2454. Sipo-SD, "Lagebericht für die Zeit vom 16. bis 28. Februar 1943," 5 March 1943, BA Berlin, R 58/ZR 945 A.01.

3. MBF, Verwaltungs-Stab, "Lagebericht über Verwaltung und Wirtschaft, Januar/ März 1943," 22 April 1943; and "Lagebericht über Verwaltung und Wirtschaft, April/Juni 1943," 21 July 1943, AN Paris, AJ⁴⁰, 444. Abert, "Aufzeichnung für Herrn Kutzschenbach," 23 July 1943, PA-AA Berlin, Paris 1119 B. Grimm, "Bericht über meine Reise nach Paris vom 12.–26. Juli 1943," 27 July 1943, ibid., 1330. See Eckard Michels, "Die Stimmung in Frankreich aus Sicht der Besatzungsbehörden 1942–44," in Martens and Vaïsse (eds.), *Frankreich und Deutschland im Krieg*, pp. 145–61.

4. Sauckel to Bormann, 10 August 1943, AN Paris, AJ⁴⁰, 846.

5. Knochen to RSHA, 2 August 1943, BA Berlin, R 58/7742.

6. Schleier to DB, Zweigstelle Vichy, 19 August 1943, PA-AA Berlin, Paris 2479. Medicus, "Vermerk," 25 August 1943, AN Paris, AJ⁴⁰, 539.

7. "Niederschrift über the Einführung der Arbeitseinsatzstäbe ... in Paris, Deputier-tenkammer," 27 August 1943, AN Paris, AJ⁴⁰, 853. Oberg, "Abschrift. Der Führer ist in Gefahr!" 15 September 1943, ibid., 451.

8. Rü-Kommando Paris-Mitte, "Kriegstagebuch," 8 October 1943, BA-MA Freiburg, RW 24/101. Rü-Kommando Paris-Ost, "Lagebericht für Monat September," 18 October 1943, ibid., 92. AA to DB, 30 October 1943, PA-AA Berlin, Paris 2479.

9. Galley (Directeur Général du Cinéma in the Ministère de l'Information), "Note pour Monsieur le Secrétaire d'État," 7 November 1942, AN Paris, F⁷, 15294. Ministère de l'Information, "Note sur la situation actuelle du cinéma français," 15 July 1943, PA-AA Berlin, Paris 1113 Z. See Engel, *Deutsche Kulturpolitik*, p. 439.

10. Abetz to Gast, 3 May 1944, PA-AA Berlin, Paris 1113 Z. Reinigger, "Geschäftsjahr 1943/44. Entwicklung des Verleihs deutscher und Continental-Filme in Frankreich," 2 June 1944, ibid., 1114.

11. Schleier to DB, Zweigstelle Vichy, 20 November 1942, ibid., 1106 Y. Krug to DB, 24 November 1942, ibid. Messageries de la Coopérative des Journaux Français, "Prises nettes quotidiennes: semaine du 3 au 9 janvier inclus," 20 January 1943, AN Paris, AJ⁴⁰, 1013.

12. Schwendemann, "Aufzeichnung: Projet de réunion des journalistes des deux zones à Paris," 25 February 1943, PA-AA Berlin, Paris 1123 A/1.

13. DB (Knothe) to AA, 25 May 1943, ibid., 1139 A. DB to Laval, 17 June 1943, CDJC Paris, II-159. Pietri (Directeur de la Presse in the Ministère de l'Information) to Bousquet, 18 June 1943, AN Paris, F⁷, 14897. Kommandant von Gross-Paris, "Standort-befehl Nr. 24/44," 29 April 1944, BA-MA Freiburg, RH 36/42.

14. DB (Bargen) to AA, 27 April 1944, PA-AA Berlin, Paris 1106 X. Messageries de la Coopérative des Journaux Français to MBF, Abt. Propaganda, 15 May 1944, AN Paris, AJ⁴⁰, 1014.

15. Groupement Coopératif de la Presse Périodique Générale to Klecker, 5 November 1943, AN Paris, AJ⁴⁰, 1013. "Note sur l'Édition," 21 December 1943, ibid., F¹⁷, 13338. DB (Kutzschenbach) to Kommandant von Gross-Paris, Verwaltungs-Stab, 21

December 1943, PA-AA Berlin, Paris 1141 B. Oberg to Schmidtke, 24 December 1943, AN Paris, AJ⁴⁰, 1009.

16. DB (Weinhold) to DB, Zweigstelle Vichy, 9 April, 6 May, and 7 June 1943, PA-AA Berlin, Paris 1145 B. Memo by Renseignements Généraux, 11 July 1943, AN Paris, F⁷, 15299.

17. Sipo-SD, "Lagebericht für die Zeit vom 14. bis 25. Januar 1943," 30 January 1943, BA Berlin, R 58/7742. Goebbels to Stülpnagel, 13 December 1943, BA-MA Freiburg, RW 35/537. Humm to Abetz, 14 March 1944, ibid.

18. DB (Kutzschenbach) to AA, Abt. Rundfunk, 20 March 1944, PA-AA Berlin, Paris 1116 B. Pressedienst (Bassewitz), "Wochenbericht vom 7. bis 13. April 1944," 13 April 1944, AN Paris, AJ⁴⁰, 1015. Abetz to AA, 24 May 1944, PA-AA Berlin, Paris 1116 D.

19. MBF, Verwaltungs-Stab, Abt. Verwaltung, "Einziehung von Rundfunkgeräten," 24 March 1944, BA-MA Freiburg, RW 35/537. Stülpnagel to Oberg, 25 March 1944, ibid. MBH NW Frankreich, "Einziehung von Rundfunkgeräten in der Kampfzone und in der Normandie," 31 May 1944, ibid. See Luneau, *Radio Londres*, pp. 201–9, 238–43.

20. Kommandant von Gross-Paris, "Kommandantur-Befehl Nr. 52," 12 April 1943; "Kommandantur-Befehl Nr. 69," 28 May 1943; and "Kommandantur-Befehl Nr. 102," 10 September 1943, BA-MA Freiburg, RH 36/39–41.

21. Abetz to AA, 20 March 1944, PA-AA Berlin, Paris 1116 A.

22. Kommandant von Gross-Paris, "Kommandantur-Befehl Nr. 69," 28 May 1943; "Kommandantur-Befehl Nr. 71," 12 June 1943; and "Kommandantur-Befehl Nr. 72," 15 June 1943, BA-MA Freiburg, RH 36/39.

23. Reichsministerium für Wissenschaft, Erziehung und Volksbildung to AA, 1 July 1943, PA-AA Berlin, Paris 1144 X. DB (Knothe) to AA, 13 October 1943, ibid., 1143 B. Kommandant von Gross-Paris, Abt. Ia, "Standortbefehl Nr. 134/43," 19 December 1943, AN Paris, F⁷, 15142.

24. "Théâtre National de l'Opéra. Mois de mars 1944" and "Théâtre National de l'Opéra Comique. Mois de mars 1944," (?) March 1944, AN Paris, F¹⁷, 13391.

25. MBF, Abt. Propaganda, Gruppe Kultur, "Bericht über den Monat April 1944," 30 April 1944, ibid., AJ⁴⁰, 1001. DB (Gerlach), "Vorschlagsliste des Deutschen Instituts Paris für das Veranstaltungsjahr 1944/45," 6 May 1944, PA-AA Berlin, Paris 1115 A.

26. AA to DB, 4 May 1944, PA-AA Berlin, Paris 1113 X. Telegram from DB (Bargen) to AA, 24 May 1944, ibid. On Karajan, see Annemarie Kleinert, *Berliner Philharmoniker. Von Karajan bis Rattle* (Berlin, 2005), pp. 33–71, and, concerning Frau Gütermann, note 35 in the chapter entitled "Das Orchester auf Reisen." Unfortunately, the notes are available only on the Internet.

27. AA (Luther) to DB, 29 January 1943, PA-AA Berlin, Paris 2382. Schleier to AA, 1 February 1943, ibid.

28. Ribbentrop to DB, 14 February 1943, ibid. DB, "Konzept eines Berichtes an das Auswärtige Amt. Betr.: Errichtung eines Ehrenheims im Bois de Boulogne," 2 June 1943, ibid., 2381.

29. "Heldengedenkfeier des Standorts Paris," 12 March 1944, ibid., 2382. Abetz to AA, 17 March 1944, ibid. Mächler (NSDAP Auslands-Organisation, Landesgruppe in Frankreich) to DB, 3 April 1944, ibid.

30. Kutzschenbach to Schwendemann, 6 May 1943, ibid., 1136 A. Kutzschenbach, "Aufzeichnung" (for Abetz), 22 April 1944, ibid., 1113 X. DB (Bargen) to DB, Zweigstelle Vichy, 23 May 1944, ibid., 1106 X.

31. Knochen to DB, 15 May 1943, ibid., 2481. Schleier, "Aufzeichnung," 15 May 1943, ibid. Schleier to Krug, 15 and 22 May 1943, ibid. See Duquesne, *Les catholiques français sous l'Occupation*, pp. 299–338.

32. Schleier to Krug, 24 June 1943, PA-AA Berlin, Paris 2481. Schleier to Suhard, 28 June 1943, ibid.

33. Kaltenbrunner to AA, 5 July 1943, ibid.

34. Knochen to RSHA, 2 August 1943, BA Berlin, R 58/7742. Memo by Dr. Klassen, 2 December 1943, PA-AA Berlin, Paris 2481. Telegram from Abetz to AA, 8 February 1944, ibid.

35. Faÿ, "Rapport à Monsieur le Ministre de l'Éducation Nationale sur la discipline de la Bibliothèque Nationale," (?) 1943, AN Paris, F[17], 13368. DB to Brinon, 8 July 1943, PA-AA Berlin, Paris 1139 B. MBF, Verwaltungs-Stab to Generaldirektor der Staatsarchive (in Potsdam), 12 July 1943, AN Paris, AJ[40], 571. Gerlach, "Aufzeichnung für Herrn Gesandten Schleier," 26 July 1943, PA-AA Berlin, Paris 1139 B.

36. Schleier, "Französische Schulgeschichtsbücher," 20 January 1943, PA-AA Berlin, Paris 1211.

37. Schleier to MBF, Verwaltungs-Stab, 30 January 1943, ibid., 1284. Schleier, "Aufzeichnung. Betr.: École Polytechnique," 22 March 1943, ibid.

38. FK 669 (Dijon) to the Préfet Régional, 2 February 1943, AN Paris, F[17], 13382. Préfet Régional (Dijon) to Roy (Ministère de l'Éducation Nationale), 6 February 1943, ibid. Ministère de l'Éducation Nationale, Direction de l'Enseignement Primaire, "Circulaire N° 287," 27 April 1943, ibid., 13375. DB (Schwendemann) to AA, 23 September 1943, PA-AA Berlin, Paris 1123 B.

39. "Liste des arrestations qui nous ont été communiquées à partir de juin 1940. Elèves"; and "Liste des arrestations .... Personnel enseignant," (?) 1944, AN Paris, F[17], 13360.

40. "Note pour le ministre," 22 May 1944, ibid., AJ[40], 556. Joint communiqué by the Ministre de l'Éducation Nationale, the Ministre à la Production Industrielle et aux Communications, and the Ministre de l'Agriculture, 24 May 1944, ibid. "Remarques au sujet de l'ajournement des concours en 1944," 25 May 1944, ibid., F[17], 13380.

41. Deutsche Schule Paris to DB, 25 April 1944, PA-AA Berlin, Paris 1111 A. Hepp, "Note pour Monsieur Watteau" (Directeur du Service des Réfugiés), 5 June 1944, AN Paris, F[17], 13338.

42. "Réunion du Parti Populaire Français," 24 November 1942, AN Paris, F[7], 15280. Sipo-SD, "Lagebericht für die Zeit vom 26. Nov. bis 9. Dez. 1942," 16 December 1942, BA Berlin, R 58/ZR 945 A.01. Sipo-SD to PPF, 4 August 1943, PA-AA Berlin, Paris 1306. Schleier to AA, 8 August 1943, ibid. Prefecture de Police, "Note au sujet des organisations politiques," 30 August 1943, AN Paris, F[7], 14897. Unsigned police reports of 3 and 11 May 1944, ibid. On Déat and Doriot, see Burrin, *La France à l'heure allemande*, pp. 391–402, 417–28; and Jackson, *France: The Dark Years*, pp. 192–98.

43. Schleier, "Aufzeichnung. Betr.: Besprechung mit Jean Weiland," 19 January 1943, PA-AA Berlin, Paris 1121 Y. Weiland to Schleier, 30 March 1943, ibid., 1299. Schleier to Grimm, 15 April 1943, ibid., 1115 A. Weiland to Schleier, 16 October 1943, ibid., 1121 Z. Weiland to Schleier, 21 December 1943, ibid., 1121 Y. See Corinna Franz, *Fernand de Brinon und die deutsch-französischen Beziehungen 1918–1945* (Bonn, 2000), pp. 255–60.

44. Schleier to MBF, 27 January 1943, PA-AA Berlin, Paris 1307. Stülpnagel to DB, 25 February 1943, ibid. Schleier to MBF, Verwaltungs-Stab, 26 February 1943, ibid.

45. DB to Cercle Européen, 10 May 1943, ibid., 1309. Schleier to Grosse, 2 July 1943, ibid.

46. Schleier to AA, 12 October 1943, ibid., 1123 B. Préfet de Police to Ministère de l'Intérieur, 4 January 1944, AN Paris, F[7], 14904.

47. "Statuts de la milice française," 30 January 1943, AN Paris, F[7], 15300. "Règlement général sur l'organisation de la milice française," (?) February 1943, ibid., 15301. Costantini to Schwendemann, 26 November 1943, PA-AA Berlin, Paris 1309. DB to Kommandant von Gross-Paris, 7 December 1943, ibid.

Chapter 15: A Wretched Conclusion

1. Délégué du Secrétaire Général à la Police Nationale to Röthke, 9 November 1942, AN Paris, F[7], 14895. Memo by Permilleux, 20 November 1942, ibid. Bard to Bousquet, 8 April 1943, ibid. See Berlière, *Les policiers français sous l'Occupation*, pp. 247–91; and Kasten, *"Gute Franzosen,"* pp. 166–75.

2. Knochen to Befehlshaber der Ordnungspolizei, 12 February 1943, CDJC Paris, XXVc-205. Röthke, "Weigerung der französischen Gendarmerie, beim Abtransport von Juden französischer Staatsangehörigkeit mitzuwirken," 23 March 1943, ibid., 228. "Lacking sufficient forces to do everything themselves, in numerous matters, large and small, the Germans managed to have French officials carry out their work for them," observes John F. Sweets, *Choices in Vichy France: The French under Nazi Occupation* (New York, 1986), p. 175.

3. Sipo-SD, "Lagebericht für die Zeit vom 10. bis 31. Dezember 1942," 6 January 1943, BA Berlin, R 58/ZR 945 A.01. Röthke to Darquier de Pellepoix, 12 January 1943, AN Paris, AJ[38], 9.

4. Röthke to Oberg and Knochen, 3 December 1942, CDJC Paris, LXV-12. MBF to Verwaltungs-Stab, Abt. II, 12 December 1942, ibid. Knochen to RSHA, 30 December 1942, ibid.

5. Sipo-SD, "Lagebericht für die Zeit vom 26. Nov. bis 9. Dez. 1942," 16 December 1942, BA Berlin, R 58/ZR 945 A.01. On Darquier, see especially Marrus and Paxton, *Vichy France and the Jews*, pp. 283–339.

6. Röthke to CGQJ, 17 December 1942, AN Paris, AJ[38], 114. CGQJ to Stenger, 18 December 1942, ibid. Speier to CGQJ, 19 January 1943, ibid., AJ[40], 619. Stenger to CGQJ, 15 February 1943, ibid., AJ[38], 375.

7. Röthke to CGQJ, 17 February 1943, ibid., AJ[38], 14. Röthke to Darquier de Pellepoix, 8 March 1943, ibid., 9. Darquier de Pellepoix to Röthke, 30 July 1943, ibid., 14.

8. DB to Kommandant von Gross-Paris, 14 April 1943, PA-AA Berlin, Paris 2463.

9. Darquier de Pellepoix to Stenger, 2 December 1942, AN Paris, AJ[40], 615. Memo by CGQJ, Services administratifs, financiers et généraux, 21 December 1942, ibid., AJ[38], 403.

10. MBF, Abt. Wi I/1 (Blanke), "Vermerk," 17 November 1942, ibid., AJ[40], 615. Stenger to CGQJ, aryanisation économique, 4 December 1942, ibid., AJ[38], 371. "Abschlussbericht der Treuhand- und Revisionsstelle ... für das Geschäftsjahr 1942," 31 December 1942, ibid., AJ[40], 591.

11. MBF, Verwaltungs-Stab, "Lagebericht über Verwaltung und Wirtschaft, Oktober–Dezember 1942," 27 January 1943, ibid., AJ[40], 444.

12. MBF, Verwaltungs-Stab to Stenger, 8 January 1943, ibid., 591. MBF, Verwaltungs-Stab to CGQJ, aryanisation économique, 30 January 1943, ibid., 618. Blanke to MBF, Abt. Wi I/1b, 24 February 1943, ibid., 615. Vogl to CGQJ, 2 March 1943, ibid., AJ[38], 376. Stenger to CGQJ, 12 April 1943, ibid., 378.

13. MBF, Verwaltungs-Stab, "Lagebericht über Verwaltung und Wirtschaft, Januar/ März 1943," 22 April 1943, BA-MA Freiburg, RW 35/288; and "Lagebericht über Verwaltung und Wirtschaft, April/Juni 1943," 21 July 1943, AN Paris, AJ[40], 444.

14. MBF, Abt. Wi I/1 to CGQJ, 9 July 1943, AN Paris, AJ[40], 615. MBF, Verwaltungs-Stab to General von Unruh (Sonderbeauftragter des Führers), 16 July 1943, ibid., 587. MBF, Abt. Wi I/1 to Knoke, 14 October 1943, ibid., 615.

15. "Bericht über die bei der Treuhand- und Revisionsstelle … vorgenommene Prüfung des Abschlusses," 31 December 1943, ibid., 591. "Abschlussbericht der Treuhand- und Revisionsstelle … für das Geschäftsjahr 1943," 31 December 1943, ibid.

16. MBF, Abt. Wi I to Zentralabteilung, 5 January 1944, BA-MA Freiburg, RW 35/1419. Soltau, "Bericht über eine bei Herrn Ferdinand Niedermeyer vorgenommene Prüfung," 10 January 1944, AN Paris, AJ[40], 622. Memo by Knoke, 4 February 1944, ibid., AJ[38], 100. "Mémoire sur la situation des agents du Commissariat Général aux Questions Juives," 6 March 1944, ibid., 1.

17. Klassen, "Aktennotiz," 28 March 1944, PA-AA Berlin, Paris 1319. MBF, Abt. Wi I, "Nr. 45/44," 30 April 1944, AN Paris, AJ[40], 444.

18. For example, Blanke to CGQJ, 24 May 1944, AN Paris, AJ[38], 386. Knoke to CGQJ, 24 May 1944, ibid. Schutzbar to CGQJ, aryanisation économique, 6 June 1944, ibid. See Joly, *Vichy dans la "Solution Finale,"* pp. 729–41.

19. Bouffet (Préfet de la Seine) to the Ministère de l'Agriculture et du Ravitaillement," 30 November 1942, AN Paris, F[7], 15107.

20. Himmler to Bormann, 18 December 1942, BA Berlin, NS 19/1929. Röthke to RSHA, 21 January 1943, CDJC Paris, XXVc-195. Knochen to Sipo-SD commanders, 26 January 1943, ibid., 198. See Peschanski, *La France des camps,* pp. 345–52.

21. Sipo-SD, "Lagebericht für die Zeit vom 14. bis 25. Januar 1943," 30 January 1943, BA Berlin, R 58/7742.

22. BdS, II pol to Sipo-SD, Abt. IV, 10 February 1943, CDJC Paris, XLV-62[d]. BdS, II pol, "Aktenvermerk. Betr.: Abtransport von Häftlingen," 10 February 1943, ibid., 65. Bouffet to Direction Générale de la Police Nationale, 10 February 1943, AN Paris, F[7], 15107.

23. Hagen, "Aktenvermerk," 25 March 1943, CDJC Paris, XXVc-232. Knochen to Eichmann, 29 March 1943, ibid., 235.

24. Röthke, "Gegenwärtiger Stand der Judenfrage in Frankreich," 21 July 1943, ibid., I-54. Knochen to RSHA, 2 August 1943, BA Berlin, R 58/7742. Röthke, "Besprechung mit Laval und Bousquet am 14.8.1943 in Vichy," 15 August 1943, AN Paris, F[7], 15310.

25. Röthke, "Gegenwärtiger Stand der Judenfrage in Frankreich," 21 July 1943, CDJC Paris, I-54. Sipo-SD, "Lagebericht für die Zeit vom 16. bis 31. Juli 1943," sent by Knochen to RSHA, 2 August 1943, BA Berlin, R 58/7742. "Déportations du Camp de Drancy," (?) July 1944, AN Paris, AJ[72], 288. See Brayard, *La "solution finale de la question juive,"* pp 158–63. The complicity of the SNCF in the mass deportation of Jews has stirred much controversy and some post-war legal proceedings. See Beau et al. (eds.), *SNCF. La machine infernal* (Paris, 2004); Raphaël Delpard, *Enquête sur la SNCF et la déportation* (Paris, 2005); and Christian Chevandier, "Le grief fait aux cheminots d'avoir, sous l'occupation, conduit les trains de la déportation," in Marie-Noëlle Polino (ed.), *Les cheminots dans la Résistance. Une histoire en évolution* (Paris, 2006), pp. 91–111.

26. See, for example, Henri Michel, *Paris résistant* (Paris, 1982); Rayski, *Le choix des juifs*; and Asher Cohen, *Persécutions et sauvetages. Juifs et Français sous l'occupation et sous Vichy* (Paris, 1993).

27. Similar conclusions are reached by Paxton, *Vichy France*, pp. 357–74, 380–82; and Jackson, *France: The Dark Years*, pp. 233–35.

Chapter 16: The Twilight Weeks

1. Memo by Stülpnagel to all military commanders, 11 June 1944, BA-MA Freiburg, RW 35/1420. MBF, Verwaltungs-Stab, Abt. MVZ to Verwaltungs-Abteilung, Wirtschafts-Abteilung, and Haupt-Arbeits-Abteilung, 12 June 1944, ibid. Stülpnagel to OB West, 15 July 1944, AN Paris, AJ⁴⁰, 849.

2. Boineburg, "Kommandantur-Befehl Nr. 21," 12 June 1944, BA-MA Freiburg, RW 35/1420. Hofacker, "Vorschlag betr. Neugliederung des Regts. Majestic," 18 June 1944, AN Paris, AJ⁴⁰, 451.

3. MBF, Verwaltungs-Stab, Abt. MVZ, "Reisevermerk," 3 and 17 July 1944, BA-MA Freiburg, RW 35/270.

4. More than a thousand SD and SS personnel were arrested. See Klemens von Klemperer, *German Resistance against Hitler: The Search for Allies Abroad, 1938–1945* (Oxford, 1992), pp. 363–69; and Gerd R. Ueberschär, "Cäsar von Hofacker und der deutsche Widerstand gegen Hitler in Paris," in Martens and Vaïsse (eds.), *Frankreich und Deutschland im Krieg*, pp. 621–31.

5. Oberg to Himmler, 10 August 1944, BA Berlin, SS 0354 A. See Pryce-Jones, *Paris in the Third Reich*, pp. 193–207; and Wilhelm von Schramm, *Der 20. Juli in Paris* (Bad Wörishorn, 1953), which appeared in abridged translation as *Conspiracy among Generals* (London, 1956). Best's unpublished memoirs, "Erinnerungen aus dem besetzten Frankreich 1940 bis 1942," are to be found in BA Koblenz, N/1023 12. In his diary, Ernst Jünger also wasted little sympathy for Stülpnagel, his erstwhile friend, commenting only: "For a long time I have been convinced that through uprisings little will be changed and above all nothing improved." Ernst Jünger, "Das zweite Pariser Tagebuch," in *Sämtliche Werke. Tagebücher* (Stuttgart, 1979), 3:288–90. But on Jünger's dangerous involvement with Caesar von Hofacker, see Schwilk, *Ernst Jünger*, pp. 402–4. According to Walter Bargatzky, however, Stülpnagel was for some time deeply involved in the planning of the plot, which could not have been conducted without his consent and participation. His fault, rather, was a Hamlet-like indecisiveness once the action began and Hitler survived. Bargatzky, *Hotel Majestic*, pp. 122–43. See also Klaus-Jürgen Müller, "'In gewissen Lagen wird das Verlassen des Lebens dem Tüchtigen zur Pflicht'—General Karl-Heinrich von Stülpnagel," in Bengt von zur Mühlen and Frank Bauer (eds.), *Der 20. Juli in Paris. Verlauf—Hauptbeteiligte—Augenzeugen* (Berlin, 1995), pp. 22–40.

6. Sipo-SD, "Lagebericht für die Zeit vom 1.–15. Juni 1944," 17 June 1944, BA Berlin, RW 58/790. Kiep, "Kriegstagebuch," 30 June 1944, BA-MA Freiburg, RW 49/76. Sipo-SD, Abt. IV A1, "Lagebericht Nr. 11. Kommunismus," 8 July 1944, AN Paris, F⁷, 15145. "Note sur la question des spectacles à Paris," 10 July 1944, ibid., F¹⁷, 13391.

7. MBF, Abt. Propaganda, Gruppe Kultur, "Bericht über den Monat Juni 44," 30 June 1944, AN Paris, AJ⁴⁰, 1001. Brinon to Abetz, 15 July 1944, PA-AA Berlin, Paris 1110 A. Bargen to MBF, 20 July 1944, ibid.

8. Direction Générale de la Police Nationale, "Note," 9 June 1944, AN Paris, F⁷, 14905. Sauts to Leguay, 10 June 1944, ibid., 14893. Sipo-SD, Abt. IV A1 to MBF, Verwaltungs-Stab, Abt. MVZ, 14 June and 14 July 1944, ibid., 15142. MBF, Verwaltungs-Stab, "Lagebericht über Verwaltung und Wirtschaft für den Monat Juni 1944," 13 July 1944, ibid., AJ⁴⁰, 444.

9. "Liste des victimes des attaques aériennes anglo-américaines en zone nord pendant le mois d'avril 1944," 14 June 1944, ibid., AJ[41], 356. "Bombardements de la nuit du 14 au 15 juin," 15 June 1944, ibid., F[17], 13338.

10. Police report, 19 June 1944, ibid., F[7], 15312. MBF, Haupt-Abt.-Arbeit A7, "Vermerk. Besprechung am 30.6.44 über Arbeitseinsatz von Nordafrikanern, Tunesiern und Algeriern," 1 July 1944, ibid., AJ[40], 849.

11. Sipo-SD, Abt. IV A1, "Lagebericht Nr. 14. Kommunismus," 24 July 1944, ibid., F[7], 15145. Kommandant von Gross-Paris, "Standortbefehl Nr. 57/44," 31 July 1944, BA-MA Freiburg, RH 36/42. Report by the Direction des Renseignements Généraux, 3 August 1944, AN Paris, F[7], 15313. MBF, Verwaltungs-Stab, Abt. MVZ, Gruppe 3, "7. Wochenbericht über Verwaltung und Wirtschaft für die Zeit vom 30.7. bis 5.8.1944," 6 August 1944, ibid., AJ[40], 846. FK 758 (St. Cloud), "Bericht über letzte Tätigkeit," 12 September 1944, ibid., 853.

12. "Objet. Procès Oberg (7ème note)" (session of 22 September), 24 September 1954, AN Paris, F[7], 15316. Further details, not for the faint-hearted, may be read in Giolitto, *Histoire de la Milice*, pp. 280–302.

13. MBF, Abt. Wwi, Gruppe Ic, "Lagebericht Mai 1944," 9 June 1944, BA-MA Freiburg, RW 24/11. Rü-Kommando Paris-Mitte, "Kriegstagebuch ... für den Zeitabschnitt vom 27.3–30.6.44," 10 July 1944, ibid., 104.

14. MBF, Verwaltungs-Stab, Abt. MVZ, Gruppe 3, "Lagebericht über Verwaltung und Wirtschaft, Juni 1944," 13 July 1944, ibid., RW 35/298. MBF, Verwaltungs-Stab, Abt. MVZ, Gruppe Ic to OKW/Feldwirtschaftsamt, 13 July 1944, ibid., RW 24/12.

15. Generalingenieur beim Oberbefehlshaber West, "Betr. Baueinsatz bei der Beseitigung von Luftkriegsschäden während der Invasionskämpfe," 16 June 1944, AN Paris, AJ[40], 849.

16. Rü-Kommando Paris-Ost, "Kriegstagebuch ... vom 1.4.1944 bis 30.6.1944," 30 June 1944, BA-MA Freiburg, RW 24/95. Rü-Kommando Paris-West, "Kriegstagebuch vom 1. April bis 30. Juni 1944," 30 June 1944, ibid., 112. Bichelonne to Michel, 20 July 1944, AN Paris, AJ[72], 1927.

17. Telegram from Abetz to AA, 6 July 1944, AN Paris, AJ[40], 846.

18. "Niederschrift über die am 15. und 16. Juli 1944 auf der Wartburg stattgehabte Tagung," 24 July 1944, ibid., 853.

19. "Note sur l'ingérence de la H.V.D. dans l'exploitation de la S.N.C.F.," 5 June 1944, ibid., AJ[72], 477. "Extraits du Compte-rendu de la réunion du 8 juin 1944 à la H.V.D.," 8 June 1944, ibid., 474. On the HVD, see Alfred Gottwaldt, "Die Eisenbahner der Hauptverkehrsdirektion Paris während der Okkupationszeit in Frankreich 1940–1944," *Jahrbuch für Eisenbahngeschichte* 33 (2001): 37–50.

20. "Compte-rendu de l'entretien de M. Berthelot ... avec les Abt. Präs. Kukiela et Unverzagt," 9 June 1944, AN Paris, AJ[72], 474. "Mémento du 8ème entretien du Ministre Bichelonne avec le Président Wintgen," 10 June 1944, ibid. Memo by the Direction des Renseignements Généraux, 12 June 1944, ibid., F[7], 15299.

21. Direction des Renseignements Généraux, "Compte-rendu de la réception ... au Club de la Presse à Paris," 28 June 1944, ibid., F[7], 15299. Memo by the Direction des Renseignements Généraux, 29 June 1944, ibid. "Mémento de la conférence avec le Président Wintgen à la H.V.D.," 29 June 1944, ibid., AJ[72], 1927. MBF, Verwaltungs-Stab, Abt. MVZ, Gruppe Ia to OKW/Feldwirtschaftsamt, 5 July 1944, BA-MA Freiburg, RW 24/12. MBF, Verwaltungs-Stab, Abt. MVZ, Gruppe 3, "3. Wochenbericht über die Verwaltung und Wirtschaft für die Zeit vom 2. bis 8. Juli 1944," 12 July 1944, ibid., RW

35/299; and "4. Wochenbericht über Verwaltung und Wirtschaft für die Zeit vom 9. bis 15. Juli 1944," 16 July 1944, AN Paris, AJ[40], 846. Secrétaire d'État du Ravitaillement to Darnand, 4 August 1944, ibid., F[7], 14904.

22. Memo by SNCF, Chef du Service du Matériel et de la Traction, 17 July 1944, AN Paris, AJ[72], 1927. Befehlshaber Nordwestfrankreich, Abt. Ic, "Ereignis- und Erfahrungsbericht für die Zeit vom 1.7. bis 31.7.44," 5 August 1944, BA-MA Freiburg, RH 36/51.

23. Sipo-SD, Abt. IV 1a, "Lagebericht Nr. 15: Kommunismus," 9 August 1944, AN Paris, F[7], 15145. Memo by the Renseignements Généraux, 10 August 1944, ibid., 15299. Commissaire Divisionnaire, Chef des Renseignements Généraux des Gares de Paris-Est et Paris-Bastille to Délégué du Directeur Général de la Police Nationale, 11 August 1944, ibid., 14889. Sipo-SD, "Ereignismeldung Nr. 195," 12 August 1944, BA Berlin, R 70 Frankreich/1. "Mémento de la réunion des Directeurs de l'Exploitation des Régimes et des Chefs des Services du Matériel et de la Traction," 13 August 1944, AN Paris, AJ[72], 477.

24. Memo by the Direction des Renseignements Généraux, 14 August 1944, AN Paris, F[7], 15299.

25. Rü-Kommando Paris-West, "Kriegstagebuch vom 1. Juli bis 28. August 1944," 28 August 1944, BA-MA Freiburg, RW 24/113. Rü-Kommando Paris-Ost, "Kriegstagebuch ...," 1.7.1944–18.8.1944," 29 September 1944, ibid., 96. Keil, "Kriegstagebuch des Rüstungs-Kommandos Paris-Mitte ... 1.7.44–7.10.1944," 7 October 1944, ibid., 105.

26. "Note relative à l'étude du dossier No 144.812: 'Relations entre la S.N.C.F. et la W.V.D.,'" (no date), AN Paris, AJ[72], 474. See the debates on this topic in Marie-Noëlle Polino (ed.), *Une entreprise publique dans la guerre. La SNCF, 1939–1945* (Paris, 2001), pp. 123–36, 159–72.

27. "Bulletin du Maintien de l'Ordre," 11 July 1944, AN Paris, AJ[72], 4. Boutry (Directeur du Laboratoire d'Essais du Conservatoire National des Arts et Métiers) to Ministère de l'Éducation Nationale, 3 August 1944, ibid., F[17], 13385. Directeur de l'École Normale Supérieure to Ministère de l'Éducation Nationale, 7 August 1944, ibid. Ministère de la Production Industrielle et des Communications, "Arrestations de fonctionnaires et d'agents des Ponts-et-Chaussées," 8 August 1944, ibid., AJ[72], 1926.

28. Délégué en zone nord du Secrétaire Général au Maintien de l'Ordre to Directeur Général de la Police Nationale, 25 July 1944, ibid., F[7], 15086. "À Paris," 31 July 1944, ibid., AJ[72], 288. "Déportations de Drancy," 12–17 August 1944, ibid.

29. The estimated total of more than 75,000 does not begin to account for hundreds of deaths by illness or execution in French and German camps. Among many others, see Klarsfeld, *Vichy-Auschwitz*, 2:7; Marrus and Paxton, *Vichy France and the Jews*, pp. 343–46; Zucotti, *The Holocaust, the French, and the Jews*, pp. 181–87; and Jackson, *France: The Dark Years*, pp. 360–63.

30. "Liste des approbations d'aryanisation du mois de juillet 1944," (?) July 1944, AN Paris, AJ[38], 589. "Approbations juillet 1944," 1–31 July 1944, ibid., 572. "Approbations août 1944," 1–7 August 1944, ibid., 574. "Bericht der Gruppe Wi I/2 über die Behandlung des feindlichen Vermögens im Geschäftsbereich des Militärbefehlshabers in Frankreich (20.10.1940–15.8.1944)," 15 August 1944, ibid., AJ[40], 589.

31. MBF, Gruppe Wi I/2, "Bericht der Gruppe Wi I/2 (Feindvermögen) über die Tätigkeit vom 20.10.–15.8.44," (no date), BA-MA Freiburg, RW 35/257. "Die Entjudung der französischen Wirtschaft," (no date), ibid., 2. See Philippe Verheyde, "L'aryanisation économique. Le cas des grandes enterprises," in Bensoussan (ed.), *Aryanisation. Le vol légalisé*, pp. 7–30.

32. See Joly, *Vichy dans la "Solution Finale,"* pp. 606–9.

33. Prost et al. (eds.), *Aryanisation économique,* p. 168. Yet "a bottom line ... remains difficult, indeed impossible to establish," writes Jean-Marc Dreyfus, "L'aryanisation économique. A-t-elle été l'un des instruments du pillage de la France?" in Martens and Vaïsse (eds.), *Frankreich und Deutschland im Krieg,* pp. 529–40. See also Calvi and Masurovksy, *Le Festin du Reich,* pp. 7–24.

34. MBF, Verwaltungs-Stab, Abt. MVZ, Gruppe 3, "7. Wochenbericht über Verwaltung und Wirtschaft für die Zeit vom 30.7. bis 5.8.1944," 6 August 1944, BA-MA Freiburg, RW 35/300.

35. Secret report by Agent D.J.5 of Renseignements Généraux, 8 June 1944, AN Paris, F[7], 15301. Unsigned police reports, 13 June 1944, ibid., 15312. Struve to DB, 13 June 1944, PA-AA Berlin, Paris 2380. Memo of the Direction des Renseignments Généraux, 16 June 1944, AN Paris, F[7], 15300. "État numérique récapitulatif des attentats signalés," 19 June 1944, ibid., 15312. Unsigned police reports, 19–24 July 1944, ibid. See Giolitto, *Histoire de la Milice,* pp. 419–64; and Kasten, *"Gute Franzosen,"* pp. 219–22.

36. "Déclarations de Monseigneur l'Évêque," 21 June 1944, AN Paris, AJ[41], 60. Secret report by Agent D.J.5 of the Renseignements Généraux, 26 June 1944, ibid., F[7], 15292. Cabinet du Secrétaire Général au Maintien de l'Ordre to Darnand, 27 June 1944, ibid., 14898. Without explanation, the number of victims is set at 634 by Crémieux-Brilhac, *La France Libre,* 2:1257. See Meyer, *Die deutsche Besatzung,* pp. 149–70; Henry Rousso, *Le syndrome de Vichy de 1944 à nos jours,* 2nd ed. (Paris, 1990), pp. 72–75; and Sarah Farmer, "Postwar Justice in France: Bordeaux 1953," in István Déak et al. (eds.), *The Politics of Retribution in Europe: World War II and Its Aftermath* (Princeton, 2000), pp. 194–211.

37. Secret report by Agent J.P.7 of the Renseignements Généraux, 22 June 1944, AN Paris, F[7], 15300. Charlet, "Rapport pour Monsieur J. Darnand," 12 July 1944, ibid., 14900. Abetz to AA, 19 July 1944, PA-AA Berlin, Paris 2479. "Compte-rendu d'un incident survenu entre francs gardes et police," 7 August 1944, AN Paris, F[7], 14886. Secret report by Agent D.J.5 of the Renseignements Généraux, 14 August 1944, ibid., 15300. See Burrin, *La France à l'heure allemande,* pp. 444–64.

38. Presse-Nachrichtendienst der Deutschen Botschaft, "Nachrichtenspiegel Nr. 316," 17 June 1944, AN Paris, AJ[40], 1575. Sipo-SD, "Lagebericht für die Zeit vom 1.–15. Juni 1944," 17 June 1944, BA Berlin, RW 58/790. "Exposé du Capitaine Schott," 27 June 1944, AN Paris, F[7], 14886. DB to AA, 11 July 1944, PA-AA Berlin, Paris 1110 A.

39. MBF, Abt. Propaganda, Gruppe Presse, "Presse-Parole Nr. 382," 4 July 1944; and "Presse-Parole Nr. 397," 25 July 1944, AN Paris, AJ[40], 1008.

40. DB (Gerlach) to Schwendemann, 12 July 1944, PA-AA Berlin, Paris 1110 A. Reports by MBF, Abt. Propaganda, Gruppe Presse, 27–28 July 1944, AN Paris, AJ[40], 1008. A more plausible estimate is that between 1940 and 1945, about 67,000 French civilians were killed by Allied bombing, of which slightly more than half died in 1944. See Olivier Wieviorka, *Histoire du débarquement en Normandie. Des origines à la libération de Paris 1941–1944* (Paris, 2007), p. 159.

41. Abetz to Brinon, 31 July 1944, PA-AA Berlin, Paris 1345.

42. Abwehr, Feldpostprüfstelle (Rödert), "Tätigkeitsbericht für August 1944," 8 September 1944, BA-MA Freiburg, RW 49/78.

43. Reports by MBF, Abt. Propaganda, Gruppe Presse, 7–9 August 1944, AN Paris, AJ[40], 1008. On the military events leading up to the liberation of Paris, see Crémieux-Brilhac, *La France libre,* 2:1250–1318; and Wieviorka, *Histoire du débarquement,* pp. 217–47, 373–429.

44. Generalabteilung der Militär-Verwaltung, "Vorbereitungen für einen 'Besonderen Fall,'" 9 August 1944, AN Paris, AJ⁴⁰, 451. Abwehr, "Vernichtungsverhandlungen," 12 August 1944, BA-MA Freiburg, RW 49/93. Klatte, "Kurzer Abschlussbericht über meine Tätigkeit," 20 October 1944, AN Paris, AJ⁴⁰, 588. See Jasper, *Hotel Lutétia*, pp. 321–40.

45. Report by the Direction des Renseignments Généraux, 14 August 1944, AN Paris, F⁷, 15307. Hötzel, "Reisebericht," 21 August 1944, ibid., AJ⁴⁰, 847. "Erlebnisbericht über den Rückmarsch des Stabes des Chefs der Militärverwaltung aus Frankreich," (no date), ibid., 444. On the "Rückzug und Ende" of the Occupation, see Jäckel, *Frankreich in Hitlers Europa*, pp. 344–71.

46. "Situation dans Paris," 21 August 1944, AN Paris, AJ⁷², 61. Bernard, "La libération de Paris," 24 August 1944, ibid. General Billotte to Choltitz, 25 August 1944, ibid. Choltitz, "Befehl. Der Widerstand in dem Stützpunktbereich und Stützpunkten ist sofort einzustellen," 25 August 1944, ibid. Transcript of Choltitz's testimony in court, 13 September 1948, ibid., F⁷, 15317. For a general summary of the liberation, see Azéma, *De Munich à la Libération*, pp. 335–44; and Jackson, *France: The Dark Years*, pp. 554–67.

Epilogue: The Long Handshake

1. Titled "Erlebnisbericht über den Rückmarsch des Stabes des Chefs der Militärverwaltung aus Frankreich," copies of this document are preserved both at the Archives Nationales in Paris (AJ⁴⁰, 444) and at the Bundesarchiv-Militärarchiv in Freiburg (RW 35/267).

2. The text reads as follows: "Die Vertreter der Behörden und französischen Dienststellen erschienen wie bisher zu Besprechungen im Majestic und liessen sich in den meisten Fällen kaum anmerken, dass sie mit dem baldigen Abzug der Deutschen aus Paris rechneten. Nur wo sich aus längerer Zusammenarbeit ein persönlicheres Verhältnis entwickelt hatte, konnte man wohl aus dem länger als üblichen Händedruck entnehmen, dass der Franzose sich wortlos verabschieden wollte."

Appendix: Classified French Police Files

1. The files in question are AN Paris, F⁷, 15326, 15327, 15329, 15331, 15332, 15337, 15375, 15389, 15669, 16073, and 16127.

2. Knochen to RSHA, 12 February 1943, ibid., 15337.

3. Telegram from Abetz to AA et al., 7 January 1944, ibid., 15331. Memo by Abetz cited in records of the Tribunal Militaire Permanent de Paris, 15 January 1949, ibid.

4. Scattered dossiers collected in ibid., 15327.

5. In connection with these investigations, a host of prominent Vichy officials were detained for questioning at Fresnes: Jacques Barnaud, Jacques Benoist-Méchin, René Bousquet, Max Knipping, François Lehideux, Paul Marion, Xavier Vallat, etc. Direction des Renseignments Généraux, "Liste des personnalités incarcérées à la prison de Fresnes depuis la libération," 12 April 1946, ibid., 15331. See the chapter entitled "Die Legenden der Täter. Vernehmungsprotokolle als historische Quelle," in Meyer, *Täter im Verhör*, pp. 299–358.

6. Marc Berge and Léon Dauzas (Sûreté Nationale) to Direction des Renseignements Généraux, 27 November 1945, AN Paris, F⁷, 15332. Convicted in 1949 by a

French court and sentenced to twenty years of hard labor, Abetz was released in 1954. He died in an automobile accident in 1958.

7. Berge and René Seyvoz to Direction des Renseignements Généraux, 15 January 1946, ibid., 15329. "Le général Oberg 'boucher de Paris' va répondre de ses crimes," *Cité-Soir*, 17 January 1946, ibid. Condemned to death in 1954, Oberg's sentence was commuted to twenty years of hard labor in 1959. He was pardoned by French President René Coty in 1965 and released. He died later that year.

8. Georges Claudet (Direction de la Surveillance du Territoire), "Auditions du nommé KNOCHEN Helmuth," 24 November 1946, ibid., 15337. In the same trial as Oberg, Knochen was convicted and received a death sentence in 1954 but was later pardoned. He returned to Germany and died there.

9. "Note pour Monsieur le Directeur Général de la Sûreté Nationale. Personnes exécutées par les Allemands en France au cours de l'occupation," 30 August 1952, ibid., 15669.

10. Choltitz, "Pourquoi, en 1944, je n'ai pas détruit Paris," *Le Figaro*, 14 October 1949, ibid., 15326. This carton also contains dossiers of some of the more notorious collaborationists, notably Marcel Bucard, leader of the Francistes, who was executed in March 1946.

BIBLIOGRAPHY

Archival Sources

Archives Nationales, Paris
AJ^{38} Commissariat Général aux Questions Juives
AJ^{40} Militärbefehlshaber in Frankreich
  439-448   Kommandostab, 1940–1944
  449-867   Verwaltungsstab, 1940–1945
  868-897   Kommandant von Gross-Paris, 1940–1944
AJ^{41} Organismes français issus de l'Armistice de 1940
AJ^{72} Comité d'histoire de la Deuxième Guerre mondiale
F^{1a} Ministère de l'Intérieur: Objets Généraux
F^{7} Police Générale
F^{12} Commerce et Industrie
F^{17} Instruction Publique

Bundesarchiv, Berlin
NS 19   Persönlicher Stab Reichsführer SS
PK G66   Personalkorrespondenz Helmut Knochen
R 3   Reichsministerium für Rüstung und Kriegsproduktion
R 58   Reichssicherheitshauptamt
R 70   Frankreich: Polizeidienststellen im Bereich des
               Militärbefehlshabers in Frankreich
R 124   Verkehrswesen in den besetzten Gebieten
SSO/354A   Personalakten Carl Oberg

Bundesarchiv, Koblenz
N 1023   Nachlass Werner Best
R 43   Reichskanzlei

Bundesarchiv-Militärarchiv, Freiburg
RH 36   Kommandanturen der Militärverwaltung
RW 5   OKW/ Amt Ausland/ Abwehr

RW 19   OKW/ Wehrwirtschafts- und Rüstungsamt Frankreich
RW 24   Rüstungsdienststellen in Frankreich
RW 35   Der Militärbefehlshaber in Frankreich
RW 49   Dienststellen und Einheiten der Abwehr

Centre de Documentation Juive Contemporaine
See Lucien Steinberg (ed.), *Les autorités allemandes en France occupée* (Paris, 1966). Among the important cartons:
XXV-XLVI   Documents de la Gestapo
LXXI   Dossier du Procès Otto Abetz
CCCLXIV   Procès Oberg-Knochen

Politisches Archiv-Auswärtiges Amt, Berlin
Paris
1102-1103   Verschiedenes, 1940-1944
1104-1109   Presse und Propaganda (deutsche), 1942-1944
1110-1119   Kulturpolitik, 1942-1944
1120-1122   Französische Innenpolitik, 1942-1943
1123-1125   Arbeiterfragen, 1943
1136-1152   Kulturpolitik, 1940-1943
1153-1158   Verwaltungssachen, 1943
1170-1202   Akten der Informations-Abteilung, 1941-1944
1203-1220   Akten des Kulturreferats, 1940-1942
1270-1382   Geheimakten der Politischen Abteilung, 1940-1944
2379-2389   Politik (Verschiedenes), 1920-1944
2402-2403   Verbindung des AA zum OKW, 1940-1942
404-2406   Wirtschaftsangelegenheiten, 1939-1944
2444-2513   Geheimakten (meist politisch), 1914-1944
R 27779-27785 Handakten Ritter: Frankreich
                Nachlass Schleier

Secondary Sources

Abetz, Otto. *Das offene Problem. Ein Rückblick auf zwei Jahrzehnte deutscher Frankreichpolitik.* Cologne, 1951.

Adler, Jacques. *The Jews of Paris and the Final Solution: Communal Response and Internal Conflicts, 1940–1944.* Oxford, 1987.

Alary, Eric. *Les Français au quotidien 1939–1949.* Paris, 2006.

Amouroux, Henri. *La grande histoire des français sous l'Occupation.* 8 vols. Paris, 1976–1988.

———. *La vie des français sous l'occupation.* 2 vols. Paris, 1961.

Andrieu, Claire. *La banque sous l'Occupation. Paradoxes de l'histoire d'une profession.* Paris, 1990.

Aron, Robert. *Histoire de Vichy.* Paris, 1954.

Auda, Grégory. *Les Belles Années du "milieu," 1940–1944. Le grand banditisme dans la machine répressive allemande en France.* Paris, 2002.

Azéma, Jean-Pierre. *De Munich à la Libération (1938–1944).* 2nd ed. Paris, 2002.

Azéma, Jean-Pierre, and François Bédarida (eds.). *La France des années noires.* 2nd ed. 2 vols. Paris, 2000.

Bachelier, Christian. *La SNCF sous l'Occupation allemande, 1940–1944, Rapport documentaire.* 2 vols. Paris, 1996.

Banach, Jens. *Heydrichs Elite. Das Führerkorps der Sicherheitspolizei und des SD, 1936–1945.* Paderborn, 1998.

Bargatsky, Walter. *Hotel Majestic. Ein Deutscher im besetzten Frankreich.* Freiburg, 1987.

Barruch, Marc Olivier. *Servir l'État francais. Vivre sous l'Occupation.* Paris, 1992.

Beau, Nicolas, et al. (eds.). *SNCF. La machine infernale.* Paris, 2004.

Beaujouan, Guy, et al. (eds.). *La France et la Belgique sous l'occupation allemande 1940–1944. Les fonds allemands conservés au Centre historique des Archives nationales.* Paris, 2002.

Bensoussan, Georges (ed.). *Aryanisation. Le vol légalisé.* Paris, 2000.

Berlière, Jean-Marc. *Les policiers français sous l'Occupation.* Paris, 2001.

Betz, Albrecht, and Stefan Martens (eds.). *Les intellectuals et l'Occupation 1940–1944. Collaborer, partir, résister.* Paris, 2004.

Brandt, Karl. *Management of Agriculture and Food in the German-Occupied and Other Areas of Fortress Europe.* Stanford, 1953.

Brayard, Florent. *La "solution finale de la question juive." La technique, le temps et les catégories de la décision.* Paris, 2004.

Bucheler, Heinrich. *Carl-Heinrich von Stülpnagel. Soldat, Philosoph, Verschwörer.* Berlin, 1989.

Buisson, Patrick. *1940–1945 Années érotiques. Vichy ou les infortunes de la vertu.* Paris, 2008.

Burrin, Philippe. *La France à l'heure allemande 1940–1944.* Paris, 1995.

Callil, Carmen. *Bad Faith: A Forgotten History of Family, Fatherland, and Vichy France.* New York, 2006.

Calvi, Fabrizio, and Marc J. Masurovsky. *Le Festin du Reich. Le pillage de la France occupée 1940–1945.* Paris, 2006.

Cardon-Hamet, Claudine. *Mille otages pour Auschwitz. Le convoi du 6 juillet 1942.* Paris, 1997.

Carlier, Claude, and Stefan Martens (eds.). *La France et l'Allemagne en guerre. Septembre 1939–novembre 1942.* Paris, 1990.

Caron, Vicki. *Uneasy Asylum: France and the Jewish Refugee Crisis, 1933–1942.* Stanford, 1999.

Chevassus-au-Louis, Nicolas. *Savants sous l'Occupation. Enquête sur la vie scientifique française entre 1940 et 1944.* Paris, 2004.

Cobb, Richard. *French and Germans, Germans and French: A Personal Evaluation of Two Occupations, 1914–1918/1940–1944.* Hanover, NH, and London, 1983.

Coeuré, Sophie. *La mémoire spoliée. Les archives des Français, butin de guerre nazi puis soviétique.* Paris, 2007.

Cohen, Asher. *Persécutions et sauvetages. Juifs et Français sous l'occupation et sous Vichy.* Paris, 1993.

Cohen, Richard I. *The Burden of Conscience: French Jewish Leadership during the Holocaust.* Bloomington, 1987.

Cointet, Michèle, and Jean-Paul Cointet (eds.). *Dictionnaire historique de la France sous l'Occupation.* Paris, 2000.

Cotta, Michèle. *La collaboration.* Paris, 1964.

Courtois, Stephane, Denis Peschanski, and Adam Rayski. *Le sang de l'étranger. Les immigrés de la M.O.I. dans la Résistance.* Paris, 1989.

Crémieux-Brilhac, Jean-Louis. *La France libre. De l'appel du 18 juin à la libération.* 2 vols. 2nd ed. Paris, 2001.

Déak, István, et al. (eds.). *The Politics of Retribution in Europe: World War II and Its Aftermath.* Princeton, 2000.

Delacor, Regina (ed.). *Attentate und Repressionen. Ausgewählte Dokumente zur zyklischen Eskalation des NS-Terrors im besetzten Frankreich 1941/42.* Stuttgart, 2000.

Delarue, Jacques. *Histoire de la Gestapo.* Paris, 1962.

Delpard, Raphaël. *Enquête sur la SNCF et la déportation.* Paris, 2005.

Delporte, Christian. *Histoire des médias en France de la Grande Guerre à nos jours.* Paris, 2003.

Diamond, Hanna. *Fleeing Hitler: France 1940.* Oxford, 2007.

Doktor, Claude. *Les ennemis de l'intérieur dans la France occupée, 1940–1944.* Paris, 2004.

Drost, Wolfgang, et al. (eds.). *Paris sous l'Occupation. Paris unter deutscher Besatzung.* Heidelberg, 1995.

Duquesne, Jacques. *Les catholiques français sous l'occupation.* 2nd ed. Paris, 1996.

Duroselle, Jean-Baptiste. *L'Abîme 1940–1944.* Paris, 1982.

Ehrlich, Evelyn. *Cinema of Paradox: French Filmmaking under the German Occupation.* New York, 1985.

Eismann, Gaël, and Stefan Martens (eds.). *Occupation et répression militaire allemandes. La politique de "maintien de l'ordre" en Europe occupée 1939–1945.* Paris, 2007.

Engel, Kathrin. *Deutsche Kulturpolitik im besetzten Paris 1940–1944. Film und Theater.* Munich, 2003.

Farmer, Sarah. *Martyred Village: Commemorating the 1944 Massacre at Oradour-sur-Glane.* Berkeley, Los Angeles, and London, 1999.

Fouché, Pascal. *L'édition française sous l'Occupation.* 2 vols. Paris, 1987.

Franz, Corinna. *Fernand de Brinon und die deutsch-französischen Beziehungen 1918–1945.* Bonn, 2000.

Garçon, François. *De Blum à Pétain. Cinéma et société française (1936–1944).* Paris, 1984.

Garnier, Bernard, and Jean Quellien (eds.). *La main-d'oeuvre française exploitée par le IIIe Reich.* Caen, 2003.

Gildea, Robert. *Marianne in Chains: Daily Life in the Heart of France during the German Occupation.* 2nd ed. New York, 2004.

Giolitto, Pierre. *Histoire de la Milice.* 2nd ed. Paris, 2002.

Gordon, Bertram M. *Collaboration in France during the Second World War.* Ithaca, 1980.

Grenard, Fabrice. *La France du marché noir (1940–1949).* Paris, 2008.

Grynberg, Anne. *Les camps de la honte. Les internés juifs des camps français, 1939–1944.* Paris, 1991.

Halimi, André. *La délation sous l'Occupation.* 2nd ed. Paris, 2003.

Haussmann, Frank-Rutger. *"Auch im Krieg schweigen die Musen nicht." Die deutschen wissenschaftlichen Institute im Zweiten Weltkrieg.* Göttingen, 2001.

Herbert, Ulrich. *Best. Biographische Studien über Radikalismus, Weltanschauung und Vernunft, 1903–1989.* Bonn, 1996.

Hirschfeld, Gerhard, and Patrick Marsh (eds.). *Collaboration in France: Politics and Culture during the Nazi Occupation, 1940–1944.* New York, 1989.

Jackson, Julian. *France: The Dark Years, 1940–1944.* Oxford, 2001.

Jäckel, Eberhard. *Frankreich in Hitlers Europa. Die deutsche Frankreichpolitik im Zweiten Weltkrieg.* Stuttgart, 1966.

Janssen, Gregor. *Das Ministerium Speer. Deutschlands Rüstung im Krieg.* Berlin, 1968.

Jasper, Willy. *Hotel Lutétia. Ein deutsches Exil in Paris.* Munich and Vienna, 1994.

Joly, Laurent. *Vichy dans la "Solution Finale." Histoire du Commissariat général aux Questions juives (1941–1944).* Paris, 2006.

Jünger, Ernst. "Das erste Pariser Tagebuch." In *Sämtliche Werke. Tagebücher,* 2:223–406. Stuttgart, 1979.

_____. "Das Zweite Pariser Tagebuch." In *Sämtliche Werke. Tagebücher,* 3:9–294. Stuttgart, 1979.

Kaspi, André. *Les Juifs pendant l'Occupation.* 2nd ed. Paris, 1997.

Kasten, Bernd. "Gute Franzosen." *Die französische Polizei und die deutsche Besatzungsmacht im besetzten Frankreich 1940–1944.* Sigmaringen, 1993.

Kedward, H. R. *Resistance in Vichy France: A Study of Ideas and Motivation in the Southern Zone, 1940–1942.* Oxford, 1978.

_____. *Occupied France: Collaboration and Resistance, 1940–1944.* Oxford, 1985.

_____. *In Search of the Maquis: Rural Resistance in Southern France, 1942–1944.* Oxford, 1993.

Kershaw, Ian. *Hitler 1936–45: Nemesis.* New York, 2000.

Kitson, Simon. *The Hunt for Nazi Spies: Fighting Espionage in Vichy France.* Chicago and London, 2008.

Klarsfeld, Serge. *Vichy-Auschwitz. Le rôle de Vichy dans la solution finale de la question juive en France.* 2 vols. Paris, 1983–1985.

Klarsfeld, Serge, and Léon Tsevery. *Les 1007 fusillés du Mont Valérien parmi lesquels 174 juifs.* Paris, 1995.

Klemperer, Klemens von. *German Resistance against Hitler: The Search for Allies Abroad, 1938–1945.* Oxford, 1992.

Kupferman, Fred. *Laval.* 2nd ed. Paris, 2006.

Laborie, Pierre. *Les Français des années troubles. De la guerre d'Espagne à la Libération.* 2nd ed. Paris, 2003.

_____. *L'opinion française sous Vichy.* Paris, 1990.

Lambauer, Barbara. *Otto Abetz et les Français ou l'invers de la collaboration.* Paris, 2001.

La Martinière, Joseph de. *Le décret et la procédure Nacht und Nebel (Nuit et brouillard).* Orléans, 1981.

Lévy, Claude, and Paul Tillard. *La Grande Rafle du Vel d'Hiv (16 juillet 1942).* 2nd ed. Paris, 1992.

Lindeperg, Sylvie. *Les écrans de l'ombre. La Seconde Guerre mondiale dans le cinéma français.* Paris, 1997.

Loiseaux, Gérard. *La littérature de la défaite et de la collaboration.* Paris, 1984.

Lottmann, Herbert R. *The Fall of Paris: June 1940.* New York, 1992.

Luneau, Aurélie. *Radio Londres. Les voix de la liberté (1940–1944).* Paris, 2005.

Luther, Hans. *Der französische Widerstand gegen die deutsche Besatzungsmacht und seine Bekämpfung.* Tübingen, 1957.

Marrus, Michael, and Robert O. Paxton. *Vichy France and the Jews.* New York, 1981.

Martens, Stefan (ed.). *Frankreich und Belgien unter deutscher Besatzung 1940–1944. Die Bestände des Bundesarchiv-Militärarchivs Freiburg.* Stuttgart, 2002.

Martens, Stefan, and Maurice Vaïsse (eds.). *Frankreich und Deutschland im Krieg (November 1942–Herbst 1944). Okkupation, Kollaboration, Résistance.* Bonn, 2000.

Meinen, Insa. *Wehrmacht et prostitution sous l'Occupation (1940–1945).* Paris, 2006.

Messinger, Sylvie (ed.). *La France et la question juive, 1940–1944.* Paris, 1981.

Meyer, Ahlrich. *Die deutsche Besatzung in Frankreich 1940–1944. Widerstands-bekämpfung und Judenverfolgung.* Darmstadt, 2000.

———. *Täter im Verhör. Die "Endlösung der Judenfrage" in Frankreich 1940–1944.* Darmstadt, 2005.

Michel, Alain-René. *La jeunesse étudiante chrétienne face au nazisme et à Vichy (1938–1944).* Lille, 1988.

Michel, Henri. *Histoire de la Résistance, 1940–1944.* Paris, 1950.

———. *Paris allemand.* Paris, 1981.

———. *Paris résistant.* Paris, 1982.

Michels, Eckard. *Das Deutsche Institut in Paris 1940–1944.* Stuttgart, 1993.

Milward, Alan S. *The New Order and the French Economy.* Oxford, 1970.

Mitchell, Allan. *A Stranger in Paris: Germany's Role in Republican France, 1870–1940.* New York and Oxford, 2006.

Moll, Martin (ed.). *Führer-Erlasse 1939–1945.* Stuttgart, 1997.

Mühlen, Bengt von zur, and Frank Bauer (eds.). *Der 20. Juli in Paris. Verlauf—Haupt-beteiligte—Augenzeugen.* Berlin, 1995.

Müller, Rolf-Dieter, and Hans-Erich Volkmann (eds.). *Die Wehrmacht als Mythos und Realität.* Munich, 1999.

Nestler, Ludwig, and Friedel Schulz (eds.). *Die faschistische Okkupationspolitik in Frankreich (1940–1944).* Berlin, 1990.

Novick, Peter. *The Resistance Versus Vichy: The Purge of Collaborators in Liberated France.* New York, 1968.

Ory, Pascal. *La France allemande (1933–1945).* 2nd ed. Paris, 1995.

———. *Les collaborateurs 1940–1945.* 2nd ed. Paris, 1980.

Oustry, Ian. *Occupation: The Ordeal of France 1940–1944.* London, 1997.

Paul, Gerhard, and Klaus-Michael Mallmann (eds.). *Die Gestapo im Zweiten Weltkrieg. "Heimatfront" und besetztes Europa.* Darmstadt, 2000.

Paxton, Robert O. *Vichy France: Old Guard and New Order, 1940–1944.* New York, 1972.

Perrault, Gilles. *Paris sous l'Occupation.* Paris, 1987.

Peschanski, Denis. *La France des camps. L'internement, 1938–1946.* Paris, 2002.

Pinault, Michel. *Frédéric Joliot-Curie.* Paris, 2001.

Polino, Marie-Noëlle (ed.). *Une entreprise publique dans la guerre. La SNCF, 1939–1945.* Paris, 2001.

——— (ed.). *Les cheminots dans la Résistance. Une histoire en évolution.* Paris, 2006 [in *Revue d'histoire des chemins de fer,* N° 34].

——— (ed.). *Transports dans la France en guerre 1939–1945.* Rouen, 2007.

Polonski, Jacques. *La presse, la propagande et l'opinion publique sous l'Occupation.* Paris, 1946.

Poznanski, Renée. *Les Juifs en France pendant la Seconde Guerre mondiale.* Paris, 1994.

Prost, Antoine, et al. (eds.). *Aryanisation économique et restitutions. Mission d'étude sur la spoliation des Juifs en France.* Paris, 2000.

Pryce-Jones, David. *Paris in the Third Reich: A History of the German Occupation, 1940–1944.* London, 1981.

Rajsfus, Maurice. *La police de Vichy. Les forces de l'ordre françaises au service de la Gestapo 1940/1944.* Paris, 1995.

———. *Drancy. Un camp de concentration très ordinaire.* Paris, 1996.

Rayski, Adam. *Le choix des juifs sous Vichy. Entre soumission et résistance.* Paris, 1992.

Rayssac, Michel. *L'exode des musées. Histoire des oeuvres d'art sous l'Occupation*. Paris, 2007.

Rémond, René. *Le "Fichier Juif."* Paris, 1996.

Richard, Thibault. *Vivre en région parisienne sous l'Occupation. La Seine-et-Oise dans la guerre (1940–1944)*. Condé-sur-Noireau, 2004.

Rioux, Jean-Pierre (ed.). *La vie culturelle sous Vichy*. Paris, 1990.

Rousso, Henry. *Le syndrome de Vichy de 1944 à nos jours*. 2nd ed. Paris, 1990.

———. *Les années noires. Vivre sous l'occupation*. Paris, 1992.

———. *Vichy. L'événement, la mémoire, l'histoire*. Paris, 2001.

Sanders, Paul. *Histoire du marché noir 1940–1946*. Paris, 2001.

Schramm, Wilhelm von. *Der 20. Juli in Paris*. Bad Wörishorn, 1953.

Schwilk, Heimo. *Ernst Jünger. Ein Jahrhundertleben*. Munich, 2007.

Smelser, Ronald, and Rainer Zitelmann (eds.). *Die Braune Elite*. 2 vols. Darmstadt, 1993–1994.

Steinberg, Lucien. *Les autorités allemandes en France occupée*. Paris, 1966.

———. *Les allemands en France, 1940–1944*. Paris, 1980.

Steur, Claudia. *Theodor Dannecker. Ein Funktionär der Endlösung*. Essen, 1997.

Sweets, John F. *Choices in Vichy France: The French under Nazi Occupation*. New York, 1986.

Thalmann, Rita. *La mise au pas. Idéologie et stratégie sécuritaire dans la France occupée*. Paris, 1991.

Tooze, Adam. *The Wages of Destruction: The Making and Breaking of the Nazi Economy*. London, 2006.

Umbreit, Hans. *Der Militärbefehlshaber in Frankreich 1940–1944*. Boppard, 1968.

Veillon, Dominique. *La Mode sous l'Occupation*. 2nd ed. Paris, 2001.

———. *Vivre et survivre en France, 1939–1947*. Paris, 1995.

Venner, Dominique. *Histoire de la Collaboration*. Paris, 2000.

Verheyde, Philippe. *Les mauvais comptes de Vichy. L'aryanisation des entreprises juives*. Paris, 1999.

Vinen, Richard. *The Unfree French: Life under the Occupation*. New Haven, 2006.

Welch, David (ed.). *Nazi Propaganda: The Power and the Limitations*. London, 1983.

Wellers, Georges. *L'étoile jaune à l'heure de Vichy. De Drancy à Auschwitz*. Paris, 1973.

Wieviorka, Olivier. *Histoire du débarquement en Normandie. Des origines à la libération de Paris 1941–1944*. Paris, 2007.

Zuccotti, Susan. *The Holocaust, the French, and the Jews*. New York, 1993.

Name Index

Abetz, Otto, 11, 19, 26, 28–31, 34, 36, 40–42, 48, 51, 53, 57, 60, 66, 73–74, 76–77, 79, 87–89, 95–96, 108, 122, 125, 140, 157–59, 211n
Adenauer, Konrad, 155
Aragon, Louis, 157

Bach, Johann Sebastian, 28
Barckhausen, Franz von, 21
Bard, François, 17, 47, 51, 58, 102
Barnaud, Jacques, 66, 69
Baudrillart, Henri-Marie-Alphonse, 33, 79
Beaverbrook, William Maxwell Aitken, 158
Beck, Ludwig, 4
Beethoven, Ludwig van, 27, 124
Benoist-Méchin, Jacques, 75
Berlioz, Hector, 124
Best, Werner, 6, 10, 19, 30, 34, 40, 42–43, 49, 52–53, 57, 60, 75, 87, 135, 165n
Bichelonne, Jean, 112, 118
Bizet, Georges, 124
Bloch, Marc, 78
Blomberg, Werner von, 4
Boineburg-Lengsfeld, Hans von, 139–40
Bonnard, Pierre, 141
Bormann, Martin, 121, 133
Bourgin, Georges, 126
Bousquet, René, 60, 62, 90, 99–102, 117, 136, 157, 159
Brauchitsch, Walther von, 5, 14, 29, 41–42, 65
Brehmer, Walther, 140

Breker, Arno, 77
Brinon, Fernand de, 76, 78

Canaris, Wilhelm, 5, 96
Carcopino, Jérôme, 32
Carpentier, Georges, 123
Cathala, Pierre, 86, 112
Choltitz, Dietrich von, 149,160
Churchill, Winston S., 158
Claudel, Paul, 27
Clemenceau, Georges, 76
Cocteau, Jean, 27
Curie, Marie, 32
Curie, Pierre, 32

Dannecker, Theodor, 39, 41, 53, 81, 83–84, 87–89, 129, 135
Darlan, François, 44, 54, 69
Darnand, Joseph, 99–100, 102–3, 106, 127–28, 136, 141, 147, 153, 157, 159
Darquier de Pellepoix, Louis, 85–86, 130–33
Darrieux, Danielle, 76
Déat, Marcel, 35, 49, 80, 127
Debussy, Claude, 124
Deloncle, Eugène, 35, 55–56, 80
Diebner, Kurt, 32
Doriot, Jacques, 35, 79–80, 127, 147
Drumont, Édouard, 125

Eichmann, Adolf, 5, 81, 84, 87–90, 134, 157
Eisenhower, Dwight D., 140
Epting, Karl, 28–30, 32, 124

SUBJECT INDEX

ALSO BY ALLAN MITCHELL

Revolution in Bavaria, 1918–1919:
The Eisner Regime and the Soviet Republic (1965)

Bismarck and the French Nation, 1848–1890 (1971)

The German Influence in France after 1870:
The Formation of the French Republic (1979)

Victors and Vanquished: The German Influence
on Army and Church in France after 1870 (1984)

The Divided Path: The German Influence on
Social Reform in France after 1870 (1991)

The Great Train Race: Railways and the
Franco-German Rivalry, 1815–1914 (2000)

Rêves Parisiens: L'échec de projets de transport public
en France au XIXe siècle (2005)

A Stranger in Paris: Germany's Role in
Republican France, 1870–1940 (2006)

Anthologies

Everyman in Europe: Essays in Social History, 2 vols.
(3rd edition, 1990), with Istvan Deak

Bourgeois Society in Nineteenth-Century Europe
(2nd edition, 1993), with Jürgen Kocka

The Nazi Revolution: Hitler's Dictatorship and the German Nation
(4th edition, 1997)